MICHELANGELO IN RAVENSBRÜCK

MICHELANGELO IN RAVENSBRÜCK

One Woman's War Against the Nazis

KAROLINA LANCKOROŃSKA

Translated by Noel Clark

Preface by Eva Hoffman

A MERLOYD LAWRENCE BOOK
LIFELONG BOOKS • DA CAPO PRESS
A Member of the Perseus Books Group

English translation by Noel Clark

Printed in the United States of America.

Typeset by Deltatype Ltd., Birkenhead, Merseyside

Cataloging-in-Publication data for this book is available from the Library of Congress.

First published by Społeczny Instytut Wydawniczy ZNAK, Poland, as Wspomnienia wojenne in 2001. This English-language translation was first published by Pimlico in the UK in 2005.
First Da Capo Press edition 2007
ISBN 0-306-81537-0
ISBN-13 978-0-306-81537-9

Published by Da Capo Press
A Member of the Perseus Books Group
http://www.dacapopress.com

1 2 3 4 5 6 7 8 9

Contents

Translator's Acknowledgement

I am particularly indebted to Professor Zdzisław Wałaszewski for reading and checking the first draft of this translation for accuracy, and for his countless fruitful suggestions and wise comments.

N.C.

List of Illustrations

The Partition of Poland in 1939

Note on Pronunciation

The Polish language is written as it is spoken. Another advantage is that the stress is almost always on the second-last syllable of the word. Ideally, as with any language, one should listen to a native speaker for 'fine-tuning'. But the notes below should help with the pronunciation of the names of people and places in this book. Take a few personal names, starting with the author's:

Karolina Lanckorońska = Karol-EE-na Lants-kor-ONska ('i' is pronounced 'ee', 'c' like 'ts' and the Polish 'ń' sounds like the Spanish 'ñ' in 'Señor')
Sikorski = Shee-KOR-skee
Chorążyna = Hor-on-ZHINN-a ('Ch' is a 'hard-breathing' sound, as in the Scots 'loch'; 'ą' is a nasal sound, like the French 'on'; 'ż' sounds like the French 'je')
Ryszard = RISH-art ('sz' sounds like the English 'sh')
Krzeczunowicz = K-zhetchun-O-vitch ('rz' sounds like the French 'je'; 'cz' like the English 'ch' in 'church'; the frequent combination 'szcz' in Polish is pronounced like the English sound produced in 'freSH CHoice', and Polish 'w' = English 'v')
Rękas = RENK-as ('ę' is a nasal sound, like the French 'in')

Place names:
Warszawa (Warsaw) = Var-SHAV-a (Polish 'a' is always pronounced 'ah')
Kraków = KRAK-oof (Polish 'ó' = English 'oo'; 'w' = 'v', or 'f' at the end of a word)
Łodź = Woodge (Polish 'Ł' = English 'W'; 'dź' = 'dg' as in 'edge')
Lwów = Lvoof
Stanisławów = Stanis-WAH-voof
Przemyśl = PSHAY-Mishl ('ś' is a soft 'sh' and 'ć' is a soft 'ch')
Rozdół = ROZ-doow (final 'ł' sounds like 'wit' without the 'it')
Wrocław = VROTS-waff
Kołomyja = Kowo-MEE-ya ('j' is pronounced like the 'y' in 'yet')
Wodzisław = Vo-DZHEE-swaff
Brzezie = B-ZHAY-zheeay
Katowice = Kahto-VITS-ay
Łącki = WANT-skee

Preface

The publication of Karolina Lanckorońska's memoir of struggle and survival in Poland during World War II is an event of great interest. Poland, during the Second World War, was the site of two catastrophes: the Holocaust and the war of occupation and conquest against the country as a whole. While the human dimension of the Holocaust has been made indelibly vivid through a body of powerful personal testimony, the other aspects of the Polish war are known to American readers, at best, as remote history. Lanckorońska's narrative, written mostly during the war years, gives us rare insight into some of that history's complexities, while introducing us to a fascinating story and an extraordinary personality.

Lanckorońska's personality may initially seem distant from us in its social formation and almost stern code of behavior and honor, but it grows both more familiar and more deeply impressive as she moves through her dramatic and unexpected journey. Countess Lanckorońska was an aristocrat with a cosmopolitan background and strong proclivities for the scholarly life. Through the vicissitudes of Polish history, her ancestors settled in Austria at the end of the eighteenth century. During her formative years, her family was involved in the highest echelons of Austrian life, while keeping the Polish side of their identity intact. The young Countess Lanckorońska seemed to choose Poland as her homeland out of an affinity for that country's people, culture, and sensibility.

The outbreak of the war found Lanckorońska in Lvov, where she held the post of professor in Renaissance Italian art—the first woman in Poland to achieve this rank in her field.

Her decision to become engaged in the resistance movement, which arose in opposition to the Soviet and Nazi invasions, seemed to follow unhesitantingly from her convictions and affiliations. Her descriptions of working in the underground, with its dangers and its ethos of solidarity, make for some of the most fascinating sections of the book. Her activities in Soviet-occupied Lvov were mostly humanitarian, but her network of contacts was wide. As the danger of discovery became apparent, she had to flee, ironically enough, into the Nazi-occupied Polish territories where she walked a dangerous line between legal and illegal activities, organizing relief efforts for prisoners of the Nazi regime throughout occupied Poland. Her native German helped her in dealing with Nazi officials, whom she confronted with shrewd perceptiveness and uncompromising honesty. In one case, this exasperating combination led one of her Nazi interlocutors, Hans Kruger, to confess to—or boast of—the murder of twenty-three professors from the University of Lvov. (Lanckorońska later tried to make the knowledge of this terrible war-crime public, but was ignored by the German authorities). During the war, she was to some extent protected by her highly placed international connections, but eventually her refusal to disavow her loyalty to Poland led to her imprisonment in Nazi jails and incarceration in the concentration camp of Ravensbrück.

Lanckorońska's account of these events is unmarred by any excess, self-pity, or sentimentality; but she was driven by some powerful motives. Her youthful ambition was to be a nurse; and the instinct to help, heal, and serve clearly remained potent at the time of her most severe ordeals. In Ravensbrück, she refused the "privileged" treatment of a special solitary cell, choosing instead to share the fate of her fellow inmates, whom she tried to succor in all available ways. Her preferred duty was working in the sick bay and with the so-called "rabbits" who were the subjects of odious medical experiments. But she also gave informal lectures on art and European history to women who, even on the eve of death, seemed to be hungry for the nourishment of mind and spirit.

Indeed, this is where Lanckorońska's memoir meets with such Holocaust testimonies as Primo Levi's account of his time in Auschwitz. Like Levi, she was sustained in her bleak setting by memories of art and by literature. Like him, she took all of the world's culture as her province. Unlike Levi, however, she had actual access to books, and the readings she requested ranged from Shakespeare to Herodotus and, astonishingly, *Mein Kampf* (know your enemy!). Her breadth of perspective gave her deep and sometimes poignant insight into the behavior of Ravensbrück's victims. For instance, when she noticed that women condemned to execution frequently asked to have their hair done, she recalled Herodotus, who described how the Spartans at Thermopylae combed their hair with great care before a foredoomed battle.

In other respects, Lanckorońska's resilience was also derived from a set of attachments and beliefs which may seem to us old fashioned but allowed her to behave with a selflessness and courage that amounted to a form of heroism. She was a patriot in the true sense of the word, but her love of her homeland was untainted by nationalism, if that suggests a belligerent or insular attitude. She was also a believing Catholic, whose devotion was compatible with genuinely enlightened views and encompassing sympathies. She abhorred discriminatory provincialism, claims to racial superiority, and the ethnic stereotyping that went on even in the desperate world of Ravensbrück. Rather, she judged people by their capacity for self-discipline, generosity, and selflessness, and by how much or little they complained—in other words, by the qualities of their character.

Her own character was underwritten by values that were so internalized as to be part of herself, and that withstood the test of every adversity. After the war, Lanckorońska decided to live in exile, as it became evident that Poland would come under the Soviet sphere. She went on to live to the great age of 104 and established important institutions for the study of Polish culture and art. She clearly felt that the Poland she had fought and hoped for had been, in the end, bitterly betrayed. Her moving and illuminating chronicle is evidence that, during Poland's greatest trials, she never betrayed what she saw as its best ideals—or indeed, herself.

—Eva Hoffman

Introduction

Does one deserve special credit for devoting all one's strength to doing what one does for love of it? I think not.[1]
Karolina Lanckorońska (1898–2002).

The last representative of the clan Lanckoroński of Brzezie considered that the family history, dating back to the fourteenth century, imposed duties upon her rather than privileges. During the time of Poland's noble Commonwealth,[2] the Lanckorońskis played an active role in political life. They were appointed Deputies and Senators in the Polish Parliament (Sejm) and held various offices and functions such as Bishop, Provincial Governor, Chancellor or Mayor, not to speak of General or Chief of Staff.[3] Karolina Lanckorońska was born in the nineteenth century (1898) and lived for the whole of the twentieth century, not only witnessing but participating in many historic events. The main theme of her life throughout was service to Poland and Polish culture.

In the nineteenth century, Vienna, capital of the Habsburgs, became the principal seat of the Lanckoroński family. When Antoni (1760–1830), a deputy in the Four Year Sejm and loyal supporter of the Constitution of the Third of May, moved to Vienna after the Third Partition of the Polish Republic, he was there accorded the office of Austrian Chamberlain and appointed Speaker of the State Sejm. His son Kazimierz (1802–74) took his seat in the Upper House, and his grandson Karol – father of Karolina and distinguished recipient of the Order of the Golden Fleece – was appointed Chief Steward at the court of the Emperor Franz Josef I. Throughout the nineteenth century the Lanckorońskis became slowly embedded in the governmental fabric of the multiethnic monarchy.

The life of the last of them, Karol Lanckoroński (1848–1933), renowned collector and amateur art historian, encompassed the rise and fall of the Austro-Hungarian monarchy. A greatly respected owner of extensive properties in Galicia, the Kingdom of Poland and Styria, he was highly regarded for his academic pursuits as well as a passion for collecting, with a vigour worthy of the Renaissance era. His collection of paintings in the Lanckoroński Palace comprised one of the richest private art collections in Vienna.[4] Through his marriages, twice to Austrians and for the third time to a Prussian, Małgorzata Lichnowsky[5] (sister of Karol Maximilian Lichnowsky, German ambassador in London from 1912 to 1914), to all appearances Lanckoroński was 'completely at home in the life of the Court and of the highly exclusive Austrian aristocracy'.[6] Poland's place under the rule of the Habsburgs he saw as part of a three-nation federation, but the world of his political illusions vanished with the death of the Emperor and the subsequent collapse of the Austro-Hungarian monarchy. Though closely bound up with German and Austrian culture, he nevertheless achieved an enormous amount for Polish culture and learning. His work in this field was acknowledged by the government of independent Poland with the award of the Great Ribbon of the Order of Polonia Restituta. When, after his death, his beloved daughter Karla (Karolina) was tidying the room, she found lying open on his bedside table a copy of Poland's national epic, *Pan Tadeusz* by Adam Mickiewicz.

Lanckoroński avoided trying to influence the inclinations or choices of his children in matters national or political. Antoni, Karla and Adelajda, who were reared and educated in Vienna, felt their closest affinity with the culture and history of the old, pre-partition Poland and the new Poland now struggling for independence. At the time of the First World War, when the Chief Steward of the Habsburg court was experiencing the death of the Emperor in 1916, his eighteen-year-old daughter Karolina, with youthful enthusiasm, was collecting photographs of the Polish Legion, leaflets and Eagle badges, while supporting the central figure, 'Brigadier' Piłsudski. She also spent some time nursing sick and wounded Polish soldiers in a convalescent home (Faniteum) built by her father. She read with deep emotion *Forest*

Echoes and *Faithful River*, novels by Stefan Żeromski. At the same time, dearest to her heart was the poetry of Juliusz Słowacki, of which she memorised lengthy extracts.

By the end of the war, the secondary-school student was showing distinctly academic leanings. As a voluntary attendant, she began to follow the university lectures in Vienna by the well-known art historian Max Dvořák. In 1920, having graduated from the private secondary school '*Zu den Schotten*', she enrolled at Vienna University as an art-history student. Her choice of subject was as self-evident as her childhood contact with art had been unforced. The family collection of paintings in the Vienna palace, supplemented by visits to various European museums, had a considerable influence on her lively imagination.

Equally, in the family's summer residence at Rozdół in Galicia, where she used to spend the holidays, Karolina saw not only portraits of her ancestors, but examples of Polish art. The walls of the Rozdół palace, indeed, were hung with paintings by – among other artists – Jan Matejko, Arthur Grottger, Józef Chełmoński and Jacek Malczewski, who was virtually 'court painter' to the Lanckorońskis. Karolina was not at her happiest in the vast, neo-baroque Vienna palace, as she recalled years later: 'For more or less seven months of the year, we eagerly looked forward to the longed-for visit to Rozdół where we stayed from June to mid-November, when we returned to Vienna. The important feast of St Karol [Charles] – name-day of both my father and myself (as well as father's birthday) – we always celebrated at Rozdół where, in the dining-room according to family tradition, on that day the chairs of the celebrants were decorated with flowers.'

It was there, in fact, that she passed the happiest hours of her childhood, climbing trees and swearing childish oaths in their shade. While still a student, observing evidence of a neglect in public health care, she took to 'chasing' after the sick. On her return to Vienna she resumed attendance at art-history lectures and studied the works of her favourite artist, Michelangelo. From time to time her father expressed discontent with his daughter's student lifestyle, arguing that 'women of the Renaissance [. . .] were educated and did not run to catch a tram at eight o'clock in the morning, clutching a briefcase'. But even before obtaining her doctorate, Karolina was thinking about her future. The desire to devote herself to the service of others, the attraction of nursing and her interest in medical matters led her to visit the School for Nurses in Warsaw.

In the end, however, following the kind advice of the Rozdół doctor, Tadeusz Rawski – 'a far better and wiser man than most' – she opted for an academic career. On the strength of a dissertation entitled 'Studies relating to Michelangelo's Last Judgement and its artistic descendants', which she had been preparing, supervised by Max Dvořák (after whose death she completed the thesis under the guidance of Julius von Schlosser), Karolina was accorded her doctorate in the history of art, at the University of Vienna on 21 May 1926.

The same year Dr Lanckorońska paid a lengthy visit to Rome, where she devoted herself to researching Italian art of the Renaissance and baroque periods. The material she gathered on that occasion bore fruit in her subsequent learned works. She was librarian of the Rome branch of the Polish Academy of Arts and Sciences (PAU), where for several years she was in charge of the art-history department, organising among other things collections of books and photographs, partly consisting of her father's bequests.

Karol Lanckoroński died in 1933, leaving behind properties in Galicia, which forged a further link between the Lanckoroński family and Poland. Karolina herself inherited Komarno and settled permanently in Lwów. Her academic interests played no small part in this decision – namely a possible university career. In 1934 she was elected a member of the Lwów Scientific Society and, in October, the governing board of the Jan Kazimierz University supported her request for admission to the oral examination to qualify for the assistant professorship of modern art, expressing the unanimous opinion that 'the acquisition of Dr Lanckorońska by the Jan Kazimierz University as Art History lecturer is highly desirable'.

The same year – as a private lecturer – she began giving lectures and conducting classes. Her examination thesis based on her dissertation, entitled 'The decoration of the Church Il Gesù in the context of baroque development in Rome', was received with unanimous acclaim on 13 December 1935 by the Council of the Humanities Department, and on 13 January 1936 by the Senate of the Jan Kazimierz University.[7] That was how Dr Karolina came to be the first woman in Poland to obtain a professorial appointment in the field of art history. Now she was able to devote herself wholeheartedly to what she most earnestly desired: the work of teaching and research at university level. However, as she used to say, her happiness was short-lived.

Her wartime memoirs begin with the outbreak of the Second World War and the invasion of Lwów by Soviet forces in September 1939. With emigration as a possible option, she chose instead the 'destiny of the belated grandchild' of her valiant forebears and refused to leave Poland while the country was occupied by foreign armies. At the turn of the year 1939–40, she was still teaching art history at the university. However, it was not long before she was actively engaged in the underground resistance. In January 1940 she swore an oath of allegiance to the underground Union for Armed Struggle (*Związek Walki Zbrojnej*, or ZWZ). The heart-rending, tragic events of that period – the deportations to the heart of the Soviet Union, the kidnappings and anarchy, the climate of human despair and helplessness – she has tried most faithfully to record in her memoirs. Numerous arrests of members of the Lwów underground, as a result of informers' reports to the authorities, brought about Karolina's hurried escape from Lwów in May 1940. As soon as she arrived in Kraków, she resumed her contacts with the underground. On the orders of Colonel Tadeusz Komorowski, commanding the Kraków regional branch of ZWZ, she undertook various duties, including the translation into German of appeals designed to demoralise the German forces. These notices were then pasted on billboards and walls in the city. Chiefly, however, she was engaged in the activity of the Polish Red Cross, in which as a nursing volunteer she brought Samaritan help to sick and wounded prisoners-of-war released from the German Stalags and Oflags. In that capacity she witnessed 'many deaths and many burials'. In the second half of 1941 the Main Council for Relief (*Rada Główna Opiekuńcza*, or RGO) entrusted to Karolina Lanckorońska the care of all prisoners in the whole German-occupied territory of Poland – the so-called General Government. She dedicated herself totally to this assignment. Her excellent knowledge of German, her aristocratic descent and her steadfastly courageous attitude towards the Germans helped her to operate effectively. Collective action organised by her for the supply of extra food in prisons, and the procurement of parcels and other assistance for approximately 27,000 prisoners, were instrumental in saving the lives of many of those in captivity.

In January 1942, as an official of the RGO, she travelled to Stanisławów. Having learned of mass murders carried out by the local Gestapo (German secret police), she sent an immediate message to General Komorowski – at the time commanding underground resistance units in the Kraków area. Although officially appointed the RGO Commission's Manager for the Stanisławów region in March, with German agreement, Karolina ran into problems, arousing ever-increasing suspicion about her activities, especially on the part of SS Hauptsturmführer Hans Krüger.

On 12 May 1942 she was arrested during a committee meeting of the RGO in Kołomyja and was later taken away to the prison in Stanisławów. While she was being interrogated, her persecutor, Krüger, exasperated by the unflinching demeanour of his prisoner, her display of Polish spirit, and convinced that a sentence of death awaited her, confessed to the murder of twenty-five professors of the Lwów colleges of higher education. Thus she became the first witness in the case of a crime that has remained unpublished to this day. What Krüger had not expected was intercession by members of the Italian royal family to Hitler's Gestapo chief, Heinrich Himmler himself. This led to her death sentence being quashed. A few days later, on 8 June, the Countess found herself in jail in Lwów. There, while undergoing interrogation by SS Kommissar Walter Kutschmann, she gave an account of her interrogation by Hans Krüger in Stanisławów and, at his request, wrote a fourteen-page report in which she revealed (among other things) Krüger's confession to the murder of the Lwów professors. The text of her report reached Himmler himself and he was surely responsible for having the 'chauvinist' Polish countess sent to Ravensbrück, the women's concentration camp. On 27 November 1942, with an SS escort, she left Lwów and Poland for ever.

After a short spell in a Berlin jail on the Alexanderplatz, she was transported on 9 January 1943 to her appointed quarters in Ravensbrück. On arrival in the camp, she was allocated the number 16076. As a result of repeated representations by the International Red Cross, she was placed on her own in *Sonderhaft*, or 'special confinement'. This 'favour' Karolina regarded as humiliating and, at her own request, she was sent back to the camp as an ordinary prisoner. 'There are things going on in there,' she wrote after leaving Ravensbrück, 'which people cannot bear to hear about, things the human mind cannot comprehend.'

The memoirs present us with heart-rending documentary descriptions of scenes in the camp life of the women prisoners, of their terror and suffering, faced with disease, torture and death. The atmosphere of constant tension is almost palpable. Against this background, some outstanding women prisoners of invincible character succeeded in redeeming human dignity amid the dire conditions of the camp. They managed to organise meetings, lectures and discussions on subjects pertaining to actual normality, so proving that 'in countless cases, all this nameless brutality, all these cruelties can neither break nor destroy, nor even harm the human spirit'. Karolina Lanckorońska, in fact, has devoted to such women brief character studies and portraits from memory – sketched, as it were, in passing. She herself conducted art-history lessons for the 'rabbits' – that is to say, women who had been subjected to dangerous medical experiments.

A month before the end of the war, on 5 April 1945, as the first Polish woman to be freed, Karolina was released from the camp with a batch of 299 French women prisoners. This was the result of intervention by the President of the International Red Cross, Professor Carl Burckhardt. Along with many others, the final scene in Ravensbrück will be certain to lodge in the reader's memory: Karolina's farewell to her fellow prisoners, when, in deference to a prison superstition, she turns to take a last look at the camp as she passes through the gates.

In Switzerland, Karolina Lanckorońska handed over to Professor Burckhardt her report on the situation of women prisoners in Ravensbrück. She also published an account of her recent experiences in the columns of a French-language learned periodical '*Souvenir de Ravensbrück*' (*Revue Universitaire*, 1945, vol. 2), and in German, '*Erlebnisse aus Ravensbrück*' (*Schweizerische Hochschulzeitung*, Jg 19:1945/46 Heft 2). At the same time she began writing her *Wspomnienia* (*Memoirs*).[8] Travel to Italy and an encounter with soldiers of the Polish Army 2 Corps, who were unwilling to return to a Communist Poland, confronted her with a new and unusual task. At the wish of General Władysław Anders and with the rank of Public Relations Officer, 2 Corps (later Lieutenant, AK [*Armia Krajowa*], or Home Army, as Poland's wartime resistance was officially known), Karolina undertook to organise educational studies for about 1,300 former soldiers of 2 Corps. Her acquaintances and pre-war academic contacts made it possible for Polish students to attend Italian universities and colleges in Rome, Bologna and Turin. Later she was instrumental in promoting similar activities in England and Scotland.

In November 1945, with Father Walerian Meysztowicz and Polish émigré professors, she signed the founding charter of the Polish Historical Institute in Rome. Closely involved with this 'small nerve centre of free Polish learning', Karolina devoted herself entirely to publishing and organising activities to promote Polish culture. Many years later, speaking about her determination and options at the time, she had this to say: 'Poland's destiny guided my inclinations to such an extent that I felt obliged to abstain from my beloved art-history research [. . .] It seemed to me then – and I believe I was right – it was the only painful sacrifice of my life – that the service of Polish culture at that time required of me not the study of Michelangelo, but work of a completely different kind. It was clear to me that the need was to dedicate all my energy to researching and publishing the sources of Polish history to be found in the archives of the West.'[9] Under the aegis of the Polish Historical Institute (financed by the Lanckoroński Foundation) were published twenty-eight volumes of an annual review devoted to Polish history, *Antemurale*, and seventy-six volumes in a monumental series of sources, *Elementa ad Fontium Editiones*, as well as the *Acta Nunciaturae Polonae*. It is difficult to appreciate the scale of activity initiated in 1967 by the Lanckoroński Foundation in promoting Polish learning and science.

Karolina Lanckorońska, who dedicated her whole life to the service of Polish learning and culture, also displayed the traditional patriotism of a Polish citizen. She inherited from her father a unique collection of paintings, which, as the last of her line, she presented as a gift in 1994 to the royal palaces in Kraków and Warsaw, 'in honour of the Free and Independent Republic'. When the monthly periodical *Znak* (*The Sign*) distributed a questionnaire to distinguished personalities in the field of culture, asking 'Polishness – what does it mean?', Karolina Lanckorońska replied succinctly: 'Polishness is for me the awareness of belonging to the Polish nation. I consider we should do everything possible to provide concrete proof of this awareness, though I do not understand the need to analyse it.'

Karolina Lanckorońska's fundamental activity consisted in the promotion of intellectual life with ceaseless vigilance in order to ensure that Poland's learning and culture remain in the sphere of European and world culture. She died in Rome aged 104 on 25 August, 2002.

Lech Kalinowski and Elżbieta Orman

Prologue

This memoir, intended for possible publication after my death, was written during the years 1945–6, following my liberation from German captivity.[1] It was originally intended for publication in English, and I had a few extracts from the book translated and sent to two publishers, both of whom rejected them out of hand on the grounds that the text was 'too anti-Russian'. A few years later I sent the specimen extracts to two other English publishers, who also turned them down, this time on the grounds that they were 'too anti-German'.

My memoir is meant to be a report – and only a report – of what I witnessed during the Second World War. I know that others have lived through a great deal more than myself. I was never in Auschwitz or Kazakhstan. Nevertheless, I also know that every first-hand account contributes fresh detail to the picture of those years. I have made next-to-no textual changes, despite the fact that in some places I refer to things nowadays familiar to a wide public and better described elsewhere. I leave it to my publishers to decide on any possible future 'abbreviations', since it is impossible for me to assess, let alone rework, the contents of a book written more than fifty years ago. My one stipulation is that any omissions should be limited to matters of detail and include nothing that bears on the general atmosphere that engendered this memoir. I am confiding the editorial task in the first place to Professor Lech Kalinowski and Eli Orman. They may like to involve other friends in their discussions about any 'cuts'.

K.L.
Rome, 20 February 1998

Chapter 1

Lwów

22 September 1939–3 May 1940

During the night of 22 September 1939 the Soviet Russian Army occupied Lwów.[1]

In the morning, I went out to do some shopping. Small groups of Red Army soldiers, who had been in the city only a few hours, were already wandering about the streets. The so-called 'Proletariat' was not raising a finger to welcome them. The Bolsheviks themselves looked neither like happy nor proud conquerors. We were looking at men in shabby uniforms, with pasty complexions – plainly anxious, if not frightened. They appeared wary and at the same time greatly astonished. They stood a long time in front of shop windows with remnants of stock on display. But it was a couple of days before they ventured inside. As soon as they did, they appeared greatly heartened.

Once, in my presence, an officer bought a baby's rattle. This he pressed to the ear of a comrade and, when it rattled, the pair of them hopped around the shop with shouts of delight. Having bought it, away they went rejoicing. The proprietor, dumbfounded, turned to me after a moment's silence and asked with a baffled look: 'What's it going to be like, madam? I mean to say, if those are officers!'

We were entering the first phase of our new life. It was obvious that the Bolsheviks would be with us for the whole winter. There was nothing for it but to hold out till distant spring arrived. We had the radio and, listening in to broadcasts from all over Europe, we told ourselves repeatedly that we were not, after all, cut off. We knew all about what was happening. The first thing we knew was that Warsaw was fighting on and we were immeasurably envious. Later, however, we learned by the same means that our government was now in Paris and that, this time, 'God had entrusted the honour of the Poles to General Sikorski'*[2] Also – but this time with the help of loudspeakers, which the moment they got the power-station back in working order disclosed their presence at the corner of every main street – we heard about something quite different, namely that our Lwów was the capital of the 'Western Ukraine', which was now at last to become a new member of that great and happy family of nations embraced by the Soviet 'Union'.

For the first time, the slogan 'Workers of the World, unite!' thundered about us from all sides. Simultaneously, the radio began broadcasting abusive tirades about the 'Poland of the nobles' and her 'former army'. These broadcasts were illustrated by caricatures that appeared on the walls of houses. All these introductory steps had one important result: that of turning the Polish workers of Lwów against the new regime from the very outset. True to the innate temperament of the city, the workers were infuriated.

Meanwhile local Ukrainian committees began to sprout like mushrooms overnight. The palace of our friends, the Gołuchowskis, was taken over to serve as the seat of their headquarters. That was one of the first acts of seizure directed against private ownership. In the course of the difficult process of removing the children of the owner, I managed to salvage from the loft of the already occupied palace eleven evening dress-shirts belonging to the late Agenor Gołuchowski*, one-time Minister of Foreign Affairs in the Austro-Hungarian Government. This priceless acquisition I took right away to the so-called Kraków Committee, which was in charge of people newly arrived from Kraków. The committee was headed by the then professors Kot* and Goetel.* There was obviously a huge demand for any and all items of male attire. Ministerial dress-shirts equipped with formidably high, stiff collars, known as *Vatermörder*,[3] were received and quickly adorned the backs of the needy.

Lwów at that time was a city of about a million inhabitants. It was hard to squeeze through the crowded streets, where literally all Poland seemed to be concentrating. The roads were blocked by every conceivable means of locomotion. It was impossible to move at all

---

* Names followed by an asterisk are described in the Biographical Notes.

along the pavements. Hundreds of thousands of refugees, in thoughtless flight – frequently bombed on the way, having lost all they owned and often some of their nearest and dearest as well – were streaming into Lwów with no idea what to do next. From the moment the Bolsheviks invaded, legal exit to Romania became impossible and travel to Hungary more difficult. Despite that, a number of people continued to get out on foot or by other means, but others – far more numerous – were still pouring in. Everyone kept asking everyone else: 'What's going to happen?'

The overall refugee problem was exacerbated by the lack of food and accommodation. However, the situation was improving with every day that passed. Supplies of produce from the countryside resumed and the tide of humanity was beginning to flow westwards to 'the other side' – where the Germans had withdrawn behind the San. Crossing the river at that time was difficult, but not impossible. The street crowds were visibly thinning, and meanwhile the fabric of Lwów in autumn was enriched by a fresh strand – the appearance of a large number of men in heavy greatcoats and fur caps, landowners and gentry from rural parts, seeking refuge in the city.

They brought the first news of killings (albeit sporadic) accompanied by many arrests among the landowners in the villages. At about this time an official arrived from Jagielnica, my brother's property near Czortków, to inform me that my brother and sister had set off in the direction of the Romanian border only ten minutes before the Bolsheviks appeared. Both of them managed to get out at the last minute through Zaleszczyki, where they met a large number of relations and acquaintances. Later, they were to make their way to Geneva. The leader of the first band of ruffians to reach my brother's estate asked for him by name and said that he intended to shoot him.

The first news from my home at Komarno[4] was brought to me by my faithful servant Andzia, a simple country girl. She had lugged a heavy suitcase all the way. Behind her strode solemnly the monumental figure of her protector, seventy-five-year-old Mateusz Machnicki, a retired servant who tyrannised the household, with his snow-white mutton-chop whiskers in the style of Emperor Franz Josef. After greeting me, Andzia pointed at the suitcase and announced: 'I've brought your papers and study notebooks. Please look and see if I've got the lot.' She had, indeed, brought everything, including my manuscript [her thesis on Michelangelo] ready for the publisher – the fruit of eight years' labour. 'I have many other things as well for you. But I brought the academic papers first of all because I knew they were the most important.' In Komarno, with the departure of the Polish authorities, peasants began inspecting the manor house amid scenes reminiscent of others in previous upheavals. They were followed by the Germans who, after staying a few days and thoroughly pillaging the area, were obliged to withdraw to Przemyśl. From then on, the local Ukrainian committees were in charge and, for the time being, the influx of Soviet elements was slight.

My flaxen-haired Andzia now moved in with me. However, she made frequent trips to Komarno to fetch provisions for me and my friends, often at considerable risk to herself. The foodstuffs she brought were invaluable, but she also rescued a great many more of my personal belongings. Local peasants also came to see me with the latest news. I remember once receiving a present of cheese wrapped in a couple of sheets torn from an illustrated publication of fifteenth-century Florentine paintings, filched from my library.

The Bolsheviks now began arriving in greater numbers, men together with some unusually ugly women. They bought up everything they could lay their hands on. They crammed every shop. Scenes like the one with the rattle, described earlier, took place several times a day. Because the intended purpose of many objects was not always known to them, the buyers were apt to suffer certain embarrassments. For example, comrades might turn up at the theatre in an alluring silk nightdress, or use chamberpots for watering the flowers. Their rapacity in acquiring goods was hard to reconcile with their constant assertion of Russia's superabundance and their claim that in the Soviet Union there is everything the soul desires. Asked by one native of Lwów whether, for instance, one could find a Copenhagen in the Soviet Union, a Russian assured him that the Soviets had millions of them. What about oranges, then? Any number of them! Of course, there were always plenty, but, now that we've built so many new factories, we've got even more.

It wasn't long before we encountered the new authorities on our own ground – the university. Professors, readers, lecturers, students and janitors were invited to a meeting in the Collegium Maximum on 29 September. It was a very large gathering. High above the podium hung a gigantic portrait of Stalin, in profile and full colour. Such huge dimensions were familiar to us only from Byzantium. But the portrait hanging above us bore testimony to a mentality completely divorced from the classic roots from which Byzantine culture had evolved. I looked, horror-stricken, at the features and forehead, which were to confront us henceforth always and everywhere, whether in shop windows, restaurants, on street corners or in trams. That face seemed to me fundamentally different from our own faces, which reflect our thoughts and emotions. That is characteristic of people's faces in the West. But the features now before me appeared totally to hide thought and feeling with an impenetrable veil. From this face – at that time so strange to us, but later to become so well known, though always to remain just as foreign – we came to learn, in a way both bitter and irrefutable, that we were being ruled by a mentality absolutely alien to our own.

Meanwhile, Soviet personalities had entered the hall: the Russian Commandant of Lwów in a heavy greatcoat, accompanied by a tall man with plump but unusually intelligent features, wearing a Bolshevik tunic, whom the Commandant clearly treated with deference. They mounted the podium and invited Rector Longchamps* and the deans of the various faculties to join them. First to speak was the Commandant, in what struck me as very good Russian. He greeted the audience, declaring that he himself had wished to open the first meeting in this building, which would henceforth serve to educate not gentlemen but ordinary people. He then gave way to comrade Kornijczuk*, a member of the Kiev Academy.

Kornijczuk stood up, walked slowly to the rostrum and from there began to address us in a deep and forceful voice. He spoke in Ukrainian, the Kiev dialect that is slightly different from that on our side of the river. He talked of the greatness and power of truth and knowledge, and of how much Polish culture had contributed to the culture of the world; paid tribute to the greatness of Adam Mickiewicz, the national bard, in exceptionally fine words; went on to speak in moving tones of the power and value of learning, which unites humanity, and about the mission of universities, particularly the University of Lwów, whose task was to weld two cultures – Ukrainian and Polish – into a single whole. Although I did not understand every word and more than one sentence escaped me, I will always remember that speech as one of the most gripping I have heard in my life.

When Kornijczuk had finished, the future high-flyers of a Communist university took the floor – Ukrainians, Jews and Poles. They began to shower us with demagogic phrases. When there was talk of excluding members of the former 'privileged class' from the university, old Professor Krzemieniewski* asked to speak. He had previously been Rector, had participated in the struggle of 1905 and was a former political prisoner. When his majestic figure appeared on the stage, we received him with a spontaneous burst of applause.

Krzemieniewski turned, ostentatiously bowing to the Rector, and began in a loud, calm voice: 'Your Magnificence!' then, looking towards Kornijczuk: 'Academician!' Finally, he turned to the audience: 'Ladies and gentlemen!' The rather short figure of the Commandant of the city, whom the speaker had not deigned to mention at all, stirred uneasily in his seat. 'The honourable gentleman who has just spoken [the man referred to, now sitting among the audience, was seen to curl up] wants to exclude part of our society from admission to the university. I would say this to him: if Learning is indivisible as Truth is indivisible, if we do not now recognise class distinctions, it is because, so far as I'm concerned, all are equal – peasant, worker, intellectual and gentry. I shall educate peasants, workers, intellectuals and gentry. The social origin of anyone who wishes to serve the cause of Learning and Truth is none of my business!'

Ignoring the strident outcry of his opponents, Krzemieniewski strode from the platform amid wild applause from almost the entire assembly. The town Commandant stood up, looking a bit unsure of himself, as though something were amiss, though he himself was unable to understand what. He then read out the text of a telegram from the meeting, addressed to Stalin. It was couched in cautious language, not excessively obsequious and obviously intended not to antagonise us. 'All in favour of sending the telegram, raise your hands.' Out of the few hundred present, only a few dozen raised their hands. 'And who is against?' Not surprisingly, not a single hand went up. Then, with a broad smile, he declared: 'The motion to send a telegram is approved unanimously.'

We left with a feeling of distaste. It was already dusk. Yet despite everything, after Kornijczuk's speech we were full of hope that the Jan Kazimierz University could still be saved and that we would manage to preserve it unharmed till spring, as a memorial – a sort of *naufragio Patriae ereptum monumentum*.[5] A few weeks later we were to learn that, the very same day at nine o'clock in the evening, Kornijczuk had made another speech every bit as fiery – but this time at a meeting of Ukrainians – promising to exclude all Polish elements from Lwów University.

We continued to wait. We had the impression that Providence was leading us into the Unknown, and our curiosity was boundless. I must admit that, so far as I was concerned, the curiosity of a historian – before whom was opening up the possibility of being in contact with one of the leading movements of our time – outweighed all else. If it had to be that the whole country had to lose its independence for months on end (till spring, say), then I was glad to be in the Russian-occupied part. The experience was bound to be more interesting and, besides, the concept of human dignity, which provides the basis of our inner being, occupies much space in the theory of Communism, whereas Hitler had abolished it in favour of the zoological cult of racism.

The information that reached us from 'the other side' appeared to support this assessment. On the radio we heard about mass executions in our western provinces and finally got to know about the arrest of professors at the Jagiellonian University in Kraków[6] and their dispatch to a concentration camp. That piece of news hit us like a thunderbolt. It was followed by an endless stream of reports about the destruction of all cultural centres and archives – in fact, of all traces of our past history. Though we still clung to the illusory hope that all of this could not be true, that some of it, at least, must be attributed to anti-Hitler propaganda, one had to admit that the Soviets, by contrast, were demonstrating a respect for learning and culture that would surely enable much to be saved. That impression persisted once the university was fully open. We were all to carry on with our lectures as normal. That was the recommendation. So we set to work as though nothing had happened and I, among others, resumed my lectures. Those who attended, however, were a rather odd selection. Of young Polish males there was not a sign; they were in hiding. The students came one at a time to our apartments for books and guidance on further reading. Former girl students came to the lectures declaring that the hours they spent with me somehow helped them to carry on. There were also some new girl students, not of Polish nationality, sent along by the authorities. Because, in keeping with the original programme, I was peacefully lecturing away on the world of the fourteenth-century Siena school of painting, the unfortunate newcomers sat hopelessly hour after hour, eyes fixed not on the transparencies on the screen, but staring into space ahead of them. They were obliged to attend the lectures because we were all under strict supervision. Often they fell asleep and accompanied my lectures with their rhythmic snores while I tried to explain the importance of Simone Martini, friend of Petrarch.

Our legally elected Rector Longchamps, in the penultimate academic year of his term of office, carried on with his duties, till one day he was replaced by a Professor Marczenko* from Kiev University. He told everybody he was the son and grandson of day-labourers, but nobody could really get much out of him because he was simply not very intelligent. The same could not be said about his unapproachable companion, Lewczenko, who was the 'Political Commissar' of the university. We didn't know quite what that meant, but we didn't like the sound of it. Comrade Lewczenko also took a keen interest in us all, but never in an obtrusive fashion. We were given forms to fill in, much like a *curriculum vitae*. Only two sections of the questionnaire really mattered: social origins and the number of your inventions. The second question puzzled us considerably. I tried to explain to Lewczenko's secretary that a teacher of the humanities, and a historian in particular, does not regard the object of research as 'invention'. She looked at me in amazement, but remarked with an air of tolerance: 'Oh well, that's a pity, comrade. If you haven't made any inventions, that's what you have to put down.'

This Lewczenko also ordered us to form a cooperative of all permanent staff members of the university, from professors to janitors. When after a couple of weeks there was no food in the cooperative store, the Commissar demanded that the janitors be expelled. When we pointed out that such a measure was not in accordance with our social ethos, Lewczenko replied impatiently: 'That's because you have that so-called equality too, do you? Well, we don't.'

The next thing was the constant, as it were imperceptible, creation of more and more Chairs of new subjects: Darwinism, Leninism, Stalinism, and so forth. The incumbents of these Chairs were all newcomers from Kiev. One day, the Faculty of Medicine was detached to form an independent so-called 'Medinstitute', which clearly further slimmed down the body of Polish professors at the university. Simultaneously, a whole series of Chairs were done away with, one after another, at certain intervals. These included the Chairs of Law and the Humanities. Very soon, nothing at all remained of the Law Department, and our own staff was shrinking daily.

With the beginning of winter, we had a visit from a party of professors from Moscow. They behaved soberly and sedately. Some even betrayed partial acquaintance with civilised conventions. The History Department was visited by Professor Galkin, with whom I had a meeting in the Dean's office. Our exchange of ideas ran into serious technical difficulties when my interlocutor – a Professor of German History – turned out not to know any language except Russian. Since he insisted on asking me questions about my studies and speciality while failing to understand my answers in any language, I tried a few shreds of Latin in despair. At that, the Muscovite nodded vigorously, but did not himself reply in Latin. However, he refrained from asking any more questions. During this 'conversation', in walked Professor

Kuryłowicz*, one of my Polish colleagues. When he heard me addressing the Muscovite in broken Latin, he made a lightning exit, unable to contain his mirth. Finally Galkin declared in Russian that the whole department, especially Archaeology and Art History, needed thorough reorganisation because there were no museum specialists on the staff. He added that I ought to come and look at the *Hermitage*[7] as soon as possible. That was the end of the matter.

When they came to leave a few days later, the Russian professors, in bidding us farewell, earnestly entreated us to contact them in case of any future difficulties. Whence such difficulties might arise became apparent almost immediately after their departure. Even while they were still with us, it was easy enough to discern the tension between the Russians and incoming professors from Kiev. As long as the Muscovites were in Lwów, the Ukrainians seemed to understand Polish perfectly. The delegates from Moscow, for their part, constantly stressed that they were not in the least concerned about a professor's nationality, or about the language in which he lectured. As soon as the colleagues from Moscow were out of the way, however, those from Kiev immediately forgot their Polish and were unable to understand a word of the language. At the same time, the pressure for all lectures to be given in Ukrainian amounted almost to compulsion. Only a minimal number of professors and readers, myself among them, were never confronted with a demand to lecture in Ukrainian. But bursaries were made readily available for Ukrainian studies. The weakest among us submitted to the pressure, but – in defiance of everything – a great many continued to lecture in Polish.

Some time in February 1940 there appeared a new Dean of our History Department, Professor Brachyneć*. In a fur cap and boots that smelled strongly of tallow, he received me in the Dean's office and suggested that I should give a general course under the title 'Baroque Renaissance, Renaissance Baroque'. The strangeness of the title was probably due to my new chief's uncertainty as to which of the two words to mention first. Later I found out that one of my Ukrainian girl students had reported, for my safety's sake, that my lectures were highly specialised. As yet, there had been no instance of the removal of any professor teaching a specialist course recommended by the Soviets themselves. Comrade Brachyneć seemed not to know the Latin alphabet. In any case, throughout his tenure as Dean he was never known to read anything written in that script from end to end. As he was the Professor of Leninism and Stalinism, of course he had absolutely no need of Roman letters.

When a professor was squeezed out, his faculty would also have a way of disappearing at the same time. Books dealing with non-materialist philosophy, and other books that did not refer in glowing terms to our eastern neighbours (and there were many such works), found their way on to the *Prohibitur* (Index), or were immediately taken away and passed to the 'community' for destruction as pornography.

Being employed by the university offered a twofold guarantee of protection: first, for oneself, and second, for one's abode. I had a chance to satisfy myself on this point when I encountered Captain Pawłyszeńko of the Red Army.

On 19 November 1939 this Soviet officer arrived at my flat and occupied one room. I explained that I had brought family to live with me because their home had been destroyed by bombing during the fighting in September. Furthermore, as a university employee I was entitled to three rooms, as I was living with a foster child (Andzia) as well as possessing a library. All to no avail. He pushed his way in and made himself at home. While I was in the flat,[8] he was more or less quiet. When I went out, he played the devil. The first night he tore round his room like a madman while Andzia and I sat and waited, armed with the largest possible frying pan. At last, at about two o'clock in the morning, he began moving all the furniture, building barricades between his door and my room. Clearly he was worried about the fate of some Soviet tenants of Lwów workers' flats, who had been ushered into the next world during the night. However, we found this manoeuvre of his reassuring, and clearly his nerves, too, relaxed. It was not long before we heard his powerful snores. We too dozed off and slept like logs.

Next morning, the performance began again. Having found out about me from the concierge, he burst into the flat with a loud yell and ordered Andzia to hand over the gold furniture I was hiding from him. He knew perfectly well, he said, that pre-war Polish landowners had solid-gold chairs and tables. He wasn't such a fool as to believe that I lived with such miserable sticks of furniture (my furniture was old, Italian and unpolished) as I now had on show. He stormed into my room and looked at my bookshelves, on which there were a lot of Italian books in particular. Baring an improbable array of white fangs in his fury, he started screaming: 'Fascist library!' At that moment I happened to arrive home and entered the room. Pawłyszeńko declared in Russian: 'I am going to arrest you!'

'Not just now. I haven't time,' I replied gravely and with dignity. 'I'm due at the university.'

He then asked, in a noticeably quieter tone, when I would be free. We fixed a rendezvous for three o'clock in the afternoon. Naturally enough I did not turn up. Instead, he was confronted by Andzia's three brothers – peasants from our part of the country, now working in Lwów. At the sight of these three hefty youths, it seems, he turned pale as they assured him in no uncertain terms that if he so much as touched a hair of their sister's head, he'd have the three of them to deal with. The youngest of them told me that evening that Pawłyszeńko had looked like a 'cartoon tiger' painting – a very apt description. Over the next few days we removed everything of value from the flat and stored it for safe keeping with people we knew. That brought home to me how very uncomfortable it is to have possessions – though I was soon to learn that it's equally uncomfortable not to have any.

Communal life, however, proved totally impossible. Pawłyszeńko attempted to smash everything whose purpose was beyond him. He threw out all the more complicated kitchen utensils and adopted a particularly threatening attitude towards the plumbing. Andzia had warned me that something was amiss, because 'he's started washing in the lavatory basin'. The next day he ran up behind her, waving his revolver, and accused her of sabotage. The trouble – according to Andzia – was that after he pulled the chain, the water stopped flowing before he had time to finish washing his hair. There was not a moment's peace in the house. When I went out I never left Andzia on her own, for pretty young girls were in ever-increasing danger. On arrival home, we were always faced with some fresh catastrophe. At last I decided to go to the Military Prosecutor General's office and commence battle against my tenant. My friends were aghast: 'One step inside that building and you'll never get out again.' However, I had no wish to wait till Pawłyszeńko finished me off. And I went along to the office in Batory Street accompanied by Andzia and my 'sub-tenants'.

The Prosecutor received us and listened intently. Andzia, who had a good command of Ukrainian, spoke up sensibly and very boldly. The Prosecutor told us to put our statement in writing and come back the next day. I wrote a full account of the affair, which my sub-tenants translated into Ukrainian. The next day the Prosecutor had another chat with us and told us again to come back 'tomorrow'. The fifth time this happened my friends bade me farewell as though I would be gone for ages. After I had to write down precise details about myself, including my pre-war possessions, we were told to go home and there we would receive our answer. When I got back in the evening after my lecture, I faced a novel situation. There was a notice hanging on the door, which said that a university professor lived there and the apartment was not to be requisitioned. Andzia and the sub-tenants were waiting in the hall and, at the sight of me, burst out with the full story, all talking at the same time. Shortly before, the Deputy Prosecutor had been to the flat with Pawłyszeńko – the latter unarmed, stripped of his officer's badges of rank and, instead of a fur cap on his head, wearing a kind of knitted cotton helmet, as worn by a private soldier. The Deputy Prosecutor ordered him to collect his kit and told the astonished women that the comrade had been punished for disgracing the Red Army and that the *chadziajka* (owner) could henceforth continue her scientific work in peace.

Unfortunately, this last wish was not to be fulfilled. The peace of the following days was seriously disturbed by innumerable visits from acquaintances as well as total strangers, who had Soviet soldiers billeted in their flats and insisted on knowing how to get rid of them.

Some of the subsequent callers were less innocent. The military occupation of Lwów was now ending and the NKVD (the Soviet secret police) began to take over. The whole atmosphere of the city changed from one day to the next. At all hours commissars in civilian dress and brown leather jackets, or militia in navy-blue peaked caps, would barge into the flats of those suspected of 'anti-revolutionary views'. I was a particular worry to them as a notorious 'landowner', as well as enjoying, thanks to the university, something akin to parliamentary immunity. That made them awfully angry.

'And what did you do before the war?' they would ask ironically.

'The same as now – I taught at the university – only then I had peace to get on with writing my books as well, whereas now I can't even prepare my lectures, what with your rifle-butts battering my door every morning. In you come, sit down and start asking questions – every day the same – making it quite impossible for me to do any work at all. On top of it all, the Soviets are said to attach great importance to education.'

'You're a countess, aren't you?'

'I don't know about your country, but there aren't any countesses in Poland.'

'What do you mean, none in Poland?'

'The Constitution doesn't recognise titles.'

At the mention of the sacred word 'Constitution', they stood nonplussed. I showed them my identity card and documents, none of which, obviously, mentioned any hereditary title.

'Doesn't say so, true. But what was your father?'

'My father was a patron of the arts.' Dismay came over the questioner.

'Come with us to NKVD headquarters.'

I went along. The same thing all over again. The phrase 'patron of the arts' proved very useful. Nobody knew what kind of an animal that might be. On one occasion there was a commissar who was almost on the right track. He was a huge peasant in a fur cap. He flashed a toothy smile from ear to ear and said: 'Look, we know that a countess is something passed on in families – like father to son.'

'That may be so, but in Poland it isn't – because the Constitution does not recognise titles.' And so it went on, in a sort of vicious circle. Things were also advancing swiftly on the political front. Since, according to the Constitution, only the country itself could decide whether it wished to accede to or, rather, ask to be accepted into the USSR, the Western Ukraine had to declare the will of its people fairly soon after its 'liberation'. A plebiscite was announced and the campaign got under way. The Polish Radio, broadcasting from France, was encouraging citizens to vote, in the name of the Polish Government, because a plebiscite before signature of a peace treaty would be *ipso facto* invalid, and the government of the Polish Republic did not wish any of its citizens to put themselves at risk by failing to vote. It was very unpleasant, but almost everybody voted. Thanks to my name being misspelled on the electoral roll, I succeeded in not having to do so, but that was sheer luck.

That evening at 11 p.m. – the polls stayed open till midnight – a patrol of militia called at my flat, armed to the teeth and amid much shouting, and asked me why my husband hadn't voted. I replied that I could not answer for him as I had no influence over him. Our guests' irritation with my husband grew apace. It was not until I got them to understand that I could not lead a non-existent husband to the polls that they finally roared with laughter and departed.

Later there was a second plebiscite. After a spontaneous manifestation of the will of the people – many million strong – the USSR deigned to receive this Benjamin, the Western Ukraine, into the bosom of the family, and the newcomer had now to elect its representatives. Photographs of the candidates together with their printed biographies appeared on house walls. One of the leading representatives of Lwów was Professor Studyns'kyj*, who, for distinguished research in the field of Ukrainian literature, had been proclaimed Professor Extraordinary by the Austrians for his outstanding services. When, however, in 1918 the enemy, Poland, emerged triumphant, Studyns'kyj was downgraded to Ordinary Professor (*sic*). This time the Polish Government had adopted the same attitude, so we all voted. I knew there would have been no point in resisting, but all the same I must admit that such an action leaves one with a sense of profound disgust. The voting was secret. A militiaman led Andzia and me behind a curtain to the urns and watched while we cast our votes on the cards handed out in advance. Thus did the will of the people manifest itself in order that the provisions of the Constitution might be fulfilled.

Meanwhile, all about us the atmosphere was becoming ever more stifling and oppressive, and the days shorter and darker. The severe frosts of that exceptionally cold winter had begun, and every day the most dreadful burden in the world – the loss of freedom – weighed more and more heavily upon us. The higher the mountains of dirty snow piled up before us in the streets of Soviet Lwów, the deeper we sank daily into our captivity. More and more people were arrested, mostly young men. The Brygidki prison was full of them. Apart from that, boys were simply vanishing without trace – somewhere. The first to go were young lads arrested for singing patriotic songs at school. They just disappeared. Then, for the first time, a sinister rumour began to circulate: 'They've been taken away to Russia.' It was word-for-word the story of Sobolewski in Part Three of *Grandfathers' Eve*.[9] The only difference being that this time a great many children, and later adults too, in no small numbers, started to disappear without trace, apart from occasional postcards found lying between the railway tracks: 'We are being transported to Russia. We beseech you to remember us after the war.' Messages like that, followed by a row of signatures. But they didn't take teachers. In the early days the only persons to disappear were Leon Kozłowski*, Stanisław Grabski* and Ludwik Dworzak, the Prosecutor in Communist trials. After that, there was peace. But there were many arrests among the intellectuals, not to speak of officers, just after the capitulation, many of whom sent word from Russian prisoner camps in Kozielsk and Starobielsk. We were glad that they seemed to be in groups. They would have a better chance of survival.

Among those taken away were people who were particularly dear to us. One Sunday one of our assistant lecturers took me along with him to deliver some food at the former Insurance Companies' Hospital, now treating war-wounded veterans. The Russians allowed us in to visit the patients, taking note of our names and then moving among the beds to eavesdrop on our conversations. A number of impoverished and starving natives of Lwów had also brought comforts for the wounded, which they themselves lacked. It was well known that these patients, if and when they recovered, would be transported into the unknown – but meanwhile let them be aware that they were still in Lwów. In one of the wards there was a door leading into a small room. Both the sick and their visitors eyed this door with visible disquiet every time it opened.

'He's not in need of anything. He's got it all. He was in a bad way, but he's a bit better now. They'll soon be taking him away. Nothing to be done about that,' whispered my companion. He must have realised that I had no idea about whom he was talking, because he added at once: 'That's General Anders* in there.'

Meanwhile, the outward appearance of the city had changed. Polish street names were being replaced by Ukrainian ones, and Polish signboards were removed from shops and business premises. The Polish proprietors of these concerns, now dispossessed, were allowed to occupy a single room in their former apartment, and the same applied to former owners of whole apartment blocks. They sat waiting. If their property – goods and chattels, as well as homes and businesses – had been confiscated and they pointed out that the Constitution guaranteed their right to these possessions, they received this exhaustive reply: 'We apply the Constitution where order already exists. Here, our first job is to *restore* order; only then can we put the Constitution into action.' After such an answer, they simply went on waiting for destiny to run its course.

As for the liberal professions, the doctors came off best at the beginning. Their housing was protected. The Russians went to them for treatment, especially for Soviet children, who were frequently in a life-threatening condition. The incidence of bone tuberculosis was exceptionally high. Even when well, the Russian children were strangely unchildlike. They roved the streets, pale-faced and solemn – never laughing, never running, their large eyes full of immeasurable sadness, resignation and what seemed to be hopeless exhaustion. They would stand staring into shop windows, just looking, but even then their eyes were unsmiling.

The shop windows, in fact, were emptying. There were no goods to display. Their place was taken by portraits of Stalin. Second-hand shops alone were more crowded than ever, with more and more beautiful objects coming up for sale. Lwów was selling out its tradition and culture simply to stay alive. That was the hardest thing of all. Not only foodstuffs, but all kinds of consumer goods could now be found only outside the regular shops. The first free market of this sort came into being in the Mikolasz Passage in the very heart of the city. I used to go there regularly and spend a lot of time looking round. I managed to buy medicines, syringes, cotton wool, wood wool and all kinds of dressings. The first thing to be done, it seemed to me, was to lay in stocks for that coming spring, which was to be so 'rich with events'.[10]

I bought these articles – obviously stolen from pharmacies before they became State property – from the most unlikely traders. These treasures I then stashed away at home or with friends, and it seemed to me that I might still be of some use. Obviously, secrecy was of the essence in affairs of this kind. I was very angry one day when I happened to be at home sorting out a large batch of bandages on the carpet with the help of my friend Jadwiga Horodyska*, a sculptress, when in came a friend of hers, Renia Komorowska*, whose husband was a colonel. I was very upset that somebody I hardly knew should have seen what was going on and might well not keep it to herself.

A few months later the militia began to take too close an interest in that market passage. Twice they closed down all the traders they managed to catch, so we switched to the Skarbkowski building in the Jewish suburb of Lwów. There, on a large square covered by uncommonly huge heaps of muddy snow, there were swarms of people – all sorts and in all conditions, from the dregs to the cultured upper reaches of Lwów society – buying and selling absolutely everything, whether or not it was in demand. There were articles of furniture; parts of cars and other bits of machinery; a black market for dollars and paintings; blankets and bedclothes; rings; pillows, new and old – some amazingly dirty; men's trousers new and second-hand, in good condition or torn, some darned, some not; in fact, every item of clothing needed to stock a wardrobe, male or female, from evening dresses to flowery, fustian dressing-gowns; keys and screws; articles of china, cracked or pristine; buttons and needles; silver – real or fake; instruments, both musical and medical; and translations of thrillers by H. G. Wells.

All this buying and selling was going on amid tremendous uproar and jostling. I had only to appear for my suppliers of bandages and dressings to materialise at my elbow. They called me 'Doctor' and advised me to sell my patients this or that remedy – 'very dear' because there'd soon be no more left. Meanwhile another merchant close by was selling brand-new handcuffs from a wide range slung over his shoulder, while beside one of the booths I caught sight of a yellow rubber ring (the sort invalids use) gently hugging the waist of a mandolin. I've remembered that particular 'still life' all these years. I looked round at it all and terror seized me at the sight of this fragment of Asia that had descended on Lwów. It was so tragically evident that the East was devouring us. We were being swamped.

The Soviet ordinance of 21 December 1939, abolishing the Polish currency, paralysed all commercial and investment enterprises in train at the time. From one hour to the next we were face-to-face with ruin – nothingness. It was an enormous shock to everybody, a tremendous blow to the city's morale. People who had not heard the news went into shops as usual, only to be asked by shop assistants whether they had Russian roubles, since the złoty no longer existed. Dumbfounded and empty-handed, the would-be customers had to be shown the door. Others boarded trams. When they tried to pay the fare and had no Soviet money, the conductor stopped the tram and the passengers had to alight. People were at a total loss to understand. Everyone was asking: 'Where, and at what rate, can we exchange our złotys for roubles?'

'No rate, and there's nowhere to go. Złotys are no longer legal tender.' Only a very few Poles had roubles at that time. They needed to be working for Russians. By Christmas time the situation was becoming desperate. Then, to some extent, things began to improve, thanks to the black market. The Jews bought up the złotys – still valid on the 'other side' under the Germans – and vast quantities of złotys changed hands for a very small number of roubles.

The holiday season was very difficult, not only for want of cash. Worse still was the total lack of political information. The prevailing silence everywhere was deeply depressing, despite the fact that everyone felt sure it could not last for long. Come the spring, we believed, the Allies and the forces in the Middle East would attack the Germans and, obviously, the Bolsheviks would 'automatically clear out'. There were those who said it might take just a little longer, but never for a moment did we doubt the outcome.

Since there was no good news to report, the most astounding prophecies began to circulate by word of mouth. What was worse, people frequently wrote them down and kept them at home, where they were later discovered in house-to-house searches and used as highly incriminating evidence. A particular favourite was a rhymed prophecy, which, it is true, spoke of a four-year war – which at the time, so the propagators claimed, did not mean that the war in Europe (particularly in Poland, where it had started) would necessarily last that long because, as the prophecy went on to assert, the 'obscene cross'[11] and the Hammer would both be destroyed and Poland 'would extend from sea to sea'. During the winter, a prophecy attributed to St Andrzej Bobola was especially attractive. This held that the Russians would leave Poland on 7 or 9 January. Children who repeated this prophecy in school were arrested. Wernyhora,[12] too, continually disturbed us with fresh revelations. The struggle against these prophecies was hard going. People used them as drugs and, as is well known, that is a habit not at all easy to break.

The war between Russia and Finland[13] also gave us fresh hope and a belief in some inherent Soviet weakness. But the capitulation which ended that episode unleashed a major wave of depression. The news from across the River San, separating us from the 'German side', was deeply disquieting. The radio reported ever-increasing mass expulsions of Poles from Pomerania and the Poznań region to the General Government, as the Germans called that part of Poland where Poles were still allowed to reside. According to the radio, families, old people, women and children with no possessions, travelling in the bitter cold, were being hunted down and expelled from Polish towns and villages. They travelled for a week or more, and the corpses of those who died on the journey were often never unloaded. We heard about these things and were appalled, but were unable to grasp the full horror because it is never possible to comprehend fully what one has not personally experienced.

We constantly gained the impression that the West had no idea what was happening in our country. This weighed terribly on our minds, but there was one chance encounter at that time which delighted me greatly. I do not remember the precise date. All I know is that one evening during that ghastly winter I was on my way from one of our frequent meetings in the 'House of Professors' in Supiński Street and hurrying along Długosz Street, where the pavement was, of course, separated from the roadway by a rampart of snow. I was just passing under a street-lamp, with the light full upon me, when a sledge drew to a halt in the roadway. A fur-clad figure, standing up in the sledge, was trying to attract my attention by waving his arms. Beside the driver was a large suitcase. Much intrigued, I scrambled through the heaps of snow and into the roadway. The man in the sledge was Professor Wacław Lednicki*, who now apologised in elegant French for failing to get out of the sledge to bid me farewell because he was afraid of losing his suitcase. That night he was travelling to Kraków and from there, he added quietly, 'to Brussels, God willing'. I hurriedly told him how delighted I was that he was going. There was nobody better able to tell the West about the true state of affairs over here. He asked about my plans. I said I was staying on at the university where I belonged. The sledge was moving off. '*Buon viaggio*,'[14] I called out. '*Buona permanenza*!'[15] came the answering shout already from some way off.

In those depressingly monotonous days, the last evening of that tragic year was for me quite eventful. When I got home in the afternoon, I found a hopeless situation. In front of the house stood a long line of lorries – nineteen of them in all. One of them was being loaded with coal from our cellar. On orders from above, the militia had arrived to 'nationalise' all the coal from our block – coal bought before the war by our tenants' association. It struck me that Andzia was not about. A little later she appeared, running towards us and out of breath. 'I've been to the Prosecutor's office. He says they're not allowed to take our coal!' she shouted at the sight of me, still some way off.

I went to look for the previous owner of the building and found him sitting in his last remaining room, terrorised by the concierge, who would not let him out. Seeing that we had nothing to lose – the weather was already freezing – I started to go round all the flats in the building, hammering with my fists on every door and shouting for the women to come out. Remembering that during the *Terreur* of the French Revolution the women were the most dangerous, I decided to follow their example. 'Women, get out on the streets! This is revolution!' Within minutes, a few dozen women were out on the stairs. I explained that Andzia had word from the Prosecutor's office that the militia had no right to take our coal, and that we must try to save it by staging a demonstration and making as much noise as we could. The women expressed a readiness to join in, so out we all rushed – accompanied by three or four men, who were seemingly more frightened by us than by the militia. Having created a hideous uproar outside, we invaded the cellar from which the militia were heaving our coal out on to the street. When they saw us (and even more so when they heard us) the militiamen, in a panic and perfectly understanding our Polish, started appealing to us from the cellar to calm down. Meanwhile, a couple of Lwów street urchins were passing. Said one: 'They ought to call up a few battalions of women and Poland would be freed right away!' This laudatory comment fuelled our stomach for the fight to such an extent that the militia came up out of the cellar. Meanwhile a crowd had gathered around us, through which a Russian in uniform was shouldering his way. We threw ourselves on top of him, explaining that the militia obviously thought they were no longer living in a law-abiding state and that this coal was Communist coal, being the property of our tenants' 'Soviet'. The Bolshevik, relishing his role in the dispute, hurried away to the militia headquarters. When he returned a few minutes later there was no longer any sign of the militia or their lorries. Two lorryloads of coal had been driven away before we began our demonstration, but we did not feel the effect of that till the end of March, by which time there was no coal at all. For the time being, however, on New Year's Eve – worn out by our shouting and screaming – we returned to our own warm flats to rest on our laurels.

The year of 1940 began for me under a new and more promising sign. On 2 January I swore a military oath as a member of ZWZ (the Union for Armed Struggle). I had long wanted to belong to a military organisation, but had postponed the decision because secret societies were springing up all over the place, like mushrooms after rain. Many of them, however, bore a pronounced party-political stamp. I wanted to make quite sure that the group I joined was a genuine military organisation subject to the Polish Commander-in-Chief of the Armed Forces in France. Only then did I apply for membership, my efforts eventually being rewarded by being sworn in on the crucifix on 2 January, by the hand of Colonel Władysław Żebrowski*.

From that day onwards, for the next two and a half years, my thoughts and emotions centred on the contents of that oath. I believe that anybody who worked in the underground resistance, even if it was not given to him to perform great deeds, would admit that the experience gave more to us than the other way round. The resistance movement was the unfailing source of our strength to endure. Constant danger engenders the atmosphere in which the majority of Poles feel at their best. At the same time, we do not suggest that courage is not in itself deserving of reward. Besides, every one of us is grateful for those wonderful moments of exaltation; likewise for the gift of friendship tempered by fire. But there is another side to conspiracy. By its very nature, it is – or rather should be – a short-term enterprise. Thanks to the preparatory effort, which demands both ingenuity and caution, the deed is assured of success, which in turn inspires fresh courage. The resistance of the Polish underground – the Home Army – lasted for so many years! At the same time, its activities brought out the worst in some people. Vanity, one of the greatest perils to which mankind is prey, always falls on fertile ground whenever there is a chance to brag about something that nobody else knows anything about. This vanity, or boastfulness, was responsible for many of our misfortunes. Moreover, there were other dangers – including those of rash judgements, whether positive or negative. These were very plentiful in the prevailing conditions, especially because of our excessive fondness for going to extremes in nominating heroes and traitors. Above all, the weaker characters become warped and grow accustomed to continual lying, insincerity and mutual distrust. They also grew used – the danger was enormous among young people – to completely irregular occupations and often to wasting several weeks just waiting. They shed the burden of regular duty, disciplined effort and the continuity of work: guiding principles of every person of character, in whatever walk of life, who wishes to avoid becoming corrupted.

Conspirators of that kind are certain in future to talk a great deal more about themselves than those who spent all those years wandering – with neither a true name nor a roof over their heads, being hounded night and day by one or other of the enemies, often with no food and practically no clothes, living in forests and filthy basement cellars, yet performing feats of daring worthy of an epic by Homer.

At that time I knew nothing about things of that sort. All I knew was that I had been accepted and would be employed. At first, however, there was almost nothing to do. I used to transcribe radio news bulletins and, every few days, officers would meet at my home for briefings, consultations and discussions with other groups. Of all the people with whom I came into contact, there was one man whose image remains in my memory and my heart. He was not a professional military man, but he was the strongest and toughest, his courage the coolest and, at the same time, the most circumspect. This man was the parish priest of St Mary Magdalene, Father Włodzimierz Cieński*. I once confided to him a reaction of my own so powerful that I was at a loss to understand it.

One of the meetings at my flat was attended by a tall major, codename 'Kornel'*. At first sight of him, I experienced a violent repugnance mixed with downright fear. I found it difficult even to shake hands with him. To look back, years later, on the early days of our resistance efforts is enough to bleach the hair. Those meetings were held regularly at the same venue, the home of someone who, by reason of family origin, was particularly at risk – in a flat with no back-door kitchen entrance and constantly under surveillance by the authorities (a fact which, of course, I had reported to my superiors).

Worse still, Colonel Władysław Żebrowski, our District Commander, codename 'Żuk' (Beetle), stayed briefly at my flat. But the meetings went on taking place. Remembering what it was like, I can only conclude that we were extremely lucky. It does not say much for our common sense!

It was about now that we began to appreciate certain political aspects of our situation. The Soviet Constitution gave the various republics of the USSR a fair amount of autonomy. Moscow, at least nominally, reserved for itself only the conduct of foreign affairs, military matters and 'the security of the Revolution'. The rest was left in the hands of the various 'Soviet governments' – in our own case, that of Kiev, the Ukrainian capital. Constantly and at every step of the way we sensed that, in our daily life, we were being ruled not from Moscow but from Kiev; that we were dealing not with Russia, but rather with the problems of our tragic seventeenth century, the legacy of the rebellion in the Ukraine, led by the Cossack Hetman Bogdan Chmielnicki. From the east our lands were inundated (as they were after King Władysław IV) by a wave of socially inchoate barbarism, fighting against us under the banner of social slogans deriving in large part from an inferiority complex and a hatred of the indigenous culture which the invaders did not possess. Because that culture happened to be Polish, everything Polish had to be destroyed.

So far as the business of everyday life was concerned, we had to contend far more often with simple and coarsely simplistic Ukrainian nationalism than with Communism or Russian imperialism, which did not 'get involved in trifling affairs'.

On the other hand, this imperialism proceeding from Moscow was promising us – mainly by radio and often in very plain language – that the time was not far off when Russia would conquer all the Polish lands, and the border 'which now causes you such pain' would disappear. The Russians, too, had their own great science and culture before the war. These had been drowned in a sea of blood. Some spheres of science – in contrast to those of culture – had been successfully adapted, but without tradition there can be no culture. The Muscovites were well aware of this, which is why they treated educated people with respect, provided they could be absolutely sure that the results of their research would never and nowhere conflict with their conception of the class struggle, their materialistic philosophy or Russia's imperialist principles.

We at the university witnessed the struggle between Kiev and Moscow over the symbolic, but nevertheless important, matter of the university's name. It all hinged on a single word. Kiev turned to Moscow to approve the following title: 'The Ukrainian University of Lwów, in honour of Ivan Franko'. Moscow concurred, having struck out the word 'Ukrainian'. Seemingly, Moscow had nothing against dedicating the university to a Ukrainian poet, but the centre of learning itself should not be qualified by an adjective of nationality. There then appeared notices and announcements attributed to the 'University of Lwów in honour of Ivan Franko'. We knew, however, that the Ukrainians were not beaten, and that this 'decapitated' title continued to annoy them. The matter was referred back to Moscow, with the strong backing of some influential comrades. At last, one fine day, two large notice-boards painted crimson appeared at the entrance to the university, with the full title: on one board in Russian and, on the other (in second place, rather than first), in Ukrainian. Kiev had triumphed over the Ukranian University of Lwów in honour of Ivan Franko.

Kiev, however, had other problems of its own. To start with, it could count on the unswerving support of the local Ukrainian population, including its intellectuals. After a short while, though, it became apparent that the difference between our own people (who until recently – the First World War – had called themselves '*Rusini*') and the Kievans was a bottomless chasm. From Zaporoże to Red Russia is a long way, and 700 years of neighbourly relations with Western culture are simply not be wiped out. People reared for generations in a Polish cultural atmosphere – although politically hostile towards us – often came to us in despair, just to confide that this Ukraine that had suddenly taken control of them was unspeakably barbaric and diametrically alien. Such conversations imbued us with the boldest hopes of future concord and understanding.

We were also deluding ourselves about other Soviet internal difficulties. Some of the more cultured officers of the Red Army, especially Russians born and bred, made no secret from the hosts with whom they were billeted of their lively antipathy towards the NKVD and its methods. Particularly noteworthy was the NKVD's extreme anti-Semitism towards the Jews, who were numerically predominant in this institution. It seemed to us that there were already radical cracks in the Moscow edifice.

We were surprised by the daily increase in the amount and precision of information about individual citizens required for the record: their social origins and occupations. The only exceptions were refugees 'from the other side', who admittedly had to register, but immediately thereafter were left in peace. In any case, their numbers were decreasing. In November the Germans and the Russians reached some kind of agreement that was valid for a few days, to let a large number of refugees cross the River San boundary with official permission.

All pre-war inhabitants of our district – except for old people and children – were compelled to work. A work-card was the sole guarantee of one's right to existence, accommodation, food – and very nearly air and water as well. Anyone who did not work was an enemy of the Revolution. According to Article 118 of the Constitution, every citizen had the right to work and to be paid wages commensurate with the amount and type of work done. Society might well agree unreservedly with these basic principles. The sole employer, however, was the State. If anyone who did not work was supposed to perish and if the State alone could give him work, then the only one with the right to exist is he to whom the State (that is, the Party) sees fit to give work. In other words, if the Party does not like him, he will not get a job and will be bound to die. For us, this discovery came as a profound shock.

Everywhere and at all times private life was controlled by the authorities, who allocated to each his prescribed cell. Every contact with officialdom – and there was no way of avoiding it – entailed further consequences. The citizen was ceaselessly chivvied and required to voice his opinion of the regime, the changing social order, the new conditions; he was constantly being pressed to say whether he thought the Soviet solution of social problems was fair and just, whether he liked the reforms introduced and – this was the most frequent question – whether he felt at home with the Russians and was glad of their presence. Evasive replies were very much frowned upon and every word was subjected to well nigh microscopic examination.

At the same time, educational problems were becoming more acute. The schools had reopened swiftly after the Soviet invasion and a new syllabus had quickly been introduced. Many hours were to be devoted to the study of the Ukrainian language. This also applied to the university. Russian was not taught. Polish study was reduced to reading and writing, and religious instruction was entirely forbidden. In its place pupils were given talks about the Soviet paradise, the kindness of dear 'Daddy' Stalin, the best social security, the cruelty of the Polish landowners and their persecution of the workers. This propaganda caused serious concern to parents, because the children reacted to it so badly – or so well – that the number of arrests grew daily.

As far as the history and literature of Poland were concerned (and likewise religious instruction), children educated in wartime undoubtedly learned more about these subjects than the preceding generation. The banned subjects were studied at home with a passion not previously seen. Knowledge of Poland and its religion flooded their young minds as an indissoluble entity in accordance with tradition, just as the shedding of blood – shed for these ideals by school-age youth – was also strictly in line with tradition.

It has to be admitted that, apart from the forbidding of religious teaching in schools, there was, contrary to expectations, no religious persecution in the true sense of the word. Priests obviously found themselves under strict surveillance, but no clergy were arrested other than on solid political grounds. The authorities dealt with religious life by other means. They imposed an enormous tax burden on the churches. I was kept regularly informed about these developments from my home district. In the all-Polish village of Chłopy, near Komarno, we had just built a big, new church[16] when war broke out. On that account, the Soviet authorities levied a huge tax on the village, which, in the course of the war, earned a great deal of money and paid off the tax at once. Not content with that, the peasants vied with one another to speed up completion of the building work and also paid to equip and furnish the interior of the church.

Once, while walking along Sykstuska Street, I heard behind me a demonstratively loud shout: 'May the Lord be praised!' It was one of the peasants with an immense sack across his shoulders. 'Bet you don't know what I've got here, m'lady!' he declared with a promising wink.

'No idea,' I replied, 'but I'm immensely curious.'

'It's the blessed St Anthony. Just bought him!' came the triumphant response. 'I ask you, ma'am, they're so stupid! Such idiots! As they passed by the building, they shouted at us, called us madmen. What they don't know is, it's people who don't believe in a God are the real lunatics and fools!'

Some of the Bolsheviks seemed to share his opinion, sneaking out to Confession very early in the morning while it was still dark and, having confessed their sins, going on to take Communion at the Lord's Table. It was said that one day a priest who was distributing the holy wafers suddenly paused and hesitated at sight of a Soviet soldier, kneeling in front of him. Understanding the priest's problem, it seems, the soldier raised his head and said under his breath: '*Davajte mi Boha*!'[17] upon which the priest granted his wish.

Peasants used to visit me fairly often, bringing news of happenings at home. Things, it seemed, were going badly. The main purpose of their visits was to collect information about public affairs. They wanted me to tell them how much longer they would have to wait. 'When are we finally going to get this new Poland?' Farmland had been distributed among them, but they were not satisfied with the distribution, complaining that the individual shares were too small. Moreover, the fact that they did not have to pay for the land filled them with distrust of those who were handing out what they did not own. At least when they were speaking to me, they stressed that they regarded the present state of affairs as provisional. They were also uneasy when they became aware that, personally, I was in no hurry at all to see an eventual return to the conditions obtaining previously: great responsibility on the one hand, and, on the other, great resentment among a large portion of society, which had, of late, surrounded the so-called major landowners. When the visitors returned home after seeing me, they told people in Komarno: 'She's not doing at all badly without us, earning a good salary at the university and she's got some peace at last. She's not in a hurry to come back to us and that's a bad thing.' However, it was only when there began to be talk of creating collective farms that people started to panic.

The situation of the farm owners was particularly difficult because the localities affected were the traditionally all-Polish villages: Chłopy, Buczały, Tuligłowy and the age-old Kazimierz settlements.

Even before the war there were always violent squabbles among these villages, whose inhabitants were deeply aware of their nationality and spoke a charming, slightly archaic brand of Polish, surrounded – as it were – by a sea of Ukrainian. For the time being, they were very well behaved, but life was not easy for them. One day a farmer from a neighbouring village, Klicko-Kolonia, came to see me. That was a new settlement that sprang up after the First World War, when my father parcelled out the ancient farm of Klicko. Those who received the portions of land were exclusively Polish peasants from the villages round about. There were no outsiders at all. My guest was clearly worried and depressed. After a lengthy talk about commonplace matters, he suddenly said: 'I came here today because something new is going on over our way, but I don't yet know what it is.'

'What? Come on, out with it.'

'They're making us all register.'

'Who?'

'Us, all of us who bought farmland after the last war – that's the whole of Klicko-Kolonia.'

'Who's making this register?'

'The Russians who've come here. What are we to do?'

'Do your best not to let them make detailed lists.'

'And what about our Ukrainians, who are always spying on us, counting every soul and checking every child? Hope to God it isn't another deportation to Russia. That's what the Ukrainians have been talking about.'

'They're just trying to frighten you. The idea's unthinkable!'

Off he went. That was a morning in January, very early and very dark. On 11 February, a day that was equally dark, there arrived at my flat a peasant from Buczały village, who struck Andzia and me as totally demented. He was babbling and crying. 'They've gone!' he shouted. There were thirty degrees of frost outside and I tried to bring him to his senses with the help of a hot drink. He swallowed it and sat down. I then heard how, during the night, the military had in a very short time rounded up the whole of Klicko-Kolonia – that is to say, all the families from the neighbouring Polish villages who had settled on the former farmlands after the First World War. Half an hour after our people had been driven out, while it was still dark, Ukrainians from nearby villages moved in and occupied their homesteads. The Polish deportees were allowed to take with them only what they could snatch and pack at the last minute, a little food and eiderdowns or quilts. According to our visitor's account, they couldn't have had more than an hour in which to clear out.

'Where have they taken them?'

'By train.'

'Train? Where to?'

'It's still standing in the local station, but the soldiers aren't letting anyone near it.'

Throughout our exchange my mind was obsessed by the thought that they could not just be isolating Klicko-Kolonia. Something far worse might be under way.

'Have they taken anyone from Buczały?' I asked.

'Nobody. Nor any of us at Chłopy.'

He left after an hour, promising to return as soon as he had fresh information.

Around noon there was another visitor, someone I did not know personally, but who was just as frantically distraught as the first man, though he showed it in a different way. This time it was not a peasant, but an engineer from Lwów. He neither babbled nor wept, but talked awfully fast, in broken sentences that were terribly hard to follow. Moreover, he frequently interrupted his repetitive account with straightforward requests for help from me. After a while I realised that he was the brother-in-law of a forester who during the night, together with his wife and two-month-old baby, had been kidnapped from the Komarno forests. The engineer said that the train was still standing in Komarno station, and that the forester had been able to hand the baby over to his wife's mother, who had managed to approach the carriage, but she was seen by a Russian soldier who made the grandmother give the infant back to its mother. From the same engineer, I learned that at a few stations between Komarno and Lwów were standing other trains, guarded by soldiers, from which the sound of singing could be heard.

About noon came a third visitor – this time an elderly farmer from Chłopy. This man said almost nothing, but sat in the kitchen clenching his fists. When, after a short while, he had thawed sufficiently, he told me – as though savouring every word – that he knew exactly who the Ukrainians were who had listed the so-called 'colonists' for the Russians. Not one of them would escape him alive, as soon as Poland was free once more. Having delivered this declaration, he left the flat, with hardly a word of farewell. It was then that I realised what an enormous source of strength the craving for revenge is, and what naïve dreamers we were who often imagined that, after this terrible remedy, the two communities might one day find it possible to live together, or even share a platform.

The next day, 12 February, Lwów was gripped by panic. More and more trains appeared at all the railway stations. Long lines of cattle-wagons stood waiting on the tracks. The singing of hymns could be heard. The hymn most often sung was '*Gorzkie Żale*'[18] for this was the season of Lent. The trains were closely guarded by the military. Meanwhile, the locals and people from the surrounding areas were flocking to the stations. If a wagon happened to be guarded by a Kirghiz or a Kalmuk, there was nothing one could do. If the soldier standing guard was a Russian, more often than not he would turn a blind eye, and sometimes even take it upon himself to distribute food, water, milk or medicine, pushing it in through the small, barred window set high up.

The cold was appalling. The winter's unbroken succession of freezing days was as full of despair as the uninterrupted run of fine weather in September 1939. Trains continued to pull into the stations. But the wagons were kept closed. The occupants were allowed only to get rid of corpses – and sometimes not even that was permitted. The bodies were picked up from the tracks in the evening; there were many frozen children among them. It seemed that, contrary to what happened in Klicko, many deportees were not even able to take an eiderdown or a rug with them. In some villages – if the local Ukrainian Soviet so ordained – they were forbidden to take anything at all. The trains were arriving from areas west and north of Lwów, and news of what was going on filtered through from the provinces and districts all over the Russian-occupied sector. Poles from all the neighbouring villages who had bought land after 1918 were being deported as foreign elements, artificially planted in the region by the then Polish government. Apart from such families, they took away only the professional foresters of the region. On sidings at all Lwów railway stations stood lines of cattle-trucks, averaging eighty persons per wagon. Some people died; others were born. The bitter cold persisted. Finally, the first trains began to move – eastwards. Always, without exception, at that last awful moment of departure, the same song – or rather, the same two songs – resounded: '*Rota*' and '*Boże, coś Polskę*'.[19]

Around this time (I cannot recall the exact date) I received one of the most memorable visits of my life. The man who came to see me was Father Tadeusz Fedorowicz*, who used to drop in from time to time for a word about various aid matters. When I opened the door for him, I was immediately struck by his expression: peaceful, almost joyful, glowing – as though with some inner happiness. This was in strange contrast to the suffering by which we were surrounded just then.

'I've come to say goodbye.'

'Where are you off to, Father?'

'I don't know.'

He sat down and drew a small crystal glass from his pocket.

'Just a little something from home,' he said with a smile. Then, from another pocket, he produced a tiny book in which was printed the Ordinary of the Mass. Now, I understood.

I knew that some priests had been trying to squeeze into the cattle-trucks that were about to head eastwards. Despite all the guards could do to stop them, some had managed to get through. My guest told me that permission for his journey had already been granted by his spiritual superior and that he was hoping to sneak aboard one of the cattle-trucks as it was moving. He was counting on that happening within the next two days. He asked me to say a prayer for his success. Then off he went, smiling as he bade me farewell. His eyes were shining. As I closed the door behind him, I had the impression that a trace of his radiance remained. A few hours later, my door-bell rang. A workman of some sort – quite unknown to me – was standing outside. He did not greet me and would not come in. He merely said: 'Father Fedorowicz has gone. He succeeded.' With that, he turned and walked away. I had time to call after him only a single word: 'Thanks!'

These events were taking place all over eastern Poland between 10 and 13 February. Ten days or so later the local command of the ZWZ – my branch of the resistance – already possessed information that about one million Polish peasants had been deported. Later, the estimate was found to be fairly accurate.

The only thing to do was hold on. But even that was becoming increasingly difficult. Spring – so long and eagerly awaited – was swift approaching, but there was no hint of a change on the political horizon. We consoled one another with the thought that the radio obviously could not report what was really happening, at a time when preparations were surely under way for a general offensive. The weather was still dreadfully cold and there were more and more arrests. More frequently, too, there were reports of torture being used to extract confessions. These tortures (apart from beatings that drew blood, and so forth) were sometimes modelled on oriental practices, often with nails being driven under the fingernails. Sometimes the torturers were Jewish. A large number of Jews were involved, working for the NKVD together with Communist-inclined members of the Jewish proletariat, which had largely supported the Bolsheviks from the outset. Happily, however, I can assert that there were also Jews of another kind. I was brought up in a spirit of hostility to anti-Semitism, which has remained my attitude throughout.

One day a stranger called on me, apologised for not revealing his name and explained that he was a Jew, which was why he had approached me. He begged me to remove everything I valued from the flat, or I would lose the lot. They were going to deal with all Poles, he said, and the most vulnerable of all, of course, were those with 'counter-revolutionary antecedents'. He finished by saying that he had come as a Jew because, although he did not know me personally, he felt it his duty to call on someone who, at the university, had opposed the beating up of Jews. With that, he went away. There were two more visits of this sort – one with an offer of money.

Polish society continued to wait. We had a lot of spare time and it weighed heavily upon us. There was nothing to do at the university. The lectures were of such poor quality that they were barely worth preparing, and research was out of the question. The quality of the students, too, was steadily declining. The tremendously debilitating absence of all initiative was paralysing not only the university, but all Lwów. Everyone – not only Poles, but Ukrainians, too, as well as imported Bolsheviks – was theoretically employed, but nobody was actually working. The atmosphere was characterised by a dull lethargy and a boundless indifference towards work, in which nobody believed. During this period I started giving English lessons to one of our professors. My pupil turned out to be very capable and, after a couple of months, we were able to progress to reading. I chanced to have a book that I thought would be specially appropriate: Lord Acton's *History of Freedom.* I doubt whether that magnificent work has ever been read with greater excitement and understanding than it was by us at that time, having just lost our own most precious possession – the book's exalted theme. Reading it was for us a kind of protest, the only form of protest available to us, a protest of the spirit against everything that was going on around us.

At about the same time, various items of news reached me from Komarno. The Director of Forests, Karol Dudik, the most devoted friend of our family for more than thirty years, had been arrested. He was to pay with his life for his attachment to his work, for he had refused to leave Komarno despite my earnest pleas. The Muscovites lost no time in deporting him to the trackless wastes of Russia,[20] where – somewhere – he perished. His family was deported to Kazakhstan after his arrest.

I also got to hear that the NKVD in Lwów had sent an enquiry to the local authorities in Komarno concerning my pre-war relations with the people of the area. The local council committee gave me a flattering testimonial, a copy of which they sent to the university. I had an unpleasant presentiment of trouble when I heard about this, but soon we were all preoccupied with more important matters. Easter came and went, and with it the period of the Church's deepest lamentations, ending with the glorious Resurrection hymn '*Wesoły nam dzień dziś nastał*' ('A happy day is come to us today'). The holiday fell at the end of March. On 10 April, Europe was shaken to its foundations. Hitler had occupied Denmark and attacked Norway. We awoke as from a nightmare sleep. At last! It seemed to us as though, at the very season when mountain torrents – freed from their wintry fetter – were once more stirring, this sudden deluge of events promised to burst the loathsome bonds by which we ourselves were bound. We sat glued to the radio. We could think of nothing else. All unpleasant personal matters, even dangers, seemed of no account. In any case, we thought: 'It can't last much longer, now!'

I was not particularly worried even to hear from Andzia that for the past two days a tall Russian major had been asking for me at the flat. Andzia mentioned that he was wearing a blue-peaked cap. At last he managed to find me at home. He was a Russian all right, but with nothing coarse about him – rather well-mannered in fact, tall and fair-haired. He introduced himself as Major Bedjajev. He sat down and informed me calmly and politely that he was moving into my flat. I replied that I already had sub-tenants and, besides, since I was a member of the university staff, my flat was exempt from requisitioning.

I pointed to the notice hanging on the front door to that effect, still in position after the defeat of Pawłyszeńko. The Major listened to all this, after which he said quietly: 'You are no longer at the university.' He handed me a letter that he took from his wallet. It was very short and addressed to Bedjajev from the university, informing him that I had been relieved of my post. I said that until I received official notice in writing, I could not consider myself as no longer employed. What was more, I needed to go at once to the university, where I was due to lecture. The Major replied courteously that he quite understood and that I would be receiving official confirmation.

I went along to the university. Nobody in the Secretariat knew anything about it. So I went to deliver my lecture. At the entrance to the hall, a woman I did not know barred my way and requested a short conversation in private. We went into a side corridor. There she told me that there had been a leakage of information from the local branch of the ZWZ, that it was probably a case of treachery and that a couple of persons in my section had already been taken away. An engineer acquaintance living in the same apartment block had sent her to warn me. At that moment I remembered seeing her name on the door of the ground-floor flat in our building. She told me I must get away at once, without even first calling at my flat. I believed what this person said, but I was not allowed to enter into a conversation with her unless authorised to do so. Besides, I knew that the engineer, though thoroughly trustworthy, was also rather apt to fuss and I did not think what she had told me was sufficiently precise. I told her I knew nothing whatsoever about the matter and must get on with my lecture. Into the hall I went and began talking about the early sculptures of Donatello. That same day I received by special messenger what was known as a 'Category 1 Passport', describing me as a university professor and a Soviet citizen of the highest value to the State. I knew that such a passport, rarely granted, gave 'absolute' protection against deportation and that this was the Soviet way of making clear that my academic qualifications ranked more highly on the agenda than the shame of my social origins.

The next morning, 11 April, I received a letter identical to the one Bedjajev had shown me, releasing me from my work at the university and addressed to the university itself. Professor Podlacha*, then head of the department, went to see 'Rector' Marczenko, who informed him that his duty was not to concern himself with professors such as me, but to educate future professors from among the sons of workers.

That evening friends advised me not to sleep in the flat for a couple of nights, since, having lost my job, I was now just an ordinary 'lodger', with the added disadvantage that a major in the NKVD had his eye on my flat. I did not care for this advice, but I gave in on the grounds that, in such a situation, bravado was inadmissible. So I spent the night at Wisia Horodyska's place, on her spare sofa. We gossiped for hours, both of us being severely shaken by the numerous arrests of recent days. In many cases, heads of families had been taken away, particularly doctors and landowners. We knew that some of them were still in Lwów in the Brygidki prison.

The following day, 12 April, was normal enough. At noon I gave my usual English lesson in my library at home, after which I left the flat. After supper at a friend's flat, an acquaintance took me to the place where I was to spend the night. About ten o'clock we passed by my house, and I went to lie down on a hospitable sofa elsewhere. We slept badly. The traffic was unusually heavy, with cars and cabs streaming past all night. At dawn we were roused by the concierge with the news that, overnight, 'half Lwów' had been taken away. We went to the windows. By the very pale light of dawn, heavy lorries were driving past, crammed with people. The passengers were smartly dressed. I remember seeing women in mourning veils, sitting in carts, as stiff as statues. They were guarded by Red Army soldiers and militia, standing on the running boards. As we were watching, in came the acquaintance who had brought me here the previous evening. With a strange expression on his face, he silently handed me a small parcel. I opened it and found that it contained my toilet requisites and some underwear. 'Miss Andzia has sent you these. She says you cannot return to the flat. They're already inside waiting for you.' It seemed that they had arrived during the evening and were already in my flat when we passed by the building on our way back from supper. More of them had arrived during the night, fully armed. In the end, there were eight of them in the flat. They tried, machine-carbines at the ready, to frighten Andzia into betraying where I had gone for the night. The girl stubbornly insisted that she hadn't any idea. They finally left after daybreak, but continued to observe the house from the street. Meanwhile, Andzia went out, but instead of coming to me, she set off in the opposite direction to mislead the guards. She then ran to my friends and asked them to warn me.

Meanwhile, news was coming in from various parts of the city. By noon, we already knew that the people arrested were packed into the now familiar trains waiting at the city stations. This time those arrested were exclusively residents of Lwów city: officers' families, retired officials, doctors and landowners. These four groups were being terribly depleted just then. Furthermore, among the other groups affected were all families whose fathers had been arrested a few days earlier. Of the 'runners' – those refugees from the west, German-occupied part of Poland – not one was arrested. Among the landowners, the first to be taken were those about whom the Soviets had received flattering reports from the inhabitants of their former properties. A landowner who was not only not a bloodsucker, but displayed a social conscience, would give the lie to their propaganda and, by the same token, was a dangerous enemy of the Revolution.

Once again, the urban and suburban population rushed to the railway stations; once again, they pushed everything they could into the wagons for the deportees; once again, priests were smuggled aboard.

The property of deportees was subject to immediate sale, and the funds realised were meant to be sent to the former owners in cash. I know some cases where that actually happened. From the first day, my own flat was occupied by Major Bedjajev. Part of the furniture he had burned because 'nobody wanted it'. Some of it was stolen by the concierge. Gone were my notes and, above all, the contents of my reference library (not to speak of other things, such as personal mementoes of the dead). I know that thousands (even millions) of people in Europe have had the same experience in recent years, but not only is awareness of this no consolation; on the contrary, it only makes matters worse. The more people we have among us robbed of their past, the greater the threatened decline of tradition and spiritual continuity – in a word, culture.

In the meantime I was forced to hide. I could not stay with people who were known to be my friends, because I knew I was a wanted person. Yet acquaintances with no obligations of friendship towards me took me into their homes. This particular three-week period was unspeakably unpleasant for me. To know that I was constantly exposing my protectors to danger weighed on me more than I can say. I was expecting the NKVD every time the door bell rang. I trembled for my hosts' safety, yet I myself hardly knew what to do. It seemed to me there was no point in creeping into the German-occupied zone. It was impossible to work under Hitler. Here, on the other hand, my task was to hang on while waiting for the approach of the 'moment of resurrection', which would see me safely across the border, first to Italy and thence to the Polish Government in France and the Anglo-Saxon countries.

I thought at that time that the West really did not know what was going on in Poland, that it lacked information, since the radio broadcasts reported always and only the terror and cruelty of the *German* occupation!

As if out of spite, the border crossing across the Carpathians to Hungary or Romania was impossible just then. The last groups had been picked up to a man, and nowadays the borders were so strictly patrolled that none of the guides wanted to risk it. Today, as I write these words, my heart is filled with gratitude to Providence which by making those unreasonable plans impossible allowed me to stay and work for another two years in Poland. But it meant continuing to wait, and that was the worst thing about it. I tried as far as possible to put the time to good use by attempting to prepare for work abroad. For the moment, what mattered was the first step: Rome.

Having made contact again with Father Włodzimierz Cieński, I asked if I might see him before my departure; since I was set on going to Rome, I would like to take any messages and be given some guidance on what to tell the Vatican. One day Father Cieński sent word that he would be at the Main Post Office in Lwów at five o'clock in the afternoon, and that from there Wisia Horodyska would lead him to me. I prepared a series of questions to ask him and waited impatiently for the man in whom I had such confidence. I felt sure this parting conversation, which meant so much to me for personal reasons, would provide me with crucial guidelines for work in the field of information, for which I was preparing myself. Six o'clock passed and still nobody appeared. At about seven Wisia finally arrived – alone. I took one look at her and said: 'Cieński's been arrested.'

'Yes.'

Her information was that the priest had been abducted from his own parish presbytery that afternoon, wearing his soutane, which was just as he would have wished. More than once he had said to me: 'They're bound to come for me one day, so let them take me wearing my soutane. It's often necessary these days for a priest to wear civilian clothes to avoid endangering anybody he calls on. But I've no desire to travel to the depths of Russia in disguise.'

His arrest caused great depression in Lwów, the more so because at the time the shock of the recent deportations had by no means worn off. For months people slept with food and ski-clothes by their beds. There were some who even wished to be deported because they could no longer bear the strain of waiting. Despite everything, I was determined to obtain guidance about seeking an audience with the Pope. I sent word to find out whether Archbishop Twardowski* would see me before I set out for Rome. In response, he named a day for me to attend seven o'clock morning Mass in the monastery where he was living after being evicted from his palace. After Mass, I was to follow him as he retired from the chapel to his room. For the occasion I dressed in clothes as far removed as possible from my normal day attire – scarf round my head, spectacles on my nose, and a bottle of vodka in a small basket under my arm – and set off for the monastery in question. I attended the Archbishop's Mass and followed him as he came out. I was told to wait a few minutes in a small parlour, so that I just had time to shed my alien accessories before he returned. Once we were seated, I told him that I was going to Rome and would surely have an audience with the Pope. Would he advise me what to say?

The old man listened intently. When I had finished, he said with a smile: 'Please tell the Holy Father that all is well with us. Tell him that the entire clergy – I mean it literally, because a very few weak elements fell away at the outset and their defection was actually to our advantage – tell him that the entire clergy is now in very good shape. Tell him that quite a number of priests have succeeded in travelling to the depths of Russia with the deportees, and that others – possibly all of us – are waiting to be deported or whatever else lies ahead of us, but that the anti-religious propaganda in the schools is not catching on; that the population, above all the intelligentsia who previously kept their distance, is now rallying to us. A large number of people are receiving Holy Communion, as we can tell by the unusual increase in the demand for Hosts. Tell the Holy Father that I, and all the clergy and faithful of my archdiocese, send him our assurance of boundless affection and, for the Holy See, of our readiness to sacrifice our last drop of blood, if need be. But please don't fail to assure him that all is well.'

I looked and listened. I had heard that this elderly priest was a modest man, with no very pronounced personality![21] At that moment I could understand how the power of an idea can raise its exponent high above all human suffering, anxieties and fears – even above the strain of heroic conduct – into a sphere of cheerful buoyancy, where only what is true and essential exists. When he had finished speaking, he blessed me for the journey and I could see the depth of his emotion at bidding farewell to somebody who was to establish what might be the final link between himself and Rome. Then he said in a changed, almost light-hearted voice: 'Now please get dressed here beside me!' He much liked my headscarf, but when he saw the bottle of vodka protruding from my basket, he seemed to beam with almost childish delight. I came away feeling very small.

Spring arrived – that spring so long awaited and desired – but with it came not liberation, but the dreadful news that the Allies were evacuating Norway. So it was not over yet! It was still going to drag on.[22] How much longer could it possibly last? At about that time I had to change my quarters yet again and move in with some other acquaintances. I could not stay any longer in the previous flat, since the only window in my room looked out on a small courtyard with a militiaman living opposite. Although the only ventilation I had was through the little doors of the stove, the militiaman was beginning to take an interest in me. The windows of my new room gave onto a scrap of wasteland with a big old birch tree, the branches of which were just then covered in little green leaves. I had not the least doubt – and said as much to everybody – that before the birch shed its leaves I would return to a free Lwów. For me, the thought of leaving the city was inexpressibly hard. This time, however, I really must get out. The route through the mountains was still impossible. We got word, however, that the crossing to Hungary by way of Zakopane was very much easier. I was therefore obliged to consider something which so far I had not dreamed of – namely, 'going over to Hitler' and then crossing into Hungary. About then, a second train was being made ready for the return of another batch of 'runaways', people who after the September campaign had fled eastwards 'to be safe'. The arrangements were being worked out by a Soviet and a German commission. Friends helped me, and an acquaintance without the least obligation on my account proposed something that I felt I had to accept, though with a heavy heart. There was simply no other way out. He had all his papers and was travelling to Kraków and offered to take me with him.[23] At first, the situation appeared to be that I could travel only as the wife of this gentleman, and that I would therefore have to contract a Soviet marriage with him – a so-called 'five-rouble' (that being the official fee). When it later turned out that I need only be his sister, we breathed more easily, I must admit – both of us. So papers were forged for me in his name. A chemistry professor at the university, working by night in his department, managed to remove the name from my green identity card without the colour fading, and wrote in the surname of my 'brother'.

The moment of separation and departure was approaching. Although I knew that I was only a burden to everybody, I still felt like a deserter. Apart from that, I was oppressed by the knowledge that I was endangering still further a man I hardly knew, who was already being hunted by the Soviets. I took leave of my closest friends and my ever-loyal Andzia. For all anybody knew, these people might be heading for the heart of Asia, or wherever else barbarity might drag them. True, I was myself heading into the unknown, but at least I was moving westwards and, whatever became of me, I was escaping. The parting might perhaps have been a little less painful, had I known at the time that it was not because of my family origins that I was being hunted, but as a result of 'leaks' from inside the ZWZ, for it was 'Kornel', the tall major whom I had instantly found so repugnant, who betrayed us. Today, at time of writing, out of our entire Lwów group, only three are still alive: Father Cieński, Jan Jaworski* and me.

The painful moment of departure fell on the evening of 3 May. It was a clear, warm spring night. A hackney-cab drove us through that city so dear to me; to this day, I remember the slender silhouette of the Church of the Bernardines in the moonlight. We drove to a large garage from which a goods lorry, due to start before dawn, was to take us all to Przemyśl. We were late leaving. The sky was already growing light as we drove out of Lwów, seeing on our way the dome of St George's Church and the towers of St Elizabeth's. There were about twenty of us, but nobody said a word to anyone else. We passed the Jagiellonian Castle and the road that branches left from there. There was a signpost inscribed 'To Komarno'. It was not until we had already passed it and were driving on that, suddenly, for the first time, I no longer had a link with any place on Earth. I had severed all personal connections. I was now about to set off into the wide world.

Przemyśl was swarming with acquaintances of mine. People kept running up to me in the street with a cry of joy, having heard that I had been dead for some time; that I had slipped into the gutter from a drain pipe while escaping from my flat; that I had been shot on the 'green border'. These shouts and the vexatious chatter came, of course, from various politically 'unorthodox' individuals who happened to be travelling to Przemyśl and for all concerned the encounters were extremely inconvenient.

That day I called on the Suffragan Bishop of Przemyśl, Father Tomaka*, whom I knew well. It occurred to me that he might have some news to impart to the Ordinary Bishop on the German side. Bishop Tomaka received me with genuinely paternal concern.

'What are you doing here?'

'I am trying to get out, Excellency,' I replied.

He gave me quite a lot of news for Bishop Barda*. At last, on the third day, we had to undergo a final Soviet inspection. It was unusually thorough. Jewellery was confiscated and a large amount of money in Polish złotys, for which the guards hunted with rapacious zeal, despite the fact that for some months (since December, to be precise) the złoty had been abolished in the Russian sector. Notwithstanding, they failed to discover a considerable sum of money hidden in the lining of a leather bag, nor did they find the pearls I had sewn into the collar of my overcoat.

After that our documents had to be examined. My papers did not attract all that much attention, probably because my 'brother's' documents were exemplary. Next we were formed up in fours and told to proceed to the bridge. As we walked past the Russian guards, they shouted : 'See you in Kraków.'[24] They were like all Red Army soldiers: dirty, unshaven and in poor-quality uniforms. When we got to the middle of the bridge, we saw coming to meet us a group of German soldiers: splendidly built men, looking extremely smart in their spick-and-span turnout. With them were Red Cross nurses in white aprons. More than one of us was heard to comment. 'Whatever else, this is Europe.'

Chapter 2

Kraków

May 1940–June 1941

We crossed the bridge and there we stood on the soil of German-occupied Poland. German soldiers were all around us. After a brief pause, the order was given to march. So, four abreast, we paraded through Zasanie 'Deutsch-Przemyśl'. For eyes weary of deciphering Cyrillic script, it was a real joy to read notices in Polish on the signboards. Not far off, small groups of people stood around gazing at us. Now and then women would wave their headscarves in our direction. They obviously did not dare approach us and looked terrified. We were escorted to a barracks where extreme filth was the dominant feature. There was nowhere to sit down, and a wash was impossible to imagine. The first two days we spent sitting on our suitcases.

At last, the women and children were called out with their belongings. Once again we had to form fours and were marched to a bath-house. There, women in aprons ordered us to undress completely and put our things in a numbered bag. The same number was burned on a small wooden tag that we were ordered to hang round our necks. My number was fifty-seven. I remember it well, since I managed to hide the plaque and smuggle it out. I kept it for ages. I wanted to have something to prove, after the war, that I had been ordered, while stark naked, to parade with a number round my neck. I was still a trifle over-sensitive in those days!

Next, we were lined up again in the bath-house, this time in pairs, and chased under the showers amid shouts of '*Ratten hinaus*!'[1] From there, to the same accompaniment, we were made to walk with hands raised along a narrow passage leading to another hall. Two men in white coats were posted at the entrance. Standing opposite were a number of eleven- or twelve-year-old boys, specially selected from among us for the purpose of humiliation. We were then moved on, no longer in pairs, but one at a time. The men in white coats peered into our mouths, and anyone not holding her hands high enough had them roughly forced up by the searchers who were examining our armpits, clearly on the look-out for gold or jewellery. They found quite a lot.

After this so-called 'disinfection' – as thorough as it proved rich in booty – the search was extended to our bags and other belongings, then we were ordered to put on our clothes again and chased into the yard. One woman fainted. A German Red Cross nurse approached her, uttering such a yell that the woman instantly recovered. After that, we were again made to form fours and were led away to a much cleaner barracks, where we were even allowed to lie on straw.

On the evening of the fourth day we were marched to the railway station for the journey to Kraków. When the train finally began to move, most of the passengers expressed their joy aloud: 'At last!' Many of them, overcome by an immense weariness, fell asleep at once. Others stood watching in the warm spring darkness as the lights beyond the River San and the gentle contours of the hills behind slowly vanished from sight – along with the eastern region of their birth.

The morning of 8 May 1940: Kraków. A city of sun and movement. No destruction. Lots of Germans in the streets. The best shops and restaurants had signs saying '*Nur für Deutsche*'.[2] All the same, the tenor of external everyday life appeared a hundred times more normal than in Lwów and with far fewer changes on the surface. The majority of my acquaintances were still living in their own flats and inviting friends to meals (albeit frugal ones), always served on genuine porcelain with silver spoons and forks. This we found astonishing after the tragic 'clearance sale' of goods and properties in Lwów. Only now did we finally realise the full import of that Soviet ordinance abolishing the Polish złoty. The German-occupied zone of Poland was spared that economic catastrophe. Nor, above all, did it undergo the total Asianisation of its lifestyle, or the abandonment of certain ingrained European conventions.

I remember how amazed I was during the first few days of my stay to find, waiting for me when I got home, the visiting card of Professor Stanisław Kutrzeba*. What strange people, I thought, still finding a need for such antediluvian niceties! A month later I was ordering my own visiting cards. But in the first days we found this superficial continuity of an earlier lifestyle painful and offensive. All our thoughts were focused on Lwów. Who else had been deported? We repeated this dread question to one another and every morning to people, known and unknown, whom we saw at the station when the train arrived from Przemyśl.

I used to complain, among friends, that I could hardly bear knowing that I was relatively safe, while people at home might at any moment be heading into the heart of Asia. At first, I couldn't make out why my concern seemed to amuse my hosts so much . . .

'You're obviously a newcomer if you still feel relatively safe. Think yourself lucky. The feeling will soon wear off.'

What hurt me most after my arrival was something I really couldn't talk about: the fact that I had left Lwów in circumstances that prevented me from contacting the Kraków command of the ZWZ.[3] I therefore had no hope of resuming my efforts to realise my dream of being sent as a courier to Hungary, Italy and beyond.

However, four days after reaching Kraków I was visited by a certain Maria (codename Dzidzia) Krzeczunowicz* from Lwów. This call from someone I hardly knew puzzled me. Maria sat down and said: 'You are a member of the ZWZ.' That surprised me even more. 'Somebody who's come over from Lwów has vouched for you on oath. So our Commander knows all about you and he's expecting you at half past two tomorrow.' She then gave me the address and told me precisely how to knock on the door.

When I arrived the following day the door was opened by Dzidzia and Renia Komorowska, who had dropped in on me in Lwów one day while I was winding bandages. Both were present throughout my interview, which was conducted by a middle-aged man of rather short stature and a swarthy complexion, who looked at me intently from very dark eyes.

He asked about Lwów, wanted details of the betrayal and questioned me about my work. Then he informed me that there was nothing for me to do just then in Kraków. I spoke of my hopes of going abroad and did my best to justify my motives. The response was immediate approval and a promise of being dispatched to Hungary as a courier in about a fortnight. The next day Dzidzia told me that I had been speaking to the Commander of the Kraków District, Tadeusz Komorowski*, who was also Renia's husband.

I had to make ready for the road, but meanwhile – to wait. The Commander had ordered me to start training for a long trek across the mountains. So I started running about all over Kraków and the immediate neighbourhood for several hours each day. Acquaintances who chanced to meet me thought my nerves must have been shattered by the stress of life under the Bolshevik occupation, since I always seemed to be racing at full pelt when supposedly just out 'for a stroll'.

I also went to see the Metropolitan Archbishop of Kraków, Prince Sapieha*, who had known me all my life. He greeted me warmly and remarked with a twinkle in his eye: 'There's a certain story about you going the rounds – something to do with plumbing and a Bolshevik in your flat. I know you can't go into details, but I'd very much like to know whether it corresponds to the truth.' I thought he must be referring to Pawłyszeńko, who washed his hair in my lavatory. I assured the Archbishop that what he had heard accorded with the facts, if indeed he was referring to a certain hair-washing problem. The Archbishop was tremendously amused.

We then turned to other matters. Requesting secrecy, I told him that I was about to cross 'the green frontier' to Hungary and Rome. I asked what I should say when I got there. The Archbishop's handsome features assumed a look of extreme dejection, which I had never previously observed in him.

'Please tell them that they must inform the Pope that his failure to speak out about Poland is having dangerous consequences with regard to the growth of anti-Rome sentiment in our country. We are doing what we can, but we have no means of counteracting the fact – because it is a fact – that in this dire catastrophe that has befallen us the Pope is not addressing the Polish people. Secondly, please tell them to instruct the Papal Nuncio in Berlin, Orsenigo, that he should not visit Dachau, and particularly not our imprisoned priests. His visits arouse immense bitterness, because, to put it mildly, he is not impartial, but besides that he is awfully tactless.' As I was saying goodbye, the Archbishop asked me to come and see him again immediately before my journey.

Apart from that, I did my best to find out as much as I could about what was going on in the German-occupied zone and the tragic western provinces of Poland, which had been incorporated into the Reich. Long trains had been arriving, crammed with displaced Poles from those parts. Now that the weather was warming up, the transports were fewer. I was told that the Germans carried out mass deportations only in the severest cold. The truth of this observation was strikingly confirmed the following winter. Meanwhile, Kraków itself was severely shaken by a wave of mass street arrests on 3 May.[4] This operation was clearly timed for that particular day – there being no demonstrations. A large number of young men were seized on the streets, in pubs, cafés and at the railway station. It was then that I heard for the first time a word that came to figure so largely in everyone's vocabulary – namely '*ŁAPANKA*' (round-up).

From then on, that word entered so deeply into our lives and consciousness that one couldn't imagine a weekday without it. Where are they taking them, we used to ask? 'To forced labour in Germany, especially the stone quarries or the concentration camps,' came the answer. At that time the existence of German concentration camps was to some extent known to us, largely as a result of the so-called *Sonderaktion Krakau* (Special Operation Kraków), the notorious affair of the Jagiellonian University professors, about which I finally learned the truth. In May, when I arrived in Kraków, those of the older professors who had not died in the camp were already released. The younger ones, up to forty years of age, were still being held in Dachau. They later returned, one by one. Meanwhile, every Thursday a special Mass was celebrated at the Church of St Anne, in front of a painting of St Jan of Kenty, at which wives and mothers prayed for the deliverance of their husbands and sons. As for me, I came to realise that circumstances do arise in which the words of a prayer you've repeated thousands of times in your life stick in the throat. In this case the words were: 'As we forgive those who trespass against us . . .'

It was at about that time I received word that I would have to be patient a little longer. Somebody else, who was wanted by the Germans, would be going out as courier this time. Since I was not under any immediate threat, I would have to wait for the next occasion.

In the outside world, events were moving swiftly. Belgium and Holland had fallen, while Italy had entered the war.[5] France was seriously in peril. We had all of us believed implicitly in France, with the unshakeable faith, admiration and affection that we had been brought up to feel, supported by memories (still vivid among the older people) of French heroism in the First World War. In early June, to celebrate the capitulation of France,[6] the bells of every church in Kraków rang out – loudest of all the great bell of Zygmunt.[7] This was a special mark of respect, performed by express order of the highest German authorities. The people of Kraków, on that scorching June day, closed their windows and stuffed their ears in order not to hear those bells. That afternoon I went to listen to the radio. It was the only illegal thing I did at the time, but I made a point of doing it fairly regularly. Churchill delivered a speech that day on the BBC. Just a few sentences, in a changed voice: 'The news from France is very bad . . . but we shall not forget the gallant French people. *As the only champion now in arms, we will do our best to defend our island and we will fight until the curse of Hitler is lifted from the brows of men.*'

Kraków was drowning in flags. All around the Market Square enormous white poles had been planted, every one and a half metres, from which fluttered blood-red banners, many metres long, with an embroidered white circle, inside which was to be seen that weird black sign – the symbol of evil. These battalions of swastikas were supposed to express the rejoicing of '*der urdeutschen Stadt Krakau*'.[8] That same night, in Kraków, more than sixty persons were registered as having committed suicide.

However, even among those who wanted, despite everything, to carry on living and fighting, many no longer believed in victory – even those to whom it was given (as a special gift of Providence and source of strength) not to doubt for an instant Germany's ultimate defeat, even those knew from that day on that the end was now a long way off and the war might last another whole year, perhaps even two.

Europe's fate was now bound up with that of England. The words of Churchill – '*we will do our best to defend our island*' – were terrifying, as a clear indication of the danger now facing the Island of Freedom.

At this period, there grew within us all a deep-rooted emotion, which for several years was to play a great role in our thinking and in our hearts: a love of England. This emotion had many components: awareness of England's great role in European culture; of England as the last stronghold now of this culture, as a creative force in the spiritual being of the Poles. There was also terrible disappointment at the French collapse – France to whom we had all looked up for so long. This frustrated love of France was redirected all the more intensely towards England – powerful, wise, immeasurably upright and yet, so far, hardly known to us. We clung to this belief with all our strength and boundless confidence. The knowledge that our great ally might shortly find herself in peril still further strengthened our affection and our selfless desire to dedicate ourselves to England's cause in order to build together the new Europe, including a new and sturdy Poland.

There were people, admittedly very few in number, who dared to declare that the English were a very practical nation, who were fond of us Poles just now because they had need of our blood – being loath to shed their own. But their attitude towards us, they said, would later change. Persons expressing such opinions were cold-shouldered.

The new political situation – the total occupation of Belgium, Holland and France by the Germans – had a tremendous influence on the underground resistance in Poland. Contact with the Polish Government in London became that much more difficult, and the dispatch of couriers abroad was dreadfully complicated from the moment of Italy's entry into the war. From then on, we were simply encircled. For me, it seemed, there was now no chance of getting further than Hungary or Yugoslavia. I therefore requested that the Commander be asked not to send me abroad, because my plan was no longer practicable. With little hope of taking part in any underground activity, I began trying to make myself useful by undertaking some legitimate charitable work. I applied to the Polish Red Cross and, after a lengthy wait, was allowed to start work on a temporary basis.

For the time being, at my own suggestion, I began compiling a register of people deported from the Soviet-occupied zone of Poland to the heart of Russia. Crowds used to gather every morning outside my office. There were large groups of people related to officers confined in camps at Kozielsk and Starobielsk, who were then still able to send word of their whereabouts. Others were the families of deportees who had received news from the depths of Asia and brought along postcards to show me, convinced that people registered with the Red Cross would immediately be deported from Russia to America, India or Canada. They beseeched me to discharge the task assigned to me by the Americans with all possible speed. Most of the news from deportees came from Kirghiz farms in Kazakhstan, where the Polish families of officers and landowners reported that they were living in sheep-pens. They wrote that water had to be fetched by bucket every morning and carried three kilometres across the steppe. After that, with the help of a lasso, they had to round up the bulls that grazed all night on the steppes and harness them for ploughing. All of these activities were performed by women – often, naturally enough, women quite untrained for physical labour. One of the women wrote: 'I am at present reading a fascinating book called *Dante n'a rien vu*',[9] while another expressed her one real fear – that of dying before seeing her children: 'Pray for death to observe a logical sequence . . .'

The forester from Komarno reported that he was working in the Urals and that the child was well. Although I was cut off from my own family lands, I also received a little news from the peasants of Klicko-Kolonia who wrote from different parts of Asia. All the postcards sent from those regions were similar in content.

On the wall of our office hung a map of Russia on which we marked the various localities, or at any rate the *oblasts* (regions) from which the letters came, by pinning little flags. Kazakhstan and the Altaj area had the thickest clusters. We felt ashamed to be so much safer than these people. The Germans could transport us no further than the heartland of Germany, simply because they didn't have an Asia. It was soon to become apparent, however, that they would not need to transport anyone even as far as the German heartland, on the first stage of a road that usually led a great deal further afield than Kazakhstan.

In the roasting days of that 1940 summer, rumours spread in Kraków that great preparations were under way on the Silesian border. It appeared that a large barracks, or block of buildings, was being constructed, completely surrounded by barbed wire, and everything top-secret. Even had it all been quite public, none of us could have conceived the point of it, for the Germans were building AUSCHWITZ.

For me, the summer passed with a series of occasional jobs for the Red Cross, interspersed with a few trifling assignments for the ZWZ resistance. It irritated me more than I can say never to be given a mission of any importance. My immediate superior in the Polish Red Cross was at the same time my chief in the underground. Lieutenant Colonel Adam Szebesta*, a neurologist and a man of great energy and intelligence, had a splendidly distinguished record of service in the September campaign, during which he had taken part in the defence of Zamość. Towards me he had always behaved with the greatest reserve, and this reserve was quite clearly the reason for my inactivity in the resistance. That infuriated me.

I once succeeded in obtaining a rather valuable piece of information and duly reported it to him. He listened to me very attentively and replied with a trace of irritation, which surprised me.

'You have brought me an important item of information, acquired at considerable risk to yourself – and I was always so prejudiced against you.'

'You never kept it a secret from me, Colonel,' I retorted.

He stood up and began to pace the floor.

'What do you think was the reason for this prejudice of mine?'

'Since you never gave me a real job to do, it couldn't have been that I ever let you down. It could only have been something for which I am not responsible – my social origins, very likely.'

'That's right.'

Now I've got you, I thought to myself. Here was the country spilling its blood, yet these trifles were still creating barriers between Poles fighting for their country's freedom.

'If you did not like my class origin, Colonel, why did you never ask me what I myself thought about it? And if the trouble is my name – which wasn't my choice, either – I consider that merely increases my obligations to Poland. If the name is well known, it's because people of that name fought – and not at all badly, it would seem, since they were so often in command! They fought at all the periods of Poland's greatest need: from the Battle of Grünwald to the Siege of Vienna.[10] That's my family background! And today, not wishing to bring shame on those ancestors, I am entitled to ask for the chance to risk my life on a worthwhile job. Is this any time for such nonsense as class prejudice?'

At that, point I had to break off my monologue. Adam Szebesta, standing in front of me, had taken hold of both my hands (none too gently) and begun kissing them alternately at high speed. From that day on, he was one of my closest friends.

The world news was becoming ever more alarming; the Battle of Britain[11] was warming up, and German propaganda was promising a swift end to the war. The whole nation was at one with those Polish pilots to whom it was given to take a direct part in the terrible ordeal. Our love for England grew by the hour. It was a love imbued with faith, hope and boundless solicitude, with fear for the future and with envy of England's ability to struggle openly for her survival and that of Europe.

I remember the pontifical High Mass of 15 August 1940, conducted by the Metropolitan Archbishop Sapieha in the Mariacki Church. We were all very conscious of the fact that on this – the anniversary of the Miracle on the Vistula[12] – the Archbishop was praying for a Miracle on the Thames. All Kraków knelt to pray with him. When Sapieha strode out of the cathedral, he was greeted with a thunderous ovation from the waiting crowds, who were unable to find seats in the church. Anxious Germans, who asked what the exact significance of this commotion might be, received the answer that it was just the Polish custom for people to shout loudly at the sight of a bishop.

A few days later an episode occurred that sticks in my memory. I was instructed to go to the Metropolitan Archbishop and to ask him, in the name and by order of the officer commanding the Lwów district branch of our resistance – at that time, Tadeusz Komorowski –

whether, on Sunday 1 September, the first anniversary of the outbreak of war, in all the churches of Kraków he would permit the faithful after High Mass to join in singing the patriotic hymn '*Boże, coś Polskę*'. Komorowski was not asking the clergy for active support, but he did not want anything to take place in the churches without the advance knowledge and agreement of 'the host' in those churches.

I went to the Archbishop. Since I had been more than once to Franciszkańska Street on Red Cross business, my arrival at visitors' hour attracted no special attention in the waiting room, nor was the Archbishop himself surprised to see me. He received me with his usual extreme kindness and warmth, and asked what I had come about. 'This time, I'm not here on my own initiative, but by order,' I said, speaking very slowly and composedly. The reaction, however, though silent, was neither slow nor composed. The Archbishop's noble, expressive features lit up, his dark eyes flashed and a vivacious, almost youthful smile played about the fine lips. The man who was sitting in front of me, leaning across the table towards me and waiting tensely to hear what I had to say, was at that moment, above all, the Sapieha for whom a suit of armour would have been more appropriate than a bishop's violet vestment. So I told him what had brought me there. The Archbishop listened intently, then repeated verbatim what I had said, as though the better to remember it. Meanwhile his expression had changed to one of concern. At last, he told me to come back in two days' time and he would have his answer ready. I was about to stand up, but he stopped me.

'There now, you have fulfilled your mission. I want to ask you, strictly between ourselves, what you would do if you were in my position. It would interest me to know. Would you agree to that – or not?'

'Never,' I replied without pausing to reflect. 'Thank God, just now there's absolutely no need to boost morale, and the Germans would take advantage of any demonstration to carry out more arrests, deportations, even murders. Our duty is to lay down our lives for the struggle, if need be, but not for a song!'

'Thank you. I'll expect you the day after tomorrow.'

I went back as arranged and the Archbishop's answer was negative. Before leaving, I wanted to agree with him on the subject of our discussion. With that in mind, I gave him a few details about my Red Cross activities. He looked highly amused.

'Who is going to ask us what we were talking about?'

'The Germans, of course, when they arrest me.' His question struck me as no less amusing.

A few days later I asked Renia what her husband's reaction had been to the Archbishop's refusal. 'He sighed and said he had been counting on the Archbishop's wisdom.' Only then did he admit to his wife that he had been having trouble with the young people. They had been very set on having the demonstration, while he himself had strongly opposed it. He had explained to them that they must abide by the Archbishop's decision.

Sapieha, our moral leader in those days, was not to any extent involved in the underground resistance. On the contrary, the movement had deliberately distanced itself from the Archbishop in order not to endanger him. This discretion had a mildly amusing side-effect. Prince Sapieha was in despair about what he thought was the 'inactivity' of those in his circle. He used to grumble: 'Where are they at a time like this? Sitting quietly in their manors – that's all!'

He had no idea that practically every manor house and palace, where the owners were still in residence, was as good as a fortress. He subsequently became aware of this.

Later, as the situation grew more dangerous, tension among the public was reaching a climax. A woman who happened to be taking her child for a walk in the Planty[13] fainted on the spot when told by an acquaintance they met that England had capitulated.

During these troubled months I visited Warsaw for the first time since the outbreak of war. I was sent as a courier to deliver mail to the Warsaw underground. Though my contacts were fleeting, I came away from Warsaw with a profound impression of a courage and resilience even greater than that of Kraków. People were more optimistic – not merely hoping, but in sure and certain expectation of that great success for which we had the honour to be struggling. It was pleasing to note far fewer Germans on the streets of Warsaw than there were in Kraków, and equally far fewer establishments labelled 'Germans only'. However, the city itself – the scale of its destruction – plunged me into depression. Although the rubble and debris had quickly been tidied up, I could not reconcile myself to the disappearance of whole streets, such as Świętokrzyska and Foch – and the fact that such architectural gems of the capital as the Raczyński Palace on the Krakowskie Przedmieście, or the Zamoyski Palace on the Senatorska, were missing. Worst of all, the Royal Castle was no more. It seemed to me that probably no city had ever suffered so appallingly. The journey to Warsaw also involved my travelling by rail for the first time since the war began. Out of sixteen carriages on the train, thirteen were reserved for Germans. These were often practically empty or with only one passenger in the compartment, while in the Polish carriages it was standing room only, all night – one foot at a time for a change, since there was no room to stand on both feet together. For the first time, too, I was slapped by a German ticket collector for standing, because of the crush, in the entrance to one of the carriages reserved for Germans.

At the same period, there being still very little work for me, I continued my study of English, as well as trying to acquaint myself with the literature of our ally. The finest hours of those gloomy months I spent in the library of Roman Dyboski*, our Anglicist, who spared no pains to make available to me the treasures of the English spirit. I remember how impressed I was at the time reading a poem by Arthur H. Clough,[14] which Dyboski himself translated into Polish. That poem reached the ZWZ, was printed by the underground press and much admired. Simultaneously, I had my first encounter with the monumental figure of Emily Brontë, the spontaneity and vehemence of her subject matter and her blunt, unpolished but powerful style. Her poem 'No coward soul is mine . . .' was later to accompany me on my long and far-from-easy travels.

The hours I spent in Dyboski's library were the happiest during the whole six years of war, for reading was interspersed with conversations about English, French, German, Latin, Greek, Italian and, above all, Polish culture. For the first time since the war started, humanism had once more begun to appeal to me, in the person of one of its most illustrious Polish representatives. Those conversations proved a great source of strength for me in the future. Professor Dyboski, meanwhile, was preparing himself mentally for the responsible tasks that would await him after the war, in his endeavour to enlighten the Anglo-Saxon nations about who the Germans are and what their relations with us and our culture have been.

'It will be very difficult,' he said, 'because, knowing them as I do, I doubt whether they are at all capable of understanding what is happening here. Peoples brought up with a concept of human dignity regard war as a kind of chivalrous trial of strength and do not believe that a whole nation can possibly revert to barbarism.' And, indeed, it was becoming increasingly hard for us to understand that nation.

I once told the Professor that, out in the country where some of my relatives live, there was a so-called *Treuhänder*, an official whose job it was to administer properties and who, together with his wife (as a rule), would collect from a house such items as old clocks and so forth.

They had a son called Helmut who used to play with my cousins' children. My cousins allowed that because they did not want their children, so young, to grow up hating another child. But one fine day the children stopped playing together, although they had got along very well up to then. Asked why, the children did not want to tell their parents. It was quite a long time before the eldest daughter at last confided in her mother: 'Mummy, we can't play with Helmut any more.' 'Why not?' 'Because he told us he wished he was a grown-up so that he could be an airman and then he'd be able to drop bombs on our house.' We ruminated – the Professor and I – on the instincts inherent in that nation.

We also spent the evening in discussion the day the Mickiewicz Monument[15] was smashed. Both of us were desolated not so much by the loss of such a beautiful memorial ('We'll erect an even finer one after the war'), as by such eloquent proof of what the Germans were like. Dyboski had wrung his hands in grief and pointed at the German literary masterpieces on his bookshelves.

'Are you quite certain this has happened? I haven't been out today.'

I told him that I had been to the Market Square twice since the morning – first, while they were preparing to do the deed, and the second time only a short while ago. Crowds had gathered all round the police cordon. Women were weeping loudly. Every so often the police chased the people away, beating and arresting numerous photographers. Incidentally, that action, like so many deeds perpetrated by the occupiers, missed the mark. Within two days, scores of photographs of the statue toppling were circulating in Kraków, and boys at the Sukiennice (Cloth Hall) were going up to people, restoring their confidence and selling at a fairly steep price postcards with the caption 'Mickiewicz being overturned'. Naturally, I bought one and much enjoyed showing it to foreign visitors after the war. For two more days the statue, with its head smashed, was left lying in the Market Square. A few women were arrested for strewing flowers on the remains.

Peaceful Kraków was shaken to the core. For the first time, simple people who had initially been impressed by the Germans were stirred to fury. My friend Dzidzia's maid, who was illiterate, wept for three days, though it was hard to believe that *The Improvisation* or *Pan Tadeusz* were part of her spiritual baggage. When Dzidzia asked her why she was in despair, the girl replied: 'I feel dreadfully insulted.' The destruction of the Battle of Grünwald memorial immediately after the occupation of Kraków[16] was at least understandable, inasmuch as it was clearly anti-German. The removal of the Kościuszko Memorial at the

Wawel Castle passed almost unnoticed as the Wawel was so inaccessible. The fortress, surrounded by black-and-white-striped Prussian barriers, guarded by huge sentries with bayonets, had become, as it were, quite alien. I must admit that this strange – I might say – 'absence' of the Wawel Castle always seemed to me to symbolise most eloquently the absence of our most precious possession: independence. Besides, the Kościuszko statue had not been there all that long and was not an integral part of Kraków, unlike the Mickiewicz Monument in the Market Square.

Moreover for many generations we had grown accustomed to a certain conception of what this poet stood for, regardless of nationality – a conception of what is generally meant by art and culture: a whole body of ideas which, after only a year of enemy occupation, we were in no hurry to discard. That day, coming back from the Market Square, where the shattered statue of Mickiewicz was lying, I walked along Sławkowska Street. My eyes came to rest on the bronze plaque, decorated with laurels and bearing the legend 'Goethe lived in this house'. Reading it, I couldn't help reflecting that no Pole had so far thought of smashing this tablet, or at least removing it, despite all the unprecedented crimes committed in the world by the nation of Goethe. The point was that we were not at war with Goethe. I called to mind the visit of Mickiewicz to Goethe in Weimar and the golden quill that he received as a gift. Will humanity, these days wallowing in the mud, ever again be capable of raising itself to such heights?

I told Professor Dyboski that evening that appalling as it might be, I could not rid myself of the impression that even an occupying power capable of such an exploit was less of a danger for Poles than the one over in Lwów, which placed immense wreaths at the feet of that same Mickiewicz. My exchange of ideas with Professor Dyboski was not destined to last long. It was very hard to give up these lessons, which meant so much to me. Despite new commitments, I tried not to interrupt them until, at last, in December, I simply no longer had the time.

From October onwards I had been given fresh duties. Just then Polish prisoners-of-war were beginning to return from Germany: 'other ranks' and a small number of officers, the state of whose health precluded all future military activity on their part. Up to then they had been arriving as individuals or in small groups until, at the beginning of October, a transport of 500 tuberculosis victims arrived in Kraków. They were accommodated in the Jesuit College in Copernicus Street. The Polish Red Cross (PCK) had been informed that these men were badly under-nourished. Renia Komorowska, some other young women and I got hold of everything we could from the PCK and raced to Copernicus Street. The Red Cross delegation was admitted by the German military guards. Carrying our baskets, we made our way down a long corridor. We were directed to a large hall, where an unexpected sight met our eyes. Besides the wounded in bed, there was a sizeable group of officers still able to walk. When they saw us, they got up and came to the door to greet the first Polish women they had seen for a year. They were in uniform, wearing decorations and merit badges – everything about them we found astounding. We hardly knew how to conceal our emotion. The big hampers of food were our salvation. Leaning over while unpacking them enabled us to bow very low.

Then we went to the smaller cells where the seriously sick were in bed. Two died that first day. A few living skeletons waited their turn. Wives and fiancées were sitting beside some of them, looking with fear in their eyes at some loved one who had only just returned and was now about to leave again, this time for ever. Among others, there was the defender of the Hel Peninsula,[17] Engineer Second Lieutenant Lech Stelmachowski. His very young wife was sitting beside him. The sick man had already lost his voice and could barely whisper, while gazing at her with his sapphire-blue eyes. It was obvious that he was gathering strength to say something. At last he managed to find the breath to utter four barely audible words: 'Duty to Poland done.'

He died the next day. A dozen or so of his colleagues were allowed to attend the funeral. The German guards accompanied the cortège, it must be said, in a discreet and considerate manner. As the funeral procession emerged, passers-by doffed their hats, flowers rained down from windows along the route, women in a tram cried: 'Jesus, Maria!' I do not remember ever in my life being so proud of the company in which I found myself that day as I walked through Kraków with those poor, helpless consumptives. At the entrance to the Rakowice Cemetery our procession was already strong in number and very many people joined us inside the cemetery itself. In the chapel, Stelmachowski's comrades formed the guard of honour around the coffin. It was very quiet. Only now and then one could hear a dry, consumptive cough.

As they came out of the chapel, these very sick men gently pushed aside the undertakers' bearers and shouldered the coffin themselves. As we walked, I thought it was as well that a few nurses were present. If anyone could not last out, first aid would be at hand. We walked quite some distance to the new cemetery, in the sunlight of a wonderful,

Polish autumn day. Somebody did need treatment on the way – not one of the invalids, but a nurse who fainted with emotion. There were a great many flowers, appropriately in the Polish national colours of red and white. As the coffin was lowered, there came to mind those words written on the occasion of another hospital burial:

> At least, Lord, from Thy heaven out of reach –
> Hurling Thy bolts that fall upon the brave –
> By this handful of bones we Thee beseech:
> Thy sun let blaze as we go to our grave!
> Let daylight stream through heaven's portals wide
> That all may see and know when we have died![18]

There were to be many such deaths later on and burials, too, though nothing like that first time. Once was enough for the Germans. A few days later the prisoners were released. The sick soldiers became civilians. Those who were fit to travel were transported to various parts of the German-occupied sector. The travellers were not entitled to wear uniform, but if they had no civilian clothes, uniforms were allowed, without badges of rank or decorations. This last proviso was hard to interpret. Somehow the men could not understand it. While the painful task of stripping their uniforms of ribbons and badges was in progress, the sick men – with many a face already marked by impending death – came up to us with whispered requests to slip those items into a pocket, 'since I'll be needing them again very soon'. They were at last beginning to learn a little caution. In the early days they said aloud whatever they thought. It had to be explained to them, at all costs, that they were surrounded by spies; that the hospital nurses were *Volksdeutsch*[19] or, unfortunately, Ukrainian girls; that the occupation regime was not that of a prisoner-of-war camp, and the Gestapo (German secret police) not the same as the Wehrmacht (German Army). They were horrified. 'If that's so,' said one sergeant, 'having been prisoners-of-war, we're now to become slaves.'

At last they were discharged. Only those who were seriously ill, or who came from our territory on the far side of the Ribbentrop–Molotov Line, remained in Kraków. Often they were fathers whose families had been deported to the depths of Russia. For them, as well as the bedridden cases, we had to provide nursing care and regular feeding, which was not difficult at that period, since the attitude of the local population towards them was one of selfless generosity.

Equally generous were the Jesuit Fathers who agreed to let the invading females make use of the priests' private kitchen. Our ladies, numbering the evangelical total of twelve, took turns cooking for the patients. Much more difficult was protecting these invalids from the manifold irritations and denunciations by the Ukrainian doctors and nurses who filled the hospital.[20] Their physical and moral leader was one Sister Józefa, the Mother Superior of the Basylian Order. Her bony face, usually all smiles, her small, half-shut eyes and her very wide, very thin-lipped mouth, as well as her black habit, were for us a fearsome sight. After her visits, personal articles were always missing; also food, even hospital equipment, blankets or sheets. Some of these items reappeared after a time, but as the personal belongings of Ukrainian soldiers, while the food was used to grace receptions for Russian priests in the private parlour of the 'little sister'. This charming Samaritan bestowed her special antipathy on me. That in itself was as much an honour as it was troublesome because, as a result, I had constantly to deal with the German authorities over her numerous denunciations of me. Fortunately, nothing came of all that.[21] At the same time, the struggle to achieve a modicum of cleanliness in the hospital yielded no result.

In December another large transport of consumptives arrived. The Germans made no provision for food or accommodation. Bedridden patients were again crammed into the Jesuits' hospital. The German soldiers simply dumped them on the beds. The patients were very weak. One of them had tears streaming down his face when he was given a little milk. 'But it's Polish milk!' he kept repeating, while his fingers, lacking the strength to hold a cup, slipped among the pleats of my apron. Meanwhile, in a neighbouring bunk a man had begun to die. Eyes shut, a gurgling in his throat, a few broken words: 'At least . . . I've got here . . . and I'm dying . . . in Poland . . .'

A priest, a dedicated young Jesuit who looked disturbingly lacking in immunity to this ever-increasing epidemic of deaths, amid which he moved so calmly, recited the last rites at one bedside after another: 'Deliver, O Lord, the soul of Thy servant, as Thou didst deliver Noah from the flood, the youths from the fiery furnace and Daniel from the jaws of the lion.' Though every such occasion demanded swift and punctilious action, each time I heard those words, an image of the Roman catacombs thrust itself before my eyes. The verbal content was the same as that of the prayers said over the tombs of the first Christians buried there. For the past two thousand years the Church has been escorting the faithful to the gates of eternity in the very same way . . .

Those less seriously ill were left waiting in a corridor till the Germans came to collect them in the evening. They found accommodation for the patients simply by requisitioning the last Polish Red Cross establishment to be built – a freshly equipped and not yet completed hospital on the Prądnik Czerwony. That is where they sent the consumptives who could still stand – to a house with no heating whatsoever and without any light. We managed to take them cauldrons of hot soup, with the help of some German lorries, after explaining to their drivers in an imperious manner that they must take us there at once. We knew perfectly well that a polite request would have been flatly refused. The result was highly satisfactory. The drivers even waited for us outside the hospital and drove off with the empty containers. The fact that I was bilingual in German was a considerable advantage on that occasion.

Another problem arose at the Prądnik Hospital. A number of the healthier soldiers – relatively speaking – simple souls, reacted to all this by singing patriotic songs, which was strictly forbidden, especially '*Boże, coś Polskę*'. It had to be explained to them that they were endangering themselves, without helping the cause. They listened reluctantly and finally promised 'to behave themselves at Sunday Mass'. Indeed, during Mass they sang only religious hymns. But after Mass they rose to their feet as one man, stood to attention and nobody was in any doubt about what was to come – suddenly: '*Serdeczna Matko*' . . . At least, the melody was the same.[22]

At last these men, too, moved on. There was one final hitch at the railway station, where we were thickly beset by Germans who never took their eyes off us. When everybody was aboard, a few relatively mobile patients jumped down from the carriage and stood before me in a compact group, whose senior member declared in a very loud voice: 'NCOs and men of the Polish Army wish to warmly thank the Polish Red Cross and Sister, and hope to meet again soon doing even better work.'

After their departure I was again able to return to the Jesuits where, until then, I had gone only in the evening on my way back from the Prądnik. In the meantime, Renia had been in charge of the work there. I had a special reason for hurrying back. A friend was waiting for me. People on the point of leaving, particularly young people at the moment of departing this life, sometimes develop a strong attachment to one of those around them, specially an older person whom they find supportive, clinging to that person with all the strength with which they desire to cling to life as it escapes them. Sometimes, on a death-bed, the friendships formed are of immeasurable intensity and substance.

The soldier who had wept on arrival when I gave him a drink of milk, Bronisław Kozłowski, died shortly afterwards, for his already depleted strength had dwindled day by day. He could no longer lift his head, but his mental alertness (as is so often the case with consumptives) seemed even keener than before. He wanted me to sit beside him every evening. He talked a great deal and exhausted himself in the process. But physical tiredness was no longer a problem, so I did not interrupt him. The whole twenty-three-year life of this peasant from Trzemeszno was spread out in front of him and paraded before me through his accounts of his parents' house, the neighbours, even the dishes his mother used to cook for him. All of this he described for me in detail. But he also voiced his opinion on serious matters. He must have had a tremendous thirst for information on subjects that he could not have studied at the communal school. He spoke passionately about the public library in Trzemeszno, where he had read everything. I once sensed that he was curious to learn something about me, but was too shy to ask. So I told him in passing that I came from around Lwów and taught at the university before the war. At this, he appeared strangely moved. He suddenly stopped addressing me as 'Sister'.

'Just fancy, you know how to teach at a university, and here you are giving a drink to somebody like me!' From then on, he treated me with something like respect. For my part I reflected, for the thousandth time in my life, that to make education available to all who want it, without lowering standards, is one of humanity's highest ideals.

He was always harking back to times past: 'I liked . . . I thought'. He recalled that Louis XIV, on the day he died, said: '*Quand j'étais roi.*'[23] This young soldier was very much aware of his impending death, and so was I. Nor was I against his mentioning it. He had one wish, only one: to live till Christmas Eve. Every day, in the evening, he would say: 'I so looked forward to your visit today and now there's only four, three, two days . . . perhaps we'll still be able to break a holy wafer[24] together. I know I'm very weak already, but I think I'll probably just be able to make it.' On 22 December his condition worsened, so I called at the hospital early the next morning. I was too late. He had passed away in the night. Suddenly, it seems, at the last moment he had rebelled against death and died calling out: 'I want to live!' That morning – with the whole hospital full of patients, the work that so appealed to me – all seemed frighteningly empty and pointless, but there was no time for moping.

Christmas Eve was approaching and, with it, a Homeric battle with the Germans for permission to hold a joint celebration. I rushed around the various commands, explaining that these soldiers would probably be celebrating this solemn feast for the last time in their lives, and it would be very hard to forbid them to do so.

'All they want is permission to pray together.'

'But they'll just start praying for Poland's freedom.'

'I promise that they won't do that out loud.'

At that point, the man I was talking to – a former Austrian army captain – burst out laughing.

'All right, I will give permission for the ceremony, but what any of you pray about in your hearts will be no concern of mine.'

So Christmas Eve was celebrated and afterwards, for those who were well enough, Midnight Mass with carols. It was my only truly beautiful wartime Christmas. After the holiday, the burial of Kozłowski took place. Whenever one of our patients died, the nurse who was with him till the end walked behind the coffin and placed a couple of white and red flowers on the grave. This time, once again, it was my turn. In a terrible blizzard I stumbled along behind the coffin, quite alone, thinking as I walked of all the countless others in whose name I was acting at that moment.

Around this time my duties at the Jesuit Hospital were supplemented by the task of caring for the military wounded in other wards of the St Lazarus Hospital. There, still more difficulties were put in our way. In this connection I had to call on the Medical Director, Dr Fischeder from Berlin. I had been advised to go early in the day, as he was always drunk later on and in such a state that it was difficult to get any sense out of him. Whatever you said, he would insist – wherever he went – that everyone cheer him and that all (including women) should first bow to him. I went to his office at 9.30 a.m. On arrival, I could see at once that I was far too late. This dignitary, built like the dwarf former King of Italy, Victor Emmanuel, greeted me with almost comical politeness and told me to be seated – a rare thing among Germans. I said that I would like written permission to visit and distribute food to the military patients. He interrupted me with a torrent of words, to the effect that he had been waiting to see me for a long time to tell me something very important, namely that he was prepared to sign anything I wanted – absolutely anything – on one condition only: from now on, all Polish Red Cross employees would bow first, the moment they met him. I listened in silence. He repeated his demand several times while signing – with a hand that visibly trembled – the entry permits we needed as I placed them before him.

At last, my silence began to get on his nerves. He asked several times in an increasingly loud voice whether I had understood him and why I was such a disappointment to him, when he, for his part, had been placing such trust in me. '*Ich habe doch geglaubt, eine Gräfin ist ein kultivierter Mensch*,'[25] he added dolefully. I struggled gallantly to keep a straight face and sat stock-still. At last this confrontation with an ageing Joan of Arc incited him to a fit of drunken fury.

'At least tell me what was your month of birth!' he yelled.

'August.'

'Naturally! And it's bound to have been before the twenty-first?'

'I was born on the eleventh of August,' I replied in total amazement.

'I might have known it,' he shouted angrily, 'one can just about put up with people born at the end of the month – they're Virgos. But you are a Leo! You would be!' he bellowed, pounding the table repeatedly with his fist. I only wish he knew, I thought to myself, that I have that lion on my coat of arms and it's belching fire.

I do not know what turn that scene might have taken. I was afraid that he might take back our signed passes, which were already in my handbag. But for some unknown reason he suddenly calmed down, declaring his delight that we had got on so well and had reached agreement '*bis zum nächsten polnischen Freiheitskampf!*'[26] That was how it ended. After that we had no further problems over access to any of the hospital wards.

Instead, our troubles with Sister Józefa resumed with redoubled strength. Her aversion to us and our work was to some extent understandable. Among our sick soldiers there were quite a lot of Ukrainians and, since we were responsible for all soldiers of the Polish forces entrusted to our care, we naturally treated the Ukrainians in exactly the same way as the Poles. This maddened Sister Józefa, particularly since these soldiers were on very good terms with us. So she went to the Germans, who held her in high esteem (she baked them very good cakes), and denounced us, the Polish nurses, for allegedly staying overnight in the hospital and creeping out through the back gate in the morning. The moment I was summoned to the Director's office, his deputy, a very Prussian type (Dr Fischeder himself, it seemed, was totally unconscious that day), together with the Head Nurse (a former cook) informed me that complaints had been made about the Polish Red Cross. I was angry and rather anxious, since I was always afraid that the Germans would throw us out, leaving nobody to look after our sick soldiers. I assumed the manner of an affronted prima donna and enquired what kind of complaints. The reply was that the complaints were 'of a moral nature'. I was flabbergasted. I knew the Germans would be furious if I simply burst out laughing. So I pretended to be even more deeply offended, because I could not think what else to do. With bombast worthy of a better cause, I declared that I was the only person who stayed overnight in the hospital and that all my life I had been in the habit of using only the main front entrance. Because I was speaking very loudly, the Germans began to speak noticeably more quietly. Once again, the whole affair blew over.

There was a great deal of work to be done in the hospital and much of it was unusually demanding. Constantly escorting patients to the very boundary of life, and the fact that none of our patients ever recovered, had a deeply depressing effect on us.

At this stage we kept very much to ourselves. Renia was closest to me at the time, but today, after all these years, I still remember many other very endearing colleagues. One was Stasia, whose outstanding culinary talents gave unparalleled pleasure to so many poor souls; Maniusia, so gentle and ever punctual; Wanda, strong, blunt, motherly – a native of our parts – forthright and down-to-earth, like everyone in that area. Then there was Krystyna Ładomirska, utterly selfless, charming, young, cheerful and adored by all the patients. She so much wanted her work in Poland to be worthy of her officer husband, of whom she spoke with such pride – and who had the good fortune to be in England.[27]

All around us the situation was deteriorating. In practically all parts of Kraków, people were being turned out of their dwellings. All decent apartments (as, indeed, every respectable bar and restaurant) were already earmarked for Germans only. More and more Germans were bringing their families to live in Kraków. German children were particularly impertinent to the Poles. Although there were tramcars reserved for Germans, German passengers continued to occupy seats in the few trams in which Poles were still allowed to travel. German women could be heard asking in loud voices: 'When are they going to put a stop to this disgrace of still letting Poles travel by tram?' In fact, the only area still open to Poles was that which lay between the former Jewish quarter, which was unbelievably squalid, and the railway station for Kazimierz. At that time the Jews in all Polish cities were being herded into ghettos surrounded by a high wall. Despite our horror, despite our inability to credit that anyone could conceive of and execute such a scheme, not one among us – even the greatest pessimist

– would have dared for a moment to suspect that, by confining the Jews in tiny spaces and cutting them off from the world, the Germans were acting only by way of preparation.

The existence of the Poles was also becoming increasingly difficult. Ever more strongly, and at every step, it was emphasised that we Poles were *Untermenschen* (sub-humans). Moral resistance, in the face of all this, was obviously growing; physically, however, we felt ourselves to be defenceless in the hands of the German General Governor Hans Frank*, who resided in the Wawel Castle, and whose deeds vied with those of all his predecessors who had borne that terrible title on the soil of Poland. I saw him once only. I was going through the Market near Bracka Street when five motor cars and a posse of motorcyclists, moving at top speed, emerged from Franciszkańska Street and drew to a halt in front of the Partei-Haus (Nazi Party HQ). SS men with hand-held machine carbines jumped from their cars and, at the speed of lightning, formed a double cordon from the pavement to the main door. At the same time, walking quickly, came a man in uniform with very black hair and eyes. A pace to his rear a couple of aides were almost running to keep up. Had I not recognised his face – his photograph was everywhere – I would have known who he was by the immense fear that he did nothing to hide, peering round to left and right at every step till he disappeared behind the door, which shut immediately. Probably, Alba[28] felt more at ease in Brussels. But Alba was a normal human being, which was more than could be said of Governor Frank. Roman emperors had a way of going mad, but they did so on a grand scale, like Claudius and Caracalla. This madman of ours, however, stole artistic masterpieces (the Leonardo owned by the Czartoryskis hung in his palace). He rebuilt as his private residence Kressendorf, the home of the Potockis (Krzeszowice Potockich). But, above all, this man Frank made speeches that will never be forgotten.

On the first anniversary of the General Government he publicly proclaimed that 'The Earth will cease to exist, before the swastika flag will cease to flutter above this city.' At the opening of the newly refurbished building for the Jagiellonian Library, completed just before the outbreak of war, he declared that the library was German, since only people who made history had a right to libraries and that, the English might open opium dens in the territories they conquer, '*Wir Deutsche aber bauen Bibliotheken.*'[29] These and numerous other pronouncements might well have given rise to merriment, had not the shedding of our blood in streams accompanied, or rather ratified, every such performance.

I know that in those days there existed a precisely calculated quota – that is, a prescribed number of Poles who must constantly be held in prisons or concentration camps. If, for whatever reason (such as increased mortality), the prisoner level dropped and there happened just then to be no good grounds for mass arrests, *łapanki* (round-ups) were organised. Often no cause could be found to justify the arrest and imprisonment of persons whose names were actually on the quota. Arrests had begun to multiply alarmingly. The Montelupi prison was full of people who had been tortured. Reports of even more bloodshed were coming in from all over the country, especially Warsaw. There, with the largest concentration of inhabitants, local resistance was at its strongest. At every stage the capital set us an example. The more they resisted, the greater the sacrifices. The round-ups in Warsaw, which the Germans themselves called *Menschenfangen* (manhunts), were more numerous and more intensive than anywhere else. During one of the major 'manhunts', the daughter of acquaintances, a pretty young girl, was about to enter her apartment block when she met a young man in the hall on his way out.

'Upstairs, quick. Manhunt!' she warned him. The boy turned pale. 'My briefcase!' he whispered, turning to escape. But at the same moment Gestapo men rushed into the hall and seized him. The girl at once threw her arms round his neck, bursting into tears and screaming: 'Darling, sweetheart! My only love – they're going to separate us.' Meanwhile she snatched his briefcase and raced upstairs. The boy was arrested. The girl got safely back to her flat and opened the briefcase. It was full of underground leaflets. 'Would you recognise this boy you saved from certain death?' her mother asked. 'Not for the life of me! I've no idea what he looked like.'

The enemy was powerless against the spirit of the capital, so they simply set about getting rid of the population. For them it was the easiest and most straightforward solution. Among the other Polish provinces, Radom was worst hit. There, the Germans surpassed even themselves. The strength of moral opposition to all of this was growing steadily, but at the same time we asked ourselves more and more often how it would be if, when Poland was free again, there were not enough Poles left alive . . . There were times when a hundred people a day (those that we knew about) were dying in Auschwitz. Only a part of the total had been shot or clubbed to death with rifle-butts; the majority of deaths were ascribed to 'inflammation of the lungs'. We knew for a fact that in winter the prisoners were compelled to stand for hours in the freezing cold in denim overalls, and in spring were ordered to work in water from morning to night.

The porches of Kraków churches were plastered with death notices: Christian name and surname, died in the nineteenth, twentieth or thirtieth year of his life. Funeral Mass will take place . . . If the obituary made no mention of the burial, the passer-by, reading carefully, knew what that meant – and obituaries of that kind were appearing ever more frequently.

In the whole of this inconceivable tragedy there was only one redeeming feature, compared with the arrests and deportations organised by our invader from the East. With the Russians, people disappeared like a stone in water; nobody could ever find out anything about them, let alone renew contact with them. It was different here – thanks to the Germans.

From the moment the country was occupied, Poland lived with convincing evidence of German brutality, as well as scrupulous personal honesty. Only with time, however, did we discover one very important characteristic of this occupying power: namely, the extraordinary German sensitivity to the lure of material possessions, accompanied by a total lack of sensitivity to the means by which those possessions had been acquired. The first surprise was their indescribable and completely unconcealed rapacity in looting, for example, domestic furnishings. As early as November 1939, a house for university professors in Russia Street was 'liberated' in the sense that the families of the professors, who had themselves been dispatched to Sachsenhausen concentration camp, were given twenty minutes to vacate their flats – and that in the evening, with the lights switched off. Nor was the professors' house an exception. The Germans burst in on a family we knew in Zygmunt August Street, out of breath, but yelling: '*Wo sind die Teppiche? Schnell!*'[30]

The so-called *Treuhänder* (trustees) used to operate in the same way. I do not know of any case in which the *Treuhänder* did not make off with a significant quantity of articles from a manor or palace, particularly in the case of antique furniture, porcelain and, above all, clocks. Since General Governor Frank and Field Marshal Goering did the same thing openly and officially, why should not lesser people, too, on a correspondingly lesser scale? But for us, this was not the most important aspect of the German lust for possession. That was something else again – namely, corruption. We were often grateful to this for making it possible to find out where an arrested person was being held. For a fat sum of money, a Gestapo man would make sure that a parcel reached the prisoner and one might even succeed, for a still fatter sum, in getting the prisoner set free. During the long years of the occupation a vast amount of Polish money was spent for these purposes. Obviously, the objective was attained on extraordinarily few occasions.

This was the way it worked: following an arrest, somebody would call on the wife at home or at the flat of an acquaintance with an 'offer to help'. The usual promise was that if, on a given day (usually very soon) at a given place, an exactly specified, very large sum of money was deposited, the prisoner would be released. Without more ado, the desperate family – usually women, mothers or wives – sold their last remaining jewellery, gold, dollars or works of art and paid the ransom. After that, as a rule, the Gestapo man was never seen again. In a few cases a prisoner was actually released, but it happened so rarely that, in time, this method of extorting cash became more and more difficult. Then the Germans started demanding only half the sum in advance, with the second half to be paid at the time of release. Sometimes the Gestapo man would be satisfied with the first instalment; sometimes he would receive the second payment as well and the prisoner might even be released. In the vast majority of such cases, however, freedom was short-lived and the victim would often be back in prison the same evening.

More and more, we feared the news of transports being sent to the concentration camps. The mortality rate there, especially at Auschwitz, was much greater than in prison, and likewise the chance of extracting a prisoner very much slimmer. Apart from that, we lived in constant fear that, at the time of their eventual defeat, the Germans would murder everybody in the camps before capitulating. It was not until later – a lot later – when I found myself on 'the other side of life', that I learned how, for many prisoners in jail, the journey to a concentration camp represented the summit of their dreams. Death awaited you in the camps. Everyone knew that. But to be sent to the camps from prison usually – though not always – meant an end to that most terrifying nightmare, the fear of betraying secrets under torture.

Among our patients in the hospital were some who had not only been in prisoner-of-war camps. For example, Second Lieutenant Czesław Bielewicz, a teacher from Żywiec who escaped from captivity, was recaptured by the Germans and sent to a concentration camp. There he was kept almost without clothes, living in a tent during that terrible first, freezing winter of the war. This young giant, built like an athlete, contracted tuberculosis. From there, after several months, he was sent back to a prisoner-of-war camp – but he was past curing. The man was dying because he had been without proper use of his lungs for some time, but was kept alive by sheer strength. So this strongman in his early twenties panted his way through the long hours, for days and weeks. All he asked was that there should always be somebody with him, as he put it, 'somebody else to take over half of my pain.' At last, on 5 February, he, too, ceased to suffer.

Meanwhile, the flow of new sick arrivals was beginning to decrease. More were fated to die in the Reich, and the hospitals in the German-occupied sector of Poland were clearly being vacated. That cheered us, as did every other indication that what we had all been dreaming about was now in preparation. We had been praying to God 'for a universal war for the freedom of all peoples'. We believed that a German-Russian war was the only way to solve the Polish problem and were impatiently looking forward to its outbreak. We firmly believed that the Germans would beat the Muscovites, after which the Germans, already weakened, would be finished off by the Allies. Then, both our enemies having fallen, Poland would rise between them, morally powerful in the unity and collective harmony imparted to us by this terrible struggle. We knew that the ransom – the price to be paid in blood – would be immeasurable, but we felt that we possessed today something that many nations (Poland among them) had never possessed in their history, for we were creating a national unity in the face of which class or party political differences would be seen as mere childhood illnesses outgrown, never to return.

The intensified activity by the underground resistance during those critical months gave me something to do, admittedly in a modest way, but interesting all the same. My orders were to translate into German, or to rewrite in the appropriate style, leaflets aimed at demoralising the German army of occupation.

On another occasion, Basia, my liaison officer with the underground, called in during Red Cross office hours. I did not like her doing that, but I knew it must be something important.

'Do you speak English?' she asked, to my astonishment.

'I do,' I said.

'Thank the Lord, you are Jan's only hope.'[31]

'But what's Jan got to do with my English?'

'There is an Englishman.'

'Where?'

'He's at Queen Jadwiga Street. They want you to go along this afternoon because nobody can speak to him. He's probably a parachutist. He's staying with two of our ladies. You'll need to submit a report tomorrow when you see Prawdzic.'[32] She then gave me an address to go to and a password. I thought I would never contain my impatience till the afternoon. The whole thing sounded rather odd to me – the idea of dropping a parachutist who couldn't speak Polish. But that did not lessen my curiosity.

The hours of duty and my lunch break were over at last. I hurried away. I needed to go to the Kościuszko Mound.[33] The house was one set a little apart from the others. I found the flat. An elderly woman opened the door. Password and reply matched and I entered a room where a young, fair-haired man was sitting, with his back to the door. He did not interrupt his game of patience at the arrival of a stranger. Nor did he turn his head. There could therefore be no doubt about his nationality. I walked round the table at which he was sitting, stood in front of him and held out my hand. 'How do you do?'

At that the fair-haired, rosy-cheeked young man did stir himself, but, with a contented smile, stretched out a huge paw.

'How did you get here?' I asked.

'I escaped.'

'Where from?'

'From the prisoner-of-war camp – a Stalag.'

'Why?'

'Because it wasn't much fun being there. A young worker who knew some English talked me into it and gave me some overalls and a bicycle. Then he took me to Piotrków – to some people in your organisation.'

'How did you come to find yourself in the camp?' I asked.

'Captured at Dunkirk,' he replied.

'Then you're not a paratrooper?'

'Not at all. I was at war for two days in all, then I was in the camp, and then I did a stupid thing and escaped.'

'Why stupid?' I asked.

'Because I'm putting you all at risk, I know that. There's no way of getting out. Back at the camp, they didn't know it was so difficult.'

I took his name and his unit. I remember his first name was William. He was a mechanic by profession, with a mother in London. The next day I told the whole story to 'Prawdzic', who would certainly much have preferred a parachutist. He gave me a new address in Rakowice Street, behind the cemetery, and told me to take the Englishman there. First, I was to ask William whether he agreed with our handing him over to the Bolsheviks across the River San. There was no other way to get him out. We would give him a letter to the Russians, written in Polish, English and Russian, explaining that he was such-and-such an Englishman who had escaped from a German POW camp. For his security, precise details would be radioed to London, for the information of his commanding officer and his mother. This was clearly explained in the letter to the Russians. We had done the same thing a couple of days earlier for two Frenchmen, who – so we had heard – were well received on the other side of the river.

When I put all that to William, he displayed great enthusiasm for going over to the Bolsheviks. I got the impression that he was anticipating some sort of fantastic Red Indian adventures, as it were. At the same time, he asked insistently to be allowed to stay a week or two longer with us. I really could not make him out. Hiding a man in Kraków, who did not know a word of any language except English, was exposing the lot of us to being shot. He himself had mentioned that danger to me. An escaped soldier-prisoner would also face severe punishment if recaptured. He seemed keen to go to Russia, so why would he want to delay . . .? He finally admitted that he had left some presents with his former hosts at Piotrków, which they had given him for Christmas, particularly a pair of cufflinks to which he was much attached. He would like to have them returned to him before venturing on his way. For me, that was just a bit too much! I told him in no uncertain terms that if I was shot looking after him, that would be perfectly in order, since he was an Englishman, but that my readiness to die definitely did not extend to his cufflinks. He looked dejected. 'Then I'll just have to come after the war, visit my friends again and collect the cufflinks when I leave,' he said, and followed me.

We had to walk quite a long way to the Dębnicki Bridge. I had wrapped his neck and part of his face in a scarf, for he looked desperately English, though fortunately he was not too tall. When we got into a hackney-cab I thought we might be in trouble. The driver was bound to be puzzled by these two silent passengers he was taking all the way to Rakowice. So I started, as we were driving along, to point out and explain – in Polish, of course – the monuments and churches of ancient Kraków that we were passing. He responded quite aptly with assorted murmurs of understanding and admiration. At last, towards dusk, I handed him over to his new guardians. 'Once again, nobody'll be able to understand me, once you go,' he said. A few days later I heard that he, too, had been well received on the far side of the San.

Meanwhile I had spells of night duty with another patient. This time it was a thirty-three-year-old doctor of the Polish Navy, Chief Medical Officer on the Hel Peninsula, Zbigniew Wierzbowski, who was dying of heart disease. He seemed not to be aware of his condition and was always cheerful and full of life. In more serious moments he talked about the war, and about Hel and its defenders. He was deeply religious. Having received the Holy Sacrament at Easter, he made me promise on my word of honour that if his condition worsened – but there seemed no reason to suppose this was likely – I would immediately send for a priest.

Just then I did not have much work at the hospital and so was able to spend a lot of time with him. The deterioration in his health took place very quickly. He was already unable to speak, but continued to delude himself, although I said nothing to encourage his illusion and my word of honour began to weigh more and more heavily on me. Finally I went to the priest whom Wierzbowski had been with at Easter and told him all. The priest came to see the doctor and suggested that he bring Holy Communion to him the next day and he could receive it without Confession. The sick man was happy about this, though somewhat surprised.

I then asked the priest whether, since Wierzbowski was in a private room, he would bring Communion for me too, so that I might receive it with him and the officer would not have the impression that this was the *viaticum*. The priest readily agreed and asked me to wait for him early next morning after duty, at seven-thirty. It was a difficult night and I realised the time had come.

That morning the priest was called to another dying man and so was considerably delayed. I waited with a heavy heart because I had to be with Jan, our Chief of Staff, before nine o'clock, in connection with some spare parts for our radios, which I had to extract from the Main Council for Relief (RGO). Apart from that, I needed to let Jan know the address of my new flat in Venice Street, where I was due to move that day, so that he would have a fresh point of contact. But if I failed to wait for the priest and went away, such an action, in the prevailing atmosphere, would be tantamount to betraying the resistance movement. So I had to wait.

The priest arrived at eight-thirty, and by the time I could leave the hospital it was nine. However, I was not allowed to contact Jan after nine. I was very sorry and it hurt me to fail in my duty for the first time, but I couldn't help it. I had to postpone our meeting to the next day, Sunday 20 April. After a night at the hospital with Wierzbowski, I left at eight-fifteen and arrived at Sławkowska Street, to see our Chief of Staff, at eight-thirty. I knocked in the usual way, but there was no reply. I waited and tried again, knocking hard and long; waited a long time, then knocked once more, this time very loudly, casting caution to the winds. It made me angry to think that he was sleeping so soundly on a Sunday morning.

At last I went away, furious with myself, with the priest for being late the previous day, and with this morning's further lack of success. Moreover I knew that this was delaying the solution of a serious problem, so I decided to try just once more. Strictly speaking, we were forbidden to call on Jan after nine o'clock, but surely that prohibition could not apply to Sundays . . . So I went to Mass in the nearby Church of St Mark. I was in good time. After half an hour I left and returned to Jan's place. Once again, I knocked and banged – nothing. Finally I gave up, at a loss. I dropped into a café for breakfast on my way home and got to Venice Street at about ten. I was looking forward to going back to bed very shortly. As I approached No. 1, my new residence, I noticed that in front of the house, but on the other side of the road, Renia and Stasia were waiting. I also observed that Renia was holding under her arm a vase from the Carpathians that had been standing on my cupboard, and in the bottom of which, hidden under wax, were some gold coins belonging to the Home Army. 'They must be in my flat,' I thought, so I walked on past the building without approaching the two women.

Renia saw me and followed. 'You didn't go to Jan's place, then?' she asked.

'I certainly did go there, like a fool, and achieved nothing. I couldn't manage it yesterday because I couldn't get away from the hospital in time, and today I've been twice, before and after Mass. Both times I hammered. I can't think what that Jan can be up to.'

Renia listened with visibly increasing bewilderment, and only then did I notice that she was very pale. 'The fact is, Jan was arrested the evening before last at five o'clock and the Gestapo have been sitting in the flat ever since, catching all callers.'[34]

It was my turn to look astonished. Neither of us could understand how the Gestapo could have been deaf to my pounding at the door. Stasia said that late the previous evening she received a card with an order from 'Prawdzic' to inform Renia and Karolina that Jan had been arrested. When she called on Renia that morning, Renia told her that I had probably already been picked up, since I was supposed to be leaving the hospital early and going straight to Jan's place. Stasia went to the St Lazarus Hospital, where she was told that I'd left fifteen minutes earlier. Meanwhile Renia had rescued the Home Army's gold from my flat.

That being so, there was nothing else for it but to take back the gold and go to bed. Later we found out that the Gestapo had sat in Jan's flat from Friday evening until Sunday evening and had taken away seventeen people. On Sunday morning the flat had been closed – but only for an hour and a half – because the Gestapo men had to attend a parade for the Führer's birthday. When one of us reported in the afternoon that the Gestapo had arrested everybody who called on Jan in the morning, our District Commander said: 'Yes, but somebody came to report to me after calling at the house *twice* that morning. How do you explain that? Somebody was born under a very lucky star . . .' Then out came the story of Hitler's birthday celebration.

The next day, 21 April, I was as usual in the forenoon at the Red Cross office in Piekarska Street. I had been out for a while. When I got back, one of our volunteers told me that Renia was looking for me and would like me to meet her at my flat. At moments of crisis, human instincts (like those of animals) are suddenly sharpened. At that particular moment, only with difficulty could I conceal the sense of awful fear that gripped me. Renia waiting for me in my room in duty hours? What else could that mean but that something very serious must have happened. I felt irrationally certain that our Commander's safety was threatened. I had to rush round the office and tidy up a series of trifling matters before I could set out for my flat, trying not to walk too fast. There was nobody on the stairs, so I took them three at a time . . . Before I could get out my key in a rush, Renia opened the door. 'They've got Leon,' was all she said, closing the door behind me. I took one look at her and was afraid to ask any more. Leon Giedgowd[35] was our unit treasurer as well as being the owner of a stationer's shop in Zwierzyniecka Street, where our Commander 'Prawdzic' used to work as an assistant under the name Wolański.

Renia looked calm, only rather less animated than usual, but tight-lipped as though preoccupied. I risked a question: 'So, what now . . . ?'

'I was there. The Commander was sitting in the shop and told me to leave at once. The Gestapo came in the morning with Leon, while Tadeusz was sitting there, then they went out. I wanted to take him away at all costs, but he insisted on staying to wait for some contact or other. I gave him your address. It was the only safe place for him to go, because none of the Gestapo who came to the shop could yet have known your new address. All right. Stay here. Don't go out. I'll go there, but I'll be back later.'

'Come back soon' was all I had time to say as she rushed downstairs.

I went into the flat and sat down near the door. The waiting had begun. What day was this? – 21 April, since yesterday had been Hitler's birthday. I ransacked my memory: 21 April was some kind of date . . . Aha! That's it! PALILIA, symbolic birthday of Rome. At this reminder, bygone years – those brilliant years of my 'previous incarnation', the years of scholarly work in Rome – flashed before my eyes with incredible intensity. It was a warm spring day. I went and stood by the window of my new room and saw those visible traces of our tradition, so unattainably distant at the present time and yet so near – the towers of the Wawel Cathedral. The sight of them revived my spirits . . . Acropolis. Half an hour had slipped by. Clearly Renia had not yet been able to come. It might be a long wait – a very long wait. Perhaps she would never come.

At that moment the door-bell rang. I rushed to open it and Stasia darted inside.

'Don't wait – there's no hope for Renia or for him!'

'What do you mean?'

'They're both in the shop and there are other people with them. Bound to be Gestapo. They're done for!' She was under great stress. 'You've no idea what's going on in town. They're shooting in the streets. One of our people went out carrying a briefcase with something important inside. A bullet hit him, but, while he was still lying there wounded, he managed to kick the case with such force that it flew into the canal. They didn't get it.'

I understood that day how, in situations involving great nervous tension, facts tend to get mixed up with literature, as in the present instance. Stasia's account owed something to the description of the death of Hubert Olbromski in *Faithful River*. Heaven help us, but I never thought that I, who have so much to be grateful for to the author Żeromski, would one day meet him in such a predicament! But Stasia needed calming.

'Where are you supposed to be?'

'In the chemist's opposite the shop.'

'Well, please go there.'

'I'll go back presently. I just wanted to let you know how things were, and to give you this piece of Renia's property.' Stasia pressed a gold bracelet into my hand, which I came across a week later in my handbag. I must have stuffed it in without thinking at that critical juncture. Stasia then left me.

I returned to my chair near the door. An hour now – and still nothing. For somebody under great stress, but condemned to inactivity, it is natural to concentrate entirely on observing what's happening and if, as in this case, there is no external action whatsoever, to resort to introspection. I remember as though it were yesterday observing impartially, as it were, the growth within me of a new emotion, which I had never previously been aware of – an immensely powerful feeling of limitless devotion to our Commander. This enforced inactivity, waiting while he was in danger, was indescribable torture. I suddenly understood clearly and simply why this emotion has impelled so many people in the course of history to perform heroic deeds. And here I was forced to sit nailed to my chair feeling my hair grow grey. Not a word of this to anyone. I've been waiting an hour and three-quarters. Suddenly – the bell.

'He's walking. He ordered me to go on, a short distance ahead. He'll be here presently.'

Indeed, he actually appeared in a couple of minutes. In a very calm, almost expressionless voice, he remarked: 'Things were getting a bit hot where we were.' That was all he said.

In the afternoon Renia, Wisia Horodyska and I went out for a change, to gather information, look up contacts and make preparations for the Commander's temporary absence on reconnaissance in the region. The news was dismal: all cells were under attack and there were more and more arrests. The Commander's thoughts turned constantly to Montelupi.[36] People were being tortured inside.

In the evening he ordered me to take the keys of the shop to Mrs Giedgowd's friend. We later learned that this lady was terribly concerned about Mr Wolański because she didn't know whether his wife was the petite, graceful one or the very tall one . . . I also had a different assignment that day. I had to go to Mr Wolański's flat to collect some papers, which he had hidden in a crevice in the bathroom wall. The woman who owned the flat was an acquaintance of people I knew, so I had an excuse to call on her in connection with news from Kazakhstan. As I went in, while I was still in the hall, I felt a little 'unwell' and needed to go to the bathroom. (The Commander had described the layout of the flat for me in detail.) There was a ladder in the bathroom, which I climbed, and, with the help of a pair of pliers that he had also given me, I managed to extract the papers from the crack in the wall. I waited a little while till I felt 'well' again, and left the flat, having said goodbye to the lady of the house, whose speech was sprinkled with French words and who was very *inquiète*[37] about my health.

In the evening I called on Doctor Szebesta*, to whom I was to report the facts of what had happened. He had heard nothing about it as yet. When I finished my account, I added that I had waited for an hour and three-quarters. He looked at me and said: 'It's nothing. That gave you time to think what it means to be a Commander and what a person will do for such a man.'

'How did you know?' I asked.

'I could tell as much by the look on your face.'

That evening Renia and I explained to our hostess that a cousin of mine who was sick, and waiting to be admitted to hospital, was due to arrive and had nowhere to spend the night. I don't know what she thought, but she agreed to let the Commander stay the night in a small passage room opposite mine. He left two days later.[38]

I returned to my recently neglected, though constantly dwindling, work at the hospital. The Jesuits' Hospital had been very nicely renovated and refurbished. On 4 May Wierzbowski finally died in his ward. For the last several days he was often unconscious and, in his unconscious state, he was still defending the Hel Peninsula. As I laid him in his coffin, I reflected how I had been unable to save his life, whereas it was to him that I owed *my* life. Had I not taken Holy Communion with him that morning, I'd not still be alive . . .

Towards the end of May I sent word to our Commander, who was absent from Kraków, to enquire what plans he might have to find me a new job, since my work at the hospital was nearly over. The answer I received instructed me to join the so-called 'Protectorate', a committee of ladies looking after the inmates of Montelupi, because the Commander wished to have 'his own man' in the prison. So I made some efforts to join, with no success. In charge of the Protectorate was an honourable man, very devoted to the work, a Socialist and a trifle doctrinaire, who was opposed to my admittance to the Protectorate 'on grounds of principle'. He is no longer alive, but as long as I live I shall remain deeply grateful to him for turning me down, otherwise I might very well have been stuck with the 'Protectorate' for good.

It was now June and we were living from day to day and hour to hour, constantly awaiting that longed-for event. The Germans were making simply colossal preparations. By day and night, troops were passing through Kraków, equipped with the latest weapons, gleaming uniforms, marvellous horses and huge, shapeless tanks. The whole cavalcade – gigantic, limitless in numbers and scale – rolled on and on, as though it would never end. The procession lasted all day and all night, through the next day and on into the night. One had the impression that it would go on for ever. It streamed out from the railway station, along the Planty Promenade, then disappeared down the Karmelicka and beyond – moving east. Only one thing was in strange contrast to this show of strength by the *Herrenvolk*: the faces of the soldiers showed no sign of joyful ardour in keeping with such a palpable display of physical strength. The men, it's true, looked determined but often sad, uncannily resigned, jaws tightly clenched.

It was at this stage that a German who was staying with people we knew returned from leave. The lady of the house, Hungarian by birth, asked him what the situation was like in Germany. He was silent for a little while, then he replied: '*Glänzend, aber hoffnungslos*'.[39] The whole General Government sector was changing visibly, day by day, into a war zone. The hospitals stood waiting. The strictest orders were issued regarding the blackout. The feeling of tremendous tension in the air was like the build-up of electricity before a storm. Added to that, the Polish population had a fresh problem: anyone heard discussing the possibility of a new war would be punished with arrest. We never could understand whether the Germans really believed that the Muscovites knew nothing about their fantastic preparations, or whether they were simply looking for a new way of irritating the Poles.

At last, at seven o'clock in the morning on 22 June, Wisia Horodyska dropped in, having just returned from our part of the country. I had slept very soundly and she had to shake me awake. 'Karla, get up. It's war!' I looked at her, afraid to believe her. 'Yes, it's true. The chaplain who lives in the monastery near my mother heard the German radio through the wall, and he rushed in – still in his nightshirt – to tell the old lady. The Germans are telling the whole world they're going to war against Russia and Communism!'

I got up and dressed and went to the church. Everyone was there already, kneeling and giving thanks . . . From the church I went to pay a Sunday visit to some friends with a radio. Moscow was broadcasting in all languages to the workers of the world, that this day, on the anniversary of Napoleon's declaration of war on Tsar Alexander I, Hitler's armies had crossed the border of the Soviet Union. The Poles were going mad with excitement. That border, the blood-stained Ribbentrop–Molotov Line cutting Poland in half, had ceased to exist from this day onwards. The thought that the dreadful 'boundary' was vanishing at this very moment, once and for all, filled us with a frenzy of delight. Let the Germans drive into the heart of Russia for the pyrrhic victory that awaited them. They would never come back, because the Allies would put paid to them in the west. And we could then return to our east – to Lwów where we belonged.

The following day I listened to General Sikorski's speech. He spoke about the terrible weakening of the Germans, and their crazy policy. He also said he knew that in Poland people were deeply convinced that the Germans would win against Russia, but he did not consider that a foregone conclusion. It might turn out otherwise. We pondered those words. Could it really be possible? Would Eastern Poland again be threatened if that were to happen? But no, it didn't bear thinking about! The mere idea was an insult to those who, in alliance with ourselves, were fighting to protect Western culture. They would never sacrifice half of Poland's territory along with their entire honour, in disregard moreover of their own interests. Bearing all that in mind, it would be sheer lunacy to let the Russians advance as far as the River Bug. No, in any case, the Germans were too powerful ever to be beaten by Russia. The Soviets would teach them a lesson, but would not defeat them – just drain Germany's resources to the last drop, in time for the Allies to finish them off.

A few days later news came that the Germans had taken Lwów and the city was not too badly damaged. We were going to have to wait a bit to make direct contact. Meanwhile, we agonised over a most distressing rumour. The Germans were said to have arrested a large number of professors attached to Lwów University. Different names kept being mentioned. But so far nothing was known for certain.

At last, the first smuggled letter came through addressed to me. Enclosed was a list of twenty-two professors and lecturers who had been arrested – some with their wives and grown-up sons – two days after the German invasion and were now being held, presumably, as hostages. The place of confinement was not known.[40] It emerged from the list that the Department of Medicine was mainly involved, but professors at the Polytechnic and the High School of Commerce had also been seized. From then on, that mysterious affair was constantly on our minds.

Meanwhile, I was making some plans of my own. Since I had not been successful in applying for membership of the Protectorate committee, I was at a loose end. I had to find something to do. Just recently we had been getting some very distressing reports about prison conditions in the provinces. Some particularly tragic facts had come to light from Tarnów, where there was a very big jail, which from the beginning had been receiving food aid from the local Red Cross. This was later forbidden by the Germans. The food that they themselves provided was such that eighteen to twenty-three prisoners were dying from starvation every day. We had precise evidence, because the local community welfare was paying for the coffins. The bodies were transported in full view, and the sight of them left not the slightest doubt about the cause of death. So I went to the President of the RGO, Adam Ronikier*, and asked whether he would not like to extend his welfare function to the prisoners and take me on as administrator. I based my suitability as candidate for this post on three criteria:

1 The administrator must be a woman, for a man would be too vulnerable.
2 This woman should not have a husband or son, who might be liable to pressure.
3 The woman must also speak fluent German.

The President agreed on the spot, for which I shall be grateful to him for as long as I live. The Council approved the President's proposal. Because one could not belong to both the Red Cross and the RGO at the same time, I resigned from my job with the Red Cross and became an official of the RGO.[41]

Chapter 3

On Tour in the 'General Government'

July 1941–March 1942

Now began a series of lengthy visits to German administrative offices in an effort to devise some central system for tackling the problems of prisoner welfare. The RGO, in the person of myself, approached the authorities for permission to supply foodstuffs to all people in prison, regardless of the grounds for their arrest. What we were aiming for was a general, anonymous supply to all prisoners, political or criminal. It was clear that there was no other way to ensure access to political prisoners. The German judicial authorities did not pose too many problems. Nor did another office, something akin to a Ministry of Internal Affairs. Eventually I arrived at the Social Welfare Headquarters of the 'General Government',[1] where I had to deal with a Dr Heinrich who was a young super-German, looked rather like a barber and, as everyone knew, belonged to the Gestapo. After some immeasurably long and exhausting conversational duels with one another, he finally sent me to the Gestapo. Personally, that suited me very well. Things were getting a little too hot for comfort in my vicinity. I had been under close observation ever since the security leaks in April 1941. I had received a few warnings and pieces of sound advice to the effect that I 'would do better to leave Kraków'. I knew that if I did, I would be burying myself alive; besides, I would have to go into hiding till the end of the war.

Going straight to Gestapo headquarters seemed to me by far the best defence. I reckoned the Germans would think that anyone who ventured into the lion's den itself was sure to be in order. I was received by a very tall, black-uniformed Sturmbannführer (Major), with a monosyllabic surname that I do not remember. He looked me up and down very intently and we discussed various matters. I felt that he was investigating me. Fortunately, on entering, I had quickly sat down with my back to the window before he had time to show me somewhere else to sit. As a result, I felt quite at ease with my face in shadow, whereas he was dazzled by the light. Suddenly he asked me why I was so interested in the care of prisoners. I said that since I could no longer care for the sick, I wished to concern myself with a similar category of people – that was to say, prisoners, and so forth. He asked what quantities of food we wanted to send. He warned me that I would never – but never – be allowed to ask about the number of prisoners detained. I declared that I knew the total number of prisoners was no business of mine. My interlocutor sounded very satisfied with this idiotic answer. He instructed me to come back in two days. Meanwhile he would consult his superiors.

On my next visit I was kept waiting a very long time. As I sat there, a prisoner was led in, who peered at me intently for a short while and was then led away. I got the impression that this was an unsuccessful confrontation. Afterwards I managed to confirm that the prisoner brought before me was very probably none other than that same Leon who was just then in the process of 'spilling the beans'. The confrontation failed because Leon had never seen me. For that, I could thank our Commander 'Prawdzic', who, despite my requests, had never allowed me to come to the shop.

At last, I was admitted. A second conversation took place during which I was again asked why I was particularly concerned about prisoners. This time my answer was hardly politic. I replied simply, in exasperation, that I regarded it as a national duty, which I wanted to fulfil, not illegally, but in a frank and open manner. The result was unexpected. From that moment on, the Major was favourably inclined towards my proposals. He clearly thought that anyone who could say such things could also safely be allowed to work, since she was obviously very naïve. Only towards the end did he start shouting at me in a theatrical fashion, resorting to familiar bully-boy tactics. He said he wanted to draw my attention to the fact that, should I use my office to express dangerous views, or at the very first sign of a message being smuggled through in foodstuffs sent to the prisoners, I would be arrested. I asked how it would be possible to smuggle a message in food sent anonymously, in cauldrons, for all prisoners, whether political or criminal. He replied that everything was possible, but calmed down. At last I was able to go. I left that building, symbol of our enslavement, full of hope.

When I got home that evening I noticed that, for the first time, my block was no longer under surveillance. The cunning of our western invader was decidedly not in keeping with his cruelty!

Not long afterwards I was again admitted to the presence of Heinrich who, after long telephone calls and discussions, issued me with a card bearing a swastika, the German eagle and all kinds of other decorations. The card stated in black and white that I was empowered by permission of the Gestapo and the *Sicherheitsdienst* (security service) to deliver anonymous consignments of foodstuffs for prisoners, on behalf of the RGO on the territory of the General Government. With this document, he declared, I could travel to Tarnów. I snatched the card and raced home. I read it over and over again and noted that my date of birth was given as 11 August. That Prussian barber could never have imagined that he was giving me such a royal birthday present! That evening I wrote, or rather encoded in a harmless brochure, a fairly long letter to the Commander. With this cipher – quite a simple one at that – based on the positioning of tiny dots on the various letters (sometimes in the reverse direction), I used to send him broadcast news and other information. On this occasion I reported that I had assumed responsibility for the care of prisoners all over the German-occupied sector of Poland (the General Government). I remember that for the first time I added a brief personal message: 'A huge responsibility. Please help me with your thoughts.' After a few days came a short answer ordering me to break off all contacts and relinquish all other activities so as to concentrate exclusively on my new assignment.

The day after acquiring my card, I set off for Tarnów. The prison there was not administered by the SS, but by the justice authorities. As a former Polish prison, Tarnów jail still had its Polish warders and the entire prison staff. There, the Gestapo kept its own prisoners and was responsible for 'looking after' them. I was received by the Governor of the prison, an elderly man called Günther. He read Heinrich's card and satisfied himself that I was 'in order', but was unable to do anything without an instruction from the Justice Department in Kraków. I would have to go back to Kraków at once. I would be given a lift there by the President of the RGO, Adam Ronikier, who happened also to be in Tarnów that day. On the journey we called on various acquaintances. Among others whom I knew was Mrs Bnińska, who had moved from Samostrzel, near Poznań. I asked her about conditions there. She told me that she had been allowed to go on living in her publishing house for a year, but had then been put out on the street. During that year in spring and autumn, under the windows of her printing house, a fire was lit every day under the boiler of a steam engine and stoked with great vellum-bound volumes from the shelves of the celebrated Bniński Library in Samostrzel.

By evening I was back in Kraków. There, with the help of my famous card, I managed to clear up the last remaining problems in Tarnów. A couple of days later, on 25 August, I was able to telephone the Committee in Tarnów with a request for 1,200 portions of soup for the following day. (That was the number given me by the previous Governor of the prison.) When I went along in the morning, I found that Günther had agreed to delivery of the soup for that day. The atmosphere in the Committee was hectic. At midday I climbed into a battered old rattletrap of a municipal wagon, with six cauldrons of soup for company, and drove to the jail. A group of people were waiting for something or somebody, listening constantly to the chorus of groans and appeals for help or food that issued ever more loudly from the numerous barred windows of the prison. Later I was told that the people waiting were prisoners' relatives trying to get parcels of clothing and so on passed on to their husbands and sons. I will never forget the indescribable expression of emotion and tension on the faces of those people at the sight of the truck with the cauldrons of soup and, above all, the sight of the great iron gate of the jail, which just then clanked open. I sat beside the driver, still not knowing for sure whether this was a dream, reality or theatre. To think that there were so many Polish freedom fighters locked up in Tarnów!

Into the prison we went and the gate shut behind us with a crash. We stood in the vast courtyard. A Polish warder appeared, visibly moved. A little later two or three prisoners, looking like corpses, followed him. To judge by their faces, these were criminals. The warder ordered them to pick up the cauldrons and carry them into the building. One of the youngest of them, having lifted a cauldron, staggered and lost his balance. It was easy to see how they were all stupefied by the aroma of the meat soup. Before they came back for the remaining cauldrons, an elderly man joined in, very red in the face – looking like a caricature of a criminal.

'What's all this?' he shouted at the sight of the cauldrons. Then, as he approached, he called loudly in our direction: 'You're obviously trying to help the Social Security save cash on coffins, eh?'

Presently, the truck drove off and returned with some more cauldrons brought by Maryla Dmochowska, the soul and brains of the Tarnów Welfare Committee. When all the cauldrons had been handed over, I felt my strength ebbing away, my façade beginning to crumble. I told the ladies that I would come to the office later and quickly escaped to the cathedral. There I gave thanks, sobbing helplessly. After a time I noticed that a woman kneeling nearby was looking at me with profound pity. She was convinced that I must have suffered some major misfortune, because in those days it was inconceivable that anyone would be crying for happiness. In the afternoon, back at the Committee, I came across some unknown persons who had just come from outside the prison. They reported hearing yells from the cell-windows: 'We got the soup . . . go and tell whoever's concerned that they gave it to us . . . Thank them . . . and ask them for more.'

From that happiest of all days, 26 August 1941, Tarnów – in exemplary fashion and regularly – fed its prisoners both amply and efficiently.

Tarnów was unique in the whole German-occupied sector of Poland for the fact that surrounding villages donated, and transported weekly, supplies earmarked for the prisoners – and, with arrangements in the hands of Maryla, the food was as tasty as it was economically prepared.

After Tarnów we turned our attention to Jasło and Sanok. In Jasło, the Governor of the prison was a Ukrainian who, to our great delight, was obviously afraid of me. He surely assumed that I came on behalf of the Germans, bowed very low and – most important of all – was very submissive. Sanok was more difficult. There they had a notorious Gestapo executioner, Stawitzky (it seems that was a pseudonym). Sanok was literally awash with blood. Despite that, amid constant arrests and executions, the Committee continued working with great courage. Nuns cooked for the jail because, by a curious coincidence, Stawitzky (comparatively speaking) hated them less.

Next, we turned our attack on the Nowy Sącz prison, which was administered by the Gestapo. There the lord of life and death, or rather death in particular, was one Hamann, who was in the habit of shooting Poles with his own hands. On arrival, I made my way as usual straight from the railway station to our local committee, where I was received by an intelligent, energetic-looking young woman official. I was struck by her strangely tense facial expression, the more so because, even out in the street, it seemed to me that here in Nowy Sącz people looked as though they were under the impact of something unknown and terrifying. I even met a couple weeping openly.

When I gave the young woman my name, she said in a strangely unnatural voice: 'You've come today, madam – today of all days!' I did not know what she meant and asked to see the Committee Chairman. A young man with tightly pursed lips came out to meet me and invited me into his office.

'You've come about the prisoners,' he said shortly.

'Yes, as I let you know in advance,' I said with growing astonishment.

'This morning the Germans themselves informed us that all our hostages have been shot,' he replied, slowly and emphatically.

'What hostages?'

'Almost the entire local intelligentsia, headed by our priest. We knew about it yesterday, for they managed to send us a farewell letter, signed by them all. They wrote that their wives and mothers should not weep for them, but be proud that they were found worthy . . . Across the corner, under the signatures, they had added: "*Dulce et decorum est*".[2] The entire, most valuable segment of our Nowy Sącz community has gone, including some of my closest friends.'

'Why?' I asked.

'For no reason' was the answer.

The quota, I thought to myself, and asked no more.

Given this state of affairs, I decided not to visit Hamann that day, since I would surely be refused admittance by a man still intoxicated with the reek of fresh blood. Besides, there was almost nobody left to feed in this prison . . . However, I stayed a few hours longer in Sącz, because I thought there were people there who would gladly talk to somebody who, as far as general matters were concerned, was one of themselves, but whose nearest and dearest had not been killed that day. Until late that night the Chairman of the Committee,[3] pacing up and down his sitting-room, talked about them all – every one of them individually, and then about their wives and children . . . By early morning of the next day, back in Kraków, I felt I had known them all personally: the teachers, engineers and local officials, all those who were gone, without living to see that for which it was so sweet and praiseworthy to die. That Poland of the future, I thought to myself, a Poland redeemed by such incalculable sacrifice, will need to be a very happy and moral society.

The next prisons in Częstochowa and Piotrków Tribunalski were not too difficult to 'conquer'. I had been told in advance that Częstochowa would not be a special problem. It was a known fact that the German administration there, despite many and varied irritations, was less cruel than in other localities. Up to that time there had been neither mass executions nor even large-scale round-ups. The local populace attributed this to a certain fear instilled in the Germans by the sanctity of the place: 'The Swabians [Germans] are afraid of the Mother of God.' When their leaders – such as Frank and Goebbels – came to Częstochowa, they visited Jasna Góra (the Shining Mount). They ordered the icon to be unveiled and, at that moment, Goebbels even raised his hand and greeted the Virgin of Częstochowa with the Hitler salute. As for the jail, I encountered no undue difficulty. Admittedly, the Gestapo men received me very ungraciously, with much shouting of threats, but they agreed to the food distribution.

The next morning I was at Jasna Góra, which was just then wearing its martyr's crown of leaves, withering in this third autumn of the war. At the entrance to the church hung a large notice, complete with swastika, from the *Parteivögel*[4] strictly forbidding the military to behave indecently in the church or to bring in dogs – not too much to ask of an army of professed *Kulturträger*.[5]

In the confessional was seated an old Pauline Father with a snow-white beard. When I told him that my soul was dominated by hatred and the desire for revenge, but not on my own behalf, he consoled me by saying the Lord God is admittedly slow to act, but is nevertheless very just. As for loving our enemies, the old priest – praise be to God – did not press the point.

Late that evening I reached Piotrków. There I was to be put up for the night by a local photographer, his wife (who was a teacher) and his son (a student of Polish language and literature). They were delightful people, very active in social welfare work, and received me with great warmth and simplicity. To this day I remember many coloured and black-and-white portraits of the lady of the house decorating their walls, in which one could trace the history of portraiture over the past twenty-five years. Every time during the next few months that I needed to visit Piotrków, I looked forward to the hours I would be spending with my hosts. The Chairman told me about the affairs of his committee, where the poverty was worst, and about the prison and that, living opposite as he did, he frequently heard very clearly, particularly at night, groans and people crying out for food.

When I went there, I was received by the Austrian Commandant, who engaged me in a long conversation on the subject of the prisoners' needs. He brought in the prison doctor, a Pole. The conversation was in German, and I suspect the doctor did not realise he was talking to a Polish woman.[6] Instead, it would seem, he assumed that he was required to give a factual account of the prisoners' state of health for the benefit of some German charitable institution. He asked, for example, who was supposed to be fed – all the prisoners, or only those who could still be saved? Speaking as a doctor, he doubted the possibility of feeding those who were '*unmittelbar vor dem Hungertod*'[7] because they would need to be kept for long weeks on an incredibly strict diet, which, he thought, would be virtually impracticable. I tried to explain to him as matter-of-factly as possible that the food was for all the prisoners. As I was going out, the Commandant turned to the doctor and said: 'You used the expression "death by starvation" just now. I must warn you, for the future, of the consequences of using that term.' He also drew my attention to the fact that it would not be in the best interests of my work if I were to make use of that 'irresponsible expression' employed by the prison doctor. It was lucky for me that the Commandant was an Austrian.

Off I went. Having a couple of hours to wait for a train, I spent the time visiting some of the many monuments in Piotrków dating from the fourteenth to sixteenth centuries. I did not know the town. But these reminders of the times of the Piasts and the Jagiellonians[8] was at that moment a source of strength. The radiance that shines to this day through the Piotrków monuments in living memory of the great Jagiellonians strengthened my faith in Poland.

That was the start of work in Piotrków, particularly complicated by reason of the almost total lack of foodstuffs locally and the exceptional difficulties made by the German authorities in preventing imports. Despite that, the prisoners of Piotrków henceforth received regular assistance. The next time I visited the place, the doctor reported that they were all doing well.

The continual travelling that filled my life included a trip to Warsaw once a month, to see the Commander, who was permanently based in the capital as deputy of the Commander-in-Chief, Grot Rowecki*. I submitted regular reports on the whole previous month's work, on the prisoner total in particular jails, as well as information of all kinds gathered on my journeys.

I must admit, this new life was very interesting. I tried every month to be in each of the jails, so that the number of towns on my list steadily increased. With every month, my travel technique improved. In the end, I was able to sleep wonderfully well in the middle of a group of sixteen black marketeers sharing the one compartment, or kneeling with one knee resting on a parcel at the entrance to the coach. The worst thing of all was having to change trains on the way. Given so many delayed arrivals in wartime, connecting trains never waited. A particularly menacing location on my monthly journey between Warsaw and Piotrków was a place called Koluszki. There, I never managed to catch the connection and so had a nine-hour wait every time. Poles were not allowed to wait around on the station; equally they were forbidden to enter either of the two decent restaurants. That left only a tiny tavern of sorts in which a Pole could sit and read. I once asked a companion in distress if he'd mind looking after my suitcase while I went to buy something. 'Would you be kind enough to lend me that book you were reading while you're away?' he asked. 'I so much envy you having something to read.' So I gave him the book and made for the door. Happening to turn round, I saw him greedily open the book and look stunned as he did so. It was a small book with a green binding. The traveller must surely have thought it was *The Vampire of the Sleeping-Car* or something similar, whereas the foreword read: '*Romam Urbem in principio reges habuere*'. Perhaps the story was as much of a thriller as the *Vampire*, but of a slightly different sort: the *Annales* of Tacitus. When I returned, he was furious.

'Here's your book back, and many thanks. I don't read Latin. Forgot all I knew long ago.' I explained sweetly that he himself had asked me for the book. That didn't help. I got the impression he would never again ask to borrow a woman's book on a rail journey. As we at last started moving, an elderly country woman in the carriage, after staring at me for a long time, quietly remarked: 'This is the third time I've travelled to Piotrków with you. Do you really find it pays you? The prices are very little different from Warsaw!'

In the last days of September something of great importance to me happened. I travelled to Lwów. From the day the Russians moved out, I had dreamed of nothing else, but until then it had remained just a dream. The 'border' in Przemyśl was hermetically sealed for Poles, hardly less so than in Bolshevik times. Nothing was crossing, apart from long processions of heavy German lorries, making their way through the German-occupied sector back into the Reich, packed with everything left behind by the retreating Russians. Because the latter, at the last minute, managed to take very little since they had no time, a great many things – above all vast quantities of objects of cultural value and works of art, formerly in private ownership – were looted by the Germans. Ukrainian middle-men, active on the journey, stole various items from the Germans and sold them in Kraków. In this way numerous 'pieces' from Eastern Poland started reappearing in the west, including some things belonging to my brother from the family home at Rozdół.[9] The Poles continued to be cut off from their ancestral lands by a Great Wall of China, as it were. It was widely said that a great Ukraine would arise on the far side of that wall, with far-reaching autonomy, stretching all the way to Kiev.

Then suddenly, like a bombshell, the news burst upon us that Eastern Małopolska was to be joined to the German-occupied sector of Poland as the so-called District of Galicia. We could not believe it. But very soon Governor Frank travelled to the area, was greeted by the Ukrainians with a triumphal arch and pronounced a moving speech in Lwów, which the newspapers headlined '*Die Rückkehr von Galizien in das Deutsche Reich*'.[10] I believe that German readers in those days would hardly have been surprised to hear that India or Paraguay was returning to the maternal bosom of the German Reich; they would greet the news about Galicia as cause for glad celebration, but an entirely normal event. We expected at the time that the famous border at Przemyśl (between the Russian and German sectors of Poland) would now disappear, but it was not to be. Instead, the Germans merely began to charge a fee for allowing people to cross the bridge over the River San. I was one of those who crossed.

There was a problem about spending the night in Przemyśl, for the town was crammed with people, many of them waiting and hoping to go further east. In the event, I slept very soundly that night in a dentist's chair. In the morning an SS man led us across the bridge, not free of charge. On the far side there was no shortage of second-hand bargains. Late in the day we drove into Lwów. I got out near the Stryjski Park on a fine autumn evening, unable to conceive or understand how at last I was back in Lwów. I was so bewildered that I stood in the street as though rooted to the spot.

A small elderly woman studied me with her wise eyes. 'And where have you sprung from?'

We fell into one another's arms. She was Helena Polaczkówna*, a history lecturer. A quarter of an hour later I was again among friends,[11] a year and half after my escape by night that 3 May. They talked continuously, at length and exclusively about the Bolsheviks. It seemed that only by a miracle had they escaped being deported to the depths of Russia. After my departure, in the summer of 1940, long trainloads of deportees had again moved eastwards. This time the passengers were 'runners' – that is to say, people who fled east from the west of Poland after the German invasion in 1939 and who did not return to live under German occupation. After that major deportation, things were quiet. In May 1941, before the war started (meaning Hitler's invasion of the Soviet Union), the familiar long rows of railway wagons were once again being lined up on the tracks in preparation for another mass exodus. But this time the trains were not for Poles, but for Bolsheviks, who could now (in the military trains made ready to deport more Poles) themselves be swiftly and efficiently evacuated to the heart of Russia. Later we learned that it had been planned to ship out almost the entire Polish intelligentsia.

When bombs again began falling on Lwów, it was noticed that in the case of many houses a small, mysterious mark was to be seen under the front door-bell. In the course of one night, all persons whose bells bore that sign were earmarked to travel . . . They did not, in fact. Instead, they lived to see Asia withdraw from Lwów and Poland to be reunited. In defiance of all evidence and despite everything, they still experienced an encouraging sense of having 'returned to Europe'. To certain reservations voiced by me, people replied: 'The Germans are terrible enemies, but they surely cannot be compared with those others. You were not in the Brygidki jail, so you don't know what the Bolsheviks are like.'

Brygidki, the famous prison in Lwów, was something else that nobody could discuss calmly. The Bolsheviks had murdered all the prisoners before they withdrew, and a few days later the Germans allowed the inhabitants to visit the completely devastated jail in the state in which the Bolsheviks left it. Half of Lwów went to the prison to search for their dear ones amid corpses so mutilated that, in most cases, recognition proved a hopeless task. There were priests crucified on a wall: one with his rosary beads strung through both eye-sockets; another with the shape of a cross marked out by nails hammered into his chest. And much else besides . . . Despite everything, a few of the corpses were recognised by their next of kin, sometimes by shreds of clothing or teeth. Everybody was talking about these scenes because, even three months later, they could still think of nothing else.

The people of Lwów knew little about Germany and asked a lot about conditions in the west, of which they knew almost nothing at all. In conversation they referred constantly to those twenty-five professors and lecturers who were abducted at the very start of the German occupation and begged us to search for them in the west. They were worried about whether these hostages were being ill-treated and constantly agonised about where they might be, since not one of them had ever given any sign of life. Among them was Professor Ostrowski*, highly regarded both as a man and a surgeon, who had been seized with his wife and two sub-tenants; 'Boy' Żeleński* and Father Komornicki*; there was Rector Professor Longchamps with his three grown-up sons;[12] there was an old man of eighty, Professor Emeritus Sołowij*, who vanished with his grandson, Adam Mięsowicz; there was Professor Rencki*, who was jailed for eighteen months in Brygidki prison and managed to free himself two days before the German invasion through a hole blown in the wall by a bomb, thus escaping certain death at the hands of the Bolsheviks. He was able to enjoy his freedom for barely four days.

'It was very sad, they did just the same thing in Kraków. They went for the professors and teachers. They'll release some of them after a couple of months, but they could still be rounded up again as victims – same as over there.' The people of Lwów continued to take the view that, in contrast to Kraków, no information about the professors in Lwów had ever been forthcoming, because Lwów was still cut off from the west.

The material condition of the city at that time was frightful. Starvation was rife. There were no shops and the total destruction of economic life brought about by the Bolsheviks was all the more terrible in its consequences because the Germans would neither allow anything to be brought into the city, nor import anything themselves. There were no shops apart from a few state-run establishments, manned by Bolsheviks and now, naturally, for 'Germans only'. So we went hungry. Suddenly, my former maid Andzia appeared, bringing ample provisions from Komarno. I can hardly describe what it meant to me to be reunited with this most faithful of friends after the eighteen-month break. Andzia, unlike some less simple souls, had no illusions whatsoever about the Germans. She declared to me right away that a people who can sing about their own country 'Germany, Germany above all' could not be worth much, because 'pride like that is just laughable'. Recalling how they behaved in the countryside, she thought they were no better than the Muscovites – only a bit more stupid, which would enable her to get food to me and to friends. She was right. They were more stupid, but they also had other commendable features that became apparent only when compared with the invader from the east. In the course of my first stay in post-Bolshevik Lwów I noted, to my horror, something that struck me as very strange, given the proverbial high spirits of this city. The Russian domination had left in its wake deep traces of terrible depression. Even phlegmatic Kraków, not to mention Warsaw, was nothing like as depressed.

We could now understand how it was that the reactions evoked in us by the German occupation differed so fundamentally from those produced by the Soviets. The German way of going about things irritated and incensed us to a very high degree. On top of that, the persecution of *all* Poles aroused in our society something that nobody who experienced that occupation will ever forget – the consciousness of complete unity among the Polish people. Amid the general great misfortune, there was a period of the most intense happiness, when nobody bothered about anybody else's class origins or party affiliation. There was only that collective moral strength, which was *Polishness.* Notwithstanding our total individualism, each one of us felt part of a monolith. As a result, something akin to mass ecstasy evolved, which naturally intensified in each of us in proportion to the increasing imminence of death, merely by virtue of being a true Pole. That incredible strength in tension still had its roots somewhere else as well.

The sentiment with which each of us, and all at the same time, was charged to the brim was by no means solely nationalism. Clearly, love of our country, whose existence was threatened, gained strength with every day that passed. But the struggle was being waged not only about the life of the nation, but simply about everything that made life worth living – all the ideals dear to each one of us. It was about Christianity, the rights of the individual, the dignity of man. We often gave thanks to God for the one thing left to us: the awareness that we were dying in defence of the highest values of humanity. Based on this consciousness, an atmosphere developed that was often reminiscent of what we know of the spirit of the Crusades. The very fact that there was present a spiritual and universal element in this struggle provided a firm link with the Middle Ages.

It fell to us to defend our ideals in struggling against a nation that itself once possessed them, but which today wilfully rejected them in order to secure physical authority and dominion over others – thereby erasing its name from the book of civilised nations. We often used to reflect on the terrible moral dilemma confronting any 'good' German. For such Germans *did* exist and, in a nation that size, there had to be quite a few of them. We imagined that with them, in contrast to the complete harmony among us, the conflict between the basic principles of any sort of ethic, on the one hand, and the duty to sacrifice one's life for the Fatherland on the other, must be quite intolerable. That conflict must presumably lead to some collective action by these people, who by sacrificing themselves might, even if only in part, wash away that stain on Germany's national honour. That was what we were waiting for, but we were unable to wait long enough – so we went on dying.

For the unity of our nation, the category of *Volksdeutsche*[13] proved very useful. Worthless people seeking very considerable advantages of a material nature – not to mention their own personal safety – thus separated themselves from us for ever. In buying people in this way, Hitler relieved us of individuals – albeit very few in number – constituting the chaff and dregs of society, who shunned the rest of us, those destined for elimination.

Things were different under the Soviet occupation. Before the war it was possible to be a worthwhile human being and a good Pole, as well as a connoisseur of Communism in theory, for nobody in Poland (apart from paid agents) knew anything about Communism in practice. As a result, the ethical boundary between those who did not oppose the Soviets right from the start, when they invaded, and the rest of us was that much less clear-cut. Anybody in Poland who was with Hitler was by definition a scoundrel; but anyone who, at first, had illusions about the Soviets was not necessarily a villain since, in the theory of Communism, there was a good deal of idealism.

One could hardly be surprised at the reaction of people who had always had a bad time of it and were now promised an era of social justice. That there is no such thing, and never can be, that is something unknown, not only to those who are waiting for a better life, but also to others. I am talking about those who have not themselves emerged from the masses, but who are concerned above all with this problem; to whom the old, obviously unjust order of things appeared intolerable, but who were not to know that, within a few years, the past would be 'paradise lost' for all decent people, regardless of how they managed beforehand, their social convictions or class origins. It was only after closer acquaintance that people's eyes were opened to the endless desert of lies, terror and cruelty, to the real aims of Moscow. By then, it was often too late to return to us, and extremely dangerous – almost impossible to disentangle themselves from a situation with no way out. But even those who were firm supporters from the beginning were also unspeakably distressed by this Asiatic duplicity, the unending surprises and, above all, the ceaseless repetition of idealistic bombast.

My impression is that, after the arrest, deportation and murder by the Germans of so many Polish university professors, clandestine university courses in the German-occupied sector of Poland produced far better results than the official 'work' of the Lwów professors, who were smothered in make-believe honours and unspeakably boring. From their barren existence in Soviet times, they took away with them only one very interesting memory – that of an excursion to Moscow. Transported there by official command to attend a banquet, they were ceremonially welcomed with a beautiful speech about the greatness and oneness of learning. Rector Krzemieniewski rose to reply and, in Polish, thanked his hosts for their fine words. Then, continuing in the purest Russian to make sure he would be perfectly understood, he added that despite such splendid words and this sumptuous reception for the Polish professors present, a dark shadow overhung everything. The cause was very simple: each one of them had somebody dear to him who had been transported from Lwów to the heart of Asia. The Rector sat down and nobody chose to speak after him.

The next day they called on old Krzemieniewski and took him away with them. His colleagues were horrified. After a short while, however, he returned. He had been at the NKVD headquarters. There they had asked him whether any member of his own family had been deported. He told them that his only daughter and her husband had been taken in May 1940. They noted his address, promised to send them back to Lwów,[14] and there the matter ended.

When I was in Lwów, this sturdy old man came round to see the friends I was staying with and asked me (his request sounded like an order) to search for those twenty-two colleagues 'until you find them'. On the same matter, another of our university professors advised me finally to abandon the search.

'These people died a long – a very long – time ago. I am convinced that of all the varying accounts in circulation about their fate, only one is true. According to that one, the same number of people were seen at dawn of the morning after the night of their arrest as they were being taken to Wólka – known as a place of execution since Bolshevik days. Among them was one wounded or dead man who was being carried by two others and a woman who was limping badly. In fact, Mrs Ostrowska had been having trouble with one of her feet for a long time.'

A few days later my stay in Lwów was over and I had to return to the west. I took with me my manuscript about religious problems connected with the works of Michelangelo, which Andzia had salvaged ages ago from Komarno. It had been saved by a miracle following my escape from Lwów, thanks to my having lent it to a colleague two days earlier. I came across it again in Lwów, where it was being looked after by friends.[15] I also took with me two of their children to live with relatives who could provide them with better material conditions. I loaded the two children into a trailer, quadruple-locked and towed by a German lorry. In that way we travelled to Kraków as military luggage.

Once there, by every possible means, overt and covert, we set about trying to find the Lwów professors in prisons, concentration camps and quarries in Poland and in the Reich. There was absolutely no trace of them. They had simply disappeared, like a stone dropped into water. The President of our relief organisation, Adam Ronikier, addressed questions both oral and written to every kind of German authority, but could obtain no answer. Our Commander sent a written message by courier to London asking for the case of the professors to be recalled in broadcasts. I myself wrote to Switzerland asking for intervention from that quarter, but there was not a sign; nothing for long months, till at last came a reply from Switzerland: 'The Germans have informed us that the Lwów professors are *an sicherem Ort*.'[16]

In October I was again in Sącz, but there was no sign of Hamann. Finally I went back on 4 November, my patron saint's day. On my way from the station I dropped in at the church. Mass was in progress, so I knelt down near the entrance.

'Charles Borromeo,[17] this is your day and I received your name when I was christened. What is happening here is a thousand times more terrible than your Milan Plague! By a strange dispensation of divine Providence, it falls to me – on this special day – to implore your help for those here who are suffering so abominably. Charles Borromeo, stand by me today!' I prayed through clenched teeth. And out I went.

Not long after, I was admitted to face the executioner. The man looked more like a butcher than a sadist: calm, rather plump, coarse, with big hands and fat, stubby fingers – hands that I caught myself staring at every so often during that forty-five minute interview, those hands with so much Polish blood on them. Fortunately he would not extend his hand to a Polish woman, so I was not obliged to touch it. Between us throughout stood a huge dog of which, frankly, I was more frightened than I was of Hamann. I had assumed in advance that he would not arrest me there and then. But I don't remember ever in my life having seen a dog with such an evil expression on its face. Several times it betrayed a wish to tear me to pieces, but was restrained by its master. I was told later that the dog was Hamann's one inseparable companion and ablest assistant at work. From the outset of the conversation, my interlocutor showed no signs of willingness to allow the feeding of prisoners, but in the end he gave his permission, promising to arrest all concerned with any 'abuse' – that is to say, caught smuggling letters.

Before leaving Sącz, I retired to the church and again knelt down in the same spot: 'Charles Borromeo . . .' I had never before felt so strongly that measureless bond between the Church Militant and the Church Triumphant.

One of the next stops on my way was Pińczów. I had received from a private source there some information that was both special and highly detailed. A woman unknown to me, who had been 'bought' out of prison there, informed me about the penal methods being applied in a special department for women political criminals from all over the Radom area. So I set out for Pińczów. This turned out to be a far from simple performance. After several hours by train, I got out at Kielce. There I dealt with arrangements for the prisoners, with the generous help of a priest and without major problems. After a night spent with a deportee family living in a quaint, dilapidated drawing-room, I managed – despite my innate lack of gymnastic or boxing skills – to fight my way aboard a vehicle known locally as a bus, and so arrived in Busko. There the local office of my relief organisation (RGO) provided onward transport in the form of a seat in a cart. A pair of very tired horses were driven by a Ukrainian engineer and I had the company of a Jew who, for the time being, was still allowed to move freely, provided he wore an identity badge.

After more or less five hours on the road, towards dusk our cart reached the ruins of Jewish Pińczów, which was totally destroyed in September 1939. Signboards with Hitlerite street names attached to shattered walls gave the place a singularly grotesque appearance. The cart stopped. I got out and soon ran to ground a man I had heard about who was working there at great risk to his life, helping the prisoners. He was a judge by profession. From him and two other local dignitaries I managed in the course of an evening's conversation to arm myself with the details I needed to talk to the Germans. I knew that there were a couple of hundred prisoners in a not very large jail with a quite separate, special women's section, to which were sent the most serious female political prisoners from all over the Radom district. These women lived in the worst conditions, subject to harassment and torture. One of them had recently given birth to a healthy son and had not so far been told that her husband had perished in Auschwitz. She was in urgent need of babies' nappies. Some must be sent to her without delay. I also learned that there were two Polish warders who were heroically risking their lives for these women.

In the morning I went to the prison. A friend of the women inmates led me almost to my goal and, without my knowledge, waited for me to emerge. When I entered the building (with the help of Heinrich's Gestapo card), I was instructed to stay inside and not leave the prison offices. On the wall was hanging a large school blackboard with the total numbers of male and female prisoners in their respective sections. It was clear from the board, in black and white, that there were fifty-four persons in the special section for women. Only Germans would have ordered me to stay close to that board! Naturally, I jotted down the figures in my notebook.

At last, I was admitted to the tyrant's lair. This time I was received by a not very prepossessing, coarse, low-calibre German official, who agreed readily enough to the feeding. I repeated emphatically several times that the food was to be given to all prisoners without exception, and that was by order of the German authorities. That stipulation seemed to worry him.

'Well – almost all. I'll agree to that.'

'No, *all* – without exception,' I repeated.

'But I have one section here which, if you only knew what they call it, you wouldn't ask for them to be fed. These are women . . .' He broke off, as if afraid of having already said too much. '*Unmöglich! Unmöglich!*[18] Unless you can bring me a permit from the Gestapo in Radom.'

I said that Radom had nothing to do with me, because the whole thing had been organised by Kraków, and so on. Then I began to explain that I had bacon and sugar; he took the bait and softened. I had arranged in advance – in case of success – a private delivery for the Commandant. I had no doubt that he would keep his promise because he was aware, from anonymous letters, that the Poles were watching his every step inside the jail and constantly threatened revenge. After a while, he even told me that these women needed underwear and warm clothing.

'Imagine what you would look like after a year, if you were arrested in what you're wearing now – with not even a spare blouse. Another thing. Fairly soon I'll have a small child – a boy, born here – to hand over to your Committee. Will the Committee accept him? We can only give him without a name.'

'With or without a name, we'll take him,' I replied, adding (but only in my thoughts): 'And he'll grow up to be an avenger!' (In any case, I already had his name.) Meanwhile, I proposed to send a supply of nappies, to which he gave his consent. In the end we reached agreement on all points.

On my way back I was just approaching the nearest railway station when I was greeted with a touching show of pleasure by the old friend of the women prisoners. This time we talked for so long that the good man must have felt he'd found yet another woman to 'look after'. I then called in at the Renaissance church, before embarking on the business of getting back to Kraków.

'What? You're wanting to travel today?' asked the Pińczów booking-office clerk in amazement. 'Impossible, we have only two connections a week with Kraków.'

When it turned out that the next train was in three days' time, I said I would go without a connection. The booking clerk and my new-found friend exchanged glances full of consternation, as though somebody were asking to go to the moon. At last, by dint of forceful insistence on my part, I was found a seat in a wooden cart bound for the township of Kije. The friend gave me a letter to the local stationmaster. I might find a train leaving from there 'by chance', he said. I do not remember how long the ride lasted, only that I was soaked to the skin and frozen to the marrow. The rain slanting down made my eyes sting. All around us the November fields, slithery with the damp, loomed darkly. 'Żeromski's[19] native countryside,' I thought, surveying the undulating horizon by the same kind of light as was described in '*Rozdziobią nas kruki, wrony* . . .'[20] The thought warmed me up. 'They will not peck us,' I vowed, clenching my frozen fists, partly in anger, partly for fear that they might be frost-bitten. I thought about my present way of life and it seemed to me that, travelling from prison to prison, I was constantly inspecting, one after another, the gravest wounds in the body of the Republic.

At long last, as it was already growing dark, the driver raised his whip to point out a very low building: 'The station.' We drove up, and I climbed down, with the water pouring from the folds of my sheepskin overcoat as the cart drove off. The surroundings gave no sign of human beings within reach. Eventually, with much expenditure of energy, I found an old, rather deaf railway employee.

'When is there a train for Kraków?' I asked. He looked astonished. 'Kraków?' he repeated very slowly, as though he had never heard of the place. I was in despair.

'Where's the stationmaster?'

'He's asleep.' It could have been five o'clock in the afternoon.

'Where can I wait?'

'The waiting room.' He opened the door to a small room deceptively similar to a place with which I had yet to become more closely acquainted: a prison cell. Moreover, it was the only waiting room in the whole of German-occupied Poland that was not marked 'Germans only'. Even the Germans did not come here! After some time the stationmaster woke up (I think my presence helped to rouse him), came out and asked what I wanted.

'A train!' I groaned, not even mentioning the lunatic word Kraków.

'Probably in a couple of hours. It's only just left. Hard to say when it'll be back.'

'And where is it going, this train?' I boldly enquired. He looked amazed.

'To Jędrzejów, of course! Where else?'

'That's fine. Of course, that'll do nicely,' I replied, hoping to soothe him. Then I remembered the letter in my pocket.

'I have a letter for you.' He took it, opened it, read a few words of the note and radically altered his tone.

'You're welcome here, ma'am! It's cold and you're wet through!' He conducted me to a cosy sitting-room, whispering in his wife's ear as we entered, and she in turn received me so warmly that, seeing the state of my clothes, she chased her husband out of the room without more ado and ordered me very energetically to get undressed and dry myself, after which she brought me a hot drink.

After a couple of hours there was, indeed, some sign of activity. Five or six people arrived wanting tickets. At last, with a piercing whistle, the little train pulled in. The platform was in almost total darkness. At the very last moment the stationmaster brought along a very tall young man with a pronounced limp, into whose ear he again whispered something, then turned to me and added: 'This gentleman will look after you, ma'am, on the journey.'

We took our seats in the unlit carriage. My unknown companion found me a seat, sat down beside me and started asking me about the care of prisoners. He spoke the Polish of an educated man. I answered evasively.

'You may talk. It helps us to see that important work is being done. And I, too, know it's safe to speak.' I responded with a few generally well-known facts.

'And you work here, do you?' I asked.

'In the stone quarries with the labourers. They need somebody there,' he added. And so we chatted for quite a long time, neither one of us seeing the other's face and knowing nothing about one another, except for what was most important. As we approached Jędrzejów, he stood up, said goodbye and jumped out before we reached the station. I was alone again.

During the journey I began to reflect for the first time on how a historian of the future, in presenting the history of this war, will need to adopt a distinctive method. Obviously he will have to describe the causes and effects of important command decisions as well as celebrated actions. If, however, he fails to grasp the very essence of things, if he fails to present the outstanding hero of the war, his work will fall short of its goal and future generations of Poles will not learn the truth. The real hero is the average citizen of the Republic, peasant or intellectual, landowner or priest, country girl or university woman. The *dramatis personae* are the torture victims of Pińczów, their guardians – those warders who were risking their own lives to save the women from starving to death – the stationmaster of Kije, the Unknown Stonebreaker who had been sitting beside me a short while ago.

The little train was now stationary in a broad field. Somebody shouted: 'Engine's broken down! We're three and half kilometres from the station. The train for Kraków will be leaving from there in half an hour.' At the sound of that magic word, I and a few others leaped out of the train and began to run in a group across the field, floundering at every step. When we reached Jędrzejów station we were told that the train was running three hours late. I was in Kraków the next morning.

At this time, a certain change took place in the nature of my work. Obviously the funds provided by our relief organisation had to be accounted for to the RGO in the fullest detail, but our work for the prisoners began to offer increasing possibilities of gaining access to them with more extensive (but already illegal) assistance. In every town or village, the more often I could get there, the more the locals trusted me and people approached me who, by bribery or other methods, had personal means of distributing food and clothing to individuals. Their commitment and courage, however, tended to outstrip our material resources. They needed more money. Then the Commander of our resistance organisation, on my next visit to Warsaw, put me in touch with the underground delegation in Warsaw of the Polish Government-in-exile, based in London. Every time I visited Warsaw, from then onwards, I was able to collect some cash from this 'second' source. It was not long before almost every prison had two relief schemes in action – one legal, the other clandestine – which complemented one another. The local Committee, however, remained unaware of the source of the cash that I delivered in person to our collaborators. I quietly congratulated myself on having 'extensive contacts' and 'generous friends'. One problem, among others, was my continuous fear that the amount of cash at my disposal would in the end attract the attention of well-disposed people who were not, however, privy to the secret source; or, equally, that this two-track supply route would finally explode and come to light in one or other of the prisons. Meanwhile, somehow, our work went ahead.

Towards the end of November I was again on my way to Lwów, this time in the company of the President of our relief society, Adam Ronikier, his deputy Dr Seyfried* and the President of the Aid Committee for Jews, Dr Weichert*. This man of outstanding intellectual and spiritual culture, but above all a great-hearted man of immense courage, achieved miracles in his terrible outpost. I had the privilege of being in contact with him a couple of months earlier and proposing that we cooperate in the prisoner field. Since then, the Jewish Committee had been supplying us regularly and punctually with foodstuffs with which we fed Jews in prison. I was grateful to our resistance Commander, too, for supporting the enterprise right from the start. The moment I asked him about it, he ordered everything possible to be done to help the Jews as well.

This time in Lwów we had to concern ourselves with the prison on Łącki Street. We had been getting frightening reports of infectious diseases, above all typhus, as well as extreme hunger. The mortality rate was enormous. I had one plan and a single thought. In this one jail, in this my city, I wanted to fulfil my dream of being able to arrange for the common feeding of Poles, Jews and Ukrainians. The last-named did not at first agree, so we started the work with Polish-Jewish cooperation only, though the Ukrainians, too, joined us later. We worked together for many long months and I shall always remember with the deepest gratitude all those who participated, foremost among them Father Michał Rękas*, of hallowed memory.

Meanwhile there was a great deal of other work to be done in Lwów. The object of the visit by the President and Director of our Main Council was to extend the influence of the RGO to all of the eastern region (Małopolska) and the creation of a strong base in Lwów. The persistent depression and apathy of the populace (as well as, sad to say, Ukrainian intrigues) greatly hindered the work at every step. The Germans gave permission for the RGO to operate, then did everything possible to impede progress, with the help of the Ukrainians. And just as 'on the other side', so here in the east people approached us asking us to intervene in various matters. The affair of the missing professors was again much to the fore in these requests. President Ronikier received the wives and mothers of the missing men to gather precise information, which, of course, yielded nothing of substance. Among them was Mrs Longchamps, wife of the university Rector, whom I failed to recognise at first sight. I remembered her as a lively, cheerful blonde, but the woman who appeared was subdued, grey-haired, elderly.

'Probably no one on earth has ever had to endure a march-past like that. I was standing at the door when they took them away: first came my husband, then our eldest son, then the second boy, then the third. They all walked past, looking at me.' The composure with which she spoke was scarcely bearable. There were other women, too. All of them had been to the Gestapo and all had received the same reply: that the arrests had been carried out by a special department of the Feldgestapo, which was now with the army moving further eastwards, leaving no documents behind. That being so, nobody was at present in a position to give any information. Professor Nowicka*, whose husband and son had also been taken away, and who was herself of German extraction, had been told that since she had married a Pole, she should have divorced him already and had no business complaining. Only Professor Ostrowska and Professor Grekowa* were not present, having disappeared with their husbands. Everybody had been taken from their two luxuriously furnished dwellings, including sub-tenants, and even kitchen maids. The last were released the next morning. But both flats had been pillaged at once.

The news from the provinces was also gloomy, especially everything to do with the teaching profession. In Stanisławów itself, immediately following the withdrawal of the Hungarians, who had occupied this area for a few months and had enjoyed great popularity among the Poles, 250 persons were arrested – virtually the whole intelligentsia of the town, or at any rate the most valuable members of the teaching body and the liberal professions. From that time on there was neither sight nor sound of those arrested. In Stanisławów, President Ronikier was told by his delegate that absolutely nothing could be done, for the township was ruled by the local Gestapo chief, Krüger*. It was the first time that name had been mentioned in my presence.

Not only in the provinces, but in Lwów itself meanwhile, people were beginning to become more closely acquainted with the Germans and to get the measure of 'our guests'. Two months had elapsed since my last visit and these had brought many changes in that respect. Nobody was talking any more about the 'European' quality of the occupation or the personal probity of the occupiers. Innumerable anecdotes were going the rounds in Lwów, among them one about a German officer who moved into a flat in Lwów with 'his' furniture. When after a few weeks, having found a better flat, he started to move out again, his soldiers began carrying away armchairs belonging to the owner of the flat. 'But those are my armchairs,' she politely pointed out, convinced that it was just a mistake. '*Ja, aber sie passen gut zu meiner Garnitur*,'[21] said the departing tenant. '*Weniger gut zu Ihrer Offiziersehre*,'[22] retorted the owner. The armchairs stayed put.

The affair of the vanished professors, the dismal reports from the Łącki Street jail and from the provinces, all combined to let people know that one occupying power was no better than the other, or rather nobody knew which was worse. Meanwhile, Norwid's[23] poem '*Pieśń od ziemi naszej*' had begun to circulate. Everyone was jotting down the two tercets in which one of the most profoundly thoughtful of Polish poets, in just a few words, seized and expressed the characteristics of our two neighbours once and for all:

From East – the wisdom of deceit, dark all about,
Golden lures, the discipline of knout,
  Plague, poison, filth.

From West – the lies of learning, flashy skills deployed,
The Formalism of Truth, internal Void –
  And pride of prides . . .

At this period I made an interesting excursion beyond the bounds of the so-called General Government. For some time persistent reports had been circulating in Lwów to the effect that a number of local people, who had been transported to the east by the Russians before the city surrendered, were now being held in a German camp for civilians in the neighbourhood of Równe, where they were starving to death. I asked our President to support me in approaching the military authorities for permission to travel to Równe. Acquaintances gave me long lists of the missing persons, as well as the address of a local doctor active in social welfare before the war, although nobody knew whether he was still alive. It seemed mad to suppose that the Germans would give a Polish woman a permit to travel to Wołyń Province. Yet, somehow, they did. So I set off, caught a German military train that left from Brody, travelling east across the dividing line, and by evening I was in Równe. I did not know this part of Poland. I was therefore travelling with great curiosity, although the season of the year was not propitious for exploring the countryside. From the station I went to the doctor's house. Unfortunately I cannot recall their names, but the people themselves I shall never forget. They received me like next of kin visiting relatives. There was the lady of the house – charming, vivacious and caring; the doctor – taciturn, serious; and his mother in her eighties, who hardly said a word. I thought she must be deaf as she took no part in the conversation. But I was struck by her keenly observant glances.

They started to question me about where I had come from and why.

'From Lwów? And all the way from Kraków! Jesus and Mary, do tell us what's going on over there.'

They listened with obvious emotion to the little I told them, continually interrupting with questions that I hardly knew how to answer, for they were so far removed from a reality of which these people could not conceive.

'Have you the slightest idea what this means to us to be visited for the first time by someone from the heart of Poland?' the doctor suddenly asked. 'Can you possibly imagine what it's like for us? We here in the borderland have been cut off from the rest of the Republic since 1939. First, they deported our nearest and dearest. Then, at the last moment, the Bolsheviks carried out mass executions. Somehow we were preserved. Some escaped by a miracle, like our monsignor. The Muscovites fired at him, but missed, and a couple of hours later he managed to struggle free from under a heap of corpses.'

'We must let him know, and the others as well,' the lady of the house exclaimed, disappearing into the kitchen. In a short while back she came announcing that she had sent out messengers. A few people quickly assembled, of whom I remember a woman secondary-school teacher, full of faith and imagination; an elderly, rather morose landowner couple; and finally the young priest, glowing with health and energy after his macabre ordeal. He appeared wearing his violet waistband, and the astronomical number of buttons of the same colour on his soutane reminded me vividly of Rome and times long past. His ceremonial dress evoked amazement.

'Could there be any greater occasion for Równe than the arrival of a guest from Kraków?' he asked as he greeted me. I had to begin my account all over again. Finally I was able to ask some questions myself. I was particularly interested in the reported camp for civilian prisoners, the reason for my journey. Unfortunately, I was unable to find out very much. This much was certain: there had been such a camp up to a couple of months ago, but it had been removed, nobody knew where to. The overall situation of Poles in Wołyń Province differed fundamentally from that of Poles in the German sector. There was no persecution in the strict sense of the word, inasmuch as, after the initial, immense Bolshevik deportations, the Poles did not present a serious danger. For the time being they were just badly treated, but not tormented. The Jews, on the other hand, were being persecuted in a hitherto unheard-of fashion, amounting quite simply to mass murder. One of them, a young intellectual, hid in my hosts' home. This was the first time I had directly encountered the wholesale extermination of Jews and heard of the bodies of wounded and unconscious victims, together with corpses, being thrown into mass graves. The landowners recounted these most recent cases with horror, especially since they had factual accounts from other localities in Wołyń Province. They said it was just the same in the Ukraine, in Kiev itself and even worse in other towns.

Next morning I went along to military headquarters. With great effort I managed to get to the commanding General – a jovial, very Austrian, middle-aged gentleman who received me with great courtesy. He listened intently, reflected and looked dejected, after which he called in a series of adjutants and administrators. The upshot of the whole conference was to establish the fact that the political prisoners brought to Równe by the Russians were indeed being held in a camp, where the advancing German forces came upon them. After a little while, the front line having pushed still further east, the prisoners had been handed over by the military to the Gestapo authorities. I asked what these people – arrested by the Russians – had done to the Germans to warrant being taken charge of by the Gestapo. I received no answer to this question, but the General gave me a long look amid the general hush that suddenly fell on the room.

'That being the case, I shall have to address myself to the Gestapo to enquire about these people,' I said.

'Yes – but I will help you,' the General replied. He ordered his officers to fetch maps of the Ukraine and pointed out to me three localities where there were civilian camps.

He told somebody to jot down the names and handed me the note. Finally, he asked whether I would be prepared to go to Kiev the next day. Naturally I agreed enthusiastically. There could not have been a more tempting proposal. He asked me to come back to him in two hours' time. I left him. It was Sunday, so I went into a church and chanced upon a High Mass. The church was packed and the singing testified to a large number of Poles still in Równe. After Mass, I returned to the General. He told me that an SS officer would shortly arrive, with whom the details of my departure would have to be arranged, because there in Kiev I would be seeing the General of the SS, Dr Thomas, the highest-ranking officer of that authority in this country. After a short while a very tall and very Prussian SS officer came in and greeted the General rather coolly. The General explained my business and added that I would be travelling to Kiev in his car the next morning. The Gestapo man drew himself up in his chair and replied in very harsh German that it was totally out of the question for any 'civilian person' to travel to Kiev. The General replied: 'She will travel, because I want her to present her case in person to General Thomas. I shall provide her with the necessary papers. Kindly inform your authorities in Kiev about her arrival there tomorrow afternoon. The army will provide overnight accommodation.'

I again spent the afternoon with my friends, but in the evening came word from the General that I could not go to Kiev after all, because, as it happened, SS General Thomas would be in Równe. I was angry and at my wits' end. Thomas received me about midday. I presented my case to him in the presence of two or three other Gestapo men. I told him (as I had been advised by the Austrian general) that I knew from the military authorities that there were three civilian camps in the areas mentioned in the note. Thomas listened in silence. Suddenly he asked, 'How did you get here?'

'I received permission from General Rotkirch in Lwów.'

'Show it to me, please.'

When I pulled out the paper, he ordered one of his entourage to make a copy of it. Then he declared that he could not give me an immediate answer. He would first have to obtain precise information and would communicate the result to the President of my Main Council (RGO). I knew that the cause, in which from the beginning I had placed little hope, was already lost. I went back to my friends in the evening, where I picked up a few letters for Lwów and Kraków. We said goodbye with genuine regret. The old doctor declared that all would remember my visit for the rest of their lives. The old lady continued to sit still and observe. At the last moment her daughter-in-law turned to her and said: 'Come on, Mama, tell us what you think of it all.'

The old woman, with a dismissive gesture, spoke for the first time:

'It's nothing new. There've always been these problems. I remember well, it was no better after the 1863 Uprising.[24] I was nine at the time.'

The next morning I went to the railway station. As I was waiting for the train, I noticed that I had a 'minder'. A uniformed Gestapo man, whom I had met the previous day, was also waiting for the train. We travelled together. At every stop he got out and walked to and fro under the window of my compartment. I made a point of remaining on show in the window at such times, in order not to worry him. When at last we crossed the 'border' near Brody, he crept into my compartment and asked for the General's note, which, of course, I already knew by heart. I formally demanded a receipt for parting with a document I was carrying on duty. He held the paper in one hand, while holding his head with the other and muttering, '*Wie könnte nur der Herr General . . .?*'[25] But, in any case, he gave me a receipt, which I presented to General Rotkirch in Lwów. It seemed too good an opportunity to miss for creating a bit of bad blood between one German and another. Rotkirch was comically frightened and thanked me effusively for warning him in advance.

The affair had an aftermath in Kraków, where the Gestapo interrogated the RGO President Ronikier and threatened him with my arrest, on the grounds that he had obtained military permission for my trip to Równe.

I returned to Kraków at the beginning of December. There, apart from the Montelupi jail, I had to deal with St Michael's prison for criminals, because I needed to prove to the Germans that we really did feed prisoners of all categories. In this connection I already had plenty of problems in my own community. I was sometimes criticised for feeding thieves while children went hungry. In Radom, for example, there were so many complaints that I could feed the prisoners only in secret. Not everybody understood that the only way to help political prisoners was to treat them on a par with the thieves.

Those were not my only problems. My regular visits to the Gestapo attracted such lively comment that the authorities were warned against me several times, and I was driven to appeal to my military superior to make sure that my name would be cleared after the war, in case of my death. At that period I learned for the first time just how easy it is to lose one's good name.

Before Christmas, it was again time for another visit to Pińczów. Having learned from experience, this time I went armed with underwear and warm clothes for the women prisoners. I also managed to commandeer a Polish Red Cross wagon, shaky on its wheels but still mobile, and set off at noon on Christmas Eve. The vehicle broke down a couple of times and it was almost dark when we arrived at some little town or other, where the driver informed me that this time the repair would take at least an hour and a half and advised me to go to a restaurant to get warm. I got out on the typically square market place and asked where we were. 'In Wodzisław,' a passer-by told me. God bless us and save us. Wodzisław! My family had been settled there for centuries.[26] My ancestors were buried in and around the church. I must get there at all costs!

It was pretty dark and the wind was blowing the damp snow into my eyes. With some difficulty I covered the short distance and found myself facing the portal on which our family crest – Zadora, the fire-belching lion – greeted me energetically. The church was open and decorated with Christmas trees. Soon everyone had gone and I was standing alone in front of the carved black marble tomb of Maciej, the Governor of Braclaw, my father's great-grandfather.[27] I read, as though for the first time, the long Latin inscription, praising the achievements of the deceased, who died, broken-hearted over Poland's downfall. I read on with increasing excitement. This inscription, already known to me and similar to those of so many of his contemporaries, gripped me today, as a distant grandchild, with compelling immediacy. At a period of renewed decline in the fortunes of the Homeland, I too was a soldier on active service. For a time I could not get over the sudden awareness, seemingly new to me just then, of the unprecedented *continuation* of our tragedy. I shook myself free at last and went back to the car.

An hour or two later I narrowly missed laying my bones to rest for ever alongside those of my ancestors, for the car broke its axle. However, we escaped alive, bound up the axle with wire and drove on. About midnight I roused my friend in Pińczów, gave him everything I'd brought, listened to an up-to-date account of his excellent work, read some smuggled letters that he showed me, which acknowledged receipt of the nappies and the food, and was back in Kraków by morning. Already my brief visit to Wodzisław seemed as unreal in memory as a film sequence, and a kitschy one at that. It was, nevertheless, a simple fact. I spent Christmas visiting various homesteads where some member of the family was missing . . . and New Year's Eve with friends in Lwów.

This time I managed to get to Stanisławów. I remember it was a bitter day – minus twenty-seven. We spent four or five hours sitting in a railway carriage in Lwów station, then six or seven hours travelling. When I got out at Stanisławów, at eleven o'clock in the evening, I felt like a frozen hare. After wandering for a long time through the blacked-out town I came upon a fantastic 'hotel' where I awaited the dawn. I found the Committee in a strange mood. Everybody was speaking very quietly with an eye on the door. I asked what the matter was. I was told it was impossible to talk normally because Krüger's people were everywhere. I was given a very much fuller account of the disappearance of those 250 members of the Stanisławów intelligentsia, abducted by Krüger the moment he took control. That was literally the whole of the town's intellectual elite, above all school teachers (middle and secondary) and all members of the liberal professions, including many engineers and lawyers.

Among these was the very well-known hospital director, Surgeon Doctor Jan Kochaj*. I talked to his wife, who showed me grateful letters from German airmen whose lives had been saved by her husband, at the risk of his own because he was operating on them after they had been shot down, with the town still in Soviet hands. There was even a letter of thanks, following a report by these airmen, from the Reichsluftfahrtsministerium (German Air Ministry) signed by Goering himself. But Dr Kochaj had already been arrested. I asked his wife whether she still had the letter. She told me that it had disappeared in the German offices, where it had been shown to support the appeal for his release. From the time of that mass arrest, Poles had continued to disappear singly or in larger groups. I asked whether the prison was large enough to hold them all or whether they were being transferred to Germany. I was told that nothing was known of any prisoner transports bound for the Reich, but that the jail was very extensive, consisting of two neighbouring buildings, one administered by the justice authorities and the other by the Gestapo. The latter was run by Krüger himself, and the other by State Attorney Rotter, whom I intended to see first, having been told that he was not ill-disposed towards Poles.

I went there and was received by a man of about forty, rather short of stature. He came out to meet me, talked an awful lot with exaggerated courtesy and staggered slightly as he led me to his office. He was drunk. I explained my business. He listened and I could see that, despite the state he was in, Rotter understood very well. When I had finished, he said that he was aware of the activity with which I was entrusted and that he had no objection to it being extended to the prison of which he had charge, but there were no Poles in his prison.

Then he interrupted himself: 'I'm very sorry about the state in which you found me. But probably you had already been told about the drunken attorney. I had, in fact, once again drunk too much vodka, but I know what I'm saying. I do not lock up Poles. I came here from the Reich as your enemy, but since being here I have learned to respect you, so I reserve my jail for Ukrainians. There are just one or two – very, very few Polish offenders.'

'So all the political offenders are in the other jail?' I enquired.

'All? What do you mean – all?' he asked with mounting excitement.

'All those arrested since the beginning, after the Germans crossed the border, especially the 250 persons, teachers, engineers and doctors who were arrested at once, and then in the long series of arrests ever since.'

'Krüger certainly has quite a lot of prisoners over there, but I doubt whether he would agree to their being fed.'

I had a feeling that the attorney-Governor was not fully expressing his thoughts and that, given his fuddled state, I might be able to squeeze a bit more out of him.

'That jail must be enormous, since he's arrested many hundreds of Poles,' I went on. Silence.

'There are not many people there,' he said at last, his manner frank.

'Then I must ask you, Governor, where are the rest? Where is the entire intelligentsia of Stanisławów?' I asked loudly. The Governor, supporting himself on an armchair, leaned towards me over the backrest. There was a moment of silence.

'*Die sind alle längst tot!*'[28] he shouted suddenly. '*Tot, ja tot!*' he went on repeating, since I was silent. '*Krüger hat sie erschossen, vor ich kam, ohne Recht, ohne Gericht. Wissen Sie, was das für einen Staatsanwalt ist?*'[29] You can go to him, tell him the lot. I couldn't care less what they do to me!' At last he turned round and sat down. There was a sudden deadly silence after his shouting. After a few moments I said that I must now go to Krüger and try to persuade him to let me deliver food to those who were there at present.

'I will take you to him, or else you won't get near him.'

Rotter telephoned in my presence and asked Krüger if he could come with me. After telling him to have some vodka ready for the three of us to have a drink, he replaced the receiver.

'He has agreed. Let's go.'

As I was going out, his assistant with a Polish name whispered swiftly in my ear as he was helping me into my fur: 'He's drunk right enough. But what he said is true. I heard it in the room next door.'

We went out into the frost and Rotter sobered up. As we were walking, he looked at me and began speaking quite calmly, saying that he was not surprised I had been severely shaken by what he had told me. I did not answer. We reached the second building in Biliński Street – now called Police or Gestapo Street, I cannot recall. We were admitted without any problem and went up to the top floor. A typist was working in the anteroom. We sat on chairs upholstered in raspberry-red damask. After a short wait the door was opened. I entered first, followed by the attorney. At the far end of a large, oblong room, a very tall, rather portly man, young – thirty-two or -three at a guess, with very fair hair – stood up from behind his desk. He had a very large mouth that jutted far forward, thick lips and a massive jaw. The lower part of his face was more strongly accentuated than the upper section with its unusually pale, protuberant, steel-blue eyes behind rimless spectacles. He bade us sit down in the armchairs.

The attorney explained to him why I had come. Krüger studied my papers with care, after which he looked me over even more intently, slightly narrowing his eerily pale eyes. I returned his gaze as calmly as I could, but I found it amazingly difficult this time to retain my objectivity and conceal the passionate revulsion that overcame me as I entered the room. It was only minutes since I had learned just what kind of man this was. And now, right away, I was required to talk normally to him. That was difficult. He spoke at last, explaining briefly that since it was impossible to segregate the prisoners by nationality – Polish, Ukrainian or Jewish – it would not be possible for Poles to receive special feeding. I replied that they could be fed along with the others, as in Lwów. He declared it would be impossible, without giving any reason. He would allow only blankets, combs, toothbrushes, and so on to be sent. This was the first and only prison that, despite our best efforts, RGO food failed to reach.

We left, I said goodbye to the attorney and was once again alone. Walking through the town, the cold helped me regain my composure and I returned to the Committee. I did not check into a hotel, but spent the night with a very hospitable social worker, who concealed her seven service awards from the occupying powers by sewing them into the eiderdown which covered me that night. Before falling asleep, she insisted on letting me touch the medals, explaining in detail the circumstances in which she had received them. Her recital had a soothing effect on me. I grasped the fact that human weaknesses remain unchanged, regardless of the magnitude of the events we live through.

The next day I returned to Kołomyja. There, matters at the prison went very smoothly and I returned to Stanisławów in the evening from where, the next day, I set out for Stryj, arriving in the late afternoon after travelling for many hours. The local Committee put me up in a cloister, where they gave me a hot meal, a cosy little room and warm water to wash in. I went to bed, but was unable to sleep. I was kept awake by impressions gathered in recent days and something else as well, which I had not known was alive in my memory. I had often been in Stryj, but in an earlier incarnation. So I lay there in the darkness, repeating to myself that here I was in Stryj, about forty kilometres from Rozdół, our family home – the place where I had spent the happiest years of my childhood.

The following morning I settled the prison affairs in Stryj almost without any trouble. But the Committee session that followed revealed that – as in Kołomyja and Stanisławów – there had been tremendous food-supply problems for which the Ukrainians, unfortunately, were largely to blame. There were also complaints in particular about difficult relations between the smaller centres in the surrounding area and about the slow pace of establishing local branches. I asked whether a branch had already been set up in Rozdół. They told me that our committee secretary would be going there in the next day or two. I suggested that if he were to travel the next day, we could be in Rozdół together, which might help matters. This proposal was accepted.

We left Stryj in the small hours of the following day. At Mikołajów, on the Stryj to Lwów line, where I had been countless times in my life, I alighted once again. The remaining twelve kilometres we covered by wooden sledge or on foot. On the way, my companion managed to slip off the sledge into the snow. It was some little time before I noticed and I had difficulty in persuading the driver to wait for him. I was travelling as though in a dream. Here, nothing had changed: cottages, village churches with cupolas, the soft outlines of wooded slopes on the left and the huge, snow-covered valley of the Dniester on the right-hand side and in the distance, barely discernable, the Carpathian chain. So on we went, sitting in our uprooted tree trunk. Rozdół at last. We got down to call on the Carmelite Fathers and were received by a priest I did not know. I asked after Father Bolesław.[30]

The answer was evasive. 'He's gone away.' When I mentioned my family name, the priest smiled. 'Since you know him, I can say that he couldn't bear to stay on here. Father Bolesław used to say that the very awareness of a Polish Army in existence while he was stuck here made life unbearable. So he left . . . in that direction.' And the priest pointed towards the distant Carpathians.

We had agreed to hold our session, aimed at setting up the local branch of the RGO, at three o'clock, which left me with some time. I went out to look round my birthplace and headed for my former family home. On the way I met a Jewish woman, who at the sight of me stood rooted to the spot.

'I want to know – do I recognise you, or don't I?'

'Recognise whom?' I asked.

'Why, Lanckorońska!'

'You're right.'

'That settles it – the worst is over. Everything's going to be all right.' With that she walked on, full of unfounded optimism.

I was standing in front of the entrance gate, which was ajar, so I walked through and into the grounds. The drive was covered by a thick layer of snow, with only a narrow path of fresh footprints in the centre. 'It's obvious somebody's living here,' I thought to myself. I walked on up to the palace, which stood on a snow-covered rise, vast and dead. At that moment from the opposite end somebody started walking up the same path. My heart gave a thump: Jan, the old waggoner! I stood there waiting. On he came, eyes on the ground in front of him, noticing the fresh tracks I had made, and clearly, as ever, in bad humour. Angrily he raised his old face, as wrinkled as a baked apple, obviously furious that somebody dared to trespass on his domain. Then he emitted a great cry of 'Jesus and Mary!' and threw himself at me. I tried to restrain his emotion in case I myself might go to pieces. It was not too difficult, because Jan suddenly turned his back on me and to my astonishment trotted back uphill the way he had come, bellowing to high heaven as he went: 'Come out everybody. Hello, there. Quick! Get a move on!'

In response to his shouts, so unexpectedly shattering the deadly silence of this park of the past, an old manservant appeared with his wife and sons, all running, terrified in case the old waggoner had been attacked. Not far behind came the same old gardener who had known me as a child. The manservant and his wife invited me to supper with them. While the meal was being prepared, we made a tour of the whole great mansion, whose rooms seemed even more spacious and numerous in their emptiness, dead and deserted. The Bolsheviks had made off with almost everything of value. The Germans had then taken whatever was left. Only in one place was an old baroque wardrobe still just standing on three legs. Peering out from behind it was a portrait of some partly crop-headed ancestor, speared by a Bolshevik or a German bayonet. Further on, an engraving of *Ossoliński's entry into Rome in 1633*, one of a series, was hanging askew above the remains of a sofa with no upholstery.[31] The bathrooms had been totally wrecked, because the Bolsheviks, who used the mansion as a rest house, destroyed them as relics of the bourgeoisie. They also turned the chapel into a canteen.

I listened to all the stories and looked around with a degree of detachment that surprised me. I was only concerned about these elderly people – everything else had become strange and distant. The great responsibility that rested on my shoulders at that period rendered me indifferent to all personal matters. Walking round the rooms of the ancestral home, my thoughts were far away – in those prisons that now filled my life to overflowing.

It was not until I went for a walk in the gardens and looked at the statues and Renaissance vases brought from Italy by my father, now testifying under their great pointed snow-caps to the artistic culture that once prevailed – and, more than anything, at those centuries-old trees standing motionless – that I had a feeling they, too, were welcoming me with memories of days long past, when I used to climb their branches, declaiming Mickiewicz's '*Oda do Młodości*'[32] and swearing childish vows in their shade. Standing there, I was overwhelmed by a tremendous sense of gratitude to the Creator and to Life, for giving me the grace not to betray my oaths . . . I heard them calling me indoors to eat. When I walked into the living-room of these honest people, I was stunned. In the centre, on a table covered with a snow-white damask cloth, far too big for that little table, was the blue porcelain plate I had used all my life and the old, familiar silver knives and forks. The manservant explained solemnly that I must forgive the absence of a butter knife. His wife had so splendidly hidden it away that now, in her excitement, she couldn't remember where. But it would certainly be there for my next visit. I listened and wiped away a tear. I felt like exclaiming: 'It must have gone with the wind ages ago!' But I felt obliged to respect the feelings of these old people, who were keeping alive in spirit a make-believe continuation of the past.

A meeting with the priest, which took place immediately afterwards, was equally moving for me for personal reasons. Also present were a few of my old friends and colleagues, especially among the teaching fraternity. On the practical side, the reunion shed light on the really frightening supply problems or, rather, the acute food shortages suffered by the Polish population in these parts. The obstacles in the way of any aid programme in this area were ten times greater than they were in the western sector. The general food situation, which in effect was paralysing assistance in what was now called Galicia, added to problems arising from specific inter-community relations in the area. All of this had the effect of making the work of the RGO more difficult here than anywhere else. This was the situation I reported on my return to Kraków.

A month later, towards the end of February 1942, I made another round of the prisons and again travelled to the east, this time accompanied by Edmund Seyfried, Director of the RGO's Kraków office. Among other centres, we visited Stanisławów, where I delivered blankets, combs and underwear – the only articles allowed by Krüger. The Director was appalled by the state of the aid work and by the problems in Stanisławów. He considered that it would be difficult to resolve this with local resources alone, particularly since the Gestapo had arrested a number of people immediately after being asked to approve the formation of an aid committee. In this situation, Director Seyfried proposed that I should move to Stanisławów for a couple of weeks as Acting Commissioner for the whole area. A tremendously difficult task, but the proposal was enormously tempting. I had only one most serious reservation: what was going to become of the prisoners' aid programme? The Director declared that this project no longer required my continuous presence in the west, as the organisation could now carry on without me. I could be spared for a few weeks to devote myself to something different. I was worried about the prisoners' welfare, but above all by the fact that my Commander in the underground resistance would not be at all happy about my having to neglect my chief assignment for a couple of weeks. But I could not exert any influence in that respect, since Director Seyfried was not allowed to know that I was a member of the underground army. On the other hand, that terribly difficult task – the struggle to help rescue the Polish population of seventeen districts of my native province in the east – was irresistibly attractive.

So the Director and I went to see Krüger, who gave his consent to my nomination and to the dispatch (care of himself) of the blankets, combs, and so on for the prison. After visiting a few more towns in the district of Galicia – Stryj, Sambor and Drohobycz – where we settled our prisoner problems without difficulty, we returned to Kraków.

Chapter 4

Stanisławów

March 1942–7 July 1942

I started work in Stanisławów in March 1942. It was a thankless task. The number of people in need was enormous, jobs strictly limited, imports from the west immensely difficult and the chicanery of the Ukrainians unbounded. Fear of Krüger persisted. The inhabitants of Stanisławów had never forgotten those first mass arrests and had never given up hope that those most revered, best loved and most valuable fellow citizens might still be alive. I found myself repeatedly forced to discuss this matter with relatives and friends, without betraying the secret confided to me by the drunken attorney. Fear of the executioner was sustained by ever more arrests. One was always hearing that somebody or other had been taken away. That was the normal state of affairs throughout the General Government, but in this respect Stanisławów was a special case. Nobody had ever received a sign of life from any of the arrested persons.

One morning a young Ukrainian SS man came to our committee and demanded to see me alone. Once the door was shut behind the others, he produced his identity card and declared that he had come to arrest Danuta Ziarkiewicz-Nowak, who was working with us. I had to take him to a neighbouring room to fetch twenty-one-year-old Danuta, the pretty young wife of an Air Force officer who was in England. She stood up, turned very pale and, hiding her face with her hands, said only two words: 'My mother!' Then, standing in the middle, she looked round at us all and, with her eyes fixed on mine, said: 'I'm entrusting my mother to you,' and threw her arms round me. I promised to do everything I possibly could for her mother. Danuta was led away. Her fellow workers were in despair. After much effort I obtained her mother's address and went there. To my great surprise, I found that Danuta and the Ukrainian SS man were there together. It seemed that she had implored him to take her home to say goodbye to her mother. Perhaps he had been moved by her exceptional beauty. He was just taking her away as I arrived. Danuta was wearing her warmer clothes, I remember. She had on a green sweater with a black design and a headscarf. Both mother and daughter were completely calm. Danuta was delighted by my arrival and assured her mother that it was bound to be only routine questioning and that she would be home directly. She gave her mother a smile and off she went. As soon as we were alone together, Mrs Ziarkiewicz broke down. But not for long. She soon regained her composure, sorted through her daughter's things and burned her diary.

Danuta's arrest plunged the whole staff into a deep depression. Despite that, the organisation of our relief effort continued slowly. At Easter I went to Kraków and Warsaw. In Kraków Professor Dyboski wanted to give me back my manuscript, which had been saved more than once by a miracle. But I did not want to take it away and asked him to continue looking after it for me: 'Who knows what will happen to me? And I'd like this book to be published when the war is over.'

In Warsaw I reported to General Komorowski, then Deputy Commander of the Home Army, on the situation in Stanisławów and asked him not to let our propaganda people in London broadcast anything about it right away, or any future activity of mine would be totally sabotaged. We had two lengthy conversations. The General told me to stay a few days the next time I visited Warsaw, so that I could meet the Commander-in-Chief, General Grot, who wished to see me to hear at first hand a full report on the prison feeding programme. I was delighted about this, because I had long wanted to meet the man who meant so much to all of us. He must have been a born leader because his presence was felt everywhere. He had earlier been briefed about my work, since he had awarded me the Cross of Valour. Now the chance of meeting him personally was an added pleasure.

General Komorowski was not at all happy about my new job. As I was saying goodbye to him, he said with unusual asperity: 'I forbid you to have contact of any sort with the military in the east. At the moment, the ground is hot underfoot over there. There have been denunciations . . . Obviously people are going to have confidence in you and will try to draw you into contacts with the underground, because they need help with their organisational work, but you must not risk it. Just finish off the present job quickly and resume your prison welfare activity.'

That was Tuesday, 8 April. A couple of days later I was again in Stanisławów, accompanied this time by Maryla Dmochowska of Tarnów, who had come along to give me a hand. Thanks to her immense efforts, the work was making considerable progress, not only in Stanisławów, but also in Kałusz and Kołomyja. Committees had been set up and children were beginning to be fed. Maryla and I counted on being able to leave in mid-May and return to normal work. Spring was late and it was cold and gloomy. On top of that, obeying the orders of our Commander was costing me a great deal. I was not allowed to contact the military, although, as he had foreseen, attempts were made several times to involve me and I had to pretend that I was engaged exclusively in legal activities. That was particularly disappointing because I knew I could be of assistance. The atmosphere in Stanisławów was, as usual, very trying. The only pleasure, apart from work, was Maryla, with whom at that time I struck up a close friendship. I tried once or twice to get to Krüger in order to 'inform him of my achievements' – as, indeed, he had asked me to do when he agreed to my presence in Stanisławów. However, he would not see me. Eventually I gave it up as a bad job and carried on working regardless.

Krüger finally summoned me to his office on Saturday, 25 April at 9 a.m. I went. As usual I was told to wait on a raspberry-satin upholstered chair in the anteroom. After a while I was called in. This time, Krüger was not alone. By his desk, at a small table, sat a secretary. Krüger did not stand up, but without looking at me, from behind his desk, pointed to a chair facing him and said: '*Ich muss Sie sicherheitspolizeilich verhören.*'[1]

I sat down and asked the reason.

'You are engaged here in Stanisławów in unauthorised activity,' he said very loudly. I showed him my plenipotentiary pass and drew his attention to the fact that I was entitled to operate on a far broader scale than I was doing at present, and that the German authorities in Lwów, in charge of the food supply, had already pointed out, when I had been to see them in connection with the food due to us, that the activity I was conducting was developing too slowly. At this, he changed tack and declared: 'The point is that your system is not so much engaged in illegal activity, but rather that you are using a charitable activity for other purposes.'

'I don't know what you are talking about.'

To which he replied: '*Ihr Geist gefällt mir nicht . . . Sie passen mir nicht in mein Reich.*'[2]

He was obviously very pleased with the last phrase, for he repeated it several times in the course of our conversation, pounding his fist on the table on each occasion.

'I must ask you a few questions. Do you recognise the break-up of the Polish State?'

I smiled and said I could see that he had decided to arrest me, because he could no longer be in any doubt about my answer to that question.

'How can you remain so calm?' he asked with mounting irritation. '*Sie schweben in höchster Gefahr!*'[3] I will ask you the question again, and just be careful how you answer. Are you an enemy of Germany?'

'You know that I am a Pole, and you know that Poland is at war with Germany.'

'You must reply to my question. Are you an enemy of the German Reich? Yes or no?'

'Yes, obviously.'

'*Also endlich!*'[4] he cried with a triumphant look at his secretary. '*Notieren!*'[5] he added emphatically. The girl nodded and began writing. He turned to me again. '*Seit wann?*'[6]

'Since I first saw the unspeakable suffering of my brothers.'

At that, he started talking about his hatred of the Poles and about the persecution of Germans by the Poles. I think he launched into this diatribe with the object of frightening me, but the more he talked, the more I got the impression that it was partly to excite himself, for he wound up shouting, stamping his feet and pounding the table with his fists, in the course of which his already prognathous mouth was transformed into something like a snout, giving him the look of an animal. I listened calmly to all of this, since I could do nothing else. Every so often he interrupted his flow of invective against the Poles, rebuking me for my placid demeanour and promising to upset my balance. That, of course, had the effect of reinforcing my calm. I told him that I failed to understand why the Germans, who valued their nationality so very highly, should be unable to respect the sentiment of national honour in other peoples. He lowered his eyes and said in a changed voice: 'Because that's a different thing altogether.'

'It certainly is something quite different,' I replied. He said nothing.

The next moment he reproached me for my particularly outrageous behaviour, since he knew moreover that my mother was a German.

I cannot today, years later, recall all the details of that dialogue, which lasted three and three-quarter hours.[7] I do know that several times he exploded in fury, abusing the Poles as the only true enemies of the Reich. Not the French, or the English, but the Poles, Poles, Poles!

Suddenly, in the middle of this scene, it obviously occurred to him that he had proved nothing concrete against me. He said he would never believe that a person like me would not belong to a subversive organisation. I said his interrogation would convince him of it. He then asked what I thought of Polish underground activity. I knew that he wouldn't believe me if I gave a negative answer to a stereotyped question of that sort. So I said that I was enthusiastic about their work. He leaped to his feet, leaned across his desk and demanded: 'Where were you working? What was your function?'

'I never worked. I had no function.' At this, he snorted.

'What's that supposed to mean? First you say that you're enthusiastic about their work, and then you try to back out of it!'

'I am a Polish woman, as you know – Polish, born and bred. So you could hardly imagine my not being enthusiastic about an activity aimed at freeing my people.'

'I ask you for the second time: where were you working?'

'Nowhere,' I replied, 'because for conspiratorial work something more than just enthusiasm is required.'

'What?'

'In the first place, there has got to be a man who suggests such activity to you. And nobody, anywhere, ever has suggested it to me.' I could see that he did not believe me and that my fate hung in the balance. So I continued: 'I think there are two reasons for that. The people who undertake work of that kind would be sure to know that I work for a legitimate, charitable organisation. They're obviously of the same opinion as me, that this is the way I am doing my duty by the nation and they require nothing more of me. It could also be that, because of my too-transparent disposition, and because I am very tall, talk a lot and loudly, with many gestures, they might well consider that I'm not cut out to be a conspirator – and that's a fact! I could never see myself, for example, planting bombs under trains.'

Krüger listened with growing astonishment. Once, while I was speaking, he turned to his secretary and said: '*Noch nie gehört. Notieren!*'[8]

Finally he faced me squarely, which he had done very rarely

throughout this long and stormy exchange, narrowed his eyes and asked: '*Oder sind Sie am Ende ganz gescheit?*'[9]

I smiled stupidly. He shrugged, but I felt he believed me. I knew that the Germans, in their unparalleled arrogance, would never opt for a way out that would make them look foolish. Krüger believed me because I had said that the reason nobody wanted me in the underground was because I talked too much. No German would ever say of himself that he talked too much. I had taken Krüger by surprise. That was why I won.

He changed the subject, reverting to my work in Stanisławów, and accused me of having helpers who were conspirators. He asked for the names of everybody working with the Committee. I said I did not have them off by heart and suggested that he send for Maryla Dmochowska, asking her to bring the lists of all my helpers (either direct or indirect). Obviously I very much wanted to see Maryla again. Krüger told me to ring her in his presence. It was some time before she arrived. When she walked in, it was clear that she had no idea what situation I might be in till she handed the nominal roll to Krüger. I tried to give her some indication by my looks. It was all I could do. She turned as white as a sheet. Krüger read through the names, counting them off on his fingers. As he was doing so, I noticed that his thumb was about the same length as his index finger. Finally he remarked that among the names on the list were those of a number of persons under suspicion. He told Maryla to go outside. She turned to me and asked whether she should wait for me. I told her to go back to work. As soon as she was gone, Krüger again began accusing and cursing the Poles. Suddenly he interrupted himself to declare that he was not going to arrest me, but that I should regard my experience as a warning and could now go to Lwów. He then escorted me downstairs in person, following me on my left side, one step behind.

I walked out into the street and found myself alone. The sun was shining. Spring. I raced back to the Committee, knowing that Maryla would be waiting and the state she would be in. I arrived to find her both strong and serene. We embraced, then she asked me whether I had noticed that Krüger's thumb was almost as long as his index finger.

An hour later I was on my way to Lwów, as planned. I was so weary I could barely stay on my feet in the station. Once on the train, I fell asleep and slept like a log, despite the crush.

In Lwów, I settled a few service matters, then had a meeting with my immediate superior who was visiting from Kraków. That enabled me to pass on a report of my interview with Krüger in Stanisławów to my military commander. I spent two days in Lwów and returned to work. I soon realised that I was under observation. Since I was not doing anything 'illegal', I was pleased about this, rather than otherwise. I thought Krüger might be reassured if he were persuaded that in Stanisławów my work was entirely above board. So I worked away in peace. Only once did I experience an uneasy feeling. I was walking along a street one evening at dusk, chatting about current matters with Maryla. Suddenly I had the impression that a third person came between us from behind and began repeatedly whispering in my ear: 'Krüger is going to lock you up, Krüger is going to lock you up . . .' Reason told me that this was simply common-or-garden nerves, and I was furious with myself. Besides, there was a lot of work to be done and as many irritations as ever. There was no time for anything else, the more so because our stay was almost at an end. At Whitsun, towards the end of May, Director Seyfried was planning an inspection visit. We wanted to have something to show for our efforts, and then return to the west.

Our work was progressing not only in Stanisławów, but also in Kałusz and Kołomyja. There, I had at last got a committee set up and, on the morning of 12 May aboard a lorry on its way from Lwów, I set out for Kołomyja. The sky was overcast, but the weather was fine. Spring had been late to ripen this year, but the surrounding countryside was green. I will never forget those woods in spring along our route. We reached Kołomyja by noon and I was able to collect receipts from the District Administrator's office for the food I had fought so hard to deliver. Within two days the school children of Kołomyja would also be receiving their food supplies. I was very happy and, in the afternoon, the sun came out. I still had a lot of problems to resolve, but towards evening I dropped in on the Parish Dean, an old and experienced social worker whose name I cannot recall,[10] to share the good news with him. In his joy he invited me to supper, which in Kołomyja at that period was a very generous present. I ate, although I had already had lunch (albeit, obviously, a very light one), then I sat with the old priest on his veranda that fine spring evening, watching the sunset and thinking, gratefully, what a good day it had been. First, the delightful journey in the morning, then – at last – the start of our work in Kołomyja, and now this peaceful evening with all the beauty of the countryside spread out before us in the golden light of the setting sun – here in this last remaining patch of our borderland that was still accessible.

I said goodbye at last and went to see Mrs Pawłowska, a secondary-school teacher in whose house I was staying, and where at 8 p.m. the inaugural meeting of our Committee was due to be held. I reported on the preparatory work that had been done, handed over responsibility to the new Committee and issued the ration cards. We were all in very good spirits when suddenly there was a knock at the door. Mrs Pawłowska went out and returned shortly with three men, one wearing civilian clothes, the two others in SS uniform. They asked for me and examined my papers. They yelled at us that this was an illegal assembly. I denied it. I told them to check with the District Administrator. They told all the others to disperse and arrested only me. As we were going out, I turned to one of the Committee and asked him in German to telephone early the next morning to the RGO headquarters in Kraków, tell them that I had been arrested and ask them to send somebody to replace me, so that our work would not be interrupted. Though it was pretty dark, I tried – by staring fixedly into the messenger's eyes – to make him aware of the great importance I attached to the mission I was entrusting to him. I knew that, provided the RGO was informed, the Resistance Command would quickly get to know, since so many of the people there were my 'dual' colleagues.

Off we went. They led me to a comfortable saloon car and ordered me to sit in the back beside a gentleman in a suit. The other two Gestapo men left us. My neighbour took a good look at me. Looking back, after all these years, I realise how very privileged I was in those days, in contrast to millions of my compatriots. Before and since, I have heard countless descriptions of arrests, and every one of them has stressed the physical and psychological shock experienced at the time. I was spared that shock, thanks to my own naïvety. I was almost convinced that the Gestapo in Kołomyja really thought ours was an illegal meeting and that the whole affair would shortly be cleared up. Despite that, it is true, I did not find my situation exactly pleasant, but I was very tired and soon fell sound asleep. After rather a long time the two Gestapo men returned in a fairly merry condition from the restaurant, outside which 'our' car was parked. They jumped in and off we went. I gathered from their conversation that we were bound for Stanisławów. That did not delight me. On the way, as we drove through the same forest-in-spring that had so charmed me that morning, I thought how already that ride appeared to have happened a very long time ago. The car broke down on the way. We waited so long that once again I dropped off. When I awoke, I was alone with my silent neighbour while his cheery colleagues set about mending the car. My neighbour was eating sandwiches. This reminded me that I had some provender of my own, which Maryla had given me that morning.

I started to eat. My neighbour stared at me with unconcealed amazement, which cheered me immensely. At last the two others fixed the engine, got into the car and we drove on. In Stanisławów we sped straight through the town to the prison. A gate in a side-street opened, we drove into a courtyard and the gate swung shut behind us. I was told to get out and was then taken to the main building, where on the first floor Krüger had his office. They led me to the ground-floor reception room and there I was asked my name, and so on, and had to produce my documents. I asked what exactly was the meaning of all this. The answer was: '*Sie sind doch verhaftet.*'[11]

A little while later I was again led across the courtyard to a low, oblong house, in which there was a long corridor, where the door of the first room was opened and the light switched on. Inside the room were two iron bunks. On one lay a small woman with black hair; the second bunk was vacant – for me. The door closed behind me. I ate an egg and a slice of bread that I still had with me and lay down, covering myself with a blanket, which I recognised as one of those I had sent to the prison in February. I noticed that my companion was staring at me with a look of increasing horror. She finally covered her face with a blanket. After all of this, I slept like a log.

In the morning I was told to get up and wash and was then led away to the administrative office in the same building. There I was received by the Governor of the prison, whose name was Maes or Maas. I asked to be interrogated as soon as possible, because I was convinced I had been arrested by mistake. Everything I had was taken away from me, except for a few essential toilet articles and a small bronze crucifix from Assisi, which I had taken care to hide. I was then ordered back to my cell. My companion turned out to be a Ukrainian actress from Czerniowiec. I got the impression that she was quite a shrewd person, from the intense way she observed me. Presently, the warder came back and ordered me to go with him. Once again we crossed the courtyard to the main building on Biliński Street, and went upstairs to Krüger's office. I was ordered to wait in the already familiar anteroom. I sat down on one of the raspberry-red upholstered chairs. The secretary went into Krüger's office and emerged after a moment or two, to inform me that the Hauptsturmführer had forbidden me to sit down. So I stood up. Only then – so long had it taken me, for want of proof – did I at last realise that Krüger was locking me up!

A person who has never been 'on the other side' of life would probably not understand this – and it is hard to explain. On the other hand, for example, a man who has recovered from a very grave physical illness certainly knows how it is that, when one's life is threatened, hope is a thousand times stronger than logic. I now know why even doctors who become very ill go on believing, almost till the hour they die, that they are certain to recover, whereas all the familiar signs of impending death would have long since opened their eyes to the truth in anyone's case but their own. A prisoner is in a very similar position – HE WANTS TO LIVE – and here, too, the powerful animal instinct triumphs over human logic or reason.

Conversely, now that my arrest (by Krüger himself) was an established fact, the certainty at that moment gave me much strength and peace of mind. I was called in and this time we were alone. No secretary. As before, Krüger failed to look up when I entered. All he said was: 'So we meet again – and I am the winner. You are going to Ravensbrück concentration camp, near Fürstenberg, Mecklenburg.'

'When?' I asked. He struck the table with his fist.

'What? You haven't changed! You've not lost your nerve?'

I burst out laughing. 'What else have I got left?' I asked. 'I want to know when I am going.'

'I don't know. It depends when the next transport is due for collection – from here to Kraków, and from there into the Reich.'

'Worse luck,' I thought to myself, 'if they lock me up in Montelupi prison on the way.' A lot of our people were there already, including a few informers.

'I want you to know,' said Krüger, 'that this decision is the result of the answers you gave me the last time. If you had answered differently, you would not now be depriving your country of the gift of your labour.'

For the first time he scored a hit with that remark. It was very difficult for me. I thought of the prisons and asked myself yet again if any of my answers had been inspired by bravado or, indeed, had been unnecessary. I thought not.

'I could not have answered any other way without losing my self-respect, without which I would be unable to work,' I replied. 'Although I am just *ein polnischer Untermensch*,[12] allow me to quote you something that Schiller[13] said:

Das Leben ist der Güter höchstens nicht,
Der Übel grösstes aber ist die Schuld.[14]

He put on a look of comic despair. So I told him: 'That's the ending of '*The Bride of Messina.*'

'Yes, yes,' he nodded eagerly.

'Well if, as Schiller says, life is not the greatest good, but guilt is the greatest evil, then guilt is what I would have felt, if I'd adopted any other attitude towards you.'

He said nothing, then changed the subject. Apart from that, he said, I was being punished for my behaviour as the daughter of a German woman. 'You are going to the camp as a renegade.'

'That is a citation in itself,' I replied. There was another silence. Then he said he had never before heard such an answer and did not know what it meant. With that, he started shouting again and abusing the Poles, whom, he said, he held in contempt for their lack of grit and fortitude. Again I could not help laughing outright.

'Even *you* cannot seriously mean what you're saying.'

Suddenly he assured me that he had at his disposal every means to prevent my committing suicide. I said that this would be easy enough for him, because I had not the slightest intention of doing away with myself. For one thing, my Catholic convictions forbade it (at this, he bared his teeth) and for another, I didn't want to. Besides, having the constitution of a horse, I was ready to stay the course even in a concentration camp. Once again, he promised to break me. I said that, of course, I could vouch for myself only as long as I was of sound mind. In case of mental illness, that was another matter. He was plainly cross with me for having raised with him any such possibility, so I said that I assumed all of this was academic, if my case were to be settled in the easiest and swiftest fashion.

'What do you mean by that?'

'That I don't expect to leave here alive.'

'Have you been counting on death ever since I told you you were under arrest?'

'Yes, of course.'

'Why?'

'Because I'm here.'

He snorted. He then asked me for details of my arrest. I told him that I had been taken away from a meeting at Kołomyja, of the local committee of the Main Council for Relief (RGO), which was wrongly said to be illegal.

'That was simply an excuse. I sent for you from your office here in Stanisławów and was told you had gone to Kołomyja. I could not risk them alerting you, so I had you brought from Kołomyja.' That was a great weight off my mind. Up to that moment I had felt certain that something terrible was about to happen to yesterday's newly constituted committee and its members.

I felt very tired. Krüger asked me what people thought about him in Stanisławów. I answered evasively. Again, he began to foam at the mouth and repeated the question.

'They are afraid of you. They connect your name with the arrest of 250 persons – teachers, engineers, doctors.'

'In a word, Polish intellectuals,' he interrupted me, smiling and nodding agreement.

'They're particularly concerned about the arrest of the surgeon Dr Jan Kochaj, who saved the lives of four German airmen, at the risk of his own, because he deemed it his duty as a doctor. He, too, has disappeared without trace. He was even thanked by the German Aviation Ministry, but the letter did not reach him.'

'Kochaj did receive his thanks. It passed through my hands.'

'And despite that, this man has not been released?' I asked.

'What has one thing to do with the other?' he replied in amazement. 'When we march into a city we always have lists, prepared in advance, of people who have to be arrested. That's always the way. Do you know somewhere else the same thing happened?' He gave a wild laugh.

I was at a loss. I didn't know what he was driving at, but he went on talking.

'In Lwów. Don't you know what I'm talking about now?' Another wild laugh. 'Lwów! Yes, indeed, the university professors. That was my work – yes, mine! Today, since you won't be leaving, I can tell you about it.[15] Yes, yes, on the . . .' (here he mentioned the day of the week, Thursday – I think it was) 'at a quarter past three in the morning . . .'

Here, he looked me in the eye. I believe he knew that this time he had scored – his arrow had hit the mark – and he was clearly enjoying himself. For my part, listening to him, I felt as if someone was hammering the words into my brain: 'So they are all dead, and the murderer – is *this* man!' Swiftly, as though in a dream, there flashed before me the figures of Rencki, Dobrzaniecki, Ostrowski and so many others. I saw the deathly-pale face of Mrs Longchamps, wife of the Rector . . . I thought about Wółka, about the way a group of people were led away at dawn, with one woman limping. Mrs Ostrowska had a bad leg . . .

Meanwhile, Krüger talked on, staring at me fixedly all the time. 'Yes,

I was only a short time in Lwów myself, with the Gestapo section attached to the Wehrmacht.' (I remembered the so-called Feldgestapo, which advanced with the Army.) 'Then we moved on, further east and I came back here later.'

I don't remember in detail the further course of this conversation. I was overwhelmed by the thought of the professors. I know only that, presently, Krüger started shouting again, that I again opposed him and he again promised to break me, and so on. After two hours he told me that I must be tired, but he was not going to suggest that I sit down because he assumed that I would not accept this courtesy and he didn't wish to expose himself to a rejection. Moreover, according to the regulations, a prisoner must remain standing.

'Would you sit?'

'Obviously not.'

'I knew it. Despite that, and despite the treatment that Poles deserve, I shall handle you another way.' He bowed. '*Ich werde Sie ritterlich behandeln*,'[16] he said with emphasis. His words made me shudder.

At that moment Krüger seemed to go berserk. I thought he would smash the massive desk he was sitting at. He pounded it with his fists and feet and howled like an animal.

'What? You reject my gallantry? I have been speaking to you as an officer, and all you see in me is a Gestapo man. Is that it?'

'Obviously,' I retorted.

'Do you think the Gestapo have no code of honour?' The last phrase he repeated several times, yelling ever more frantically. 'But I tell you that the Gestapo has its sense of honour, whatever you may think about us. Do you know what kind of honour that is? *Deine Ehre heisst Treue*. The name of your honour is loyalty. Do you understand that? The Gestapo has its honour. Its name is loyalty . . . And you reject my courtesy?'

'I'm sure you understand that, for me, it would be a humiliation to accept.'

'So what do you want?'

'I want to be treated the same way as you treat other Poles.'

'Very well!' With that, he stood up, rang for a guard and ordered me to be taken away.

I returned to my cell. This time, the interrogation had lasted two and three-quarter hours. But I was terribly tired. I threw myself on the bed and fell asleep. When I woke up the first thought that leaped to mind was this: Krüger murdered the professors. The second was different: self-centred. If he told you that, it was because he intends doing the same to you – that's clear. If he wanted to put you away for a certain time for a 'terror-cure', or even if he wanted to send you to Ravensbrück, he could not have told you that. So I had better begin preparing to be summoned again.

From that moment on, I did. I tried to ensure that the summons, when it came, would find me as well prepared as possible. But in fact, over quite a long period of time, which began for me that day, I encountered almost insurmountable difficulties. Again and again, just when I managed to attain a certain degree of inner concentration, in prayer and withdrawal from the world, something inside me would begin to cry out: 'Don't go on boring the good Lord. He's not about to call you yet . . . He wants something quite different of you. Just see to it that your character does not completely disintegrate in this prison, and don't bother selecting yourself for the next world, because you are going to live.' This presentiment – I would almost say conviction – was so powerful that it stifled reasoning of any kind and dreadfully impeded my inner withdrawal from the world.

In the meantime, my life in prison had begun. Initially my conditions were perfect. There were two of us, each with her own bunk. The washroom was clean, the window large. My cell-mate behaved very decently. Although from the beginning I had a suspicion (never confirmed) that she was there to spy on me, I watched my tongue and saw to it that there was nothing to fear from that quarter. The food, too, was bearable: morning and evening, ersatz coffee, with potato or cabbage soup at noon. Sometimes there were even scraps of meat and, most important of all, half a loaf of bread a day. I was therefore not hungry. Lice were the one major drawback – creatures unknown to me till then and remarkably painful. However, they were not too numerous and it was possible to wage a struggle against them. Above all, in prison one had time and, for me, that was something quite new. Not only during the war, but throughout the long years that preceded it, my life was so arranged that I had to rush to cope even partially with my assigned tasks and goals. The short period when, under Soviet occupation, I lacked intensive work soon sank into oblivion in the midst of all the varied preoccupations and pressures of the last two years. From the time I started working with the prisoners, my life had been just one breathless chase.

Now, suddenly, everything was different. I know it sounds ridiculous, but in the first days after my arrest I found the novelty, and the relatively good conditions of my imprisonment, not unpleasant. I had been tremendously tired and, for the first time in many years, I was having a good rest. I had no duties or any need to hurry. It was rather quiet in the jail at that period. In the beginning, I knew nothing at all of what was really going on around me. I tried indirectly to find out from my cell-mate something about conditions in the prison, but whenever the conversation turned to such matters, her face changed and she fell silent. At the word 'Krüger' she trembled all over. All she would say about him was that he played the piano wonderfully, especially Beethoven . . . Unable to find out anything more, I took to occupying myself with a pursuit I had much neglected in recent years: thinking.

Forcibly removed from everyday life and all-absorbing daily occupations, I experienced something that was probably similar (at least in that respect) to the sudden onset of grave illness. I had never, in fact, been ill and I realised that this was a serious deficiency in my spiritual development. Consequently, I decided to make use of my situation to marshal my forces, emotions, thoughts and will. But reality broke through on occasions, and at times even gained in intensity. One thing I found particularly painful: I was tortured by the awareness that I was in prison not as a result of my concern with prisoners' welfare – an activity I always regarded as my favourite pursuit, and for which I was immensely grateful to the Lord. I knew perfectly well that if, in any one of the prisons, the 'two-track' nature of my activity came to light, or the Gestapo found out what was going on, I would have been arrested in just the same way, but at least I would have known that I had sold myself very dearly and would not have the feeling that my probable death was merely the outcome of a verbal skirmish with a degenerate executioner.

On the other hand, rehearsing in my mind the subject matter of those two interrogations, I could not discern a single provocative answer on my part. On the contrary, I had struggled the whole time against a temptation to say what I thought once and for all, even at the cost of my life. It is a well-known phenomenon how awfully hard it is to control oneself during an interrogation and not let fly just once and give voice to all those feelings – accumulated over the years – of hatred, aversion and, above all, unlimited contempt. In that way, many Poles (whether intentionally or not) had hastened their own deaths. I did not, myself, feel guilty for not having done so. But the thought that the whole of my work was now under threat, and that its further development might even be prevented (our prison-welfare effort now embraced 27,000 people), was very hard to bear. Thank God that I had at least managed to inform our military Commander about my first interrogation. He would know the cause of my arrest.

My thoughts about him and the future of our work were deeply distressing for another reason. During the second interrogation, Krüger had asked with special persistence about the activity of the underground and had repeated that he could not imagine my not being involved. He had said the matter was under investigation. He knew I was based in Kraków. If it occurred to Krüger to question some of our 'informers' now in Montelupi prison, it could be disastrous, for then he could make use of drugs, which I had begun frantically to fear. I knew the Germans were using a special type of narcotic, with which full, precise answers to any questions could be obtained from a victim whose will-power had been, as it were, 'switched off'. In those days I used to curse two things: the sharing with me by more than one of my colleagues of information not strictly necessary for my work, as well as my own very good memory. I knew far too much, and it weighed terribly on my mind.

A few days after my arrest, the cell door was flung open and in came, or rather ran, Krüger, who stood in front of me and demanded angrily: 'Well, still nothing new? You haven't changed?'

We looked one another in the eye.

'No, Hauptsturmführer.'

'Just as I thought.' And out he went. The actress was terrified. Having listened, ear pressed to the door, she reported that he had left the building immediately.

'He only came here on your account and he's furious!'

That episode repeated itself in another couple of days. This time Krüger was accompanied by an adjutant and in his hand, but behind his back, he was holding a riding crop. He asked the same questions, adding that the whole truth about me was now out in the open.

'So much the better,' I said, 'I'll soon be free again.'

'Far from it! You are going down below – into the basement.' And he was gone.

Not long after my arrest, the cell door was opened at an odd hour on a Sunday evening. In came a young and very attractive blonde, well dressed, in a bluish coat and a red, waterproof cape. She was trembling and weeping. Judging by appearances, I had no doubt that she was Polish. I went up to her and said something, but she was crying so much that I could get no sense out of her just then.

Later, when she had calmed down a little, she told us that Krüger had beaten her a short while ago, after she was arrested. Without being asked, she said she lived in Kraków, with a married sister. She had come to stay for a couple of days only with her mother, against the wishes of her parents, who feared for her safety in Stanisławów. The town was notorious throughout the whole General Government area, for the constant arrest of young people. Her father, a court official, was away in another city. Here she had been seeing a number of old schoolmates, boys and girls who had visited her at home. Then, that day, the Gestapo called for her and, after conducting a search, took with them the addresses of a number of her friends.

Neither then nor today, years later, did I gain the impression that Łucja was active in the 'resistance. She was just a young, vivacious schoolgirl, brought up in very comfortable circumstances, without worries or responsibilities, who took it into her head (despite her parents' wishes) to spend a couple of days in Stanisławów, just 'because she felt like it'.

Two days after that, I was taken from the cell and led to a room where I was photographed from all angles. I was then taken out to the courtyard and photographed again. As if that were not enough, they took me across the street to the other building and there made a third series of photos, this time of a special kind. I was made to hold a large metal plate with the inscription *Kriminal Polizei* and a detachable number (116, I believe it was). I found it hard not to laugh, holding my metal plate. When I returned to the cell, both my cell-mates were also in jovial mood. It seemed that the Ukrainian actress, taking advantage of my absence, had told Łucja that when I first came into the cell just after my arrest, a strange idea had occurred to her. She thought, in fact, that they were locking her up with a woman who was mentally ill, firstly because I walked in swiftly and was not weeping, and secondly because I sat down and ate a hard-boiled egg on the spot and then went to sleep. She had covered her face with the blanket and waited till dawn for something to happen. But nothing did.

Meanwhile, I was trying to help Łucja to harden herself against the first blow she had encountered in life. The girl reacted very well and was daily regaining her balance. She was terribly worried about her mother, and told us the Gestapo had been looking round the couple's luxurious apartment with the greatest interest. I was reminded of what had happened to the flats once occupied by Professors Grek and Ostrowski. From dwellings of that sort, the Gestapo liked to remove everything.

A few days later we suddenly heard voices under our window,

overlooking the little yard that was always deserted. The actress, her lips ashen, whispered that we should pray. After a while the guards came in, closed the window and sternly forbade us to get out of bed or look out on the yard. Meanwhile, we could hear footsteps below. I finally understood what was going on. I drew out my little crucifix from Assisi and began to pray for those who would shortly be standing before the throne of God. All was silence, but not for long. There was a shout: '*Dreh dich um!*'[17] The dry crack of a shot and, at the same time, the dull echo of something falling to the ground. Again: '*Dreh dich um!*', another crack and the same dull thump, like a sack of potatoes falling off a cart. When, at last, body number five had fallen, the footsteps of three men died away in the distance. Then silence. At dawn the next day we heard the clash of spades on hard earth. Afterwards, when the window was again open, I stood on my bed and saw in the yard below a freshly dug patch of soil about two metres square.

On Tuesday, 26 May, two weeks after my arrest, Krüger dropped in again, bounded across to me as before and asked whether I had changed my mind. This time, I did not answer at all, but just stood in front of him, looking him straight in the eye. He turned to the Ukrainian and said: 'You should have been freed. Get out!' The actress gathered her bits and pieces and ran out of the cell. Next, he turned to Łucja: 'Pick up your things. You're going into another cell!' Łucja looked at me, gathered her belongings and went out. 'Fetch another Ukrainian,' Krüger commanded the guards, who made no effort to conceal their fear of him. They trembled when he spoke to them. One of them left to carry out the order and came back with an elderly country woman. 'No, not that kind!' he yelled and rushed out. After a little while back he came, smiling at me in the same ferocious way as he had during my interrogations.

'Pick up your things and go downstairs. To the dungeon!' I went with the guard, who took me down to an extremely dirty cell in the basement. As I walked in, I looked up and saw through the little window under the ceiling Krüger himself, standing in the yard and closing the iron shutter on me. The guard slammed the cell door and turned the key. I was in the dark, but I was alone. That was a pleasant sensation.

It would seem that this dark cellar was the last stop on the way to the 'courtyard' and I tried to compose my mind accordingly. Even here, however, from time to time I again had a presentiment that I was to stay alive. Executions continued in the courtyard, but from my new residence I could only count the shots . . . I was alone and at peace. Moreover, the darkness was not completely unrelieved. Three times a day my light was switched on for meals and cleaning up. I soon became accustomed to my new situation and discovered a pleasant way of passing the time. Each day I transported myself mentally to one of the great European picture galleries and viewed the paintings. Naturally, I started with the gallery in Vienna, where I was 'brought up'. Then came the Prado, the Louvre, the Uffizi and Venice. On occasions I managed to achieve an amazingly intense recall. The colours of Venice never shone for me as brightly as in the darkness of my cell. It was there that I realised the full meaning of a familiar anecdote about El Greco. A Dalmatian acquaintance is said to have visited him one day and found him sitting in darkness. When the astonished visitor asked why, the artist replied that he found daylight made it more difficult to see the inner light of his soul. In a less creative, though no less intense way, my memory of colour and form was enlivened in Krüger's sepulchre. I transported myself to a world that had once been mine, and I felt at home.

I was troubled by only two problems of a physical nature. One was the lice, which could not be hunted in the dark; the other was some sort of nervous fear of suffocating for lack of air, although I told myself that the room was large and I was quite alone, so there must be enough oxygen. On the fourth or fifth day, while I was eating, the Ukrainian prison Commandant, Popadyneć by name, came and asked me if I knew how long I had been in the dark cell. As a rule, prisoners were given only two or three days and I had already been there a long time. I said I did not know. The Ukrainian nodded his head and added in a low voice that it was not even possible to enquire, since the Hauptsturmführer himself had fastened my windows. That night a Ukrainian guard opened the window looking out on the courtyard for a few hours, making me swear not to betray him.[18] I cannot describe what it meant to me – that fresh night air, which allowed me to sleep peacefully. Once, while the light was on for room cleaning, I had a look at the 'furniture' and noticed that each article was stamped NKVD.[19] The directness of this clearly unbroken succession impressed me forcibly. There were also Polish names scratched on the sides of some broken shelves hanging on one wall. Taking advantage of every moment the light was on, I managed in the course of a few days (with the help of my little bronze crucifix) to scratch my own name and the date, in a not-too-obvious place, so as to leave some trace behind me in case I died. Doubtless it would come to the notice of AK[20] Intelligence, as soon as Poland returned to these parts.

I had two more calls from Krüger in the days that followed. The same conversation was twice repeated, and twice he flew into a rage and walked out. It was as though he were taking a look at an animal in a cage, which he intended presently to throw to somebody, or something, to devour. I felt like asking him if he knew Beethoven's opera as well as he knew his piano pieces, for he reminded me very much of Don Pizarro in *Fidelio*.

At the end of seven days, I was at last ordered out of the cellar and led before Krüger. On the way, I passed an open cell, on the door of which was chalked the inscription: '1 Pole'. The door was open and a guard was busy inside. Passing by, I managed to note that this very small cell had no window, and in one corner I saw (by the light from outside the door) sitting, or rather crouching, in a strangely constricted posture a man in shackles.

I went into Krüger's office. This time another SS officer was present, presumably his deputy. The interrogation did not take long. Krüger asked whether I had felt the full effects of having rejected his chivalry. He received no answer. He asked whether my sight had suffered in the dark cellar. I said it had not. He asked whether anything about me had changed. I said it had. He jumped up . . .

'I am very much weakened, so I suppose I will save you the trouble of sending me to a concentration camp.' Silence. He was disappointed and looked cross. He said I would be examined by a doctor. Then he ordered me to be taken to some sort of assembly cell.

I returned to the prison. Popadyneć, the Governor, opened the door of cell No. 6. I was struck by a blast of hot fug and the odour of unwashed and sick bodies. I went in. At that moment, somebody flung herself round my neck. It was Łucja, very pale and emaciated, much less pretty, but a great deal stronger. We sat together in a corner of the floor. She told me that her mother was also in the prison, but in a different cell, having been arrested the same day as herself, and that she had twice managed to see her for a second, while she was on her way to peel potatoes or scrub the corridor. They had heard from some recently arrested prisoners that their luxury apartment had been totally ransacked, not a stick left standing.

I looked round the cell. There was plenty of light, so I studied the faces of my new companions with great curiosity. There were women of all ages, and the faces were mostly of an obviously criminal type or bore clear traces of syphilis. They eyed me with grudging interest. The language being spoken was mainly Ukrainian. As I was looking round, a woman a few years older than me addressed me in Polish and asked whether I would agree to share a bed with her, because Łucja, as a younger person, would readily give up her place and sleep on the floor. I was pleased with that idea, since the woman inspired confidence. Next came a fairly young woman with raven-black pigtails, very prominent cheekbones, a large, unrefined mouth and eyes that were very black, passionate and fierce. She was wearing a black dressing-gown of silky fustian with a design of red roses . . . She asked me my name in Ukrainian and said she was the cell commandant. As soon as she went away, Łucja whispered in my ear that she needed very careful watching, for a great deal depended on her. She was a Ukrainian Communist who had very good relations with the guards and hated Poles.

The basic change in conditions, compared with my solitary confinement, was the hunger prevailing in our cell. Instead of ersatz coffee, morning and evening, all we got was brownish water, and at noon water with just a suggestion of potato flour. Our main nourishment was bread: one-twelfth of a loaf each.

After one day, I knew that only two persons in our cell played a role of any importance: Commandant Katia and the senior Polish prisoner, Michalina Kordyszowa, whose husband was a railway foreman. All the Ukrainians were afraid of Katia, and still more afraid of her were the few Polish prisoners. She left the cell a few times a day, to go and peel potatoes, wash corridors or tidy up the quarters of the Gestapo, with whom she appeared to be on very good terms. On her return to the cell, she usually fished out something to eat, concealed in her dressing-gown, and shared it with her Ukrainian compatriots. Mrs Kordyszowa explained that the foodstuffs came either from the Gestapo mess or from parcels.

'What parcels?' I asked.

'Surely you know the families bring masses of stuff for their relatives inside.' I was reminded that the families of people arrested the previous year – the wife of the surgeon Dr Kochaj, for example when she was working with our Committee – used to send regular parcels.

Katia occasionally brought with her news of the outside 'world' – that is to say, the prison. She knew whether or not 'he' was in Stanisławów (she never spoke the name Krüger, but I knew whom she meant by the fear in her eyes). She would know how many had died in the night of spotted typhus, or had been 'taken into the forest'. We learned a great deal from her mood. If she was uneasy and constantly watching the door, executions were in the wind. If Krüger was not about, she was always more cheerful, for no prisoners were being murdered. That happened only and exclusively under his personal supervision. If, on returning to the cell, she flung herself on her bed and wept for hours, that meant there had a been a fresh Soviet withdrawal, a new German victory. She had a deep-rooted hatred of Polish women, though, false to the core, she would often smile at us sweetly.

The senior Polish woman was the sole exception. Even Katia was compelled to respect her; nor would any other Ukrainian dream of treating her other than politely. Mrs Kordyszowa herself was nice to everybody and never lost her temper. After Katia, she was the oldest inhabitant of the cell, since she'd been there longer than four months, after being found with an old pair of trousers abandoned in her flat by a Russian who'd been billeted there. She was very moderate and careful in judging people. With regard to me, she was completely frank and open after a couple of days and confided in me that she trusted hardly anybody, after all she had seen and heard in this cell. All the same, she was very kind to all prisoners without exception because she knew how unhappy they were. She never thought about herself at all, but always of others and particularly of her beloved husband and his children, now grown up, whom she had loved and brought up for him as though they were her own. She had married a widower while young, but had no children of her own because she thought she would never be able to treat the stepchildren as fairly as her own offspring. Tears still came into her eyes when she spoke today of this sacrifice. She was musical as well, and in the evening she would lead a sing-song in the cell. All the women sang: Poles and Ukrainians, intellectuals and prostitutes. Mrs Kordyszowa's favourite hymn was 'Jesus, Jesus, work a miracle with us'. With her strong voice and a faith no less strong, this simple woman – physically almost totally exhausted – conducted the choir and conducted all of us, for none among us could fail to admire her.

By order of the prison authorities, the majority of the women were knitting socks or sweaters for the Gestapo. Having discovered the destined recipients of these articles, I said that my eyesight had been so weakened I could not see to work. The wool was collected from the unravelled sweaters and scarves of the dead. Once, Mrs Kordyszowa showed me a skein of black and green wool and asked whether I did not know whose it was.

'On your first day here, you asked me about Danuta Nowak, that lovely young wife of the airman. I did not know you at the time and I told you I knew nothing about her. That is Danuta's sweater. They proved that she belonged to the organisation. Before she died, she told Krüger that she believed Poland would shortly be free. Then she went out . . . just like so many others have gone out from here.'

The more awful our hunger pangs, the more swiftly we lost our strength. At the same time, the cell was filling up. Whenever Krüger returned after one of his usual two-day absences, he always brought with him a whole slew of people arrested in the provinces. There might be one or two Ukrainians among them, but the vast majority were Polish. Nearly all of them were accused of 'having contacts with Hungarians'. The occupation of the Stanisławów area by Hungarians after the Bolsheviks withdrew lasted for quite a few months, during which time contacts between the Poles and Hungarians became very close. A number of Polish girls got engaged to Hungarians, and Hungarians were guests of others. All of these were rounded up by Krüger and thrown into prison. If the people concerned were members of the more affluent classes, he would arrest them personally and with his own hands, and before their very eyes, would remove the more valuable contents of their homes – above all whole wardrobes of men's clothing, as well as provisions, while not disdaining silver or linen. All these people, most of whom had been beaten by Krüger himself, arrived at the prison in a severe state of shock and it would take two or three days to find out anything about them.

There were now considerably more Ukrainian women in the cell, and communal living with them was becoming awfully difficult for all the Poles, but especially for me. Katia (who had always been very amiable to me) now turned the other Ukrainians very much against me by telling them fairytales, culled from Bolshevik propaganda, about my 'class origin'. The Germans had told her all about me. Despite that, some of those poor creatures continued to treat me as a human being, to the extent that from time to time it was possible to chat with them about subjects of greater significance than everyday happenings. Indeed, the most important issues had to be addressed, because if, by great good fortune, one avoided being shot, the probability of death by starvation was increasing daily. I can attest that the second prospect is a thousand times more unpleasant than the first. Starvation is something too appalling to understand for anyone who has never gone hungry. Not one of all the purveyors of dogma and social reform understands or appreciates the morally destructive force of starvation.

Despite general debility, I realised very clearly that the sight of a

Ukrainian, given a potato for cleaning the Gestapo dining hall, aroused in me a deep-seated hatred and jealousy that she, not I, should have the potato. I even hated the cook who, while doling out soup (that is to say, water with a sprinkling of potato flour) to a Polish woman, chanced to find in the ladle a scrap of cabbage or a stray potato-peeling and at once threw it back in the cauldron. Such titbits were for Ukrainians only. Horrified at my own reaction, I shared my concern with Mrs Kordyszowa, who told me very calmly and with great regret that she had known for the past two months that no hungry person is devoid of such feelings. We are none of us truly kind-hearted.

When our hunger seemed to us past bearing, we decided to appeal to the German Commandant of the prison, Maes, to allow peel from the potatoes (of which vast numbers were peeled every day for the Gestapo by our fellow prisoners) to be thrown into our soup and cooked. As the only one who spoke German, I was deputed to voice the appeal on behalf of us all. Maes listened and calmly replied: 'That is not possible because we need the potato peel to feed the pigs.'

One day, Katia brought news that a priest had typhus.

'What priest?' we asked.

'Father Smaczniak* of Nadwórna. He's been here a long time.'

'We've been searching for him for so long!' I thought. From then onwards, I did my utmost to find out all about this heroic champion of 'The Cause'. Some days the news was better, some days worse. His room was cleaned by Ukrainians (Poles were obviously denied access). They told us that he was lying quite motionless with a serene expression on his face. When he became critically ill, the Germans began to give him milk. He was still plainly of potential use to them for information, though he was said to have driven them crazy by never betraying anybody. But the milk came too late. Father Smaczniak died on 17 June. The news of the death of this man, on whom I had never set eyes, filled me with a terrible depression. This continuous wastage of human life . . . steadily draining away. Who would be left, ready and able to work, when at last Poland returned? For nearly three years now, the best of people had been dying for her. But who would be left to live for her?

The corridor outside our cell was very wide. It was the scene of 'sporadic' or 'prescribed' beatings, combined with torture under interrogation. Sporadic beatings were carried out by all the guards, led by Maes himself. The prisoner was often made to run the gauntlet, there and back, between two rows of guards, under a hail of blows from leather-thonged whips. The victim could sometimes be heard screaming like an animal. Sometimes a voice would implore: '*Zabijte mene!*'[21] Sometimes nothing at all was heard except the blows, often followed by the thump of a falling body. Then Katia would say under her breath: 'Another Pole!' The cell would then be opened and the guard would order Katia to get out with bucket and floor-cloth. After a short while she would return with the news that, this time, 'There was half a bucketful.'

Meanwhile, in the men's cell next to ours, people were starting to die of 'natural causes'. The wall was so thin that one could hear what was going on. Death by starvation takes various forms. Sometimes, towards the end, the victim suffers cramps. I remember one such night when, for a change, we heard screams and the death-rattle. The guard went in several times during the night to command silence. But death-throes are strangely resistant to discipline – even by the Gestapo.

Complete quiet returned only towards daybreak. At the time Katia used to tell us that one or two corpses of male prisoners were being carried out every morning. Popadyneć once came into our cell and asked how it could possibly be that we were all still alive. 'Probably the Devil's holding on to the girls!' If so, his grip didn't seem to be all that firm. Simply crossing the cell to take a shortcut was becoming more and more difficult without the wall to cling on to, and it was exasperating to stagger. Even with the window open, the air in the room was stifling. The big building that housed the civil prison was right opposite, which allowed us to see only a tiny patch of the sky – deep blue at the time – but it reminded me of Italy and the innumerable things of beauty that life had brought my way.

The Germans had forbidden us to sing hymns when we prayed – not that we had the strength left to sing hymns – so each evening we recited the Litany of the Mother of God. The voice of Mrs Kordyszowa, already weaker but still full of expression, soared above our responses in chorus: 'Mystical Rose, Tower of David, Tower of Ivory . . . Pray for us . . .' We all of us prayed, without exception: Poles and Ukrainians; degraded women of the streets and innocent girls, once carefree and well loved – all of us beseeching salvation from a death so close and a life of hunger, sickness, lice and filth; all appealing to the supreme feminine ideal of our culture . . .

At about this time I received a parcel. Inside were a pair of pyjamas, a sweater, some underwear, a summer frock and a pair of slippers. I recognised my own belongings, sent to me from Kraków. The sight of them affected me strangely. It is not easy to convey just how much such a reminder of freedom means to a prisoner. The articles are incontrovertible proof that a former existence was real and not just a dream, proof that there are still people outside, alive and remembering . . . free to come and go.

One day Łucja was called out for another interrogation, during which she learned that her father was also a prisoner here. Later she saw him from a window, breaking stones with fellow prisoners. He had changed so much that, at first, she failed to recognise him. The poor girl was now tormented by the realisation that it was her thoughtless excursion to Stanisławów that had brought about her parents' misery.

The Germans now began to assemble the Jews in the courtyard, where they were forced to stand in the open, regardless of weather conditions. The high, hoarse voice of the Commandant could be heard constantly calling them to attention. For some days we used also to hear the whimpering and sobbing of a sick child, growing weaker by the day, until one night it stopped altogether.

All of this we discussed among ourselves in a whisper when nobody was listening. Our conversations aloud in the cell, on the other hand, were about subjects far removed from our everyday life. There were two constant themes. From dawn till midday, everybody's dreams of the previous night were retailed and interpreted. The rest of the day was passed in describing the widest variety of dishes and how to prepare them. I must admit that the latter topic, endlessly repeated, irritated me enormously by exacerbating pangs of hunger that were already painful enough. It could not be helped. Even Mrs Kordyszowa was a passionate 'cook' and insisted that it did her good. From time to time I tried to tell them something amusing. Once one of the girls asked me how it was that I seemed not to care in the least about anything at all. Katia answered for me: 'It's true, she doesn't actually care about anything, but her hair is so worried it's changing colour.'

What else did the women have to talk about among themselves? Obviously, they often had rows and stole from one another – when there was anything to steal. Sometimes they prayed during the day, though that was forbidden, or played cards, occasionally managing to combine both pursuits. I remember Katia once in her flowered dressing-gown, half-lying, half-sitting in her bunk, singing in Polish from a little book of devotions, *Godzinki do Matki Boskiej*,[22] which one of our cell-mates had managed to hide from the searchers – this at the same time as she was telling fortunes. It was then that Janka[23] came in, appearing at the cell door – a blonde in a sealskin fur coat, which meant that she had been arrested during the winter. Janka, with her tired, intelligent face, was a teacher. She had been 'inside' for a few months after being arrested while the Germans were searching for her fiancé. She had come from Lwów, the Łącki Street jail. I asked her whether the RGO food-relief service was still functioning and was delighted to hear it was working well. Janka had been among the chosen few who worked in the kitchen and had been able to see from the window a couple of times a week how the ladies from the relief committee were delivering soup, medicines and various other items.

A few days later Janka came back to the cell after being interrogated, with a radiant smile. From the questions she had been asked, it was clear to her that they had not caught her fiancé.

'Now it doesn't matter what happens to me – for my sake, or for the Cause. All that counts is that they haven't got him.'

From that day on Janka, with whom I talked a lot, sat quietly on the floor in a corner of the cell and, like the rest of us, grew steadily weaker for lack of food. The cell, meanwhile, became more crowded. There had again been a major leakage of information from within the resistance. Many of those most recently arrested as a result had been questioned about me. Nobody knew anything about me apart from my work with the Main Council. I was reminded of my Commanding Officer's last instruction.[24]

Katia brought still more gloomy reports of large numbers of prisoners being 'taken into the forest'. Larger-scale executions were not carried out in the courtyard, only in the forest.

One day a woman from somewhere local came in. Her name was Sitarska and it turned out that she came from a Rozdól family and had known my father. I can hardly say how much I was moved by this unexpected encounter with the past. We immediately began exchanging family reminiscences. With deep emotion she made me a really lavish gift of a fresh egg and a pitcher of milk, which she had brought with her. After eating that egg, my strength began to revive.

A few days later Sitarska returned from an interrogation, after being brutally beaten. The number of Polish women in the cell had markedly increased. They were constantly being summoned for interrogation and returning in a dreadful state. Now, instead of only one or two at a time, the guards would collect whole groups of Poles and Ukrainians. Among them was Nacia, a Ukrainian with very loose morals, but a very good heart and much loved by all. Sitarska and Janka were called out at the same time. Janka was radiant with delight. 'It's freedom at last!' she announced. We embraced and I reminded her of her promise that if she were released before me, she would let the Lwów Committee of the RGO know about me. She pressed into my hand her still uneaten bread ration and joined the others. They stood in pairs in the corridor – waiting. Suddenly we heard through the window the noise of heavy vehicles approaching. I looked at Mrs Kordyszowa. She gave a slight nod. Again the cell door opened and another two women were called. They left in deathly silence. The guard returned repeatedly, calling out fresh names. Finally, there appeared a ginger-haired police officer with a peculiarly Satanic cast of countenance. His arrival always heralded fresh misfortunes. We had nicknamed him 'Horse death'. He called out somebody else, then ordered the rest of us to sit on the floor. Nobody was allowed for any reason to stand or look out the window.

So we sat down on the floor and waited for the door to be opened yet again, each of us waiting to hear her own name. Somebody began to recite the prayer 'He who seeks refuge in his Lord . . .' The literal sense of those words in such circumstances impressed me with the force of complete novelty. 'A thousand shall fall at thy side, and ten thousand at thy right hand: but it shall not come nigh thee. But thou shalt consider with thine eyes and shalt see the reward of the wicked . . .'

The lorries were beginning to move. There were a lot of them, judging by the noise. Half an hour later they returned and presently there was a heap of dresses and suits in the corridor. There they were sorted out by the Gestapo, who retained the best items for themselves. Janka's fur coat was among them. I caught sight of it when the cell door was open for a few moments.

Katia was called out in the evening, for some reason I cannot remember, and told us when she got back that it was not yet over. Other excursions into the forest were planned. It was a long time before anyone got to sleep that night, all of us waiting. But finally we were all so tired that we slept very soundly. In the middle of the night, the door opened once more and a loud voice shouted: 'Karolina Lanckorońska!' I awoke, understanding that I was about to die, but in the first few moments unable to shake off my slumber. Suddenly I heard the placid voice of Mrs Kordyszowa: 'It's nothing – just the train for Lwów. It leaves at dawn.'

I could see that Mrs Kordyszowa herself did not believe what she was saying, but her voice was enough to bring me to my feet. I got dressed. The guard told me to gather my things. I said I wanted to leave them to my cell-mates and he consented. 'Pray!' I begged them, and out I went. I felt in my pocket to make sure I had with me my little crucifix from Assisi. At the time, my one and only feeling was a great regret that I was to perish at night, in the darkness, and not during the day, in the light and the sunshine. 'Father Jove – if die we must – grant that we perish in the daylight and the sun!' cried Ajax in the *Iliad*. That day, I knew from a single line of poetry that Homer was a great, a very penetrating connoisseur of the human soul. I also knew that *dulce et decorum est pro patria mori* is an immense source of strength. I was completely certain that I was about to die, yet completely calm.

As I stepped into the corridor, I noticed Krüger was not there. I knew that he ought to be there at the moment of execution, as he never denied himself that pleasure. I was surprised. My escort, an SS officer, turned right, out of the corridor. 'Why not left?' I wondered, 'that's the way to the courtyard.' At that moment, for the first time, I felt a link between me and those forebears sleeping in Wodzisław. I assured them they need have no fear. They would not be disgraced. Meanwhile we had reached the main courtyard. The fresh night air gave me strength. I looked around me as we walked – nothing . . . No sign of a lorry. Now I was quite at a loss to understand. He led me into the main building and ordered me upstairs. I found it far easier to climb those stairs than it had been in recent days to walk round the cell. Somehow I no longer felt that weakness, perhaps because I was too curious to see what would happen next.

I was led into an office of some sort, where an officer was sitting with a typist. They were to take down a statement from me. I had to recite my biography, practically from birth. They spent a long time talking and writing. I grew very tired. Coffee with milk and white cake with poppy-seed were brought in and the typist began to help herself liberally. I felt my weakness returning and I leaned on the table. The officer uttered an animal bellow, to let me know me that I was not allowed to support myself. Further questions referred to the subject of the Krüger interrogations, but the tone was much more matter-of-fact. Finally I was instructed to sign the record of my statement and return to the cell. As we crossed the courtyard, dawn was already in the sky. This, I thought, would surely be the last day of my life. Katia and Mrs Kordyszowa both used to say that nobody was executed before signing the record, because that action marked the official end of the 'affair'. The fact that I had not gone with the others yesterday but, instead, had been taken to the registry overnight, I too took to mean that I would certainly be in the second batch that had already been mentioned by Katia.

My return to the cell was greeted with astonishment. The joy displayed by Łucja and, above all, Mrs Kordyszowa was very touching. I was dreadfully weary and hungry. I still had the bit of bread Janka had left me. I ate it and fell asleep. In the morning all was quiet around us. The neighbouring men's cell was deserted, and not even the Commandant of the Jews was to be heard shouting at them in the courtyard. Katia reported that yesterday 'very, very many' had been taken away and today would be much the same. There were bound to be many more arrests. That was why they were emptying the prison.

That afternoon I was drowsing on the floor when in came the guard and again called out my name, adding: 'To be freed'. The whole cell leaped to its feet. I could not believe it, and said I was not going to let myself be cheated. But the guard swore that I was being freed. Łucja and Mrs Kordyszowa threw themselves round my neck and begged me to inform their relatives. The whole cell was in an uproar by now, for everyone wanted to pass on a message. Meanwhile the guard was trying to speed up my departure, so I gathered my belongings and distributed them in a flash. Again I said goodbye and promised to send a parcel for the cell. As I was on my way to the door, one of the Ukrainian girls flung herself on me and turned me round to face the cell: 'You have to back out of the cell as you leave. That way you draw us all out after you, and you've got to tread on a rag as you go.' So saying, she threw down a rag under my feet. Having turned one last time to face these unfortunate women, I held out my hands towards them, stood with one foot on the rag and, stretching the other out behind me, crossed the threshold backwards. Once I was out, the door shut with a crash. I stood in the corridor, semi-conscious. Twelve hours ago I had walked the same corridor. Then, I was on my way to die. Now, not only was I going to live, but to be free – a thousand times more precious!

In the registry, Governor Maes received me. He was very amiable: 'You see, your time has come.'

I was thinking to myself: 'I wonder whether he remembers telling me we could not have the potato peelings because they were needed to feed the pigs.'

Now, he was telling me to look carefully through my papers, which he returned to me, and check the money. I quickly examined the papers and saw with relief that Heinrich's Gestapo pass was among them, which meant that I could return at once to my prisoners' welfare work. Counting the money – it totalled about 4,000 złoty – I smiled inwardly at the knowledge that this money had come from the London Polish Government's delegate to the underground. I was then instructed to sign the famous undertaking forbidding me to disclose any information regarding what I had seen while in prison. I asked whether that would be all? Could I go now?

'Presently, you will be driven away by car.'

'Aha,' I thought, 'the same charade as in other towns, where they don't like anybody to know where the released person was in prison.' I recalled Krüger's phrase: '*Sie passen mir nicht in mein Reich.*'[25] I waited a short while for the arrival of a Gestapo officer, not known to me, who asked politely whether I had received all my property and nothing was missing. I assured him I had everything. I walked out to the forecourt, where a private car was waiting with open door. I got in. The Gestapo officer took his seat beside the chauffeur. Then out came Krüger's deputy once more to ask me whether everything had been returned to me. I gave a positive answer and we drove away.

Chapter 5

The Łącki Street Prison in Lwów

8 July 1942–28 November 1942

The prison gate swung open and, with it, the world. We drove so swiftly through Stanisławów that I saw nobody on the streets. When we were already outside the town, we came upon a funeral being conducted by a priest I knew. As we slowed down in passing, I made a vigorous movement, turning towards him in the hope of attracting his attention. It took only a fraction of a second, but the effect was extraordinary. The priest looked my way, started violently, stumbled and almost fell over – but by then we were already far off. I turned round to look at Stanisławów, whose church towers were still visible on the horizon.

'I will never be able to return here until Poland is liberated,' I told myself. 'Only when Poland is free again will I be able to come back and seek out the people I worked with, especially those I suffered with in prison or, at least, their families. I will come back to this place where I was within an inch of death. Since it is now abundantly clear that I am meant to live and work, the experiences of those eight weeks spent here in prison will be of tremendous value to me in future.'

Meanwhile the car was weaving its way through beautiful, fertile surroundings. It was 8 July 1942 and the ripe corn was already bowing to wind and sun. My lungs, which for so long had had no good air to breathe, inhaled the fresh, invigorating air with all their strength. I was seized by an indescribable emotion at the sight of those fields, the cottages and gardens with their mallows, the churches – Catholic and Orthodox – and the mere sight of those ancestral lands that I had not expected ever to see again. We drove on to Halicz and crossed the Dniester – the river of my youth – by ferry. I was almost on the verge of tears to think of this same Dniester flowing close to Rozdół, our family home.

I began to wonder what I was going to do when we got to Lwów. I did not know whether we would arrive in time to go to church that day. I considered whether to go straight on to friends from the Committee, where they would certainly want to drop me off, or to try to telephone Kraków first. I was thoroughly enjoying myself trying to make up my mind, conscious for the first time in my life of how wonderful it is to be one's own mistress and decide for oneself. My thoughts, however, constantly strayed back to cell No. 6. I asked my companion, sitting beside the driver, whether this same car could possibly take a food parcel back for my cell-mates, without mentioning any names. He said that if I could get the parcel to him before eight o'clock the next morning, he would take it with him and deliver it.

We bypassed Przemyślany and drove straight on to Lwów. From the last high ground before the city gate, I looked with deep emotion at my beloved Lwów, over which summer evening mists were rising, shot through with sunlight. We drove into town. I picked up my coat and various odds and ends lying in the car and held on to them, ready to get out when the car stopped at the RGO Committee's office. However, we avoided the city centre at high speed, and then it came to me that we were heading for Pełczyńska Street. That was, in fact, where we stopped, in front of the former headquarters of the NKVD, now the headquarters of the Gestapo. I was told to get out of the car and into the building. It was very silly of me, but I felt sure this must just be a formality of some sort. My companion pulled me up some flights of stairs and asked for Commissar Kutschmann. It was finally pointed out to him that it was now 7.30 p.m. and nobody was available. We returned to the ground floor. From there he telephoned to Stanisławów, after which he whispered a few words to the official on duty and came across to where I was sitting by the door.

'What's going to happen to me?' I asked.

'You'll see presently,' he replied, hurrying out of the room. A minute later in came a Ukrainian guard with helmet and bayonet. He ordered me emphatically to follow him. We went into the street outside, turned along Tomicki Street and from there to Łącki Street, site of the main prison. There, once again, my watch, my money and so forth were taken away and I was ordered into the transit cell. Once again, a door clanged shut. I threw myself down on an indescribably dirty floor and immediately fell asleep.

I did not wake up till roused by the noise of a tram and the footsteps of passers-by. Although the tiny window, set just below the ceiling of the cell, had a frosted glass pane, I could just make out that I was close to the pavement of Leon Sapieha Street and that a few metres away from me people were walking about in Lwów. I was greatly cheered and began to consider my new situation. In the course of less than twenty-four hours I had been led ostensibly to my death, then ostensibly released and now, here I was, back in prison. At least I had something very beautiful to sustain me: the memory of the previous day's drive, with all the natural wonders of my ancestral countryside, for me still bathed in the golden glow of freedom. That mirage had abruptly disappeared, yet the memory remained. I shall never understand why Dante considered there was nothing more distressing than to recall past happiness in the midst of present misfortune. Such memories, it seems to me, are a source of great strength.

Meanwhile, two heavily made-up German women had woken up. They had been sleeping in a corner of the cell on a splendid mattress and now began jabbering away. Both were officials. One had been brought in for black-market dealings, the other for hiding a friend who had undergone a clandestine abortion. Two ladies of the Lwów streets, in another corner of the cell, but without a mattress, went on sleeping. A little later a Gestapo man came in bringing 'coffee' and a slice of bread. Shortly after that he returned to fetch me. While he was waiting with me in the corridor for a minute or two, he asked why anybody would want to mess about with the black market or anything of the sort. That kind of thing always led to trouble.

Then the Ukrainian guard reappeared and took me with him. Back we went along Tomicki Street. Another fine, sunny summer's day. I looked around me carefully, but saw nobody I knew. We went into the Pełczyńska Street headquarters of the Gestapo, where we clambered up to the third floor. After my time in Stanisławów, that in itself was a feat of physical endurance. We stood outside the door of No. 310, with its signboard '*Polizei Kommissar Kutschmann. Polnische politische Angelegenheiten*'.[1] We went inside. Two persons were busy typing. The Ukrainian handed over a note of some sort. I was then led into another room where there was nobody.

Presently I was ordered into a third room and there, as I entered, a man stood up behind his desk. He was aged perhaps about forty, of medium height, fair-haired but greying at the temples and with dull grey eyes. He came over to me, asked whether I was so-and-so and apologised (!) for making me wait a little longer, but he needed to question me about my Stanisławów episode. He led me into the second room and told me to sit by the window. I asked whether I was actually under arrest, or was I free? He appeared nonplussed. I said that I had been officially released the previous day, in view of which I completely failed to understand why I was again being treated in this way. He said he knew nothing at present about my release. We looked at one another very intently. I was struck by the strangely melancholy expression of his eyes and mouth, and by his seeming embarrassment at having to confront me. He must have thought I was not looking too marvellous just then, for he asked whether I had eaten that day. I told him I had. But he went out and returned after a short while with a plate on which were five slices of bread and margarine. He suggested that I eat and retired to his office. I started to eat, but had to stop fairly quickly because this helping seemed to me enormous. So I sat by the window and waited.

An hour or so elapsed. Then Kutschmann came in and invited me into his office. He closed the door after me and told me sit down on the other side of his desk. In front of him lay a fat briefcase. Before he opened it, I managed to read a note on it in large type, which read: '*Vollständig unbelastet*'.[2] In that case, I wondered, how had my dossier become so bulky? He went on to question me about my interrogation in Stanisławów.

'Did you tell Krüger that you recognise only an independent Polish State?'

'That declaration accords with my convictions,' I replied, 'although I never said as much in my statement.'

'How so?'

'I was questioned as though by a judge, and forced to answer yes or no. He asked me whether I was an enemy of Germany.'

'That question interests me a lot,' said the Commissar.

'That was how the question was put and, when I avoided replying, he asked the same question again. So I had no way out, not being prepared to compromise my honour. In the same way, he asked whether I acknowledged the destruction of the Polish State.'

In the course of this interview I sensed that Kutschmann had a strong aversion to Krüger, as well as a growing confidence in my truthfulness. More than that, I got the impression that he found this whole affair strangely distasteful. During our exchange I recalled that

Krüger had spoken very contemptuously about the Poles and their attitude. The Commissar replied with a note of irritation in his voice: 'In fact, it's quite the opposite. We cannot help admiring your attitude.' Suddenly, he came out with another question: 'Who do you know belonging to the Italian royal family?'

I was flabbergasted. 'Nobody,' I replied, which was the truth.

'Yet the Italian royal family has intervened on your behalf with Himmler*.'

My thoughts flashed back to my beloved Italy.

'If you don't know any of the Savoy royal family and, despite that, the intervention actually took place, then you must have some powerful friends in Italy.'

In my mind's eye I glimpsed the tall figure of Roffredo Caetani*, a distant relative of mine, whose grandmother was Polish and the daughter of the 'Emir', as he was called, Wacław Rzewuski.[3] Caetani was a friend of the wife of the heir to the throne, the Princess of Piedmont, who played the violin, and Caetani, himself a composer, used to accompany her on the piano. They were both much opposed to Mussolini.[4]

Meanwhile, the Commissar continued: 'I am talking to you about this, though I have no right to, so please keep it to yourself. I wish you to know, however, that the intervention was very powerful and that your arrest was clearly *nicht zu verantworten*.[5] Himmler is very cross about the whole business.[6] Obviously he did not like being told to transfer you to Lwów. I have now got to send to Berlin a formal account of the whole affair, which we shall write together today. Then we shall see what happens.'

'Krüger promised to send me to a concentration camp,' I replied.

'I know about that. I am hoping that my report, and the light I shall shed on the matter, will reach Berlin before Krüger has time to arrange your departure. But even if that cannot be managed, you must be of good heart. I hope you will be released in a couple of weeks.'

'Didn't Krüger make a fuss about surrendering me?' I asked.

Kutschmann gave me a shrewd look. 'However hard he tried to defend himself, he had to back down in the end.' He broke off suddenly, as though waiting to see what I would say. But I stayed silent, looking him in the eye. Finally, he spoke again: 'By order of the Reichsführer,[7] you are to be treated and fed as well as possible. You will have a private cell, bedding and a certain freedom of movement in the corridor. What shall we do about feeding?'

'Please give your permission for me to receive a parcel from the Polish Committee.'

'How can that be organised? Is there somebody I can send for?'

'Just send for the woman in charge of the prison section and it can all be discussed with her.' He sent a car at once to our Committee headquarters.

At that point we were joined by an older man, taller and clearly also of higher rank than Kutschmann, who stood up as he entered and gave my name. The other man, as though introducing himself, announced: 'Kriminalrat Stawitzky!'

'Delighted!' I thought to myself, 'the executioner from Sanok in person.'

He asked whether there was anything I needed. I said I would like the Committee to send me some underwear and toilet articles, because the previous day when I was told that I had been released, I had given away everything I had to my fellow prisoners.

'What do you mean – released?' asked Stawitzky. When I told him the way it was, he changed the subject. He asked how I had been treated in Stanisławów.

'Normally,' I said. 'However, I preferred the dark cellar to the communal cell.'

'Dark cellar?' Kutschmann repeated after me.

'You don't mean to tell me that you were kept in a completely dark cell?' asked Stawitzky.

'Yes, indeed, for seven days.'

Stawitzky curtly excused himself and left us.

'You appreciate that I am carrying out the orders of Himmler himself,' said Kutschmann. 'I suppose you are probably the only Polish woman for whom Himmler has ever given such an order. That'll give you some idea of how strongly the Italians must have intervened on your behalf. What can we do for you? Cell, bedding, food, books?' he asked. 'Would you like some books?'

'Books were once the stuff of my life, Herr Kommissar,' I said.

'But where to get them? For my part, I can lend you only Strindberg and Nietzsche. They're all I have with me here in Lwów.'

'Thank you, those are not authors I yearn for. But if you are allowing me books, perhaps the Committee could send me some with the food.'

'Very well.'

At that moment an SS man came in to announce that an official from the Committee had arrived. The Commissar told me to go into the other room, where a close colleague and friend of mine, Lesia Dąmbska*, was waiting. With a slight head movement, I signalled a warning to her to watch what she said. It was wise to assume the room was bugged. There were tears of gladness in her eyes. I started to talk about food packages, adding quickly and quietly that she should let them know in Kraków that all was well.

'Were you afraid for me?'

'Yes and no. We knew that in the end nothing could happen, so many prayers were being said for you. It was like in the Acts of the Apostles, you remember – after they put Peter in prison.' I remembered the passage and was touched.

Then the Commissar came in. He turned to the new arrival from the Committee and told her that I was entitled to receive parcels of food and clothing. He told Lesia to make a note of what I needed. He then asked her to send me books, which I could order as required through the prison authorities. I asked her to send me Shakespeare in the original and the history of Rome. These books, I added, could be obtained from the Ossolineum.[8] I asked her to contact Professor Mieczysław Gębarowicz* about them. He was a devoted friend and Director of the Ossolineum Museum, through whose good offices I would receive the books. But – most importantly – he would alert those who needed to know. Lesia Dąmbska then left us.

The Commissar turned to me.

'I must go now. I'll be back in an hour and a half. Just wait here. I'll send you in a meal. Have a good think in the meantime and we'll write the deposition after lunch.'

Off he went and I was alone in the room. The door was open. Somebody was sitting in the main office . . . There was plenty to think about. The meal was brought in. I was frightfully hungry, but I managed to eat only a little. I went and sat down again by the window and tried to concentrate. That was difficult. Too many impressions, and I was very weak. One thing was clear. Kutschmann could not stand Krüger and – possibly for that reason – wanted to help me. Up to the present, I had expressed myself very moderately regarding Krüger. Possibly that was a mistake. Maybe I should tell Kutschmann the whole story, about Krüger 'chivalry', about being led to my execution, and so on. That way, he would appreciate that Krüger was persecuting me personally and that, in turn, might increase his own desire to help me personally. Then my thoughts took wing once more to my beloved Italy, and I reflected with emotion that I owed my life to that country, and that life was something very beautiful.

At last the Commissar returned. He told me to come into his own office, where a shorthand typist was already waiting.

'We shall now write our statement for the record.'

'First of all, I would like to make an additional deposition, but for that I would like be alone with you,' I said. He ordered the secretary to leave us and closed the door. He sat down and looked at me with keen curiosity. He said nothing.

'Because I can see that you are anxious to be fully informed about all aspects of my case, I want to give you certain details that will make it quite clear to you that Hauptsturmführer Krüger felt some kind of personal dislike, or even hatred, for me.'

'Just as I thought!' he exclaimed excitedly.

I then gave him a full account of my eight-week 'course' with Krüger. I talked about the chivalry, the starvation, the clear evidence in the cell of syphilis; about the dark cellar, the executions in the yard below the cell; about Krüger's visits to the cell, and how I was led in the course of one day seemingly to my death, then seemingly to freedom. I spoke as factually as possible, in an impersonal tone. Kutschmann listened intently. From the beginning I could sense in him, to a far greater degree than before, shame and humiliation followed by mounting indignation. He stood up, paced about the room and clenched his teeth. Then I began to talk about the overall treatment of Poles in Stanisławów. I said that almost the entire intellectual elite of the town had disappeared without trace after being arrested by Krüger and that, to judge by what I had seen in prison, I could not entertain the least shadow of hope that these people might still be alive. At that point Kutschmann interrupted, shouting loudly: 'Not to speak of another appalling thing that he has on his conscience, here in Lwów!'

Meanwhile, I was also on my feet, determined to tell him everything I knew about Krüger. Even today, after all these years, I find it hard to give any rational explanation for my behaviour. I know as much today as I did then. I felt that this seeming act of madness was an absolute necessity, that I must place every possible weapon in the hands of this man, to enable him to defeat his personal antagonist and our executioner. At that moment of decision, I was acting quite cold-bloodedly, obeying some inner injunction, in the conviction that this was my duty. When Kutschmann mentioned that Krüger had some other appalling deed on his conscience, here in Lwów, I answered calmly: 'I know about it.'

'What do you know?'

'That Krüger shot the professors of Lwów University.'

'Where did you get that from?'

'From Krüger,' – and I repeated what he himself had told me on 13 May.

Kutschmann stood in front of me, eye-to-eye, and asked three times with mounting intensity: 'He told you that, did he?' After I had answered 'yes' for the third time, he declared: 'The fact is, I was there. I was serving under him. He ordered me that night to bring in the second batch of university professors, as listed, as well as a number of other Lwów personalities. I reported that I found nobody at home, which is why those people are alive.'

'Where did you get the list of the condemned persons?' I asked.

'Ukrainian students who came in, of course.' He covered his face in his hands. 'When I think of that Higher Justice, I always wonder what may be in store for us one day in return for that deed.' Then, seeming to come to his senses, he asked in a changed voice: 'You won't go and repeat what I've told you, will you?'

'You need not worry about that,' I replied.

Presently, he asked: 'Would you be prepared to put in writing what you told me just now?'

'I can't do that. If I did, Krüger would murder all the Poles in Stanisławów and the whole surrounding area.'

'No, that would not happen. So far, I have never had a witness, but perhaps now it might be possible, perhaps at last . . . But you don't want to write it down?'

I was suddenly very angry.

'You don't imagine, do you, that I would hesitate to sacrifice my worthless life, if there were a one percent chance of freeing even a scrap of my homeland from that executioner? But I am not at liberty to provoke his revenge. That would not affect me, because I'm no longer in his hands – only those unfortunate Poles still left in Stanisławów!'

'I can guarantee that would not happen, and the chances of success are far greater than one per cent.'

'I will write.'

He relaxed and sat down. Then he provided me with writing materials and rang the Łącki Street prison in my presence to let them know that I was to have a private cell, bedding, and so on, and could receive parcels of food, clothes or books. I was to be given a table, because I was required to put certain statements in writing before the next interrogation. Meanwhile, he had calmed down entirely.

'Just now, obviously, I cannot promise you a rapid settlement of this affair,' he said with a smile. 'I would even prefer to tell you in advance that it will take some time, because I shall need to take your written statement to Berlin in person. Today is 9 July [1942]; it will probably be a fortnight before I leave, but I don't know when exactly.'

I assured him that, as things stood at present, my personal fate had become completely unimportant. I added that I could no longer suppose I would be released from prison. He looked at me fixedly and said he hoped that it would be otherwise.

'Now, let us write the record of this interview. I have to send that at once, whatever happens.'

He called in the typist and told me that he would first dictate a draft, which I would be asked to correct. It was a very short record. It began with a declaration that I had never worked in any secret organisations. That sentence he repeated, looking me straight and steadily in the eye, while I tried my hardest to return his gaze with equal force. As far as my so-called hostile attitude to Germany was concerned, I declared that I was a Polish woman. As such, I could obviously recognise only an independent Polish State and I was ready to bear whatever the consequences might be.

'Are you satisfied with the record?' he asked.

'I would like to ask for only one correction. The word "*sogenannt*" [so-called] before the words "hostile attitude" should be deleted.'

The Commissar acceded to my request. He then asked for the text to be retyped and gave it to me to sign. Finally, he ordered me to be taken back to the Łącki Street prison.

There I found my cell already prepared, with table and chair and so forth. The wardress (I don't know whether she was a Pole or an ethnic German) received me saying that she had special orders regarding me ('something unheard of'). When I found myself alone at last, I felt incredibly tired and bewildered. I gazed in wonder at the clean white sheets and lay down to sleep. The next day I set about writing. I found my strength returning almost by the hour, given cautious but healthy nourishment. I described everything: my interrogations and all the incidents I had witnessed in jail. I also recalled the earlier murders in Stanisławów.

A couple of days later I was again seen by Kutschmann, who asked me whether I was writing and when I would finish. I told him I would be able to bring him the complete document in two days' time.

'The lady official from your Committee is coming here again today so that you can let her know your further wishes on the matter of parcels, but she is not due for another hour.' He looked first at his watch, then very seriously at me. 'Perhaps you would like to go for a stroll meanwhile, but . . .'

I could not guess what he had in mind, but I was very keen to go for a walk in Lwów, even with an escort. I said nothing.

'What would you say if I let you go for a walk on your own?' he asked suddenly.

'How do you mean, alone?' I must have appeared rather slow on the uptake, for he repeated the question. At last I understood. I smiled and asked: 'What do you mean – on my own? If you send me out for a walk, you'll be hanging on to me by a chain of honour.'

'I knew your answer would be yes. I will lead you out of the building. Here, I'll give you my watch.' (I got the impression that he felt the loan of his gold watch gave him a certain guarantee.)

We were standing in Pełczyńska Street.

'Please be back here in an hour's time – not before – standing somewhere not too obvious, here under the trees.'

A few moments later, as we parted, he turned to me and said: 'If you don't come back, they will shoot me.'

I laughed and walked away. Supposing that I would still have a 'minder', I did not go into town, just left and right, uphill, among the villas. There to my surprise I confirmed that I was indeed completely alone. I walked as far as the meadow in the old bed of the River Pełtawa. I was very tired and sat down on the lawn. The sun was shining. I touched the soil with my hands; I looked at the green grass and the blue sky. After a short while I stood up, afraid of being late back. On my way, I amused myself by inventing a thousand possible means of escape, here in Lwów, my own city where I had so many friends. One thought only never occurred to me: that of trying to realise any of these projects. The strange turn taken by the battle with Krüger was sparing me all sorts of conflicts. I got back to Pełczyńska Street too soon. So I went a little further along Nabielak Street, where I had an amusing adventure. I met a man I knew by sight, and who at the sight of me gave a whoop of joy.

'Miss Lanckorońska! So you're free!'

I smiled sweetly and walked on. It was no good. My unknown, close friend turned out of his way and began to walk beside me.

'Do you mind if walk with you?' (Nice thing, I thought, if we turn up together at Gestapo headquarters!)

'Excuse me, I'm sorry, but I am forbidden to contact anybody,' I said with a smile.

The gentleman dropped back and did not look round. Often, in later years, I played with the thought of this good man, who must in time have come to the conclusion that he had suffered a hallucination. I reached Pełczyńska Street, at the agreed spot, just as the Commissar arrived. He did not conceal his pleasure at seeing me again. We went in. It was back to prison once more, as though nothing had happened.

A few days later I went back to Kutschmann with the complete text of my report, as though written in my own defence. Kutschmann ordered me to read it aloud. There were many facts which, in the heat of the moment, I had failed to mention before. He listened, apparently with great effort and immense sadness. As I was reading, the door suddenly opened and in strode Stawitzky, who asked: '*Was geht hier vor?*'[9] Kutschmann replied that I was reading out to him some notes that I had written, at his suggestion, in my cell. The tension between the two Gestapo officials was easily discernible on that occasion. Stawitzky hesitated for a time, looking in turn at Kutschmann and me, and finally left without saying anything. Kutschmann sat down again, but remained silent. It was not until the noise of Stawitzky's footsteps died away along the corridor that Kutschmann visibly relaxed and told me to carry on reading. When I had finished, he told me to come back the next day and dictate the entire text to the typist. The typescript totalled fourteen pages. He then asked me to sign three copies, which he carefully deposited in his desk under a very complicated system of locks. He was clearly busy at the time and, perhaps for that reason, forgot to relieve me of the original draft that I had written in my cell. I took the opportunity to ask him for permission to work as a prison hospital orderly. He agreed and informed the hospital management.

That was, for me, the start of one of the best periods I recall in all the years of the war. Instead of a cell, I was given a small room on the second floor, with a large, normal window, looking out on the prison courtyard and the sun. The window had no bars – surely among the greatest of comforts any prisoner could imagine. Another similar cause for joy was the door: an ordinary door with a lock, through which I could pass in and out of my own free will. I was free to go wherever I wished in the women's section. Twice daily I made a round of all cells, distributing medicines and applying minor dressings. The reaction of these women to the fact that they were being looked after by a woman, and a Pole, was touching.

One morning the wardress told me that she would have to lock me up in the communal cell for a couple of hours, by order of the prison Commandant. She added, lowering her voice: 'You will understand that you can't be at the window today because there's a *Himmelfahrtkommando*.'[10] So I moved to the communal cell. The women there did not know what was going on and were merely pleased that today, for a change, I had plenty of time to sit on the floor and gossip with them, whereas usually I was able only to call briefly and issue the medicines. After a while the door opened and two or three names were called out. Silence reigned. The women stood up and walked out with heads held high. The door closed, only to open again shortly. More names were called, and again we were a couple fewer. I was reminded of the prison in the Temple.[11] Only the minuet was lacking. I despised myself that day because, at the bottom of my heart, I knew I was happy with the certainty that today they would not be coming for me.

The following day life returned to normal. In the morning, after my medicine round, I went to the chief medical orderly and asked him whether he knew how executions were carried out. He told me that people were loaded into open lorries in the courtyard and told to squat down. Anyone who looked up was hit over the head with a rifle butt. There was an SS man with a loaded rifle posted in each corner of the truck. They drove like that through Lwów, and out to the suburb of Wólka. That was where the shooting took place . . .

I got on very well with the chief orderly at that time. He was a Ukrainian, a very intelligent and well-educated man, Andrej Piaseckyj, an assistant at the Lwów Polytechnic, who turned out to be the husband of one of my pupils. He sincerely hated the Germans. In his antipathy was a hint of unrequited love for that nation, for he was deeply concerned about the future of the Ukrainian people, while also towards the Bolsheviks his attitude was decidedly negative. I told him I was convinced that neither Ukrainian-Bolshevik nor Ukrainian-German friendship could alter the fact that the Poles and Ukrainians must find a *modus vivendi*. I could see that this honest and honourable man could not fail to recognise the validity of the argument, but that he could not rid himself overnight of the prejudices of his Ukrainian nationalist upbringing. He was ideal to work with. Intelligent and conscientious, he did not differentiate in the slightest between Poles, Jews and Ukrainians. He had too much work, for the number of male prisoners was enormous, whereas I had too little. So I was granted additional permission to look after one floor of the men's prison, which meant a great deal of extra work for me.

I succeeded in letting the Committee know that I needed far more food in my private parcels. The request was understood and acted upon. Since I was allowed to receive an unlimited supply of food, the prison authorities had no objection to these ludicrous stacks of food addressed to one person. As soon as the parcels arrived – usually around 5 p.m. – Piaseckyj would invent a serious reason for communicating a professional instruction to me. This enabled him to stuff his pockets with food. The whole problem was to make sure that the SS man who escorted us round the cells did not see what we were up to, but somehow we succeeded. It was easy in the women's section, because the wardresses (exclusively Polish) helped by distributing the food themselves. These Polish women had been given permission to work in the prison some time ago, due to a shortage of German personnel. Previously there had been a German woman guard, of whom the women prisoners had bad memories. She refused to allow them to take water to their cells and, during an epidemic, the women had no water for washing. They had to make do with the minuscule amounts of coffee they received for breakfast. This ban on water had not been officially imposed, but – like so many other things – was solely a case of the German wardress being officious.

Prisoners as well as personnel were all still talking about what had happened during the winter. Nobody could forget it. Spotted typhus was raging in this prison, where every morning, after the night before, disposal of the corpses posed a grave technical problem, because of the need to step over the sick in order to get to the door, while carrying bodies that were often covered in ulcers. Lack of water, indescribable filth, millions of lice and other vermin, as well as terminal starvation were rampant in this building, which had previously housed the Police Directorate. It was not till the Germans arrived that the premises were adapted for use as a prison. The city knew what was going on in there. Metropolitan Szeptycki* had intervened, but obviously without result. Now it was less crowded, there were no epidemics, there was water in the cells and, above all, there was no longer starvation, particularly by comparison with Stanisławów. Portions of bread were considerably larger, the soup a little better. Thrice weekly, indeed, very generous help arrived from our prison Relief Committee (RGO), which saved the situation with varied soups, including meat and onion. Morale was also a great deal better. There was no class or racial strife, since everyone was equally persecuted. Obviously, every cell had its 'informer', but that was normal.

Our wardresses treated the women kindly and did what they could to help. They asked me, for example, not to clean my own cell, but to give one of the prisoners, Józia, the chance of a break. Józia, a seamstress, was petite, young and gracious with regular features and thick black locks. Four and a half months ago, when she was arrested, she had apparently been very pretty. Now she had a yellow complexion and her face had a curiously drained look. She had been arrested with her brother, probably because they both owned a field on the frontier with Hungary, but Józia had never been called for interrogation. She had to be forcibly spoon-fed. 'Please give it to others. I don't need it,' she insisted. She never quarrelled with anyone, but neither did she make friends. She simply avoided everybody.

One day I was called to help, as a hospital orderly. In a storeroom that she was supposed to be cleaning, Józia had hanged herself. We cut down the body. The cooks, who just happened to be arriving with cauldrons of soup, scrambled to get hold of the length of rope, cut it and eagerly shared it out among themselves. A rope from a hanging is supposed to bring good luck. I started applying artificial respiration, but from the beginning I had no hope. I knew it was too late. A doctor came, but he, too, could do nothing. The wardress was terrified and afraid of being punished for inattention to duty. She came back reassured. The Germans told her it was a pity it did not happen more often. Less food would be needed. A little later, in a very elegant bright, floral-patterned dress, there arrived a pretty, possibly eighteen-year-old brunette – the daughter of the prison Commandant, accompanied by an SS man. She went into the storeroom where Józia was lying. There she began to rock the dead girl's head with her smartly booted little foot. Józia's raven-black locks tumbled this way and that. This was just too much, even for the girl's SS escort.

'Come on, let's go,' he said, pulling her by the sleeve.

'But why? It's very interesting,' she replied, without interrupting her activity.

'How can it be?' I asked myself for the hundredth time. 'What sort of instincts are rooted in this race?'

The death of Józia had a short epilogue, when two days later the Gestapo Commandant in charge of the case visited her cell. He asked her cell-mates about the causes of her suicide, as he was required to do in order to close the dossier. The women said that Józia could not stand any more of it; that she had been arrested more than four months previously and could not wait any longer for the hearing, about which she had at first been so full of hope.

'There was no reason to interrogate her, since there was absolutely no charge against her,' the officer muttered and closed the dossier. Thus, the Józia affair was finally disposed of . . .

Life in the prison returned to normal. Every morning and evening the men's and women's cells were opened to let me fulfil my modest but numerous functions, as I passed on my way through the long, narrow corridors. With every opportunity to compare them, I became convinced of how much greater the endurance (physical as well as moral) of women is than that of men. Woman was created to play a passive role, something that undermines the strength of a man.

It was not long before things got worse. As a result of a heatwave there was a severe outbreak of infectious dysentery, which raged with particular force in the cells for Jewish prisoners. I can still see the inhumanly emaciated face of one Jewish woman with a distinguished Jewish name that escapes me. I will call her Mrs Rapaport. This woman, whose husband and sixteen-year-old son were in the same jail, was dying from total debility, heart failure and constant diarrhoea. The prison doctor, himself a Jew, said that it was impossible to save her. The sick woman herself, lying on the floor near the door, was always waiting for my visits, imploring me every time to cure her because she must live for her son's sake. The Committee sent various medicines and the wardresses agreed to let drinks be prepared in their quarters, so I set to work. After a week I had the great pleasure of informing the doctor that Mrs Rapaport was regaining her strength. A few months later this woman was to cause me the most terrible pangs of conscience. Her husband and son were both murdered, and only when she heard about that did she herself die, last of all. In retrospect, it seemed clear to me that, by prolonging her life, I had exposed her to the greatest suffering a woman could experience. But of that I had no idea at the time.

My great interest in medicinal matters, which had always been with me, as well as my passion for nursing – albeit that of a dilettante, but no less intense for that – were nurtured by my work as a hospital orderly. I was almost happy, because I could see that here I had a position where I could achieve a lot, and for that I had to thank God. This fresh departure in prisoner welfare appealed to me enormously.

Then, on 4 August, a wardress came to me, clearly very confused, to say that she had been instructed to escort me to the 'German section'. This was a separate small building on the courtyard, freshly rebuilt and adapted, completely cut off from the rest and staffed exclusively by Germans. There were a number of German prisoners, as well as the most serious German political dissidents, the latter in total isolation.

I asked why I was being moved. The wardress said she did not know, but she had strict instructions to take all my medicines away from me and to search me thoroughly to make sure I brought none with me.

'You can probably guess what they're frightened of. In such circumstances, it would be easy to commit suicide. You are to take your own things with you.'

I packed my odds and ends and went to the German section. I was given a large, bright cell. An SS man slammed the door shut behind me and locked it, mentioning the fact that the key would be held by the Commandant and that future contact with me for feeding or the delivery of parcels would be by the little window only. I looked through that little barred window at other little barred windows of the general section opposite. I thought about my sick patients and I felt very sorry. In the evening, when the SS man passed in my food through the grating, I asked for a bucket so that I could wash the cell. He went away and returned to inform me that the prison authorities did not consider that necessary. The next day, however, I was brought a large pitcher by another German, since the grating was too small to admit a bucket.

I considered my next move. Kutschmann had told me on one occasion that in case the need arose, I should ask to be interrogated by him. I did so. Two days later, an SS man with a key arrived. I was led through a courtyard paved entirely with the headstones from Jewish graves. To any normal person, brought up to respect not only death but other people's religions, this trampling of inscriptions and sculpture would probably be unspeakably offensive.

I went to Kutschmann, who, I gathered, knew nothing about it all. He made a couple of telephone calls and visited a few other offices, but at last returned to inform me, with a certain sadness, that he could do nothing. The changes had been made on a higher authority, but I was to retain my right to receive food parcels and books. I went back to my cell. There began another stage of my captivity – the only one from which I possess my original notes in an exercise book that has survived. The first entry reads:

Lwów, September, second year of war, 18 IX 1942:

I have been studying how I may compare[12]
This prison where I live unto the world:
And for because the world is populous
And here is not a creature but myself,
I cannot do it: yet I'll hammer 't out.
My brain I'll prove the female to my soul,

My soul the father: and these two beget
A generation of still-breeding thoughts.
And these same thoughts people this little world.
(*King Richard II*, V.v)

Later, Richard says:

In humours like the people of this world
For no thought is contented ...

but I can't use these words here as a motto, since I cannot say that they apply to my own thoughts. Many thoughts of mine *are contented.* After all the immense strain of these last years, for me a period of forced meditation and concentration has now begun. Instead of work that was exclusively practical, the last possibility of effort now left to me is exclusively intellectual, for I am allowed books. From the start of this period in Lwów, I have been reading historical works: [. . .] Guglielmo Ferrero: *Grandeur et décadence de Rome* (4 vols). Style slightly journalistic [. . .] fluent, smooth, carefully avoiding the real problems and without psychological talent. Yet I do not regret reading Ferrero. Confronted with that multitude of events, one gains the benefit of distance, separation and peace of mind – *humility in the face of history.*

Renan: *Marc-Aurèle*; beautifully written. When I was younger I was very taken with the thinking of Marcus Aurelius. But now I find him alien to the very core of my being and I think I am not alone in that. *O homme, tu as été citoyen de la grande Cité va-t-en avec un coeur paisible.*[13] That is simply not enough (anyway, not in my present situation).

The closing years of the XIX century – a happy period with no major conflicts – admired and even made heroes of those who despised the enjoyment of life. For us, that is too little. Marcus Aurelius, as it were, withdrew his outstandingly noble soul from life altogether. There's something rather Indian about that. For us, that kind of virtue seems rather pale and a far cry from the kind of *virtus* we need so much. The wonderful word *virtus* combines in meaning virtue, strength, backbone and fortitude. *Virtus* is the basis of all action in general and consequently of that noblest of all actions, that which ethically influences our neighbours, which is to say, every action and every deed . . .

The relationship of Marcus Aurelius to his surroundings and to people in general also raises many doubts. If one passes evil by, as though it were a necessary component of every man, so that evil is not consciously visible, then one's neighbour, in many instances, will feel himself thereby 'excused', that is, relieved of any obligation to go to work on his own character, in order to eradicate inherent evil. However, to stimulate his neighbour to such an effort is precisely one of the main duties of every responsible person. This objective may be attained in two ways – above all, by example – but also by making more exacting demands on oneself than on one's neighbour and ensuring that the demands you impose on your neighbour do not exceed the measure or limits of his potential. Having time – and plenty of it – to ruminate on such problems during these months, which have perhaps been granted me for that very purpose, I shall try to concentrate all my moral forces in preparation for my future work, assuming I have a few more years to spend in the Lord's vineyard. My object is to adopt a standpoint in the face of these problems – a personal standpoint, that is to say – to provide myself with answers [. . .] regarding the development of my own character, which is my one and only remaining field of activity. Reading Renan is a great help in stimulating such reflections.

Sinko: *Greek Literature* (2 vols)

The chapters about Homer, particularly about the *Iliad*, I found very rewarding; above all, they enabled me to think about the *Iliad* for a couple of days and nights.

What Sinko writes about 'the atmosphere of the *Iliad*' and 'the charm of the *Odyssey*' – the comparisons he draws (to the advantage of the *Iliad*) – is beautiful and to the point, but does not appear to me to exhaust this enormous topic. The atmosphere of the *Iliad* is not only sunny, it is above all heroic. Reading the *Iliad* is not only a 'sun bath' for the spirit and does not only 'transport us to some kind of paradisiacal dawning of the world and mankind', it is first and foremost a beautiful epic, refulgent with heroism. Everyone who has read the *Iliad* will – consciously or not –

have had his conception of heroism affected by the radiance of the shield of Achilles and, possibly even more, by the aureole surrounding the sacrifice of Hector. The *Iliad* elevates us above ourselves and that is why idealists by nature will always prefer the *Iliad* to the *Odyssey* – the epic of heroes to the adventures of *andros polytropou*,[14] the heroism of shrewdness. Sinko is mistaken if he says that the young love the *Odyssey*, and their elders the *Iliad*.

Speaking subjectively, I may say that in my own case I read Homer for the first time when I was 15 and my immediate impression of the *Iliad* was like a thunderbolt, only to be compared with the impact I experienced three years later in Florence at the sight of Michelangelo's *David*. But of the *Odyssey* I remember nothing![15]

I do not in the least believe, by the way, that age changes one's attitude to works of art. Equally, I do not believe that a work of art that makes a great impression on one in youth will pall as one grows up. In the same way, youthful ideals do not pall. They develop and mature with the individual. He who vows allegiance to them in youth will always try to realise them, even if only in part, but he who, when young, swears fidelity to nothing and nobody does not suddenly later discover ideals for life, because he has none. One who is born blind does not become sighted with age.

Returning to the *Iliad*, it has surely been noticed that on the thresholds of Greek culture and Italian culture stand two epics that are the highest peaks of their respective cultures – the *Iliad* and the *Divine Comedy*. Like every masterpiece, these two epics not only mark the beginning of a new phase of mankind's development, but also the close of the preceding phase. The dispute about whether the *Iliad* belongs still to Mycenaean culture, or is already part of Greek culture, is just as fruitless as the dispute about whether Dante is the greatest poet of the Middle Ages or the Renaissance. The boundary posts, seen from far away, belong to both sides.

What is striking about this comparison is that neither in the *Iliad* nor the *Divine Comedy* – at least for the layman – are there signs of the previous culture starting to wither or of immaturity in the successor. The genius of Greece and that of Italy are born in these works already fully armoured with the Divine Spirit, as did Minerva spring from the brain of Jupiter.

Events taking place around me in the prison on Łącki Street are only indirectly reflected in these notes, which were never intended as a diary, but rather just as a soliloquy on matters of importance. Besides, I was counting on the cell being searched at any moment, as indeed happened once. However, the search was remarkably brief because the first thing the SS man came across was the Greek dictionary. He took one look, gazed in awe, then stopped the search and left.

Despite my apparent complete isolation, I did have some contact with the 'world' – that is, the prison – when I was led once a week to the showers. The very first time I went, a wardress from my former department was sent to fetch me. She told me that the so-called *Himmelfahrtkommando* had been at work once more. This time, the historian and archivist Helena Polaczkówna and her loyal maid had gone with a number of others, among them Zofia Kruszyńska, a close relative of the university Rector Władysław Abraham.

The man in charge of the showers (that is to say, controlling the flow of hot water) was a Ukrainian, an engineer from Kiev, with whom I managed to strike up a longish weekly conversation, thanks to the wardress as a rule 'forgetting' to take me straight back to my cell. The engineer's name was Tymon. He was young, sprightly and had a remarkable thirst for knowledge. Someone had told him that I was a scholar, so he behaved very nicely towards me, a little as though I were someone in possession of treasures, who wouldn't begrudge a share to anyone else. He confessed to looking forward all week to our conversation, from which there was always something new to be learned. So I would tell him during these twenty-minute sessions something about a subject that interested him and, in return, he would pass on to me scraps of political news that he picked up from the most recently arrested prisoners. He said it would take a long time yet, but not for an instant did he doubt that Germany was heading for catastrophe. Obviously, we did not discuss 'What then?' Instead we talked – or rather I told him – about what I was reading at the time. He listened as though to the Gospel and thanked me like a child. Sometimes, when it was hard going, we didn't have time for a chat, because the engineer had to tell me what had been happening during the week. I could see clearly that talking in this way helped him to relax and calm down. He spoke like a man who had something vile to spit out.

There had been another execution, Tymon said. Usually, if there had been an execution, he knew how many had 'gone to the sands'. Often he even knew who they were, especially if it was someone well dressed. All the suits taken off the dead were brought to him in the bath-house for 'disinfection'. There the SS men shared them out among themselves. A really stylish suit would not get as far as the bath-house because the SS men pounced on such items at once. There were often men's or women's fur coats – mainly those of Jews, in which they found gold or dollars sewn into the lining. That led to regular battles between the executioners. As more and more articles became available, the greater grew their lust for loot. In this connection, I was increasingly troubled by fear when I said the Lord's Prayer. My problem was the phrase '. . . as we forgive those who trespass against us'. To forgive what was happening around me was a sheer impossibility. I was not at all concerned with my own case – but with the suffering of thousands! I could not lie to God. Finally, after agonising for ages and biting myself terribly in the process, I cut those words out of the Lord's Prayer and recited my mutilated version till the end of the war. After I was freed from prison, I told a priest about this. He replied: 'A lot of people did the same.'

Things were getting steadily worse; that much I knew very well, even in my cell. If the authorities did not succeed in cutting me off from all contact with the rest of the prison, still less could they deprive me of my hearing. There were times, though, when I cursed my own ears. In total, absolute isolation, unable to help anyone in any way, it is not easy to listen for hours to the sound of others being tortured. I am not talking about the groans, which in any prison penetrate surrounding cells – that is part of prison life. In the Łącki Street prison that autumn, other things were still going on. That was when the Lwów ghetto, and Jews all over Poland, were being liquidated. I heard from Tymon that masses of people were being murdered in the city. One day, a commotion began in the courtyard paved with the headstones from Jewish graves. Large groups of Jews had been rounded up. To judge by the shuffle of feet (for I could not reach the window high up in the wall of my cell to see out), there must have been several hundred of them. The screaming of SS men, the sound of blows struck with rifle butts, and the groans of the victims at times drowned out even the shuffle of their feet. Occasionally a shot was fired. Later I learned from Tymon that it was from Pelz (one of the senior SS men), whose simple method this was of ridding the ranks of the old and sick, who could not

Karol Lanckoroński with his daughter, Karolina, *c.* 1900

The Lanckoroński family *c.* 1901 (Karol, his wife Małgorzata and their children, Antoni and Karolina)

Adelajda and Karolina Lanckorońśki, *c.* 1910

Małgorzata Eleonora (née Lichnowsky), wife of Karol Lanckoroński

Karol Lanckoroński with his son Antoni, *c.* 1915

Palace in Rozdół, before 1939

Karolina Lanckorońska in Rozdół, 1938

Dr K. Lanckorońska

Lanckoroński Palace in Chłopy
near Komarno, before 1939

Karolina Lanckorońska's concentration camp number in Ravensbrück

Carl Burckhardt, President of the International Red Cross, in Geneva

Karolina Lanckorońska in Italy, 1945

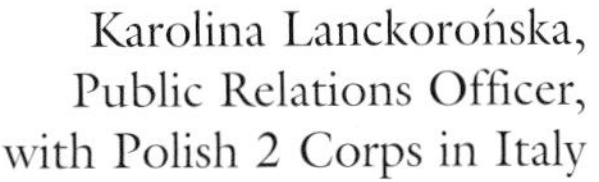

Karolina Lanckorońska, Public Relations Officer, with Polish 2 Corps in Italy

Karolina Lanckorońska in Rome, 1946.
(*Inset*) Officer's stars on Karolina Lanckorońska's uniform

Academic Reunion in Rome, 31 July 1947

Karolina Lanckorońska in Geneva, January 1947

Lieutenant Karolina Lanckorońska,
7 February 1948

Karolina Lanckorońska, lecturer

Karolina Lanckorońska with her brother Antoni in Venice, September 1954

be forced to march. As they were leaving the courtyard (I don't know whether in twos or fours) they were systematically beaten to march in step. In time, I could clearly distinguish between the dry thwack of a rifle butt to the head and the dull thud of blows landing on cloth-covered arms, backs and shoulders.

Sometimes the Jews were loaded into lorries. Once, when they were collecting women and children as well, I remember the very shrill voice of one woman. She was repeating the same sentence over and over again: '*Ich bin keine Jüdin. Bitte telephonieren Sie Pełczyńska – Zentrale Zimmer* [here she gave the number of the room and the Commissar in charge], *sonst wird es zu spät, das ist ein Missverständnis! Ich bin keine Jüdin!*'[16] The more they tried to silence her, the louder her despairing descant – the same words over and over again in broken German, about which there was nothing Jewish. Meanwhile, many more people were loaded and beaten, but that voice went on calling more and more loudly, till at last the engines roared into life. The lorries moved away, but that dreadfully high-pitched voice could still be heard: '*Bitte telephonieren!*' The lorries drove off. The courtyard was deserted, calmness reigned – till the next time.

The conversations of SS men in the courtyard outside often came through to me. I remember one night I heard them saying: 'Let's drop in on the Jew-girls. Smarten them up a bit.' They went away. I listened out because I knew that the Jewish women's collective cell was below me and the floor was very thin. After a short while, shrieks and wails from the women and children could be heard, laughter and wild bellowing from the SS. It went on till daybreak.

With the day, light returned and, with it, books and notepads.

20 IX, Sunday (my nineteenth in prison)

What, in ill thoughts again? Men must endure
Their going hence, even as their coming hither:
Ripeness is all.[17]

(Edgar in *King Lear*, V.ii)

Anyway, *supremum nec metuas diem nec optes* – death must always be present with us, so that we may despise life when higher values are at stake, but also, so that we may love this life, which we may lose at any moment, but which enables us to serve our ideals and bear witness to others. The timing of life's end is in itself a matter of no consequence. I myself not long ago experienced this proximity of death, which I do not fear, but I love life even more intensely than I did a couple of months ago.

Of all the wonders that I yet have heard
It seems to me most strange that men should fear
Seeing that death, a necessary end
Will come when it will come

says Caesar to his wife Calpurnia in Act II of Shakespeare's *Julius Caesar.*

24 IX: A fortnight ago, at my request, I was sent Shakespeare. That for me has been the most significant event of recent times. My life in prison has been totally transformed. I have read Shakespeare before and read a lot, but in my present circumstances the mind's apperception is weaker, so I did not gain as much from it as I ought to have done, whereas my sensitivity to an artistic masterpiece has decidedly increased. I have read and am reading. I note down extracts and re-read, but it is as though I had never before heard of Shakespeare. I cannot compose myself.

The whole world is probably created so as to enable genius to interact with creation. Nothing counts but the genius and his work – all else is *pulvis et umbra*,[18] unless it is of service to genius. Anyone who wants to be an educator of the people must try to gain access to the works of genius because only he who knows such works, if only in part, can know what life is really all about!

Shakespeare was born in the year that Michelangelo died. The date is, as it were, a symbol, a boundary stone. This coincidence bears eloquent testimony to the fact that, after this date, Italy no longer retains her intellectual hegemony over Europe, that the fine arts cease to be the major expression of the epoch, and that the new era stops aspiring to classicism, that is, to the triumph over nature of idealisation and sublimation. Shakespeare creates portraits of individual souls and knows that all the ills of mankind, and his destiny in general, derive from the newly discovered *ananke* or *moira*[19] – not from external causes, as in Sophocles, but only from within man himself, surging relentlessly up from the depths of his still unexplored inner being. Rembrandt's portraits are a further stage of this development.

9 X: Five days since I've written anything. I haven't had time!!! I started to write preparatory notes for a monograph on Michelangelo, thinking I might at most manage to put together an introduction. Meanwhile, however, I find that somehow or other I am really writing! What was quite beyond me during those seven months that Bolshevism frittered away my time, even though I then still had my beloved academic 'workshop', has now somehow become possible and practicable, here in my cell, without a single book or reproduction! Obviously, if I have to remain locked up here for very much longer, I will not be able to write the entire monograph. That would be a physical impossibility. But, here in the cell, I could certainly write what will be almost the most important part of the work, that which deals with Michelangelo's general significance. The foreword or introduction – a survey of the Renaissance and a chapter on the patronage of the Magnifico – I have already completed.

All the same, I sincerely hope that I do not have to stay here long enough to finish my edifice, dome and all, *sed non sicut ego volo*[20] . . . Whatever happens, I am immeasurably grateful to be able to write and prepare some intellectual nourishment for those to whom I am at present unable to offer anything in the way of physical sustenance.

> Truly: *Nor stony tower, nor walls of beaten brass,*
> *Nor airless dungeon, nor strong links of iron*
> *Can be retentive to the strength of spirit.*[21]

18 X: Yesterday I received Thucydides and, for the first time in my life, I have read in its entirety the speech of Pericles in honour of the dead in battle! On the one hand, I am ashamed of having lived 44 years and having waited to find myself in prison before reading this great speech; on the other hand, however – and this second consideration predominates – what a wonderful life it is that can bestow

> such a treasure even on a person in my present circumstances.

Around this time, certain changes occurred in me. My health, so far cast-iron, began to falter a little. To be precise, I was being kept awake at night by some strange kind of skin irritation.

On top of that, on 28 October, they took me out of the large, bright cell I had been in since 4 August and put me into another cell on the same floor, but one that was very small and very dark. This was how the transfer took place. The door was suddenly flung open by an SS man, who yelled at me to collect my things and instructed the young Jewesses who had just been cleaning the corridor to help me. One of those with regular Syrian features, like the saints in the Ravenna mosaics, picked up my books, glanced at Thucydides and one or two of the Latin authors, and stood as though rooted to the spot. When the SS man went out in the corridor for a few moments, she whispered in my ear: 'What's this? Who are you? That was once my world as well. I am a pupil of Professor Ganszyniec*.'[22] While she was carrying my books to the end of the corridor, they were moistened by the countless tears that fell from her large black eyes. But not a sob escaped her.

A few days later, while she was cleaning, she came to the Judas window of my cell – it was without a pane – and I was able to give her a little food. Soon after that there was another major exodus of Jews from the prison courtyard. The next day more Jewesses were cleaning the corridor, but my classicist was no longer among them.

The new cell was in the same corridor as my old one. This was very important for me, as I knew the SS men and I knew the neighbours – that is, those who could safely be given food to distribute, and who 'lived' where. There were various types among the SS men. Some were Austrians, some ethnic Germans. There was even a student from Lwów Polytechnic, who knew me and was obviously ashamed. The cleaners also included one eccentric, a German who said he was a priest. It was possible to give these persons small packets for the various cells, provided they were given a sizeable portion for themselves. They were usually fairly conscientious about distributing the food. To acknowledge receipt of their parcels, the neighbours would hammer on their walls. A Lwów theatre artiste living above me used to stamp his feet, and people living further away would whisper through their Judas windows as I was on my way to or from the bathroom (always on Thursday), to tell me whether or not they had received the food and how many times. When I was with the Polish wardress, I would often be allowed to pass ready-sliced quarters of onion or a cube of sugar through the Judas windows, provided, of course, there was no SS man on the look-out in the upper corridor.

For a long time one of my most valuable contacts was a ten-year-old girl, Janka, arrested for taking part in a conspiracy. Instead of denying everything, this child continually repeated that she knew, but would not tell, because she was a Pole. She lived with a woman who was a *Volksdeutsch* who, as Janka confided to me in the bathroom, was supposed to spy on her and whom because of this situation I also had to feed. After a few weeks Janka was taken away. On the ground floor there was another 'underground conspirator', an eight-year-old child. However, I could only reach her through an intermediary and then very rarely. She was under special surveillance and, unlike Janka, was never taken for a bath.

Because my permission to receive an unlimited number of food parcels was never revoked, the Germans (who, fortunately, cease to think once a *Befehl* [order] has been given) were never amazed at the continuing phenomenal appetite of this one prisoner, despite her being so hermetically secluded from the world. This minimal possibility of dispensing assistance was, for me, an immense source of strength.

The new cell resulted in a certain worsening of my physical situation. Not only was it very dark – the sky was completely invisible (whereas in the previous cell, I could see Cassiopeia through the grating every evening) – but it was also tiny. I could now only move two paces in one direction, whereas before I could walk about freely. Above all, the cell was remarkably damp. Large pipes of some sort, always wet, passed through this cell, which was unpleasant in November. Worst of all, the lighting was very feeble, so that by afternoon one could read or write only with difficulty. After a few days, my lamp was removed 'by order' and was replaced by a small blue night-light. Two things were now quite clear: that for some time I had been singled out for special interference and that, more than anything, my writing about Michelangelo and all reading would be strictly limited, since my cell was in complete darkness from 3 p.m. The evening hours I whiled away, mainly reciting aloud poems that I managed to dredge from my memory. There was one SS man, a fairly miserable type, who was clearly disturbed by my noisy behaviour in the often deathly silence of the jail. He specially disliked Manzoni's *Cinque maggio*, but above all the *Iliad*. He would then always check that the locks of my cell were in good order to make sure I couldn't slip out. When he was approaching along the corridor, I would lean against the cell door and loudly declaim, for example: '*klythi neu argyrotox*'[23] (*Iliad*, Book 1). That sent him scurrying off to the far end of the corridor.

I often repeated to myself poems by my beloved Emily Brontë. Once, I remember, I was struck by a very curious rippling sound, like the noise of large drops falling from a great height. I couldn't make out in the dark what it could be or where the flow came from until feeling with my hand on the table, I touched a paper bag containing cubes of sugar, sent to me by the Committee earlier that day. The sugar was, in fact, dissolving in the damp atmosphere of the cell and dripping from the table. So I put an earthenware plate under the bag and the next morning enjoyed a very tasty draught of sugary water for breakfast.

In entries for those days in my notebook, I discussed the problem of how to explain to academic youth the meaning of scholarly work; what in the broadest sense is Learning, and what purpose does it serve? Also, on All Souls' Day I wrote the usual notes in memory of the dead: my father and personal friends, lying in the Rakowicki cemetery.

> I have also to remember the graves of those who died in my care – Kozłowski, Bielewicz, Wierzbowski . . . and that grave in the Salvator cemetery, from which to this day there radiates – and will continue to do so – the strength of the Spirit and Faith of the playwright Karol Rostworowski. As ever, his wife Rózia and sons still visit his grave. Shall I ever again go with them?[24]
>
> There are so many these days who mourn their dead on All Souls' Day and have no grave to visit. Friendship does not come to an end with the death of the friend. The true end of friendship would be the loss of the precious standards inherited from one's friend. A friend is still alive, so long as his influence on us or his example survives. Moreover, if we succeed in transmitting those values to others, that friendship will still not perish with our death, but be passed to still more persons, even to peoples . . . We are nothing in ourselves, but we must pass on the torch of Plato . . . then we become the links of a chain that embraces the world. That is true tradition.

1 XI, cd.: Sunday again today – my 25th!!
Quousque?[25] The *Iliad* arrived yesterday.

> 8 XI, Sunday 26.
> Let us hope that *It's darkest before dawn*, but *it's very dark at any rate.*[26]

Meanwhile I learned from the SS man, who came to tell me, that I would no longer be able to take a weekly bath, and that Commissar Kutschmann (with whom I had asked for another interview) had left Lwów in September. From that I deduced that my 'case', – that is, my accusation against Krüger, had failed in Berlin and, as a result, Kutschmann had been posted away and I (at the very least) would be left here to rot indefinitely, or else quietly liquidated, when convenient. In any case, I gave the Polish wardress the original draft of my deposition accusing Krüger, having made sure in advance that she did not understand a word of German. I told her that it was a record of my depositions and I recommended her, in case of my death, to give it to a trustworthy person I knew, who, I was sure, would see that it reached the Home Army Commander. I was constantly haunted by the thought that, despite two clandestine messages that I had managed to smuggle out, the Commander might think – should I die – that I had 'disappeared' as a result of some irresponsible bragging, which the Germans would undoubtedly try to blame for my death.[27]

One day I also received indirectly some news from Stanisławów. While he was handing out some food, the new SS man asked me whether it was not so much better here than in Stanisławów, where he remembered seeing me. I asked him immediately about Mrs Kordyszowa. He was reminded of her by my description, lowered his eyes and said no more. I then asked him about Lucja. 'That pretty young blonde whose parents were also there with her?'

'I – er – there? I don't know . . . I don't remember.'

From that moment, I knew for sure that not one of those people was still alive.

Another day there appeared at my little window, while the SS man was briefly absent, Mrs Eugenia Lange-Kosicka, a former member of the RGO staff, who had been arrested before me and was now working in the prison kitchen. She was obviously very shaken and asked whether I did not know what was going on. I said there had probably been an execution, since I had heard suspicious movements inside the building and in the courtyard. She hurriedly told me that a dozen Ukrainians – all belonging to the intelligentsia – had been executed in reprisal for an anti-German demonstration by a section of the Ukrainian community in Lwów. She added that Andrej Piaseckyj was dead. Then she disappeared. For quite some time I stood by the cell door after she had gone, unable to get over the shock. I had retained a very warm memory of Piaseckyj and our intense exchange of ideas during the short time we were working together as orderlies in the prison health department.[28] Our political conversations about the future stuck in my mind. His blood, shed in the common struggle, will one day surely help bring about a new unity between our peoples!

> 11 XI: Today I am reading and translating the words of Pericles. I suppose, out of the many thousands of Poles who, in 1942, spent Independence Day in prison, I was the only one so privileged as to be able to translate in honour of that day such extracts as (11.37):
>
> '. . . in public affairs, we do not dare flout the laws or refuse to obey those who exercise authority for a certain time, nor do we refuse to be bound by common laws, especially those on which the defence of the wronged depends, but, above all, those moral laws whose transgression brings with it public disgrace.'
>
> Or this, from the second speech (11.61.4):
>
> 'You are citizens of a great Republic brought up in traditions worthy of her. It is therefore your duty to suffer the greatest misfortunes, rather than suffer any slur upon her honour. You must endure your personal misfortunes and marshal all your forces for the protection of the common cause.'

> 12 XI: Today the first snow has fallen. Half a year ago, on 12 May, I was driving early to Kołomyja. Just then, the earth was freshly covered in green. Yesterday evening, I completed my first draft of the principal Sistine cycle.

> 15 XI: Sunday again, my 27th. I feel full of strength and eager to work. *Magnificat!* Today's epistle contains the most important sentence: Plenitudo ergo legis est dilectio[29] *Rom.* 13.10.

> 22 XI: Sunday my 28th! Still waiting and translating Thucydides.

I did not have long to wait after the last note, dated Sunday 22 XI, because on the afternoon of Thursday, 26 November, my little cell window was opened and a strange SS man stuck his head in. After asking for my full name, he said: 'Get everything ready! You'll be leaving for the Reich before noon tomorrow. You can still have a bath early.' The head withdrew, the window shut and silence returned to the prison. I had trouble gathering my thoughts. 'Leaving for the Reich.' What did that mean? It meant that Kutschmann had lost out in Berlin, that he would not be returning here, and that I would be going to a concentration camp – or further still. A lot of people knew me here in Lwów, so perhaps the Germans would prefer to polish me off somewhere in the Reich.

As it was already completely dark, I started to busy myself with the foodstuffs in my latest parcels. I divided them out in portions for my immediate neighbours and the women in the communal cell. The wardress would collect the packets for distribution after the bath, and so on. I managed quite well by the blue night-light. At least there was no danger of being disturbed by anyone at that hour. Suddenly I heard footsteps approaching, the door was opened and on the threshold stood a German in uniform. It was not the usual SS man, but an officer. The silhouette of a man in a cape with a cap on his head stood out sharply against the backdrop of the poorly lit corridor. Behind him, in the corridor outside the cell, the customary SS man was standing stiffly to attention. I stood as though transfixed, greatly disconcerted by my display of food packages and in no doubt that there would now be a full-scale search of the cell before they left. There was a short silence. Then the newcomer spoke, requesting (!) me to step outside the cell. I recognised Commissar Kutschmann. I walked out.

'Now,' he told the SS man, 'take us to a place where there's some light.'

We walked along the corridor to the guards' orderly-room.

'Please lock us in and leave us alone until I knock.' The guard went outside and locked the door. The light hurt my eyes and I was a little stunned. I remember that Kutschmann had to repeat clearly his request that I should sit down, before I complied. Then he himself sat down and removed his cap.

'I was away quite a long time.'

'Yes, I know a certain amount about it.'

'Entirely on your account, and that's something you don't know about.'

'No, that I did not know about,' I replied idiotically.

'Yes, I've been waging the biggest battle of my career – and I think

I've won it. We've not got much time and there's a lot to tell. I'll begin with the most important thing. *Krüger ist gestürzt*,[30] together with his like-minded confederate [Gesinnungsgenosse] Stawitzky, my superior here, who dropped in while you were reading me your report.'

'Who read it in Berlin?' I asked.

'The Führer. All hell broke loose. Himmler was mad with rage. You would have been shot immediately, if you hadn't had the Italian royal family behind you.'

'Did Krüger try to get back at me by taking revenge on the Poles in Stanisławów?'

'He didn't have time to. He is in Berlin. So is Himmler's judge, brought in from High Command Headquarters, Sturmbannführer Hertl [or Hertel] who is waiting there for the principal witness in the case – that is, yourself. It's highly likely that you will be interrogated by Himmler himself. For months now they've been wrangling over a matter of principle – whether it's permissible at all in this case to interrogate a Polish woman as a witness. Some voted in favour, others opted for your execution. The first lot won. Krüger steadfastly denies that he told you about the murder of the professors [*von der Lemberger Blutnacht*].[31] Well, I've done my bit. I leave the rest to you. A great responsibility towards your nation now rests with you. That's why I have come here. Please, if possible, don't talk about that. *Ich musste Ihnen das notwendige Rückgrat geben*.[32] If you gain the confidence of the judges, an order will be given banning the killing of Aryans in Galicia, without the knowledge of Berlin. That would be a great thing in itself, though it can't last very much longer, for the war is lost.'

I gave a start of surprise.

'You don't know anything about it, I suppose? I'll tell you in a nutshell. The Americans are in Africa. Rommel, who was at the gates of Alexandria, has been defeated. The situation is clear. As for you, I believe that you will be able to convince the judges of the truth of your depositions and we shall win. However, it is not absolutely certain. So far as I am concerned, it came out in the course of all this that I refused to shoot when I was ordered to fire on the professors. At the very least, I could be sent to a concentration camp, but I don't think it will come to that. I shall be posted away from Lwów. After what I have done, I cannot stay here.'

'Will you be staying in Poland, I mean –' I corrected myself with a smile, 'in the General Government?'

'I hope to stay in Poland, though I fully realise that, when the end comes, I'll be hanged on the first Polish lamp-post available, *für alle*

Schandtaten[33] that we have committed here. At the same time I might still be able to help in some way. But we must agree on one or two things. What will you say if the judges ask you why I have treated you in this way?'

'I can only say that I think that you were concerned about the honour of Germany.'

'The one and only reason,' he replied. 'However,' he went on, 'I still don't know what your situation will be. Probably you won't be sent to a concentration camp. You might get *Ehrenhaft*.'[34]

'What's that?'

'Free to live at home and, for example, to move about in Berlin, on your word of honour not to go outside the city.'

'A nightmare,' I thought to myself, but I tried to explain to him that what happened to me personally, given what was at stake, was of no importance.

'Don't talk like that. You were within an ace of death.'

'I know perfectly well that I could be shot just as easily in Berlin.'

'I don't think that will happen,' he replied after a pause.

'But if it does,' I retorted, '– all said and done, *dulce et decorum est pro patria mori . . .*'

'Not sweet,' he snapped, 'and still less becoming – just common murder!'

Next, he asked me to tell them in Berlin that my treatment in Lwów had been gradually getting worse, because that was happening contrary to Himmler's orders and due to influence from Stanisławów. Finally, he stood up.

'I must go. Can I do anything for you?'

'You could indeed. I have written here in my cell part of the book I have been planning about Michelangelo. I have also got some other academic notes. Should I survive the war, they may be useful to me. If I could hand them over tomorrow before I leave, to the Prison Command, addressed to you, would you be very kind and send these notebooks, after being seen by the censor, to our Polish RGO Committee as my property? But the censor will need to be a cultured man, otherwise he'll think the Greek texts are in code.'

'Give me the notebooks, please.'

'They're in the cell.'

He stood up, walked to the door and banged. The guard opened it and we went into my cell. I gave Kutschmann the notebooks.

'There's nothing in these except academic notes?' he asked. I said that was so, which was the truth. 'In that case, I will take them. They will be sent to the Committee in the morning.[35] Anything else?'

'I would just like to thank you.'

He answered tersely that there was nothing to thank him for.

I replied that he had given me something of great importance, which is given to us very seldom – to be precise, an opportunity to respect the foe. He bowed his head and was silent for a moment. Finally, out in the corridor, he stood in front of me, straightened up and declared: 'Please accept my best wishes for you in person and –' he said slowly and deliberately, 'for your people. *Glauben Sie mir, mit diesem letzten Wunsch ist es mir sehr ernst.*'[36]

'Please accept my best wishes for your person as well,' I replied. He went away and I returned to my cell. After a while, when I had gathered my wits, I experienced a feeling of tremendous happiness. I began to recite the *Magnificat* for everything I had received in my life, as I had done daily since the time of my arrest:

My soul magnifies the Lord
Because He has wrought for me His wonders,
Has created me,
Has given me this most beautiful life,
Has put upon me this terrible torment,
Yet has given my soul the strength to bear it . . .

But from that evening onwards, I added a new phrase:

And because He has deigned to make use of me
As the instrument of His justice . . .

I felt as though I were the instrument of some Higher Will, since almost without any effort on my part, I had become the avenger of my university. The awareness that my arrest had helped bring about the liberation of my ancestral territories from at least one murderer became from that moment on a giant source of strength. Throughout the long spell of captivity that lay ahead of me, I was, as a result of this, once again privileged compared with so many others, for the presentiment never left me that the enemy was going to pay a disproportionately high price for me.

But that last night in Lwów something of more immediate importance was keeping me awake. Before leaving Poland, I must somehow let my commanding officer know who it was that had murdered our Lwów professors, as well as why I was being sent to Germany. There was a certain hint of egoism in my concern. Despite my innate optimism, I could by no means rule out the possibility of sudden death, so I wanted to say goodbye and I wanted the Commander to know that I was selling my life dearly – that I had not let myself be quietly done away with for some ill-considered anti-German demonstration. In the morning then, before it was light, I set about encrypting in Sinko's work on Greek literature, using an old cipher, a short message for the Commander. The job was made more difficult by constant interruptions. Whereas for the past few months I might have been sitting in a tomb, it had to be just this day, when peace was so vital, that people kept calling in on me with instructions on how to prepare for the journey, to take me to the doctor, to the bathroom, and so on. The message, in consequence, turned out to be necessarily a very short one, but I had finished encrypting by the time the wardress arrived to conduct me to the showers – the same Polish woman who had already successfully smuggled out for me two messages to the Commander. She threw her arms around me and bade me an emotional farewell. I gave her the books to return, as well as the food for the women prisoners; and, last of all, looking her very steadily in the eye, I handed her the *Greek Literature*, asking her to see that it was sent to Kraków, addressed to Wisia Horodyska. I repeated the request twice, very emphatically. I could see by the expression on her face that she understood this was not simply a personal matter. This was the first message that failed to get through.

After my bath I was informed that, in the presence of the prison Governor, I would be able to say goodbye to my colleagues of the RGO Committee in Lwów, for it so happened that this was 'soup day'. The two ladies (one of them was Lesia Dąmbska) were both dreadfully worried, or rather terrified, being convinced – as were the wardress and the doctor – that this journey to Berlin was final. As for me, I knew intellectually that things might not go well for me, but I had no presentiment of disaster and, in any case, I had no time to brood. At about 11 a.m. I was led out of the prison into Leon Sapieha Street and told to get into a waiting private car, where I found myself between two Gestapo men. Next to the driver was seated a young German woman. The car drove off. It was a lovely winter's day, with a light snowfall glinting in the sunlight. On our way I caught sight of Professor Franciszek Bujak, in a large fur cap, in the process of crossing Gródecka Street. I drew back my head, not wanting to be recognised by a man to whom the sight of me, in present company, would be acutely painful. At the same time I was glad, at the moment of my departure from Lwów, to have seen the pride of our university, the leading light of my department and a man who had invariably treated me with exceptional kindness.

We arrived at the station and got out of the car. One of the Gestapo men waited with me near the entrance, while the other went ahead to deal with formalities. I took a last look at Lwów. Peering up at the station façade, I noticed that although the metal letters had been removed, traces of the inscription were still easily legible: *Leopolis semper fidelis.*[37]

We went in, the Gestapo men carrying my luggage. We took our seats in a third-class compartment reserved for us. Once the train started moving, I gazed out with deep emotion at this landscape so dear to me, and which I had last seen in summer, just before the harvest. Now the fields, long since stripped bare, were covered by a thin layer of snow. As we passed through Przemyśl I was reminded of how once, two and half years earlier, I had escaped from there, pursued by the Bolsheviks. Now the Germans were transporting me from the land of my fathers. But now I was going with a concrete objective in mind. For me, that made it less hard to bear.

As dusk had already descended, I began to review in my memory the events of the period that for me was drawing to a close that day. I came to the conclusion that my four-and-a-half-month stint in the Łącki Street prison, Lwów, had been time decidedly well spent. Having narrowly escaped 'the grave-digger's spade' as we say, in Stanisławów, I had regained my physical strength. I had been able to renew and remain in contact with the great, eternal values, while being immensely privileged in comparison with so many thousands of Polish prisoners, who were starving to death or perishing in hopeless, idle solitude or amid the hubbub and squabbles of the communal cells. I had been receiving more food than I needed, and intellectual nourishment in still greater quantities: Homer, Shakespeare, Thucydides . . . I had even been able to write about Michelangelo.

Furthermore, my present deportation was being carried out under unusually favourable conditions. For very many people, the journey from homeland to prisons or concentration camps in Germany was the beginning of the end, particularly from the psychological point of view. On the other hand, I had a strictly defined task and, above all, my role for the time being did not have to be passive (the most difficult thing of all), but active. I knew that, as soon as this journey was over, the

STRUGGLE was waiting to be resumed. Awareness of that was enough to give anyone renewed strength.

We reached Kraków at two o'clock in the morning. I was thinking earnestly of friends and companions in arms, sound asleep at this time, little knowing that I was passing so close at hand.

The Gestapo men behaved decently. The function of the German female official who was with us was to make sure that I was never left alone at any time. They took it in turns to sleep at night. Clearly, they feared I might attempt to commit suicide, as sometimes happened with deportees. However, I was a very long way from being in that frame of mind. They were able to sleep soundly. Around six in the morning – at dawn – I asked the Gestapo man on duty where we were.

'We'll shortly be in Bytom,' he told me.

'That's the frontier of the Republic,' I thought. We must have crossed the border with the so-called General Government a long way back. We were now approaching the frontier of pre-war Poland. I got up and went into the corridor. I stood with my back to the window of our compartment, knowing they would not follow me out, but would leave me in peace for a moment. So, standing to attention, I crossed the Polish frontier, telling myself that I had no idea whether I would ever again see my homeland.

'I am going abroad now in your service, Poland, and I am leaving only under enemy pressure. But you, Poland – in a year, or possibly eighteen months from now – you will be free!'

I would not have stood up so proudly had I known then that I would indeed escape with my life, but as a fugitive without a homeland. At the time, I could not have conceived of anything so monstrous. So I stood and bade farewell to Poland as we rolled into Bytom. Suddenly, I felt absolutely alone. Ahead of me stretched the huge and hostile Reich.

The day was 28 November 1942.

Chapter 6

Berlin

29 November 1942–9 January 1943

I returned to the compartment, went to sleep and did not wake up until we were on the outskirts of Wrocław.[1] I kept a sharp look-out for any signs of obvious bomb damage, but there was almost nothing to be seen. We were in Berlin by afternoon. During the journey my minders had been discussing at length where they were supposed to be taking me. All they had with them was a telegraphed instruction to get me to Berlin immediately, and nothing more. We therefore made a round of various Gestapo centres and prisons by taxi. One of the latter looked very modern, and I was curious to see the inside of a Berlin prison. It was bound to be organised American-style. But once again we were refused entry because they did not accept women.

At last, in an office of some sort, following long and difficult exchanges by telephone, we discovered that there remained only a prison on the Alexanderplatz, to which they drove me with obvious reluctance. So it came about that, after extensive wandering, we finished up on the fifth floor of an immense and indescribably filthy nineteenth-century building with the look of a Roman fortress. They locked me up in a very narrow cell. The dilapidated, peeling walls and ceiling were covered with badly stained, dark-grey varnish. It was evening. I was tired. I threw myself down on the bunk and fell asleep at once.

I awoke to a grey, wintry, urban sky, which looked strangely dirty as seen through the bars of a high-set but fairly large window. I got up and wanted to wash, but at once encountered serious problems. On an ancient stool was poised a washbowl with traces of enamel still visible, but even smaller than the kind we used in Komarno or Rozdół at nursery school. While I was still standing and thinking about it, the door opened to admit a wardress with 'coffee'. From her I learned that she was to be addressed as 'Frau Wachtmeisterin'.[2] She was quite young and not bad-looking. The thought occurred to me that even a German might not like being married to a woman with such a title. The door closed again. Another Sunday in prison had begun, but this time without any books. I was not yet missing them greatly, since I still had so many recent experiences to sort out in my mind. The Gestapo man who had brought me from Lwów had told me that he would come to fetch me on Monday. I would need to prepare for a new battle.

My thoughts went back to that evening visit and the man who, so he said, had refused to fire on those professors, risking his own life to defeat his degenerate opponent; the man who had warmly wished my nation well, yet who could not bring himself to take the final step and tear the death's-head badge off his cap, but continued to wear a uniform that he knew perfectly well to be disgraced. What kind of a nation was that in which an undoubtedly honourable and, to a certain extent, courageous man fails to draw the logical conclusion and himself underwrites the very *Schandtaten*[3] he has been condemning? Will such a nation ever be able to raise itself from the depths of such a moral abyss?

In the afternoon I was visited by the Frau *Vorsteherin*,[4] in charge of all the *Wachtmeisterinnen*, an older, pre-war German woman, tall, thin, with grey hair pulled tightly back and a very proper manner of addressing prisoners. She explained to me that I had a right to electric light in the evening, as well as to make other requests. I asked for a larger washbowl. She looked at me, then at her second-in-command who was standing behind her, then turned to me once more.

'A larger washbowl?' she repeated, greatly astonished. 'No, we haven't got such a thing! What do you want it for?'

'It's just that I am a grown-up and, where I come from, bowls like that are for children aged six at most.'

'*Merkwürdig*!'[5] And out she went.

They did not give us very much food, but more than in Stanisławów. I knew that I would be hungry here, but at least I would not die of starvation. On Monday, 30 November, my Gestapo minder arrived.

We went outside and caught a tram. I was again struck, as in pre-war days, by the ugliness of the inhabitants, particularly the women. I noticed, too, that damage to the city was very slight, and it hurt me to think of Warsaw and what, at the time, I regarded as appalling destruction. Once again we wandered about, visiting two or three places, before at last arriving at a modern apartment block where, on the door of an upstairs apartment, we saw a black sign with the hideous emblem of the SS and the title '*Der Richter beim Reichsführer SS*'.[6] A clock on the wall of the anteroom said ten. I was led in at once. My minder stood outside.

I found myself in a large office. Standing in front of me was a tall man in uniform, with black hair and black eyes, no older than thirty-two or thirty-three at most. My minder had told me earlier that I was going to be questioned by Sturmbannführer (Major) Hertl. Further away, by the window, stood a second tall, lean, fair-haired man in plain clothes. Hertl, pronouncing my name fairly correctly, asked about my identity. He ordered me to sit at a big table opposite the window, so that the light fell directly on me. He himself sat at a desk on the left, with the side of his face to the window, and the lean, fair-haired man took a seat opposite him.

Hertl showed me one of the copies of my report and asked whether I admitted being the author of the document and having signed it. Next, he asked: 'Why did you write this?'

'Because Commissar Kutschmann asked me to write what I had told him.'

'What kind of impression did Commissar Kutschmann make on you?'

'*Einen richterlichen Eindruck*.'[7]

From then on, I think, Hertl no longer suspected that Kutschmann and I were in collusion.

'But why did you write it? Was it to teach the Germans a lesson?'

'Such a thought couldn't possibly enter the mind of a Polish woman living in the General Government, given the way we are treated. I wanted to save myself. I thought Commissar Kutschmann would let me go, if he knew what I had been arrested for and how I had been treated. The way Hauptsturmführer Krüger put his questions to me, I had no way out, without compromising my honour.'

'Obviously, you could answer in no other way.'

Hertl's tone was matter-of-fact, but sharp, and the speed of the interrogation abnormally swift. I suppose the judge wanted to make sure that my answers did not diverge significantly from the substance of my report. I therefore did my best when replying to use the same words and phrases as in my written report, hoping this automatic consistency would inspire his confidence. The lean, fair-haired man was completely silent throughout, but his eyes never left my face. The following facts emerged from the interrogation:

1 That Hertl had been in Stanisławów (he made me describe Krüger's office).
2 That he had questioned a whole series of Gestapo men, who bore out my account.
3 That Krüger absolutely denied the fact that he told me about the murder of the professors.

Here one could clearly sense that Berlin's principal charge against Krüger was precisely that he had *told* me about this affair, and not that he had *murdered* the professors.

Hertl kept harking back to this last point, repeating that Krüger and his secretary both insisted that I was never alone with him, that the secretary was always present and had never heard anything of the sort. I, for my part, continued to insist that during the second interrogation we were alone together. Hertl said a few times that Krüger simply could not have said any such thing, then added as though talking to himself: 'Yes, but of course, how could you have known about all this, if he himself hadn't told you?'

'That is a question I cannot answer,' I said.

Finally I replied slowly and very emphatically, fully aware that I was changing the tenor and tempo of the hearing, from the hitherto quick and quiet interrogation: 'I solemnly declare, instead of swearing on oath, that it was so.'

I looked Hertl straight in the eye while the two Gestapo men stared at me fixedly. There was a short silence broken by Hertl, who declared the interrogation at an end. He told me to go and wait in the anteroom while he wrote his report. I left the office. The minder, who had been waiting, told me that the hearing had lasted an hour and twenty minutes. After quite a while I was readmitted and Hertl read me his brief and factual report, which was faithful to the substance of my answers. The report ended with the sentence: 'I am ready at any time to repeat the above statement on oath.'

Later, I often reflected on the fact that Himmler's judge, for whom crime was the normal, everyday fulfilment of a professional obligation, was nevertheless still aware that, for a moral person, an oath makes a difference. I made one or two minor corrections, which he embodied in the report. I signed it and he then declared: 'In view of your depositions, I must put Krüger on trial. You will please prepare yourself for a confrontation.'

'It may well be unpleasant, but I have never yet said anything about anybody that I was not prepared to repeat to his face.'

'I have no doubt whatever about that. As for yourself,' he added in a different tone of voice, avoiding my gaze for the first time, 'a decision has still to be taken on your fate, after investigation of your own case.'

We left the building, caught the tram once again and returned to the Alexanderplatz. This time, in the afternoon light, the prison building, stairs and corridors seemed even more hideous, dilapidated and dirty than they had on the evening of my arrival.

When the door of the cell was again locked, I sat on my 'bed' and attempted to order my thoughts. I was basically satisfied with this first stage of my new campaign. It was my impression that Hertl believed me – and that was the most important thing.

The confrontation with Krüger would probably mark the second phase. I therefore started to prepare myself for it by working out some of my answers. I also thought about that other hearing of my own case, which Hertl had mentioned. I was anxious to know how long I would have to wait. The prospect of *Ehrenhaft* (parole), which Kutschmann had mentioned as the most likely decision in my case, was beginning to terrify me. To be treated by the enemy with a certain amount of consideration, to be ostensibly at liberty living among Germans, yet bound towards them by a word of honour, the significance of which did not depend on the person to whom it was given, but solely and entirely on the giver – all of that seemed to me to amount to an almost atrocious situation. On the other hand, I told myself, Hertl himself had told me that my personal fate had yet to be decided. It was clear that everything would depend on the outcome of Krüger's trial. It seemed to me, moreover, that if it came to a confrontation, if the Germans were prepared to go so far as to order a Polish woman to testify against a Gestapo officer in his presence, then it followed that they would absolutely have to get rid of that Polish woman. In any case, I had counted on that from the beginning. Besides, it seemed to me that if I was really to be interrogated by Himmler himself – as Kutschmann had thought very likely – then what lay in store for me was 'the sands'; this time, the sands of Berlin. In which case, there was no point in my agonising about 'parole'.

I started to take a good look at my cell. In several places the dark-grey varnish was marked with inscriptions – mostly just initials, but often full names and occasional phrases. Beside the bed just over my head I could easily read what was written in German: 'Eva, my child, you are nine years old, who will tell you the whole truth some day? Try to grow up the way I hoped', followed by initials and the date in 1942. A little further on, in minuscule French handwriting, the classic words of Chénier's *La Jeune Captive*: '*Je n'ai que* 18 ans . . .',[8] unsigned. How many women had passed this way already, and who were my present neighbours? They could be heard occasionally, even through the fairly stout walls of my cell.

An answer to the last question was no time in coming. One day, I heard a strange rustling noise under the door and saw a folded sheet of white paper being pushed in. '*Schnell, das ist für Sie . . .*'[9] It was the voice of Liesl, our cleaner, who also brought round bread – a young girl arrested on a criminal charge. I snatched the paper and found it was a letter addressed to my cell number. My neighbour on the left, introducing herself as a Berlin actress, provided me at the same time with the key to a code for tapping out letters of the alphabet. I made use of it at once and a conversation developed. To my question: '*Wofür sitzen Sie?*'[10] I received a clear enough answer: '*Kontakte mit Russland, meine Freundin schon geköpft.*'[11] Later I learned from her how to clamber up the wall to reach the window while the *Wachtmeisterin* was away at lunch. Through the open part at the top of the window it was possible to chat almost normally with the neighbours on either side: the actress on the left, the librarian on the right. They were involved in the same affair, in connection with which, at the time, fifteen high-ranking officers had been removed from High Command Headquarters. (It really cannot last much longer, I thought to myself as I listened to all this.)

I found it very interesting to exchange ideas with people who regarded their activity as a moral duty. It was the first time I had come across this way of resolving the problem that must be facing every German not totally devoid of ethical principles – and I was horrified. Hitlerism had so thoroughly erased from their consciences principles that to us would seem fundamental, that neither of these women could perceive anything wrong in their contacts with the enemy in time of war – something regarded for many thousands of years as a crime, indeed one of the gravest crimes a man can commit. They said that the Hitlerites obviously regarded their behaviour as high treason, but they could utter the term without a qualm, for they saw Russia as being at war with the Nazi regime, not the German people. They were convinced that this selfsame Russia, once Hitler had been overthrown, would bring their Fatherland an era of matchless well-being. The complacency with which both women viewed their own fate aroused my respect, though their reasoning was inexpressibly alien to mine and we often had to break off our discussions due to our inability to find a common language.

The attitude of those who sought an understanding with the enemy was every bit as indefensible as the line chosen by Kutschmann – namely, salvage as much as possible, even at the risk of one's life, but without drawing any final conclusions. I felt very strongly at the time that there really was no way out for a German. That mortal sin which every one of them had committed by permitting the authorities to perpetrate crime, and by succumbing to the tempter telling him that he belonged to a people superior to all others and promising world dominion – that was a sin that nothing could ever cleanse, not even high treason.

Once again, for the hundredth time, I felt intense gratitude to the Creator for the privilege of belonging to a nation which, in the desperate struggle for its own survival, was at the same time safeguarding the highest values of humanity.

The circle of my prison acquaintances was soon to be extended. I was asked whether I wished to see a doctor. Since my skin complaint was growing steadily worse and making it almost impossible for me to sleep, I asked to be examined.

One Thursday afternoon, the *Wachtmeisterin* came in to take me down from the fifth to the ground floor. I was told to go into the waiting room and take my turn. After the quiet that reigned in my part of the prison, suddenly going into a fairly small room, where more than twenty women were crushed together in groups, was like walking into a beehive. The women, of every type and age, were conversing with one another in whispers or low voices, hurriedly and with many interruptions, as they looked every so often at the door of the doctor's consulting room, which opened from time to time. A name would be read out and one of the women would go in. While I was standing there, a very tall, bony woman came up and asked my nationality. When I told her I was a Pole, she replied: 'I am a German, but one of those who are fighting for a united states of Europe.'

'Under the leadership of Russia?' I asked right away, already familiar with that slogan from my 'window' conversations.

'Yes, yes,' she replied enthusiastically. 'Of course, Russia would take us under her protection and we would follow her example.'

'Nice prospect, that!' I thought to myself.

I cut short our exchange because at that moment, from another corner of the room, I caught snatches of a conversation between two women speaking Polish. I therefore said goodbye to the future citizen of the United States of Europe and went across to the Poles. One of them, very young and speaking swiftly in a low voice, seemed to be submitting a report. The other, older woman was listening intently, now and then interrupting with a question.

'Good day,' I said, going up to them. The conversation stopped abruptly and they both looked me over. 'I'm so pleased to hear my own language,' I said and waited for an answer.

'Wait just a moment,' said the elder of the two, 'let me finish with this lady first.' As I waited, I gathered from the conversation, now being resumed much more guardedly, that this was a consultation on how to reply to questions under interrogation. As I moved away a bit so as not to disturb them, the German giantess at once sidled up again to assure me that Poland and Germany would prosper incredibly under Russian auspices.

'Are there a lot of people here who subscribe to that notion?' I asked.

'Not enough yet to put an end to everything that's going on. But there are quite a few Communists in this room,' and she pointed out a couple of groups. 'We were all picked up in connection with the same affair, when they arrested a certain number of officers at High Command Headquarters. Only there weren't enough of them. We're still too weak.'

Suddenly the Polish woman I'd been waiting for came over. She was aged about forty-five, rather short, slim, with a high forehead and curly hair speckled with grey, drawn very smoothly to the rear. A prominent nose and rather thin mouth lent the pale face an intense, energetic expression, and the large, very black eyes were unusually lively.

'Where are you from? Poland? What part? When did you get here?'

I answered the questions, but when she asked my name, I said that names were not necessary in prison.

'On the contrary, especially in prison, you need to know who you are dealing with. Your name, please.' It was said in a rather imperious voice. This unknown person, almost a head shorter than me, commanded so much respect that I obeyed at once. Her face lit up.

'What? Lanckorońska? Oh, what a good thing you told me!' She held out her hand and introduced herself: 'Bortnowska*. We hugged one another. Maria Bortnowska was a very well-known and highly respected member of the Polish Red Cross and a praiseworthy soldier of the AK, about whom I had heard many good things. Up to then we had not been personally acquainted, but we had long been in contact through fellow workers – both overt and covert. We quickly exchanged names and addresses of colleagues who needed to be informed if either one of us was killed or released. Bortnowska then told me that she had undergone numerous excruciating interrogations, but so far the Germans had been unable to find out anything, thanks to her stolid comportment. She asked me always to report sick on Thursdays, since that was the day she and a number of other Polish women, among them the young girl with whom I'd been chatting a little earlier, were in the habit of seeing the doctor.

'Difficult case, that. The girl had been deported to work in Germany. There, acting under orders, she drew a plan of the factory where she was working. She was arrested and the plan was found.'

Suddenly, Bortnowska was called to the doctor.

'Till next Thursday, then.' And she was gone.

I was called a short while later, but Bortnowska had already left. An elderly, experienced doctor dealt with me very decently. He listened carefully to my chest, examined me and pursed his lips.

'If you don't get out of here pretty soon, it'll be just too bad. How long have you been inside?'

'Seven months.'

'It's nerves.'

'I am not a hysterical type.'

'Unfortunately not,' the old man replied. 'If you had been, you would have got rid of the tension some other way. You would not have developed this nervous inflammation of the skin. You don't look as though you cried in your cell.'

'Of course not. What would I have to cry about?'

'I'll give you some medicine to soothe it, but I cannot halt the development of the disease.' He gave me the medicine, and some sort of *Wachtmeisterin* ordered me out. I wanted to return to the waiting room, but instead I was taken out by another door, straight to the stairs and back to my cell.

Meeting Bortnowska meant a great deal to me. I was no longer alone in Berlin. I succeeded in having another two Thursday meetings with her. Each time she looked worse; the interrogations were becoming more intensive, but with every week the strength of her morale seemed to increase. At our last meeting the young girl factory worker I had seen the first time was also present. She was pale, but composed. She had just been given the death sentence. There was still a faint hope (which, however, did not materialise) that despite the sentence she would be sent to Ravensbrück, the women's concentration camp where Krüger was once going to send me. Bortnowska thought that would be the best solution, not only for the girl, but for herself as well. It would mean no more of these interrogations, and being in the company of other Polish women. She knew many who were already there and she imagined, as I did myself, that being in the company of women political prisoners would be an enormous pleasure as well as a great source of strength.

Living among people of different nationality, but bound by similar ideals, would also be pleasant and stimulating. I had no further meetings with Bortnowska because the *Wachtmeisterin* allowed me to see the doctor only on Fridays. I think they must have sensed that I was particularly keen on Thursdays. Apart from that, I was decently treated. When one day Liesl complained to me about the *Wachtmeisterin*, I suspected this might be a provocation and replied that I had no cause for complaint.

'Of course not. They've got special orders regarding you – everybody knows you're a cousin of Mussolini.'[12]

This I denied with horror, with the result that from then onwards Liesl treated me with notably less respect.

Meanwhile, I was given permission to buy newspapers and 'appropriate' books. I ordered *Mein Kampf*[13] and immediately obtained this extremely interesting volume, in which the whole enormous blueprint for crime on an international scale was presented with total clarity. I then understood why any German who – having read that book – supported Hitler must have been completely aware of what he was agreeing to.

One day the cell door opened and the *Wachtmeisterin* announced a visit by the Herr Direktor, an elderly German in civilian clothes, who now stood in the doorway with the Frau *Vorsteherin* behind him. The Director asked me whether I wished to make any requests. Having had no success with my plea for a washbasin, I decided to try another category. I asked for the works of Goethe. After a few moments' silence, the Herr Direktor finally exclaimed: 'Are you not a Polish national!?'

I bridled. 'That is so.'

'Yet you want to read Goethe?'

'I fail to see any connection between one and the other,' I retorted.

The Director shook his head and walked out. The following day the old *Vorsteherin* called in and declared that she would be bringing me Schiller and Goethe, as she possessed the works of both authors. This, however, would take a day or two because the books did smell strongly of mothballs. True enough, two days later she brought the books, to my great delight, though they smelt strongly of the mothballs. I launched myself into the reading right away, but very soon made a most painful discovery. Not only Goethe, whom I never understood very well, but even Schiller, whom I once admired, I now found very difficult to fathom.

It was as though there were some kind of obstacle between them and me. That obstacle was the German language. That same language in which I had formerly received so many cultural treasures had today become for me, as it were, contaminated. The experiences of recent years had dishonoured it. So strongly did I feel this aversion that it was no use trying to persuade myself that only I would suffer by restricting my cultural horizon. I did, of course, read a great deal, but without deriving any real spiritual benefit.

Christmas came, a time of quiet concentration, spent in that special intimacy only obtainable in isolation and untroubled by struggle or conflict.

Almost a month had passed since my interrogation by Hertl and I had heard nothing more. New Year's Eve came and went, concluding the year 1942 – for me so rich in experiences – and heralding the new year of 1943, which must surely bring with it freedom for Poland. Then, on 8 January, the *Wachtmeisterin* came in and ordered me to get ready for the road. The next day I would be one of a batch of prisoners bound for RAVENSBRÜCK.[14]

The next day, 9 January, at 11 a.m. we were lined up four abreast in the broad ground-floor corridor of the prison. There were seventy of us. Police and wardresses ran to and fro, counting, searching and bickering. Something or somebody always seemed to be missing. Finally they started to search for a prisoner who had deposited money with the prison directorate. The name they were shouting was Bankowska. She was nowhere to be found. Suddenly, it flashed through my mind that it might be me, because I had brought with me to the Berlin prison money found on me when I was first arrested. So I raised my hand. The *Wachtmeisterin* reluctantly let me speak. However, she at first greeted with incredulity the suggestion that I might be the one they were searching for. Only after lengthy cogitation did she declare: 'We'll have to telephone to the fifth floor to find out *ob Sie nicht in der Zelle sind.*'[15] Nor did I turn a hair at the unexpected possibility of my having a double. After another fifteen minutes, however, it was established that I was not in my cell and that the money in the prison Director's office had been registered in a name that even bore a slight resemblance to my own. An hour later we finally got under way. Out in the courtyard we were loaded into two prison vehicles – big closed vans with tiny barred slits for air. We were packed like sardines, thirty-five of us to a van. I looked round at some of my companions. They were mainly German women. Oddly enough, their faces did not square with the conception I had of political deportees. They were very excited, chatting away, long and loud. They were discussing the problem of how to avoid being recognised by anyone at the station as they were boarding the train. Should they cover their faces entirely or only partially, and so on. Their dread of recognition intrigued me. When I was being driven through Lwów, I was only too eager to meet anyone who knew me, as a way of letting people know what had happened to me. What were these women afraid of, and why did they look so awful? It must be that they were simply criminals!

Chapter 7

Ravensbrück

9 January 1943–5 April 1945

We were driven to the railway station and there, under police escort, transferred to the prisoner wagons. They packed us three at a time into little boxes designed for one prisoner only. I was travelling with an immense, young Ukrainian girl who, while working in Germany, had developed too 'close' a friendship with one of the sons of the *Herrenvolk*[1] and was therefore being sent to a concentration camp. My other travelling companion was an older German woman, a midwife. After two hours, more or less, the train stopped. The door of our cage was flung open by a policeman, armed to the teeth and roaring: '*Hinaus!*'[2] We clambered out with great difficulty since our legs were numb after being quite unable to move in our box. The main building of this small railway station displayed a sign that said: 'Fürstenberg, Mecklenburg'. I was reminded of Krüger pronouncing those words. On the snowy platform stood two women in field-grey uniforms with the death's-head emblem on their forage caps. Each of them was holding a police-dog on a short leash. They ordered us to form fives and marched us to and fro on the station platform. I gulped down lungfuls of the fresh country air as I looked for the first time at the Mecklenburg landscape – flat and sad.

We carried on marching up and down till the prison van that had collected the first batch of us returned to pick up the rest. It did not take long. A ten-minute drive after boarding the van and we were ordered to get out and again form fives. We were standing in a very large square or courtyard, surrounded by low, wooden barrack-huts painted grey-green. All the huts were identical, apart from the house beside which we had stopped. This, apart from being bigger and higher, was also walled. There were women wandering about on the square, all wearing a uniform costume, as indistinguishable from one another as the buildings we could see in the distance. The women wore jackets with grey or navy-blue stripes and underneath the jackets striped dresses, with copper-coloured headscarves tied under the chin.

The most striking thing about all this at first sight was the sheer, extraordinary ugliness of the surroundings. The disproportion of those colourless hutments was simply hideous. On the far side of the square a street opened up, flanked by double rows of matching huts, stretching into the distance. They were strangely similar to the women's costumes – all the more so, viewed in the early January dusk against the backdrop of dirty snow covering the square. Together they conveyed an impression of combined opposition to anything that might once have been beautiful.

More and more women were appearing. Obviously they were returning from work, marching in groups – usually five abreast. But there were also many who were alone as they crossed the square on their way to the barrack-blocks. Among them were young and old, large and small, some moving swiftly, others painfully dragging their exhausted feet behind them. They all turned to look at us, but none approached. Anyway, the guard with her dog was standing by and not letting anyone through. Now that I could take a closer look at them, I could see that there were in fact certain variations in their costume. It was true that all the jackets had a number sewn on the left breast, but above the number there was also a coloured triangle. The colours varied: green, black or violet, as well as a great many red ones. Over many of the red triangles, a large black letter P could be seen. I was greatly cheered and attracted by the sight of these, my sisters. One of the Polish women, a young fair-haired girl, passing close to us, asked quickly: 'Any Poles?'

'There are,' I replied.

'Stick it out, it's not all that bad being here!' she said and walked on. It's not bad at all, I thought to myself, if the morale is that good. Presently another girl, petite and with a cheery manner, decided to pay me a visit, having heard my first words in Polish.

'If you've brought any food with you, you'd best eat it all up at once, or they'll take it away from you!'

'How long have you been here?' I asked.

'Three years,' came the answer and she walked away laughing.

Dusk had fallen by the time the first five of us entered our hut. The hope that we would not have to wait too long for our own turn helped to warm us, but meanwhile we were frozen to the marrow. Our names were being called out. Two or three fives ahead of me were two Ukrainian women, one of whom was called Agrippina and the other Claudia. A long way those names had travelled, I reflected, from imperial Rome to Constantinople, thence via the 'Greek' Church to the Ukraine, now to be shouted aloud at Ravensbrück, Fürstenberg, Mecklenburg. At last, they got round to me. I was admitted to some kind of headquarters office.

A woman, who was clearly the officer in charge, asked my name, date and place of birth. A prisoner seated at a sewing machine, with the letter P above her red triangle, looked at me with obvious animosity until I was asked my nationality. On hearing it, her face at once lit up. From the office, I was ordered to go to a large dressing-room where, under the command of another female guard, two German prisoners set to work on me. With a speed worthy of admiration, they took away everything I had with me and pressed a paper into my hand, on which was the number 16076. Next, I was ordered to proceed to a small cubicle, where another prisoner made me undress under her intense scrutiny. I found the situation rather laughable.

Finally, the German woman declared: '*No, Sie sind eine Polin.*'[3] Somewhat surprised, I asked her how she knew. 'I am a German, and I've been here four years already. You learn to recognise at sight, and we know you people well. It's only Polish women who march in here with their heads up, looking cheerful.'

Such a reception, of course, encouraged me to hold my own head slightly higher still. I ceased looking cheerful, however, when she ordered me to sit down and, armed with electric clippers for shaving hair, set about checking the cleanliness of my head. My two cell-mates in the Alexanderplatz prison had both complained about lice, but I didn't like the idea of having my head shaved. Somehow I was spared, however, and escaped from the 'electric chair' with very evident relief.

Next, we were sent to the main hall, where a number of my companions were already waiting. Here we were told to strip off completely and were ordered under the showers, which forced us to get our hair wet as well. After this unusually perfunctory ablution we were paraded, still damp, in front of two SS doctors, who observed the march-past with cigars in their mouths. We were then dressed in camp clothes (striped overalls and clogs) and were once again thrown out in the yard and told to form fives. By now, it was completely dark and bitingly cold. In normal conditions, exposure to freezing air with head still wet, wearing only a thin jacket after a hot shower would be enough to give any one of us pneumonia. In Ravensbrück, somehow one hardly felt the cold.

We were lined up this time by a young girl, a good-looking, very tall brunette – Polish – with a green badge on her right arm. As we moved off, she walked beside me.

'The Polish blocks already know that you've arrived,' she whispered, 'the news went round at once.'

I was more than a little surprised.

My young informant continued: 'Yes, indeed, even before new arrivals go to the showers, we are fully informed. The secretariat lets us know. The typist, who was taking down your details, was appalled at first because you were speaking fluent German. She thought you were *Volksdeutsch*. When you registered as a Polish-born national, that was a load off her mind and she let us all know you were here. You may come across some people here you know. Apart from that, the arrival of a political prisoner just now is a major event for us. It's a long time since we've had one. When did you leave Poland? Not till the end of November? God – to think you were in Poland that recently! We've been stuck here a year, two years or three. But, as you see, we're not doing too badly! Aren't you surprised we're in such good heart?'

At that moment we stopped outside one of the blocks and began to go in. At the entrance stood a sturdily built older woman, also wearing a green armband, who counted us in.

'That's Cetkowska, the block-leader. I am the room-leader. I'm in charge of half a block – that's one hut – and the block-leader is responsible for the lot.'

In we went and the block- and room-leaders assigned us our beds in a three-tiered bunk, after which we were given soup and bread. Suddenly, Mietka, the room-leader, whispered to me: 'Just slip out of the block quietly. There's somebody waiting for you outside.'

When I went out, I suddenly felt some little thing being hung round my neck and heard somebody weeping quietly. 'Madame lecturer! It's so good that you've come.'

I burst out laughing.

'No, I didn't mean –' the girl corrected herself, 'I was very upset to hear you were in the camp, but awfully glad to see you again. I was living in Lwów, in the Students' House, when you were our Superintendent. Heavens! It's so awfully long ago.'

'What are you here for?' I asked.

'A serious political affair. But it's nothing. So many the same . . . What's one more or less? Some day I'll tell you all about it.'

'Best split up. The Supervisor's on the prowl,' the block-leader whispered from the door. We exchanged a kiss. The girl disappeared into the blackness and I returned to the block. Two minutes after my return the Supervisor came in. '*Achtung*!' screamed the block-leader and we all stood up. In the doorway stood a possibly twenty-two-year-old girl, small, heavily made-up, with a head of very curly blonde hair and wearing a field-grey uniform. The block-leader reported the total of prisoners in the block and the number of new arrivals. The Supervisor, whose principal facial characteristic was a quite striking lack of intelligence, listened to the report, then walked through the block, accompanied by the block- and room-leaders. Out of curiosity I followed them at a certain remove. The building consisted of two symmetrical sections, each of which contained a dining-room and a dormitory for about 200 prisoners, a washroom and toilet facilities. At the entrance to the block was a small service room where the block-leader officiated.

When the Supervisor had left us, the block-leader invited me into this little room. I sat on a stool opposite a woman not much older than me, with a very red and extremely energetic face. There was great warmth in her eyes. She introduced herself: Eliza Cetkowska. She asked one or two short, pithy questions concerning me. Next she asked about morale in Poland and whether the Poles knew about Ravensbrück.

'Do they know in Poland about the executions and the "rabbits"?'[4]

I looked astonished.

'If you don't understand me, that's bad, very bad. It means that in Poland they don't know that Polish women – and only Polish women – are being shot here for political activity. In the same way, only Polish women are used here as "rabbits" for medical research. An orthopaedic specialist, Professor Gebhardt*, comes here from the sanatorium in Hohenlychen[5] which is quite close, and performs major experimental operations on Polish women – political prisoners only. Some of the victims have already died. Others (there are about sixty of them) will be cripples as long as they live. They're almost all very young girls, all of them with enormous scars on their legs.'

I listened and obviously I believed her, but I did not yet understand. The block-leader had something else to say.

'I cannot tell you exactly what kind of operations these are, but it seems there are a number of types. It's true that I am a nurse by profession, but I am not fully informed about these operations.'

We were still chatting when three more women from other blocks stole in to take a look at the newcomer and gather the latest news from home.

'You have simply no idea what an event this is for us, it's so long since we had a Polish "political".'

'But I thought all the women in concentration camps were political prisoners,' I countered. 'There doesn't seem to be any other kind here.'

This remark provoked a burst of hilarity all round.

'You will have to radically revise your opinion of the institution that you're visiting. The fact is that, in the batch you arrived with, there was not a single prisoner apart from you who was sent here for her political convictions. There were a couple of Ukrainians for *Umgang mit Deutschen*,[6] a couple of Germans for *Umgang mit Polen*, a couple of midwives, a couple of prostitutes and all the rest were thieves. We are in a minority. That's the hardest thing of all.'

'Well, off you go, ladies, or they'll catch you again,' said the block-leader, putting the visitors to flight, 'and we can continue training our novice tomorrow. Roll-call itself will teach her a thing or two. Now, get to bed.' I clambered up to my 'second-floor' bunk and slept like a log.

I did not stir till roused by the stentorian voice of the block-leader shouting: '*Auf!*'[7] It was six o'clock. I dressed, took my coffee and bread and prepared for roll-call. We all had to parade in front of the block. It was just daybreak. The block- and room-leaders (four all told) arranged us in ranks ten deep. Then they began to count us, dashing to and fro and visibly uneasy. Finally, they agreed on the total and the block-leader went 'up front' – that is, into the secretariat – to report the roll. Meanwhile, we stood still. It was gradually getting brighter. The block-leader at last returned with the Supervisor and called the parade to attention: *Achtung!* The German checked our total and went away, leaving us standing. My neighbour whispered to me that all the block totals now had to be checked, and only when all the tallies were agreed would the siren sound. It would take quite a time, she added for good measure. And so it did.

The sky was reddening on our right. So that was east and in that direction lay Poland, I thought. We were still standing. I started to look about me. On the left, between our two blocks, I saw a segment of high wall on top of which were twenty-six strands of barbed wire. The porcelain isolators, spaced at intervals, began to gleam white, an indication that high-voltage current was flowing along those wires . . . Beyond the wall a scrap of 'landscape' was visible, a pale-yellow, sandy precipice with a few scrawny pines.

We were still standing. It was getting cold, but that did not worry me. Another thought had begun to nag at me, or rather a thought that had long been on my mind was becoming more insistent: 'Bach . . . Dürer . . . Hölderlin . . . Beethoven – all of them actually lived and created great works and all were, in fact, Germans. Without them, world culture would not be what it is.'

I thought about German scholarship, to which I myself owed so much . . . And now these same Germans, by their very existence, were disgracing the humanity to which they belonged. Who would be blamed for what was happening today? Nobody could ever claim that it had all come about because a few criminals seized power. It was not the case that just a few individuals took control They are not just a few, but legions of them . . . legions . . . How many were needed to devise, create and administer one Ravensbrück alone. And we all know that Ravensbrück is one of the 'better' and smaller camps. In this one camp, how many Krügers are there (men and women), not to mention the millions of passive Germans who, by their indifferent attitude, not only make possible but effectively support these unseen crimes? One day they will say they did not know, and that will be partially true. They do not know because they do not wish to know. They have a blind belief in a victory which they mean to exploit in every possible way and without restraint. For that reason, they would sooner not know by what means this victory is to be achieved. Here are the underlying causes of the German moral catastrophe. That is why the relationship of the post-war world to Germany must not be conditioned by feelings of revenge or hatred, nor must nationalism of any kind be allowed to play a role. The sole deciding factor must be the effective safeguarding of humanity against comparable cataclysms in future, in order to ensure that Christian civilisation is not totally annihilated . . .

Suddenly, we heard the siren. Within a few seconds we were back in the block. Soon afterwards from the window I saw groups of women marching and singing. When I asked what this meant, I was told they were called '*aussens*'.[8] These teams of prisoners, under escort of course, left the camp every day to work outside and were under orders to sing

German songs on the march. Some of the groups even travelled considerable distances by train in the morning, returning to camp in the evening. The teams consisted mainly of factory workers, though in summer there were also agricultural labourers, who for example did very well for extra food, working on large estates in the area, owned by Himmler.

'Besides, the *aussens* are very useful to us,' said my informant in a low voice, 'they're in touch with the world outside, they relay radio news, often even deliver and collect letters. All of that is very dangerous, but without it life would be worse still!'

A little later, the block-leader came and took me with her to her small office.

'We now have to think what to do with you. Above all, we must try to prevent your being sent to Siemens.'

'What does that mean?' asked.

'It means working in a munitions factory – an affiliate of the Siemens Works – not far from the camp. But it's not only the munitions factory, but also the cloth mills and tailoring workshops where they turn out uniforms – you would find them all very unpleasant. That means directly assisting the German military. But you know some languages. In time, you could be given a green armband. You will be made a room-leader. In some respects it's a very nasty job, but it has at least one satisfaction: you avoid working for "them" and you are able to do quite a lot to help the prisoners. A block-leader can recommend somebody for appointment as room-leader. It's often successful. So far, you are not threatened with anything – here in the newcomers' block. You could help me, perhaps. I have a lot of work.'

One of my first functions was to distribute and sew on the numbers and triangles for the rest of my transport. The triangles had to be sewn above the number on the left breast of the jacket and on the left arm of the frock. The secretariat issued an alphabetical nominal roll of seventy women, with their numbers printed on cloth tags and triangles in different colours. Red ones without letters were for 'German political prisoners'. Among the prisoners who also received red triangles were a few who, as they themselves told me, had become too 'intimate' with Poles. Red triangles with the letter U or R were issued to Ukrainians and Russians respectively for 'friendship' with a German. One of them made a great fuss, objecting to the letter I had given her and claiming that she should have a U and not an R – or the reverse; I have forgotten which. At the same time, I received a P and the number 16076.

Green triangles were for the midwives and a few other Germans. Beside their names on the list were the letters BV, short for the pretty German term *Berufsverbrecher* – professional criminal. The letters 'As' beside a name stood for *Asoziale*[9] and rated a black triangle, reserved for prostitutes and Gypsies. Finally, the letters IBV (*Internationaler Bibelforscher Verein*[10]) signified a particular group of Bible Students who were given a violet triangle and were highly esteemed for their honesty. The Jehovah's Witnesses found themselves in the camp because of their conscientious objection to war-work of any kind. In a totalitarian society at war they had therefore to be eliminated. In the camp they worked as cleaners, or in the laundry, or simply exchanged gossip. In dangerous situations they displayed courage and a fanaticism peculiar to sectarians – yet worthy of unstinted admiration.

In the process of 'bestowing' black triangles on two Gypsies, mother and daughter, I asked how they came to be in Ravensbrück.

'What do you mean, how?' retorted the old witch of a mother. 'Because we're Gypsies, what else! Don't you know that all Gypsies are locked up, regardless of what tribe they belong to. Don't you know anything about us? Our tribes are known by their professions. We belong to the highest tribe. We're horse-dealers.'

'And what do the other Gypsies do?' I asked.

'The others? Don't talk to me about that lot. They're scoundrels!' The black eyes of the two women blazed with hatred and contempt.

'But what do they actually do?' I wanted to know.

'They just play the fiddle,' she muttered grudgingly. I was sorry that Kreisler or Menuhin could not have heard her.

That evening, after the second roll-call had taken place – the end of the working day for some, and for others the start of the night-shift – all of a sudden the sirens sounded and the lights were switched off. An air-raid alert! I shall never forget that first time I heard planes flying over the camp, and the sudden awareness that they were above us and still fighting – our allies, the future victors. At that moment one no longer felt that hopeless abandonment that is the hallmark of concentration-camp existence. The block-leader did not go to bed and allowed me to sit by the window in the dark, listening to the explosions. According to the recently published written orders, block- and room-leaders were forbidden to sleep during air-raids, but were required to stand in the corridor close to a shovel, a bucket and a box of sand. Prisoners were ordered to lie quietly or, if the camp was being bombed, to get dressed. Should a bomb actually hit the block, the block-leader was to lead the prisoners into the yard in fives.

While the block-leader was quoting this order to me verbatim in German, she suddenly broke off in mid-sentence. Presently, she continued speaking: 'You must be very careful if ever Hansi comes near us. She is my "green" room-leader and her job is to watch us and report everything. She is the closest friend of Marianna, also "green", the camp-senior. Both of them are Viennese, each with many previous convictions, and they carry a lot of weight with the camp authorities, especially when it comes to reporting on Poles. Among the people in charge of the camp there is absolutely nobody with the least organising ability. They all rely entirely on a very quick-witted clique of common criminals who belong, racially speaking, to the *Herrenvolk*, so that it's no harm to listen to their advice, as they're on the same cultural level as the authorities, and therefore do not evoke those feelings of inferiority from which the authorities suffer so much in their relations with the Poles.

'Obviously, I am only talking about the Polish women who are political prisoners, and there aren't many of those. The vast majority belong to the other kind. Unfortunately, we have a number of "green" or "black" Poles here. These are women workers deported to Germany and arrested there on immorality charges, or simply for theft or other petty crimes. Here, unfortunately for us, they are given our red triangle because they were originally deported to work in Germany as Polish women. As a result, there are a lot of Polish women in the camp, but they are a very mixed assortment. The great bulk of them are, to say the least, women without much in the way of guiding principles. Many are common criminals. Nevertheless, among all these, we have women and girls of the highest moral integrity who are in prison for Poland, mainly people from the western provinces, annexed by Germany, as well as from Warsaw itself.'

That night, I began for the first time to get some real idea of what it means to be in a concentration camp. It almost makes me laugh now to think I once imagined it would not be all that difficult to live with a number of women of varied nationalities, all of whom had been sent to the same place for having been opponents of Hitler. In fact, it was completely and totally different. Here we depend on our relations – good or bad – with criminals, who themselves curry favour with the authorities by providing them with reports on us. Such reports result in arrest and confinement in the 'Bunker'. I thought at first that anyone who once landed in a concentration camp would at least no longer be threatened by arrest. That particular phase would be over, I supposed.

The truth was quite the reverse. For any 'misdemeanour' or denunciation, the prisoner in question was confined in a dark cellar in a building officially known as the *Zellenbau* (cell-building), the only walled house in the camp. It was pointed out to me the day after I arrived. It had a long and very low underground storey, dug down deep enough to be nicknamed the 'Bunker'. It was fenced off and could be reached only through a special gate. The man in charge was Ramdohr*, a political commissar who had at his disposal all the 'necessary' means required for interrogations (instruments of torture, drugs, and so on). All information of this sort, which I gathered by day, I had time to digest at night, since my skin condition kept me awake.

The next transport to arrive at the camp brought a group of young German girls, aged no more than eighteen. These were meant to be staying with us for a few days while the new blocks of the nearby *Jugendlager* (Youth Camp) were being completed. To be sent here these young girls, I assumed, must be anti-Hitler youth. At last! That evening, as I was sitting in her office, the block-leader sent for some of the girls, one after another, to ask what had brought them to Ravensbrück. After listening to four or five replies, she suspended the enquiry. The girls, with obvious delight and almost always smiling, recounted their exploits, of which the one most frequently cited was incest.

Later the same evening a young Polish woman, obviously with something confidential to impart, called on the block-leader. When she left, the block-leader told me: 'The girl who was here is a cleaner in the "Bunker". She came to tell me that there's a cell with white bed-linen and flowers in readiness for you. Your name is on the list as a *Sonderhäftling* – that means a prisoner who should be given special treatment. They are expecting your arrival from Berlin. You were supposed to be coming by special transport. But in their usual state of confusion, Berlin sent you here with the thieves by mistake, and the authorities here are still waiting for you.'

'But why have I got to be put in a "Bunker" again?' I asked.

'In this instance, it would not seem to be a punishment, just a question of isolating you – separating you from the rest of us, so that you get better treatment. Down there, you'll get SS food, which is very good, not like our turnip or cabbage soup and potatoes. Tomorrow the cleaner is coming back to ask whether or not she should tell them that you're already in the camp.'

I was horrified. After so many months of solitary confinement, I was greatly enjoying the contact with my sisters as well as this 'freedom' that allowed me to walk around the block and even round the camp. But now, once again, it was back to the 'Bunker'! I begged the block-leader to say nothing to anyone about this affair and just to tell the cleaner that the last thing I wanted was to be found.

At this stage all members of our transport, as officially prescribed, were called to the sick bay for an initial health inspection. The state of my skin – in many places I had running sores – evoked a furious outburst from the local doctor, Frau Doctor Oberhäuser, at what she called 'such disgusting neglect of scabies'. When I told her that up till then I had been treated for a nervous disease of the skin and not for scabies, she only screamed at me: '*Halt deinen Mund, du freche Person!*'[11] and flounced out.

As I left the surgery, a young woman with P on her jacket whispered to me to follow her. She led the way down a long corridor. Finally she stopped and said in a whisper, 'Quick, there are no Germans about just now. Come with me to the room on the left. That's where they keep the "rabbits" who've been operated on most recently. You really ought to see them. You may get out of here alive and you know lots of people abroad. They'll believe you.'

We went into a small room where five young girls were lying in bed. My guide told them that I had recently come from Poland. They looked at me and I did not know what to say. The closest to the door was a young woman. I saw a girl, perhaps about twenty years of age and fair-haired. When I said the war would surely end this autumn, the patient obviously wanted to smile at me, but the expression on her face betrayed only suffering and boundless resignation. My guide asked them to uncover their feet. In some cases, apart from bandages, I saw two or three old scars from previous operations, about twenty centimetres long, above or below the knee. The patients asked about Poland. I said something about the high morale and the spiritual resilience of the people, but my heart was not in it. Finally I was glad to be told it was time to leave. Out in the corridor, my guide hastened to tell me that the 'rabbits' were now being looked after to some extent and nursed, which was vastly different from the first operations, when they were completely abandoned and left to look after each other. Nobody was allowed to go near them for many days. They did not even have water.

We returned to the surgery just as the last prisoners in our batch to be examined were coming out. I casually rejoined them to return to my block. The journey back was arduous on account of the sores on my feet, which made walking very difficult. Close to me, a German woman wearing a black triangle was staggering along, barely able to walk at all. She had not been taken into hospital because she was not deemed sufficiently ill and the following day, when her condition worsened, they again refused to accept her because, they said, it was already too late. When at last a stretcher was sent to our block to collect her, she was taken straight to the mortuary.

Meanwhile, many innovations – major and minor – were being carried out in my new place of residence. The continuous influx of women prisoners compelled the Germans to extend the camp by building new and more numerous blocks on other parts of the sandy dune close to our barrack-hutments, on the far side of the wall and the wire. Once this additional parcel of land had been suitably 'secured', down came the wall separating us. A makeshift barbed-wire fence was immediately installed, and an order was published forbidding in the strictest terms anyone from entering the new camp. This was seen as an obvious pretext for meting out more punishments. The following Sunday – so everybody predicted – there would be a very long roll-call at which part of our number would be transferred to the new blocks.

That day, in fact, the thermometer at headquarters registered minus fifteen degrees and we remained standing on parade in the open for more than five hours. All those in authority, male and female, including the Commandant himself, rushed all around the camp at breakneck speed, issuing orders that were mostly self-contradictory. Finally, a few hundred of the women prisoners – mostly Ukrainians and Russians – were sent to the new camp. Meanwhile, the entire camp stood still. We envied the camp authorities only one thing, namely their movement. We were slowly freezing solid, and yet, as before, nobody I knew even caught a cold as a result. A certain number of block- and room-leaders, including our own, were reassigned to the new blocks. We were given a new block-leader, Erna, a young German with a black triangle, whom I had assisted in the secretariat. At first I was a bit uneasy about how cooperation might develop with my new superior. But everything went splendidly, our relationship being based on Erna's undisguised respect for my knowledge of how to write her native language. I later discovered that this was not merely a question of spelling, but chiefly of my ability to write at all, an art in which my leader was unusually weak.

Two days after this change, the young room-leader came to me at noon looking extremely pale. 'Five people,' she whispered in my ear, 'including one of my colleagues, have been sent to the Bunker for the same offence.'

'What does that mean?' I asked.

'It means that tomorrow they will be shot. More than a hundred of us have been shot already. We know very well what's going to happen when suddenly several Polish "politicals" go to the Bunker for the same reason. They know as well. The first time – last year – nobody understood, or knew why they were given something stupefying to drink. Now they always refuse to take it. Nor do they allow themselves to be blindfolded and all of them, without exception, die shouting: "Long live Poland!"'

'But how do you know all this?'

'Very simple. There's always some contact with the Bunker, and we know exactly what happens when there are executions. Each time the SS execution-squad members are entitled to free food and drink in the SS canteen, where the waitresses are Polish. The SS men drink themselves stupid and afterwards tell one another all the details of the execution. They never conceal their boundless admiration for the Polish women. Apart from that, usually (if not always) we have another way of checking. During evening roll-call, when it's completely quiet, the shots can be heard, totalling the same number as the prisoners in the Bunker. Sometimes there's an extra shot or two, just afterwards – not so loud – because the soldiers often aim badly. Then the officer has to shoot them dead with his revolver. This time, five of them have gone. One of them was a school-friend of mine and her case is so very like my own that the next time it could be me . . . Well, can't be helped, must get back to work.' With that, she quickly ran away.

I stayed thinking about those thousands of others who refuse in the same way to let themselves be blindfolded, and who die shouting those same words . . . But they at least have the consolation that their bodies will rest in the soil of their native country. Here it must be considerably harder to die, knowing that one must rest in enemy soil. It was then that I understood how immensely practical the Germans are. Instead of murdering these strong young girls immediately after arresting them in Poland, they would transport them to Germany to work for a year or two and only then, quite calmly, shoot them . . .

One day Cetkowska, the block-leader, told me the details of how her niece Kęszycka died. The pattern was always the same: before going to the Bunker, the girls would suddenly hunt for professional hairdressers, of whom there were a few in the camp, and demand a really attractive hairdo. After that, they went . . . God Almighty, I thought, just as Herodotus describes how the Spartans at Thermopylae combed their hair with great care before the battle, knowing perfectly well that they were about to die! This was not understood by the envoys of Xerxes, who were sent to persuade them to surrender.

It was about then that I was approached for the first time on the subject of teaching. Two women from one of the Polish blocks came to ask for a 'lecture' and to fix a date and time. The problem was that 'newcomers' were not allowed to move freely about the camp, except by special order. But we arranged to meet the following Sunday at dusk. I managed to get there and found a group of people waiting for me. We seated ourselves in a corner and I began, in a low voice, to tell them about the paintings in the catacombs.[12] At first, it did not come easily to me. I did not know whether I could do it, or how I would manage without illustrations. It felt so odd to be talking about art in the way I once did. Among the six or eight of my very devoted listeners were a couple who listened with particularly rapt attention, making notes on scraps of paper. After a few minutes their concentrated enthusiasm proved infectious. Perhaps a certain thematic affinity between the catacombs and our own situation at the time was partly responsible. At any rate, I 'unwound', as it were. Suddenly the block-leader approached and yelled at us to disperse, ordering me to leave the block immediately. My audience tried to placate her with their entreaties, but the block-leader, speaking Polish with a Silesian accent, threatened to call the Supervisor. There was nothing for it but to capitulate. The women who escorted me back to my block explained to me on the way that the block-leader bore some kind of a grudge against the so-called 'intelligentsia' and took every opportunity to treat them unfavourably. She wore a P above her red triangle, but she was responsible for my first palpable impression of just how difficult it is to live in such conditions, even within one's own national group – let alone where a foreigner is involved.

Such was the role played by a Czech group: not very numerous, but closely linked with the Russians and Ukrainians, and ill-disposed towards Poles. This fact surprised me in camp conditions. I did not understand till I realised that the cause of these attitudes was ideological. The Czechs constituted a centre for Communist propaganda. As a result, they adhered closely to the Russians and Ukrainians and openly opposed the Poles, who were the largest national group in the camp and decidedly anti-Communist. Just then, news reached us of Hitler's defeat at Stalingrad. The Czechs went mad with delight. The Poles thanked God that Hitler's end was approaching, but not without uneasiness at the steady increase in the strength of Communist propaganda in the camp from that day onwards. We told ourselves repeatedly that Poland under Allied protection could have nothing to fear from Stalin. The advance of the Red Army, however, aroused within us a concern that we ourselves preferred not to admit to, but which nevertheless deepened with every passing day.

A few days later there was a radical change in my own status. My term as a 'new arrival' (that is to say, my spell of residence without being officially assigned to the newcomers' block) expired. That was the moment for my block-leader to 'introduce' me to the camp administrators and propose my appointment as a room-leader in her new Ukrainian block. She forbade me in advance to let them see the sores on my hands or – God forbid! – to catch me limping! When I pointed out to her, with a laugh, that this was not going to be easy, she declared: 'You must – and that's all there is to it!' I also said that if they wanted a really active room-leader, I would not be fit for work for the time being. She answered gruffly that we would be in a pretty pickle here, if we could not look after one another.

The proposal was accepted. Within the hour I found myself a room-leader in the Ukrainian block. At the same time, with the help of a Polish nurse in the sickbay, I wangled two things: dressings for my sores, and a *Bettkarte* (bed-card) – that is, permission to stay in bed in the block and exemption from roll-call. So I had a 'cushy' time of it, not working, and staying in bed, with Polish girls sneaking in to visit me. The second room-leader meanwhile did my work as well as her own, and I tried to repay her in part by giving her German lessons.

Apart from continuing to educate myself, I tried in every way possible to find out what was going on around me. Due to my illness I could not walk round outside, but as a result, I was told a great deal. Soon I was given to understand that Ravensbrück in 1943 was paradise compared to its earlier period, during which the 'black' German Grete Musküller, a room-leader, and Camp Commandant Koegel* with Senior Supervisor Mandel* vied with one another in cruel practices. The majority of the executioners and torturers of those days were said now to be 'working' in Oświecim (Auschwitz), where, apparently, they were more in demand than ever . . . I was told about all this in detail by tough, sober and matter-of-fact women whose accounts bore no trace of hysteria.

One day, the young room-leader called in. 'You must get up and come with me. You've got news from Poland!' I could not believe my ears, but I was up and out very quickly. In the second block a colleague whose name I knew from underground activity was waiting for me. We went to a corner of the dormitory and there she showed me a letter.

The sight of it evoked such a vivid memory of clandestine work and freedom that I was deeply shaken. Adam Szebesta[13] had written asking her to pass on to me a few very affectionate words, and adding: 'Tell her that Renia[14] has had a fine boy.' The letter was written in Polish and the subject matter was uncensored. I asked in my astonishment where she had got it. Immediately, although I had whispered the question, both colleagues pressed fingers to their lips. After a little while the recipient of the letter added, whispering even more softly: 'I go out to work every day. I received the letter today and today I must burn it.'

I returned to my block. The first direct news for ten months that my people knew where I was, and were thinking about me, put new heart into me. The thought that Renia, after many years of childless marriage, had a son was an added delight. At the same time I was imagining the complications she must have had to cope with in connection with her pregnancy, working for the RGO in Warsaw under a false name and posing as the wife of an officer transported to Russia! For two days I lived as though in a dream, constantly having to reassure myself that I had seen the letter with my own eyes, that back in Poland they were working away, and that I had actually held that letter in my hand.

Two days later, on 8 March, I was awakened from this dream – and none too pleasantly – by the block-leader:

'Get dressed at once. You're to see the Commandant. You've been sent for. This is bad news. They've got on to you at last, and they'll shift you into the Bunker.'

Out I went. A guard was waiting outside the secretariat and, after checking my number, she escorted me through the gate, turned left and led me into the big, walled building. We climbed upstairs and walked the length of a corridor to a door in front of which a soldier stood guard.

'I have brought with me prisoner 16076, summoned to see the Camp Commandant,' the German wardress told him. The soldier went in, came back and called me in. The door shut behind me as I entered. In the middle of a luxuriously appointed office stood an SS officer of medium height, lean and red-haired. I knew from colleagues that his name was Suhren* and that he had been a private detective before the war. He looked at me with pale blue-grey eyes without lashes. I reported to him in the required manner: '*Schutzhäftling*,[15] name and number' and waited. He asked how long I had been in the camp and whether I was seriously ill, as he could see that I was limping. He added that I would now be receiving regular medical care.

'There has been some misunderstanding. You are entitled to much better conditions. You will have them, starting tomorrow. In the first place you will receive far better food,' he emphasised.

'Will I be alone or will I remain with my colleagues?'

'You will be on your own – much better off. You will eat well,' he replied.

'Please let me stay as I am at present, if it means being separated from my fellow prisoners,' I said.

'That is impossible. You will leave the camp tomorrow. Until then you are bound to secrecy regarding what I have just told you.'

I went out.

That evening I gave the block-leader a short account of the whole affair of the murdered professors of Lwów, asking her to submit a report to the appropriate authorities after the war, in the event of my death. It seemed to me logical to assume that, as the possessor of such a secret, discreetly removed from the rest of the camp, I would be quietly eliminated the moment the Rome–Berlin Axis collapsed and Italian intervention on my behalf ceased.

Fellow prisoners 'in the know' greeted my impending move to the Bunker with great optimism. They assumed that I would be treated, cured and released within a couple of weeks. Though I was glad to hear them say so, I did not believe it, because it was out of the question. The cleaner in charge of the Bunker told me that my absence from the Bunker had come to light during a check on rations. For two months somebody in the SS had been quietly feeding himself with the help of my daily portions, until the previous evening, when it emerged that I wasn't there at all. They telephoned to Berlin at once and were informed that I had travelled to Ravensbrück with the transport of 9 January. That was how they finally found me. We learned at the same time that, in future, the Bunker would be staffed entirely by Jehovah's Witnesses.

Polish women prisoners came and asked me to let their relatives and friends know about them, once I got back to Poland, and bade me a very affectionate farewell. I had grown so close to them in no more than two months.

The next day, 9 March, a few dozen of us 'to be released' were led to the bathroom and the surgery. The women working there understood my impending ostensible 'release' entirely differently. One of them, passing as it were by chance, pressed a small object into my hand. It was some little while before I was able to confirm that it was a miniature figure of Christ on the cross. I had already seen such objects in the camp. They were carved from a toothbrush handle with the help of a penknife. From this gesture, I understood that the donor presumed I was going to my death. In any case, that was becoming much more than likely, and I was deeply moved by the gift.

Later, we were escorted in pairs across the sunlit parade ground of the camp. Polish women, standing close by, nodded to me in silence. At last we reached the gate into the Bunker, which presently closed behind us. We entered the building and were taken to our appointed cell, intended for one person. It was a tight squeeze, like a railway compartment during the occupation. After a short while, all my fellow prisoners – almost exclusively German women – started talking at once. At first they kept their voices low, but later they chatted more and more loudly. They were tremendously excited. One got the impression that these women scented a whiff of freedom, so very unexpected. They began to tell one another what it was like that morning when they stood for roll-call, how their names were read out, how they were ordered to line up and how eventually they understood . . . Others began to plan what train they would hurry to catch in Fürstenberg, which connection for Berlin, when – at what time of the day or night they would at last be . . . home . . .

I sat in the corner on my bunk, feeling inexpressibly alone despite the crush. All round me there was rejoicing, but I had the impression that the whole crowd was in some strange way distancing itself from me, as though between these people who were free and me, a smokescreen was descending and growing more dense with every word they uttered. Finally, they gave us a meal, then the door was opened and everyone was ordered outside, except me. The German women dashed out like a shot. Only the two last to go turned in the doorway and looked at me in horror.

'Are you not being released?'

I was grateful for their spontaneous concern and I smiled at them.

'I wish you all the best. I am staying here.' The door shut.

Presently the wardress returned and led me back to the same cell as before. But now, instead of a bunk, there was a bed freshly made with clean white sheets, a small table with a cloth and a bowl of flowers. The wardress looked at me eagerly and eventually asked: '*Schön, nicht wahr?*'[16] It dawned on me that I was supposed to be charmed by the 'luxury' of this cell. In reply, I asked her whether I could go to bed because I was ill.

'Of course, you can do anything you like,' the German replied with a courtesy which, after everything I had seen previously in the camp, made a very unpleasant impression on me. I suddenly realised for the first time that there is nothing more painful in such a situation than being singled out for privileged treatment. She left me and, instead of getting undressed, I sat down on the bed in a state of immense weariness. 'I am again to be obliged to look at the sky through a grating,' I thought to myself, lifting my head towards the barred window high in the wall. Then it struck me that I was not going to be able to see the sky at all, because the panes were of frosted glass, with wire mesh of the kind we sometimes used in the stables at home. As I sat there thinking about everything and nothing, my feelings kept returning to the others in the camp, so near and yet so far. The thought of them, and the yearning for their company, pained me very much. At last I lay down and fell asleep. When I woke up, it was already dusk. I was given afternoon tea on a tray, and in the evening a very appetising two-course meal, served on white porcelain. Each time the wardress asked whether she should bring me a second helping.

The following morning I began to take a close look at my cell. I was now experiencing what I had been curious to see when I came to the Reich – an up-to-date German prison. Instead of an iron door, scratched and rusty like the one in my Berlin cell, this door was of exceptionally stout planks of light oak, together with matching bed, table and chair of the same colour. The toilet facilities were automatic and there was central heating. The cell was painted a spotless white, apart from where a half-hearted attempt had been made to wash away a large pink stain near the radiator – undoubtedly caused by blood. Presently, a girl Jehovah's Witness came in and announced that she had been ordered to sweep my cell. I asked her to take the flowers away, but she replied that, on the contrary, her instructions were to bring me still more flowers. She went away at last and then began for me the first of many days spent on my back in the Bunker. Each day was very much like the last. For some weeks my state of health had been steadily deteriorating. The spread of festering sores all over my body caused even the SS doctor, who called in from time to time, to look increasingly pessimistic. He was the same doctor who conducted the first medical examination after our arrival. Now, however, he was all politeness, quietly spoken and almost kindly – as, indeed, were the women guards. This behaviour aroused even greater revulsion on my part than their previous brutality. It only went to prove that they were capable of doing anything to order – even down to behaving like human beings.

I consoled myself during my sickness with Tolstoy's dictum that a woman who has never been ill is a monster. Remembering how appalled I had been when I first read that sentence, I was now quite pleased at the thought of having ceased to be a monster. Moreover, despite the opinion of those around me, I felt all along that I would emerge from this abomination.

The two wardresses, Binz and Mewis, took it in turns to bring in my food, and at night peered through the Judas peephole in the door every two hours, switching on the harsh light as they did so. They were often talkative. Binz even told me that she was a cook by profession and twenty-two years old. They used to call me 'Frau Lange' (Mrs Long). Asked why, they explained that I was here under this name so that nobody in the camp would find out where I was. I do not know whether they gave me this pseudonym on account of my height or the first letters of my name. I did not like the sound of that one bit. I felt it might have to do with obscuring all trace of my existence . . .

From time to time, Suhren also dropped in to ask if there was anything I wanted. I asked to have the flowers removed from my cell because, I said, 'They are not appropriate in my situation.' He was annoyed, but I got rid of the flowers. Every time he came, I asked him when was I going to be interviewed, as promised in Berlin the previous December, because so far I still had no idea why I was under arrest. He said I was entitled to write a submission to the Reichsführer der SS, Himmler, asking to be heard. I used to receive regularly two German newspapers, the *Völkischer Beobachter* and the Goebbels paper, *Das Reich.* I remember seeing in one of them a photograph of German soldiers in Rome in Piazza Venezia listening to a speech by Mussolini. Petrarch's question suggested itself automatically: '*Che fan' qui tante pellegrine spade*?'[17]

One day, in my total solitude, I suddenly became aware in a tangible fashion that I was not after all alone in the world. The first parcel arrived from Poland. From now on, parcels arrived regularly and with them cards and letters written in German. They were short letters, but immensely precious. I was now free to receive correspondence and to write any amount of letters, whereas in the camp only one card a month was allowed, and often that failed to arrive. Meanwhile, no word at all reached me from the camp itself. Through the little window that opened only aslant, to let in air at the top, almost every day at noon I could hear a few women conversing animatedly – but in a language that I did not understand. The only other thing that occasionally wafted in was a cloud of thick smoke, which filled the cell with a strangely unpleasant odour.

A couple of weeks later, quite unexpectedly, my health began to improve and from then on the sores healed relatively quickly. When my hands were already more or less cured, I received a catalogue of books in the SS library. I decided to make myself conversant with the theory of the criminality surrounding me and ordered *Der Mythus des XX Jahrhunderts*[18] by Rosenberg*. I read with interest this volume written in bad, abstruse German, in which the mystique of physical labour and hatred for the moral strength of Christianity are combined to provide a theoretical basis for a regime of violence and compulsion. Stalin's aim was very similar, though more cleverly pursued by investing the doctrines with such an apparently democratic form of constitution, written in short passages, so lucid in form, but so ambiguous in content! Reading Rosenberg's *Myth*, I sketched out in my mind 'A Reply to Alfred Rosenberg from inside a Concentration Camp' but, naturally enough, I preferred not to put it on paper.

Soon, other books arrived, sent to me by friends. One of the first was an anthology of English poetry, lent by Professor Dyboski. Then, at my special request, came Tacitus. One day Binz told me that another book had arrived, but the Commandant had forbidden me to read it because it contained 'Catholic prayers'. I was immensely curious and asked Binz if she would mind letting me see the book through the little window of my cell. This she did. At the sight of the little volume, I calmly remarked: 'Frau Aufseherin, those are not Catholic prayers, but love poems of the fourteenth century.'

'In that case, you may take this book,' said Binz.

I did so with great delight. It was in fact a volume of Petrarch's sonnets. So ended what I am sure was Binz's only encounter with Petrarch. Presumably the phrase '*Madonna mia*' gave rise to the error.

More or less about this time the newspapers carried the news about Katyń.[19] For the first couple of days I clung to the hope that such a thing was impossible. It had to be one more macabre invention of German propaganda. But when detailed descriptions and statements began to come through, any lingering doubts about the reality of the horror were totally dispelled. The question everyone was asking, including me, was 'Who?' Surrounded as I was by collective German criminality, I naturally tended to ascribe this action, also, to the invader from the west. Two factors, however, dismissed all doubts from my mind once and for all.

I remembered that the last news of our Polish officers deported to Russia came in the spring of 1940 and that the date coincided exactly with the German accounts. The second convincing factor was that the murdered men were buried in full uniform, and even many personal items of value were found on the bodies. Anyone who lived in the German-administered 'General Government' portion of Poland would be fully aware of the German attitude towards articles of value, and would know that this in itself would preclude the possibility of Germans being capable of such 'wastefulness'. I could still see the faces of those women, young and old, who used to call in at the Red Cross centre in Kraków to ask me to 'get their husbands and sons released from the camps in Kozielsk and Starobielsk . . .'

As soon as I was able to walk again, I was allowed to stroll in the 'garden'. So out I went. The 'garden' consisted of two sections: the flowerbeds in front of the Bunker, separated from the camp by an interior wall, and at the back a narrow 'corridor' also planted with flowers, between the building and the main wall covered in barbed wire. The long narrow flowerbed was flanked on either side by a path. The camp wall was grey, like the building, which, instead of wire and insulators, had two rows of very small grilled windows – one row just above ground level and the second just under the low roof. Several of the lower windows were fastened with iron blinds, lowered from outside. 'Aha,' I thought, remembering Stanisławów and 'the dark cellars'. On the other side, above the camp wall, was an antiquated tin chimney, which was the source of that dense smoke and the extremely unpleasant odour I had smelled from my cell.

Walking along beside the wall, I could have a good look through the cell windows, and from one of them I clearly heard the sound of throat-clearing and gentle tapping. I stopped and, peering in at the partly open little window, saw the eyes and part of a woman's face. A conversation began. The woman turned out to be German and a wardress, who had been arrested on suspicion of lesbianism, which was indeed widespread among the German women in the camp. She was very keen to chat and every time I went for a walk I learned something new from Herta. She explained that the reason the smoke from the little crematorium chimney smelled so nasty was because they were burning hair.

The prisoners who were condemned to the 'dungeons', she told me, were the victims of the Gestapo Commandant, Ramdohr, who would leave them twelve days in their cells without light or food, in an attempt to force confessions out of them. If that did not work, he applied torture. She told me how furious the Germans were that Polish women who were executed went so heroically to their deaths; that Binz was a power in the camp because she was the lover of Schutzhaftlagerführer[20] Brauning; that the luxurious silk underwear, hung out to dry near the entrance, was now the property of Binz, but she (Herta) knew precisely which prisoners had been the previous owners; that Mewis was the unmarried mother of three small sons in Fürstenberg, each by a different father; that the four women who went for daily walks and spoke in a foreign language were Romanians who enjoyed special privileges as nationals of a German ally – and so on.

When I returned to my own quarters after these walks, I used to assemble this avalanche of information and trivial gossip in my memory, so enriching my own brief experience of camp life. From Herta I also learned how to climb on top of my bedside table to look out the window. From there I could just catch a glimpse, beyond the wall, of meadows and trees and the spire of Fürstenberg church. More important still, if the Supervisor was not in the corridor, one could climb up at the sound of footsteps outside, below the window. Since it was spring, flowers were being planted. The work in the garden was carried out by a Polish woman who became my first liaison officer with the camp. For some time the gardener would come every day, bringing me news and greetings from the camp inmates. At great risk, she also smuggled warm clothing from the 'store-room' into the cellar, returning with as many secrets of the Bunker as possible concerning newly arrived Polish women prisoners confined there – their ordeals, confessions, and so forth. For my part, everything I managed to glean from the different cells during my walks I would repeat to the gardener, for transmission to various persons in the camp.

The most important problem, as usual, was to reconcile the accounts. My contact with the cells became more intensive as I grew gradually more daring and as my physical strength increased. The most exacting task was how to get food into the 'dungeons' after raising the iron shutters. If the shutters jammed, the prisoner inside could not reach high enough to help, with nothing to climb on and no bunk; besides which she was always far weaker than me, her strength having been sapped by hunger. The situation appeared hopeless.

Then suddenly, while out walking, I met a German woman arrested for embezzlement. She was a camp wardress, built like a Valkyrie. In the present circumstances she sympathised with us and solved the problem in a flash. There was no great difficulty about getting food into the upper cells when the windows were open. The thing to do was to attach a stone to the string from the parcel and aiming at the slit in the partially open upper window, throw it. Then the prisoner above would lower the string, to which the small parcel could be attached.

There was never any question – any more than there had been previously in Lwów – about the quantities of food that I consumed. On occasions I would receive so many parcels at the same time that I would have needed an abnormal appetite to eat the lot, but nobody seemed to give it a thought. With the exception, that is, of the dog belonging to Miss Binz. Fortunately this animal was not a police-dog, but an awfully stupid mongrel, which threw a fit whenever I went for a walk, flinging itself at me and sniffing persistently at my pocket.

'Isn't it nice to see how much he loves you?' said Binz with a smile, clearly under orders to behave 'pleasantly' towards me from time to time. The fact was, I hated the creature and was panic-stricken in case it betrayed my secret, so depriving me of this last remaining, meagre opportunity to bring help to somebody. On occasions – very rarely – while out walking, I managed to observe Binz or Mewis re-entering the camp. That was the moment to dash headlong back to the Bunker and slip up to one of the upper cells where, I happened to know, a Polish woman prisoner was confined in the dark, and pass her something to eat through the little window in the cell door. It was most distressing that this sporadic help could get through to only half of the cells – those with windows giving on to the 'garden'. The rest, looking out on the camp and facing the Commandant's office, were inaccessible for me. That very real problem, along with many others, had to await solution by Boguś.

Some of the lower cells were occupied by male prisoners, sent here for punishment by the neighbouring small prison for men, which had no Bunker of its own. Among them was a very young lad from Silesia, who obviously spoke perfect German. Boguś was serving his term, but meanwhile he succeeded in charming both Binz and Mewis. He convinced them that he could do any work required, that his speciality was interior decoration and that the Bunker needed repainting. The two German women, always thirsting for male company, were so carried away by the sight of this curly-haired youth that finally – with the Commandant's approval – Boguś, or 'Gottlieb', started painting the cells. From then on, whenever I was walking alone, Gottlieb tried to make contact with me. As for me, seeing that he was on excellent terms with the Supervisors I made a point of avoiding him. Then Boguś began to supply me with valuable information about any Polish women who 'landed' in the Bunker, and gave me their cell numbers. I therefore decided to risk it and to adopt Boguś as a second line of contact.

My work was going very well, not only as far as food distribution was concerned, but also the business of gathering and reporting information. The various reports were being coordinated not only between the cells – with Boguś responsible for one side of the Bunker and me for the other – but also between the Bunker and camp, with the help of the gardeners, of whom there were now several. They came to work and planted flowers for us, while chatting loudly among themselves. When there were no German women on duty, I would climb up on my cupboard and join in the conversation. Occasionally the *Kolonnenführerin*, Pani Zanowa*, would appear, and, in keeping with the atmosphere evoked by her name, used to shout, as though to one of her fellow gardeners: 'Aldona!'[21] as a signal that she had something to tell me. I would then stretch one hand through the grille above my window (while gripping the recess with the other) and so receive the message. The name Aldona clung to me during my term in 'solitary', about which only the Germans could have had any illusions, for my contacts were steadily increasing. One among them I recall with particular pleasure.

Once I heard footsteps on the cinder-track below my window. I leaped on top of my cupboard and saw the remarkably elegant silhouette of a dark-haired young woman. This tall, slender girl with the hands and feet of a thoroughbred, a narrow face and aquiline nose, was dressed with unusual care and great good taste. In these hideous surroundings her appearance was so altogether unexpected that at first sight I was flabbergasted. It was only when she passed underneath my window for the third or fourth time that I called out in a prompter's stage whisper: '*Madame!*' There could not be the slightest doubt about the newcomer's nationality.

She stood still. I tapped softly on my window and stretched out my hand. 'I am Polish. You must be French. How long have you been here?'

She listened as though dumbfounded. Later she told me that these were the first words of French she had heard in many months. They had given her a great thrill, all the more so because – not knowing a word of German – she had been able to communicate only in dumbshow. Two days later, by mistake, Binz allowed us both to go for a walk at the same time. We chattered away to our heart's content. Christiane Mabire had been the private secretary of French Prime

Minister Paul Reynaud*, and for this she was being punished. She combined in one personality the elegance of a French lady of fashion with the cultural distinction of a French intellectual. We quickly became good and sincere friends.

Christiane had a large number of serious books, so I asked Binz for permission to borrow some of them, since I did not wish to expose Christiane to the risk of additional penalties for clandestine lending. Binz went to see Commandant Suhren about it and returned in a state of shock, after being told that we were not even allowed mutual awareness of one another's existence. This prohibition of course reinforced our wish for closer contact. On walks we could meet one another only under the supervision of Binz, who kept an eye on us, stretched out on a deckchair. We each had half the garden 'corridor' at our disposal. Meeting in the middle, we always exchanged a few words, but far preferable to this bizarre quadrille were our walks alone and unsupervised beneath the window. On these occasions, we could converse freely and exchange notes. Christiane was particularly fond of Latin texts referring to the Germans. I remember how delighted she was when I passed out the window to her a card with this sentence by Caesar: '*Latrocinia nullam habent infamiam, quae extra fines cuiusque civitatis fiunt; atque ea iuventutis exercendae ac desidiae minuendae causa fieri praedicant.*'[22]

It seemed to me then and, unfortunately, even more so today that those words of Caesar explain a great deal to us, first and foremost perhaps the immense success of Hitlerism among the Germans.

Unlike me, Christiane did not receive any parcels, so I was able to give her something from time to time. Once, by mistake, I mixed up two packages and Christiane received, among other things, an onion intended for the Poles. When I went out for my walk the next day, she was already waiting at the window.

'*Mon Dieu! Un oignon cru!*[23] I thought at first it was a hyacinth one could plant in a glass bowl. But, no! It's just a common onion! What am I supposed to do with it?'

'Simply eat it – all of it!' The intelligent eyes stared at me through the bars of the window with obvious incredulity.

'How do you mean – eat it?'

'Just eat it, that's all! It's very healthy. Specially good for the teeth because of the vitamin content.' At that point we had to interrupt the conversation at the approach of authority.

That afternoon Christiane stood under my window in floods of tears.

'What's happened?' I asked, fearing some calamity.

'It's just that I had so much faith in you, I ate the whole onion at once and now, strangely, my eyes won't stop smarting.'

But this encounter between the elegant Parisian and the less refined Polish onion was not her only worry. Another time, she complained to me about not knowing why she had been given a Jewish name. I discovered that they were now calling her Frau Müller, but she was certainly not Jewish. I had to explain to her at length that Müller and my own pseudonym Lange were just ordinary, very common German names, roughly corresponding to, say, 'Madame Durand' in France. The reason they had taken away our proper names was to obliterate all trace of us, so that we would become like the mysterious Man in the Iron Mask.[24] This comparison amused her and appeared to set her mind completely at rest.

Meanwhile, I made some fresh acquaintances. In one of the ground-floor cells were lodged two German women – astrologists and clairvoyantes by profession. The older and shorter of the two spoke little and was obviously bullied by the other, a slightly younger, extraordinarily garrulous, chubby blonde. From the latter's torrent of words, I learned that the authorities of the Third Reich punish those with the gift of prophecy by sending them to prison or a concentration camp. She herself had landed in Ravensbrück thanks to having had Rudolf Hess* as a client.

Once, when her colleague was out for a walk with me and patiently hunting for a four-leafed clover on the narrow band of lawn, I asked the more loquacious Sybil through the window whether the two of them had worked together before the war. She snorted with indignation.

'As if I would have anything in common with such a person – telling people God knows what rubbish for a mark and a half? A scientific seance with me used to cost twenty-five marks!'

In exchange for a little sugar, she told my own fortune in the approved fashion (from the date of my birth), including personal happiness and a future covered in glory. But the Romanian women who were in the camp because of their husbands' anti-German politicking received parcels. And by reading the cards for me free of charge, they were able to predict that I would be in prison for a long time to come.

I was shortly to learn more about that from a more authoritative source. One morning Mewis came in with one of the young 'Bible students' and set about vigorously cleaning my cell, in the course of which she told me '*ein hoher Besuch*'[25] from Berlin was expected. After lunch I was told to go out in the garden and a deckchair was placed at my disposal. This cheered me up considerably, reminding me moreover of the Third Act of Schiller's drama *Maria Stuart*, in which the meeting between Queen Elizabeth and her prisoner takes place as if by chance in a garden. Presently there appeared a very tall Gestapo officer, accompanied by Suhren and Binz. He gave his name as Dr Daumling and enquired about my health. I replied that I had been waiting since November for the interview promised me by Judge Hertl. Not only had I been sent to a concentration camp, but I was still confined in painful isolation. If I was being punished without knowing my offence, I would like, at least, to be with the other Polish women.

Daumling listened, without meeting my eye. When I spoke about returning to the camp, he cut in: 'That is impossible.' In the end, he replied vaguely that 'we shall see' and 'an effort will be made', and so forth. He went away at last and, after a while, I returned to my cell to find it full of flowers. Binz came in afterwards and removed the flowers, explaining that she had been obliged to put them on display because the *hoher Besuch* had asked to see the cell. She added that Daumling was head of the Department for Polish Political Affairs in the Ministry of Security, and that he had made a point of instructing her to treat me well because I was innocent and the Italians were backing me.

'Then why are they holding me at all?' I asked.

Binz appeared to hesitate before adding in a changed voice: 'He also told me: she knows something, which must absolutely never come out in the open. That's the way it is,' she added, 'somebody who knows too much never gets away from here.'[26]

It was spring and the flowers were blooming, even in the garden by the Bunker. Only there seemed to be no birds. Once while I was out walking, a stork flew overhead 'When storks above Poland's ploughed acres I'd see . . .'[27]

At about that time, an important piece of news reached me from the camp. Bortnowska had arrived victorious, having survived a fearsome interrogation and a serious illness. Horror-struck, I wondered how much longer this frail woman could possibly stay alive in the camp.

A couple of weeks later, Binz told me that I would be interviewed that afternoon. I tried to restrain my optimism, resisting the illusion of change for the better, . . . The gardeners at work, however, fuelled my hopes by telling me that a year or two earlier there had been a case of a prisoner being released immediately after an interrogation.

'Only please don't forget us. Give our best wishes to everyone in Kraków!'

Shortly after noon, I was led to the Bunker secretariat. There, as everywhere I had previously been interrogated, the bleak eyes of Himmler, behind their pince-nez, stared down at me from his portrait on the wall. On the opposite wall hung the motto of the Gestapo: '*Deine Ehre heisst Treue*'.[28] I searched my memory for a clue as to where I had heard those words before. Of course, it was Krüger who had boasted about the SS motto. Now at last I fully understood its meaning. He who serves loyally (and blindly) has no need of honour. What a clever way of enslaving the German soul!

Presently, an SS sergeant and a shorthand writer arrived. The hearing began. Once again: the affair of Krüger and the professors. I got the impression it was merely a matter of confirming that, after a lapse of many months, my statement was unchanged. The tone of the interview was coarse and bitterly hostile. At the finish, the Gestapo man treated me to a long monologue, delivered in a more than elevated voice. He declared that he wanted to rid me of any illusion that I was performing a patriotic deed by accusing Krüger. My accusation, he said, was of no consequence, being merely the assertion of a known chauvinist. Nobody would believe me, and so on. I thoroughly enjoyed listening to his shouting and screaming, because such a performance in itself – and the mere fact of this renewed interrogation – belied his words.

Walking back to my cell, I knew that was the end of 'my case'. They were bound to do away with me, the moment the Axis with the Italians split apart, unless, by some miracle, that event was still further postponed. The only attainable aim for me – one that I must pursue with all my strength – was to get myself sent back to the camp in order to be treated the same as the other Polish women and end this humiliating discrimination. The problem was that the authorities obviously still assumed nobody in the camp knew of my presence in the Bunker. It did not seem to worry the Germans that this order to keep me under cover made no sense whatsoever, since I had, by mistake, already spent two months in the camp and had therefore been able to confide the secret of the professors' death to other Poles (as I obviously had done). All that ever mattered to the Germans was carrying out the order, not whether there was any point to it.

Consequently, when I had to visit the dentist, he was obliged to wait specially for me until late in the evening, so that Mewis could lead me from the Bunker across the square in front of the Commandant's office under cover of darkness, without my being seen. During the day I let it be known via the gardener that I would be going out in the evening and that other Polish women 'with armbands', who could find some pretext for a late stroll on the square, should be on hand and should shout: 'Good evening, Aldona!'

My contact with the camp was developing ever more successfully. Binz had been promoted and was a now a deputy *Oberin*[29] which she richly deserved. She was more than 'diligent'. She could lay about her with all her might amid the shrieks of the prisoners, which could be heard all around, then come in to see me, all sweetness and smiles. I had to keep a grip on myself to refrain from striking her. In her place, Mewis took charge of the Bunker. She shared alternate shifts on duty with a new 'power' – a tall young brunette, who had great difficulty reading and writing . . . Boguś used to help her out. As a result, he always knew the exact number of women in the prison, and who was in which cell. By now, not only information but letters were circulating almost freely between the cells. At the same time, thanks to the gardeners and the washerwomen who called to collect laundry from the Bunker, a correspondence between the Bunker and the camp began to flourish. When, after quite a short while, 'the Calf' – as we nicknamed the new supervisor, on account of the strikingly calf-like expression on her face – fell madly in love with Boguś, who took a radio to her cell every night, every other morning he had the latest news from London. It was the end of May, beginning of June. There were no very concrete developments at the time, but all the communiqués seemed to suggest that the summer of 1943 would not pass without major events.

On one of these beautiful summer days, as I was going for a walk, Boguś was up a ladder painting the window grilles of the Romanians' cells. At the far end of the Bunker, two cells had been converted into a single room and a large window installed so that the Romanians had a 'sitting room'. I noticed a change in Boguś' manner. He was not speaking to me. As soon as there was nobody about, I went and asked him outright what the matter was. Silence. I had to repeat the question before I received the fateful answer: 'Sikorski's been killed.'

I learned the details only a little later. They told us then, as to this day, very little. The stark reality was that our Leader was gone – the man whose name, ever since the initial catastrophe of September 1939, had been our signpost pointing the way through the thick of military combat and the torment of imprisonment. We knew that our allies had great respect for him, and that all commitments had been made to him in person. He, more than anyone, was the guarantor of those promises made to his own people.

It is no secret that every man has weaknesses, which sometimes cast a shadow on a public figure. But to perceive them, one must observe at close quarters. In this case, his distant country – still struggling – glorified the name of Sikorski. For us, it was the symbol of our struggle for the highest human values and the pledge of our future victory over the Germans. England's friendship with Sikorski was our shield against the Soviets. His death, regardless of who had caused it, appeared as a fresh and monstrous burden which, in falling on the whole of Poland, had also shattered each lonely prisoner in solitary confinement. That evening at prayers, when we mentioned, for the first time among the fallen, the name of Sikorski, who hitherto had led the living – it was as though the prayer stopped short in our throats, to be replaced on our lips by words that bordered on rebellion: 'Is there any misfortune, O Lord, that you will not inflict on the Poles?'

As also happens in the case of individual catastrophes that shatter one's private life, I was astonished to find the next morning that life in the world at large – in this case, Ravensbrück Bunker – was pursuing its normal course. Even the clocks did not stop. It was just as though nothing had ever happened . . .

The next few weeks brought a great deal of news. The most significant development was the Allied landing in Sicily,[30] the first open attack on '*die Festung Europa*'.[31] From articles written by Goebbels, it was easy to deduce that Germany's situation was more than serious, and that German concern about whether Italy could hold out was growing greater every minute. The end of the war seemed not far off. For me personally, impending events could (indeed, must) have radical repercussions. It was clear that my situation would definitely change for the worse, if the House of Savoy's intervention on my behalf should cease. Logically, my execution appeared the most likely solution. Nevertheless, I felt I must now start to fight my way free of the Bunker's privileged status and get back to the camp, for which I pined with such a deep and indescribable longing.

Every time Commandant Suhren called in, I made that request with increasing insistence. Finally, I decided that the only possible way of achieving my objective was to go on hunger strike. I knew that such an action could only hope to be successful as long as they did not want me to starve to death, which would be as long as they could count on the Italians as allies. So one day, still in June, I stopped eating and told Mewis that I would touch no food until they let me go back to the camp. Here I must say that a hunger strike is something that is really very unpleasant only for the first two days. After that, the appetite somehow fades away. Even the aroma of the dishes constantly placed before me failed to make any impression. Suhren and his deputy, Schutzhaftlagerführer Brauning, now called in twice daily, urging me to eat. Their behaviour seemed to me proof that I had only to continue not eating to secure my eventual return to the camp.

These endless discussions with the Gestapo officers were tiring as I grew gradually weaker. But I knew that I was causing them problems, and that gave me added strength. Since I did not get up, simply in order not to tire myself unduly, 'my guests' stood at the foot of my bed and explained that a hunger strike was not worthy of me as a means of struggle. There was, they told me, in this very same building a person I did not know, a young French woman who was so much better behaved that she would shortly be released; and that the authorities were not in the least impressed by my type of behaviour, and so on. From time to time, during these not very interesting orations, they would glance with amused irritation at the little copper cross from Assisi hanging above my head, but they never made any comment. For my part, I repeated that since nobody had formulated any charges against me, I should finally be set free. Or, if they were holding me simply because I was Polish – which was the greatest tribute they could pay me – then I should be treated in the same way as other Polish women prisoners since I, too, was an *Untermensch* and there was no call for preferential treatment. The two Germans were stupid enough to let me sense their discomfiture, both at my assertion that, for me, it was a great honour to be in a concentration camp, and by my reminder to them that I was an *Untermensch.* They left me at last. On the fifth day Suhren came in and declared that, on the basis of a telephone conversation with Berlin concerning my case, he had come to tell me that he was giving me his word of honour as an officer of the SS – to which, he said, 'I must cease to belong, should I not keep my word' – that within two weeks of that day's date my case would be decided. He enquired whether, given this binding promise, I would eat. I agreed to end my hunger strike.

I swiftly regained my strength and waited patiently. From time to time I was visited by a new Chief Medical Officer of the SS who, after giving me a very cursory examination, sometimes launched into conversation. He once told me that he failed to understand how a person could set such store by her 'Polishness', who not only had a German mother, but whose own looks were still strikingly Germanic. I was dumbfounded. Nobody had ever told me this before. I replied that, as for my looks, my features were distinctly non-Aryan because I bore a striking resemblance to my Hungarian great-grandmother. If there was any question about my racial origins, I was a European mongrel with regard to the number of nationalities concerned in my descent, and these I enumerated for him. The doctor quickly took leave of me and never again spoke about race.

When I got the opportunity, I cautiously repeated to Christiane, in order not to raise her hopes too high, what the Commandant had told me about her impending release. A few days later she was ordered to pack her things because she would be set free the same afternoon to return to her mother in Paris. I gave her my brother's address and asked her to contact him if at all possible. I went and stood under her window for the last time. We said goodbye. I shall never forget that, despite her moment of great joy, she found room in her heart to be sad about leaving me. An hour later I heard her cell door opening and her quick, light footsteps in the corridor accompanied by the heavy tread of German feet. Suddenly, the gate of the Bunker shut with a crash. All at once I felt terribly alone and, at the same time, ashamed of myself for being overcome by selfish emotion, at the moment of release for a friend who had become very dear and was now experiencing a stroke of great good fortune.[32]

Meanwhile, the appointed day was approaching. In the course of those last two long weeks I seemed to have thought through all possible ways that they might further delay action in dealing with my case. I was mistaken. There was one thing I failed to take into account, one thing that never occurred to me: that was how Suhren would choose to act. The critical day arrived. The forenoon passed – nothing. I went for a walk after lunch. I waited till evening – nothing. The whole day went by as so many similar days before and after. There was no sign whatsoever of Suhren. I always thought he was a fool, but that day convinced me that he was wiser than the stupid prisoner who thought the word of an officer was binding.

World events were moving fast. A couple of days after that, on a very sunny summer morning, somebody tapped at my door. At the same time, as though breathless with excitement, the voice of Boguś whispered: 'Mussolini has been deposed – Italy's finished!'

I leaped to the door and listened. Boguś was already next door with my neighbour, a Czech SS man known as 'Kubuś' (Jake), whom I had met once or twice on my walks. A few seconds later he was beating on my wall with his fists. Obviously he was already beside himself, despite the fact that he still wore the death's-head emblem on his cap. Now, the end of the war could only be a matter of weeks, a very few months at the most . . .

The next day we noticed that our two prophetesses were missing. Boguś reported that they had been taken away in the night. That was more than suspicious, so we were all genuinely happy when, next day, both the old girls were back in place. They whispered to each of us that they had been in Berlin, where they were required to disclose what had happened to Mussolini. When I asked what answer they gave, both shrugged dismissively and declared that with no facts to go on – out of thin air, as it were – no clairvoyante could offer sound advice.

At about this time the Romanians left us and I was moved into their 'apartments', right at the end of the building and separated from the rest by a partition. I now had, comparatively speaking, a better chance of circulating in part of the corridor and using the interior staircase. I lived in a room consisting of two cells joined together, with two large windows. Boguś himself had painted this room to his own taste, mainly sky-blue and richly decorated, with green radiator and furniture upholstered in raspberry shades, as favoured by Krüger, I recalled. Even with the Germans, I would not have supposed possible such a juxtaposition of colours. At the same time, I had to admit that increased freedom of movement and, above all, greater access to fresh air had a very relaxing effect on me. At this period, air-raids and bombardments were becoming much more frequent and were gaining in intensity. Sleep at night was often out of the question. Meanwhile, from my windows I could see the flash of bombs exploding and a vast glow in the sky. Everyone stated with complete assurance that Berlin was over there . . .

Meanwhile, we had numerous victims. I remember one beautiful sunny day when the crematorium chimney poured smoke for a very long time. I knew that more Polish women had been executed the previous day, among them my former student from Lwów, who had welcomed me when I arrived. Round about 15 August I was ordered at lightning speed to pack my belongings and move back to my former cell. On the walk, I learned from Boguś that about ten of the 'rabbits' had been brought to the Bunker, and the supervisors were rushing about all over the place. For one or two days there were no walks allowed, nor did Boguś appear in the garden. When I got out again, I learned from Boguś that the 'rabbits' had been operated upon in the Bunker. The same day I managed to make contact with them. One of them had not been operated on that day. Urszula, who was nursing them, was waiting for me by the window.

Three days before, when they again called for 'rabbits' (who knows how often they had done so in the past?), the 'rabbits' for the first time resisted, ran away and hid during roll-call. At last, with the help of a large turnout of wardresses, SS men, dogs and so forth, the women were rounded up and forcibly led to the Bunker. Commandant Suhren then informed them that, as punishment for daring to resist, their operations would be performed not in the sickbay as before, but in the Bunker itself. My large, colourfully decorated room then became the scene of about five operations, the remaining girls being sent back to the camp. The sick patients later lay in neighbouring cells tormented by pain and fever. After a few days, however, their condition improved sufficiently to make it clear that, this time, there would be no fatal casualties, but the start of a long, difficult convalescence lasting many months, often with feverish relapses. I could do nothing for them, apart from passing on news of the camp, as well as sending in newspapers and cards with poems transcribed from memory. The poems were mainly by Słowacki, at their request. Barely a few days after the operations, one of the victims, Joanna Szydłowska, a married woman with a seven-year-old daughter in Poland, expressed her gratitude by sending me via the nurse, Urszula, an immense number of poems, chiefly by Norwid, all of whose major works she knew by heart.

Meanwhile, in the camp, Block 15 was punished for helping the 'rabbits' by being surrounded for a few days by SS guards with police-dogs, while doors and windows remained closed and the prisoners were deprived of water. Moreover, they were told that they would be let out only if they asked to be forgiven. Of course, not one of them gave in. When at last, a few days later, in the sweltering heat of August the doors were opened, they fainted on the spot. Yet they achieved a great deal, for the affair became a major talking point with women of all nationalities in the camp. From then onwards, there were no more 'rabbit' operations.

One day at the beginning of September, Urszula told me they were returning to the camp. Suhren had been to see them and she had heard him say to someone in his party that the cell had to be reoccupied by me at once, because of an impending visit from Berlin. Sure enough, the next day I found myself back in my separate apartment. I walked through those cells, with their atmosphere of suffering, in which our girls had been lying only the previous day.

On the world scene, the Germans were losing all along the line, withdrawing in Russia while Italy was toppling. As far as my own fate was concerned, I fully realised that my chances of survival were diminishing from one day to the next. I was talking about this with Boguś one day and I asked him to let the Polish women know if I was taken away. Boguś was much concerned about this possibility and the next day came up with a concrete proposal. What he had planned was nothing more or less than a joint escape! I dismissed the idea and urged him to forget such a crazy notion. Boguś then explained that the project was not impracticable, but that it would have to be carried out during an air-raid when the electric current that travelled through the wires along the walls would be switched off. We would escape through the window, after having earlier sawn through the bars, then dash to the wall. After that it would be plain sailing. However, it seemed to me that our troubles would begin only later, for want of documents. But Boguś thought not and pointed out that nobody was going to ask two people speaking fluent German for any papers in the middle of an air-raid.

Although at the beginning I had not wanted to hear a word more about all this, daily persuasion by this honest, as well as clever boy gradually began to take effect. Slowly I grew accustomed to sharing this hope and started getting ready for the road. It is easier for a prisoner to get drunk thinking about freedom than drinking alcohol. In one of the cells at my disposal were stored some long, very narrow corridor rugs. Like a latter-day (forty-five-year-old) Juliet, I thought of stitching together a portable ladder for scaling the wall. In the middle of all this, Boguś went somewhere for two days with an SS man to buy paint. He returned very depressed and did not admit till the following day that, in the course of a three-hour journey, their identity had been checked four times. So escape was an utter impossibility. But not until the plan ceased to exist did I realise, despite everything, the extent to which I had been pinning my hopes on it. I knew then that, for me, there was no way out and I experienced that sense of peace and relaxation that comes with the closeness of death.

As I was out walking in this mood on a warm autumn day, something very strange happened. 'Frau Lange' was called in from her walk to report to the Bunker office. That sort of name-change, while retaining the first syllable of the person's real name, had so far been proof that the prisoner was going to her death. I assumed that they had come for me. The sight of an SS man standing by confirmed me in this supposition. So I stood before him and waited. But he merely pointed to a table on which lay a fair-sized parcel and beside it a card.

'Please sign to confirm that you have received this parcel from the Danish Red Cross. You have to sign in your own hand on the list of contents. Only the sausage mentioned here as being in the parcel is not there any longer. It tasted marvellous.'

I stood as though paralysed. It was some little time before I could switch mentally from the direct sensation of approaching death to the problem of a stolen sausage.

A couple of days later Suhren informed me that the next day I would receive a long-promised visit from Dr Tomson of Berlin, Daumling's successor. The following day a conversation took place – a long one this time – which, like all those preceding it, produced no results. For the umpteenth time I raised the matter of a hearing. I complained that although I had sent a letter to Himmler, by hand of the Camp Commandant, requesting an interview, I had received nothing in return except – tomatoes! (For a long time tomatoes had been delivered to me daily, by personal command of Himmler, it was said.) Tomson attempted to reply, but could say nothing definite. He declared that he had so recently taken over his new position that he had no idea at all why I was here. He had simply been ordered to gather information about me. Even though there might not be any precise charges against me, he thought I would probably understand that it was out of the question to simply send me back among the Poles at the present political juncture.

'Things are not going too well for us at the front, as you are probably aware.'

That being so, I categorically demanded to be sent back to the camp. He promised to enquire about that and let me know. So saying, he left.

There began another period of waiting, enlivened only by the arrival of a new colleague. This was the notorious Gerda Querenheim, terror of the sickbay and bitter enemy of Poles. She had been sent to the Bunker for having become pregnant as the lover of Dr Rosenthal. By profession she was a nurse, and she wore a red triangle. Why she should have been sent to Ravensbrück in the first place, I don't know. I saw at once that Gerda knew all the secrets of the sickbay. While I was still in the camp, I was told that she would smother an infant and throw it into the main central-heating boiler. I decided therefore to make contact with her, which I did with no effort at all since I had food parcels. At the mere sight of the food, Gerda took a great fancy to me and told me absolutely everything she knew.

The real secrets of the 'rabbit' operations, it appeared, were not known to her. She could only say that, most often, four types of surgical intervention were involved: septic and anti-septic bone operations, as well as the same two types of operation in the case of muscles. The operations performed on seven 'rabbits' who died were mainly of a different order. Above all, the operations involved the removal of bones for severely wounded Germans and experiments with gas bombs. I asked to which group the six 'rabbits' belonged who, after recovery from their operations, were executed as Polish political prisoners. I was given the answer that those were 'normal' operations. On such occasions, Gerda told me, Dr Rosenthal had always to be present in his official capacity, and there had never been a case of any Polish woman showing the slightest fear or failing to shout 'Long Live Poland' as she died. In her conversations with me and with the prospect of obtaining food, of course Gerda was a great admirer of Polish women. She made a point of showering me personally with compliments, saying that only in my presence could she allow herself to talk so freely.

Once I asked her what happened to children born in the camp. She replied with total composure that it was a nasty subject, but since until recently under German law no child could be born in a concentration camp, the child had to be deprived of life before or directly after normal birth. Because the law had recently been changed, the unpleasant job of disposing of the bodies was no longer necessary.

Thereupon, I resolved to make use of the information I had obtained from this German girl, so gentle and well mannered in her dealings with me, and see that it reached the right quarters.

Then Boguś produced a new project. He was being sent out every day to somewhere in the Ravensbrück district on a painting job of some sort. Having managed to lay his hands on some official-looking paper, which he extracted from a drawer in the absence of the 'Calf' and inscribed with a fictitious name, Boguś wanted to escape to Poland and tell the full story of what was going on here. It seemed an idea worth taking seriously, particularly in view of the fact that fourteen gun emplacements had recently been built around us with machine carbines trained on the camp itself. It looked as though not one of us would emerge alive at the end of the war – now inexorably approaching. I then decided to write a report on a handkerchief, which the lad sewed into the lining of his jacket, and I gave him a contact in Kraków. I explained to Mewis that the paintwork in my cell was badly in need of touching up and should be put in *Ordnung*. As a result she immediately sent me Boguś. As he came in, the look on his youthful face betrayed strong emotion. He knew what was coming. Presently, in a low but firm voice, he repeated after me the words of our oath, placing his fingers on my little crucifix with the figure of Christ. It sounded so strange to be reciting that oath in the Ravensbrück Bunker!

Two days later Ramdohr ordered the arrest of Boguś, who managed to whisper through my cell window that I was not to worry. He had burned the handkerchief, but would remember the oath. At the same time, the 'Calf' was removed from the Bunker.

It had become clear to me that if I wanted to get a message through to my commanding officer, I would have to do it by my own efforts. So I set to work in the old way using the dot code with a Polish-Latin dictionary, which I had acquired at some stage with that purpose in mind, since it had such small print. I encrypted a message of 180 words, mainly on the 'rabbits' and the executions, on the morale of the Polish women in the camp and the fourteen newly built bunkers.[33] I had to complete the work in a hurry, because Mewis informed me one day that she thought it would not be long before my wish would be fulfilled and I would find myself back in the camp at last. I then made strenuous efforts to see with my own eyes the implements of torture being used in the Bunker. That was not easy, because the rooms in which they were stored were kept very securely locked when not in use. Colleagues in the camp, and later Boguś and Gerda, had described for me three pieces of apparatus. In the first room stood a wooden horse (known as the 'goat') for floggings; in the second, the 'coffin' with closing ventilation holes and 'wolf's claws', metal teeth of some kind that penetrated the prisoner's body. Unfortunately I succeeded only once, while out for a walk, in seeing inside one known torture chamber, through a door left ajar. When my Supervisor returned to the camp for a moment, I hurried back to the Bunker and went into the room. There was a wooden horse, on which was something like a saddle, with straps so arranged that it was obvious how the bodies would be forcibly restrained crosswise. I spent so long studying this apparatus intently that I missed the second room and saw neither the 'coffin' nor the 'wolf's claws', tools that were reserved for Ramdohr's use during interrogations. (The 'goat' was also used for normal camp punishment, when the noise of rhythmical strokes and groans could be heard.) I had to make a quick exit at the sound of 'authority' approaching.

I now had very good and almost direct contact with the camp. When nobody was about, I used to run to the large window at the end of 'my' corridor, which was tightly sealed. In the evening, after roll-call,

Polish women would walk past calling to one another, as though from a distance, and shouting: 'Aldona!' I would then tap my window and we would start a conversation. Because, once or twice, I had sent them by the washerwomen short talks on the history of art and culture, the girls would walk up to the window and ask questions. That camp in which there were so many girls who could have been taught seemed to me at the time like a paradise, and my longing to be with them grew greater every day.

Since the official silence regarding me continued as before, I decided to begin a second hunger strike. This one lasted a week. Each day they sent in more and more attractive dishes and left them on the table. On the seventh day there was another SS visitor from Berlin. I heard about it from the girl Jehovah's Witness who had been told to clean up my room for a '*hoher Besuch*'. She scrubbed with passion, and with equal passion attempted yet again to convert me to 'the true faith', promising that judgement was close at hand and happiness attainable, even here on Earth. The main thing, however, was that I must finally renounce my allegiance to 'the worst thing of all' – that was to say, Catholicism. Tired out by my fast, I simply lay there quietly this time and said nothing.

'I am so sorry for you,' the apostle went on as she dusted, 'just as I am sorry for my husband. He is a good man, but he won't believe. Like you, he is damned. You are both going to hell, and that is a real pity.'

The further course of these kind promises was interrupted by the arrival of Suhren, who had come to tell me that he would be returning in the afternoon with Himmler's Chief of Staff. They did in fact arrive. The 'guest' was wearing a long, brand-new leather coat of the kind that Russian secret policemen used to wear in Lwów. He stood there and solemnly assured me that the Reichsführer der SS would accede to my request to return to the camp, provided I would continue to accept SS food[34] as in the past. When I did not agree to that, he repeated – obviously counting on impressing me – that the Reichsführer was greatly concerned about that, and about my health in general. With pathos worthy of a better cause, I had to reply that the food that the other women had been eating for so many years was good enough for me.

He turned away, irritated and at a loss. He looked at the table laden with many untouched dishes. '*Mein Gott! Was ist das?!*' I could hardly refrain from laughing, when Suhren had to explain to the astounded Gestapo officer the reason for this unusual culinary exhibition. From this whole visit I gathered only that they did not want to get rid of me for the time being, and that there would seem to have been some kind of fresh foreign intervention on my behalf.

A couple of days later, I packed up a number of my books (a few English and one or two Latin authors and a dictionary) for sending back to Poland. Nobody noticed that they were not addressed to where they had come from, but to Wisia Horodyska, the same person who had once received *Greek Literature.* At the same time I wrote a letter to Wisia apologising for keeping her Latin dictionary so long, though I knew she needed it for her studies. The parcel went to the Commandant's personal censor. On my last walk I said goodbye to Boguś, who was being returned to the men's camp the same day. The following morning, as I went to the washroom for the last time, the senior Jehovah's Witness in the Bunker, Regina, was standing there. She was a strange woman, who never confided in anyone, but was always quiet and composed. However, she was not always able to control the expression of her eyes, in which could sometimes be seen, as it were, the reflection of some monstrosity she had witnessed and which she could never expunge from her consciousness. Today, for the first time, she smiled at me as I passed her on my way into the bathroom. 'Frau Lange goes in and, presently, Lanckorońska comes out,' she said, almost out loud. I was back in the camp within the hour.

I shall always recall with deep gratitude how warmly I was received. With great joy, I once more sewed the number and triangle on to my striped camp uniform and breathed a deep sigh of relief. Not only had I got rid of that unpleasant and humiliating discrimination, but I had also got rid of myself. I had ceased to be the subject and focal point of my interest in day-to-day existence – a state induced by solitary confinement. It brought home to me very clearly the extent to which man is *dzoon politikon* – a social being. I was just happy being in the camp. At four o'clock in the morning, marching to coffee with a group of *Häftlinge* (detainees), despite the dark and the cold, as we passed the Bunker I thanked God I was no longer there.

I had now been appointed room-leader of a Red Army block. There were in the block some 500 women, mostly young, of whom the great majority were very fit and strong. They had been taken prisoner by the Germans on the Russian front. They occupied a part of the camp, as it were, separate from the rest and their situation was in many respects different from that of the other prisoners. In the first place, they were held in high esteem by all nationalities in the camp, with the exception of the Poles. This bestowal of homage on often somewhat uncivilised girls by practically all the *Häftlinge*, with the Czechs at the forefront, was for me the first indication of just how far the camp had become 'Communised' by the autumn of 1943. The 'Soviets' accepted the homage and the gifts, but paid little attention to the other groups, while maintaining close solidarity among themselves. The Poles they treated with concealed ill-will, which, in exceptional cases, was displayed openly.

As a rule, one was only aware of the infinitely alien uncouthness of these girls, whose most pronounced characteristic was mistrust. This was by no means restricted to the Poles, but applied to all the women prisoners in general. In the course of a longer acquaintance, it became clear that this distrust was most marked among themselves. If one of the Soviets happened by chance to be alone with one of us Polish room-leaders, our exchanges were often quite straightforward and even almost sincere. But if anybody else approached during the conversation, the tone immediately changed, the smile disappeared and terse answers (either evasive or downright rude) were accompanied by a scowl. If there were three people, that was already a crowd and, at that moment, all individuality was lost. The Soviets hardly differed in any way one from another. They were even physically alike, and their reactions were identical to those of their leaders. During any conversation with whomever it might be – regardless of whether the subject was trivial or serious, whether there existed between them and a given person harmony or conflict – there was always a ringleader who was the one to say no, to whom they listened and whom they followed unquestioningly. One sometimes had the impression that privately, they might not agree with her, but that she held them in the grip of some iron compulsion, some incalculable terror. Once I noticed that a group of them were debating something, from time to time casting glances in my direction. Presently, one of them broke away and came over to me. Bustling about the table that I was in process of washing, she asked as though casually: '*Pani Karlo, wy religiozna?*'[35] The question surprised me, but I was afraid that a simple affirmative answer would not lead anywhere.

'Yes, I am a believer. I was not always one, but I have been for many years now and I am very happy.'

'What's that you have under your dress on a little string?' she asked, pointing to my neck. I drew out the tiny cross with the figure of Christ. She studied it closely.

'And that's your God?'

'No, it's only His image.'

'But if it isn't God, why do you carry it round with you?'

'Because, you know, here they are probably going to kill us all.'

'That's so,' she said with simple dignity.

'Well, when I come to die, I shall hold this in my hand and look at it.'

While I had been speaking, the others who had sent the girl over to talk to me had themselves come closer and stood behind her listening. Finally, she replied to me almost in a whisper: 'Life must be easier with it than without.' Suddenly she seemed to jump slightly, having only just noticed that her comrades were standing behind her. She turned round, scowled at them and quickly ran away. The others dispersed, pretending not to have heard those words – so very unseemly . . .

Once, I had to go to the sickbay to fetch one of them (a doctor, or rather, a hospital nurse) and bring her back to the block. She was supposed to visit another camp or factory an hour later. When I told the girl what it was about, it was quite clear that she did not at all like the idea of this lonely outing, but she gritted her teeth and followed me. We picked our way through the camp in total darkness. Suddenly something held me back: two powerful arms embraced me and my companion's flat face was pressed against mine. She implanted several robust and noisy kisses on both my cheeks. I was so astounded at first that I failed to react at all.

Then, the girl began to talk to me in a whisper: 'Miss Karla, we may never see one another again, but I shall not forget you because I recognised you for what you are – a human being.' She repeated it twice: '*Wy czelowiek*' and went on: 'I wanted to tell you so much, very many things, but . . . it is impossible, I cannot. With us, it's completely different from what you imagine . . . It's not the way they say. It's completely, utterly different . . . but I cannot talk about it.'

She was very excited. I embraced her, stroked her, murmured a few warm words and we walked on. When we entered the block she was as stiff and solemn as usual – like all the rest. Finally, having packed up her odds and ends and said goodbye in the hall to everyone and me in a cool, official manner, she went on her way.

Apart from the Soviets, we had four or five Jehovah's Witnesses in our block. After demonstrating opposition to Himmler himself, the Witnesses had been punished by being beaten and split into groups distributed among the various blocks. Our group included two strict observers who did not recognise the camp's roll-call. We had to carry them out and place them in the first rank, where they lay with eyes shut, then carry them back to the block when roll-call was over. I remember once, not being able to bear the gaze of an old woman who lay for hours in the slush, I found a stool somewhere and sat her on it, with the help of a colleague, but she slid back into the snow. Without opening her eyes, she shook her head angrily in my direction. From then on, I did not touch them, but during evening roll-call in the bitter cold I gazed at the innumerable stars above – for us, perhaps, the most perfect symbol of God's perceptible and infinite wisdom, sparkling in the same way on the fanatical sectarianism of the ecstatic Witnesses as on the stolid atheism of the wild women from Asia.

For me, life was not too bad because I had time for my educational work. I gave private lessons – that is to say, the pupils came over to my block after dark, or we would take an evening stroll together, while I told them about the history of Rome or explained the culture of the Middle Ages. Most important were my 'lectures' on the history of the Renaissance, delivered twice weekly to the 'rabbits'. I went to them regularly and drew strength from the feeling that I was once again of some slight use.

The contact with the Polish women was rewarding in more than one respect. One of them, for example, dictated to me from memory the whole of *The Great Improvisation*. It made such a startling impression on me that it was like hearing it for the first time. Occasionally I would lend out one of the volumes in our 'library' for a couple of days. Above all, these included the most important works of Mickiewicz[36] disguised as the packaging for bread and sugar in the food parcels. Despite frequent and thorough searches, they never fell into enemy hands.

Religious life also flourished amid the Polish women prisoners. Two consignments, each of fifty consecrated Hosts, provided by a French priest were smuggled into the camp by one of the 'outside' workers, but unfortunately that was before I was released from the Bunker.

On Sundays we often met for long conversations. Eliza Cetkowska, our block-leader, told us about a camp at Stutthof near Gdańsk, where she witnessed things that were almost unbearable to watch – for example, the brain of a Polish officer whom she knew spattered on a wall. She was very hard-worked in that camp, mostly as a washer-woman. Once, when she was cleaning the camp office, she saw lying on a table an illustrated newspaper in which there was a photograph of her cleaning a window, with the caption: 'How the Russians treat their prisoners in concentration camps.'

Some Sundays were more cheerful. Halina Chorążyna* described for us with great verve life in her block where, not long before, she lost her temper with prisoners who were forming two separate groups: one for officers' wives and the other for the wives of non-commissioned officers. One of her comrades attempted to placate Mrs Chorążyna:[37] 'Don't let it bother you too much, Mrs Chorążyna; after all, an ensign is *almost* an officer.'

Quite often, the seniors met to discuss their younger colleagues. We were deeply concerned because there could be no doubt at all that, even should they be freed, their long captivity was bound to leave deep moral scars, the great majority of which would be damaging. 'Suffering ennobles,' it has been said. But that is mostly the case when the suffering does not last interminably or sap the moral strength of the spirit, precisely during the formative years.

Apart from that, it was by no means the problem of suffering alone that worried us, but more than anything the loss of moral awareness. The relationship towards another's property differed completely from that prevailing in the 'world outside'. Only the taking of something that belonged to a colleague was regarded as a crime. Removal from the seamstresses' rooms or the workshops, or more especially from the storerooms, of blankets, quilts, eiderdowns, underclothes, frocks – anything portable – and the use of these purloined articles to buy the contents of food parcels from colleagues was considered quite normal. If a novice professed surprise that this was so, she was told not to be stupid. Hadn't the Germans taken a great deal more from us than we were 'organising'? (The word 'steal' was never used.) The expression, it seemed, had not originated with the prisoners, but with the authorities, who were 'organising' everything for themselves on such a massive scale that it was impossible to conceal it from the prisoners. For fear of being reported or denounced, they turned a blind eye to the process, so encouraging the most frightful demoralisation. It was a fact that hardly a prisoner in the camp was immune, even in the face of death, from that extraordinary lust for possession. There were even many who succeeded in amassing a complete trousseau. The demand for these articles was often – if not invariably – in inverse proportion to the pre-war level of the individual's possessions. The leaders in all of this were women prisoners with Communist aspirations: the Russians above all, but Polish women, too, were learning to attach excessive importance to such things and it worried us greatly.

Obviously, among the Polish political prisoners there were persons of varied moral values. The fact that someone had taken part in the struggle for independence could not in itself be the sole criterion of his or her standard of private morality. There were some magnificent women, totally responsible and of great integrity, who long before the war had worked idealistically – for example, a whole selection of teachers and social workers. On the other hand, there were many who, in the whole of their pre-war life, had been given no opportunity to broaden their horizons and who wound up in Ravensbrück because, impinging on their daily existence as shop-girls or office employees, they had suddenly become conscious of ideals more precious than life itself. The military career of these women, often heroic, was sometimes very brief, and they were now having to pay very dearly and at great length for their 'crime'. Admittedly, the majority of them simply gritted their teeth, paid without a murmur, and the radiance of their recollections sustained them. Then there was a third group, the saddest of all, scooped up by the authorities more or less at random as reprisals during 'round-ups' or 'traps'. They were the victims of unpremeditated, youthful escapades or of playing with fire in the resistance.

It is not always possible to deduce accurately how any given prisoner will behave in a camp on the basis of service pre-war or in the underground. There are so many determining factors involved: disposition, strength or weakness of will, social adaptability, physical endurance, nervous resilience and, above all, spiritual fortitude, which is more a gift of providence than a personal merit.

The 'rabbits' were a cause of special anxiety. The whole camp surrounded those sixty women (mostly young girls) with a certain kind of veneration related to their suffering. It was very natural, and would have been wicked had it been otherwise. Nevertheless, that fact in itself might have harmful consequences. The 'rabbits', especially some among them, were coddled like sick children and the question inevitably presented itself: if they survive, will they ever be able to live and work usefully, once the initial enthusiasm of their welcome in Poland is succeeded by the realisation that they are not heroines, but only national victims – victims of the most varied kinds, clearly totalling millions . . . The only thing we could do for them was to offer them education – and that was our consolation.

They were taught by a whole series of women, who prepared them for the *Matura* (school leaving certificate). The examination could be held in the camp because there were, among the prisoners, a sufficient number of qualified women to form a board of examiners, who met the standards laid down by the Polish Ministry of Education for secret instruction in occupied Poland. Particularly popular were the lectures on astronomy given by Mrs Peretiatkowicz*. She was the only teacher who was able to 'give object lessons', since the stars in the sky were everywhere, even in Ravensbrück. The girls loved hearing about the secrets of science, which projected their thoughts towards infinity, away from humanity and, at the same time, from Evil.

Almost immediately after my return to the camp, I was sent for by the Commandant. I cannot say I was pleased by the summons. Only a couple of days had elapsed since my books had gone to him to be censored. Obviously, that detective must have found the message in the dictionary. 'It is sure to be "the sands" for me,' I thought. 'Worse still, if they also pounce on the person the parcel's addressed to . . .' I was extremely worried. However, I breathed a sigh of indescribable relief when I arrived at the camp office. An SS man was standing beside a table, on which lay all – yes, all – of my books!

'The Commandant has directed that, after censorship, the books are to be sent to the address you gave. I'm not going to pack and address them. Here's some paper and string.'

I do not remember ever having packed and tied a parcel more zealously than the time I personally sent that dispatch to my Commander, General Komorowski, from Ravensbrück Concentration Camp. It was perhaps the only occasion on which I gave the impression of being a most obedient and humble prisoner . . .[38]

My next meeting with the authorities took place on 5 December at evening roll-call, when I was transferred to Block 27 containing French and Jewish women prisoners. This had the reputation of being the most difficult block in the camp. There were said to be intractable problems with the maintenance of discipline and cleanliness. On the other hand, the previous block-leader, a Dutch woman, was not highly regarded in the camp, so it was not clear which side was at fault.

I was therefore somewhat apprehensive as I hurriedly gathered up my belongings. At the same time I was glad to be leaving the Soviets and going to live among women who belonged to a culture and a cult that I had been brought up to respect. I told myself that there must be neither pity nor rancour in dealing with the French women here, for what had happened in 1940. The mere fact that they were here was indeed proof that they were not capitulators. Equally, about the Jews – as a people particularly persecuted by the Germans – I felt optimistic in advance, for I still cherished vivid memories of their work as orderlies in the Lwów prison hospital.

Half an hour later I was in the block, and the block-leader had assigned me to the Jewish side, together with a second room-leader, a Viennese wearing a green badge. She had many previous convictions, but was industrious, good-hearted and – while she was with us – very honest. The Jewesses were not easy to work with, mainly because of the incredible inequality of social standing among the prisoners. There were very few women from Poland, but a lot of Hungarians, Czechs, French and Spanish, as well as a large number of Germans. Many of the detainees had only a smattering of any language other than Yiddish and were extraordinarily primitive in their habits, yet gentle and considerate in dealing with other people. There were also the pre-war possessors of great wealth, amazingly pampered in the past, who boasted about their villas on the Riviera and the prizes they had won at fashion shows. They were the most difficult of all to get along with, because of their often comic pretensions. There were also highly educated women of great culture, suffering unspeakably in the company of people with whom they had nothing whatsoever in common, beyond the fact that Hitler had banished them all beyond the pale of society.

Working with the Jews was made more difficult because in no time they cottoned on to the fact that I could not make use of the only means at the disposal of block- and room-leaders to command obedience. That was to write a report on the detainee at fault, who would then be punished by the authorities. If such 'immunity from punishment' were to become widespread, the consequences would be severe. Were prisoners, for example, to see that there was no compulsion, they would report late for roll-call and for this the whole block would be punished. Two or three offenders would be responsible for the additional suffering of several hundred already sorely tried and exhausted women. The block- or room-leaders had a duty not only to the Germans, which was morally of no importance, but above all to the prisoners and to themselves. Their first obligation was to protect the block from collective punishments – that is to say, for example, standing in the cold for many hours on end, or forfeiture of dinner for five consecutive Sundays.

A room-leader who neither beat nor reported anyone was left with only one resort: to compel obedience by the strength of her own authority and, on occasions, her own toughness, in order to maintain some sort of discipline. It required a lot of effort, but in the end the Jewish women obeyed and understood the essential practicality of a degree of orderliness in collective living to ensure that contact with the Germans was kept to the minimum possible. There was one person among them to whom I am deeply indebted for her help and kindness. That was Frau Vera Strassner, wife of the President of the Vienna Supreme Court, a woman of great personal culture and innate gentleness, who performed the function of *Zimmerdienst* (room orderly), working tirelessly at the job of keeping things tidy, in the course of which, needless to say, she encountered a great deal of unpleasantness.[39]

Some of the Jewish women had children with them, big or small. The Star of David and the number, on the arm of a child only a few years old, looked huge and grotesque on the tiny sleeve.

Among them was four-year-old Stella, with large, black eyes and very poor health. Her mother had died in the sickbay of tuberculosis, and Mrs Strassner took care of the child. Once a month, signing the letters 'Stella', we corresponded with her father who was in Mauthausen (concentration camp) and carefully preserved two copies of the address of the little girl's grandfather, who lived in Barcelona.

Working with the French, of whom there were quite a number in my hut, proved to be more difficult. Most, if not all, wore a red triangle, but they were not concerned with political problems. They were known as *travailleuses libres* (volunteer workers) – some of them professional prostitutes who had volunteered to come and work in Germany and who had been arrested for an offence of some sort. Relations between them and their compatriots of the French resistance were bad. The number of French women who were in the camp for the sake of France was still small at the time. But among these were women of very high intellectual and moral calibre who, in attempting to make themselves heard in our block, came up against what was for them the very distressing opposition of their compatriots. In general they were hostile to discipline as such, regarding it as a German invention. In their view, anyone who wanted or was forced to encourage order or cleanliness was 'serving the Germans'. Many of the French women in Block 27 were also ill disposed towards the Poles. I now know this was a frequent phenomenon in concentration camps, though at the time I racked my brains about the possible causes for this attitude in my new block. French consciousness of their own intellectual superiority, which nobody of any importance or seniority denied, transformed itself in many of the women into a kind of *Herrenvolk* complex, which was very difficult for Poles to stomach, especially after the events of 1940. I soon came to understand that wartime happenings exerted a profound influence on many of the French women, who regarded the Poles as being to blame for the war and, by the same token, responsible for the French finding themselves in Ravensbrück.

Their attitude to their fate was radically different from ours. A politically active Polish woman was fully aware, from the first moment of her engagement in the underground struggle, that she might very probably pay for this activity with her life or, at least, suffer confinement in prison or a concentration camp. Much as a Polish woman might blame her fate if arrested by accident or oversight, no Polish woman, seized for political activity, would ever – absolutely never – complain. The French were different. Almost all of them grumbled and wailed, thereby weakening their own morale. These women, spoiled by years of comfort and well-being in their daily lives, did not realise that the only way to survive in Ravensbrück was to grit your teeth and clench your fists. When one of their number, Doria Dreyfus, a woman of unusual strength of character and an ardent lover of France, told them as much one day, they called her 'brutal'.

'Brutality' was the reproach also directed against many of the Polish women. One reason for this was that, to our regret, many Poles in the camp were acting as block- or room-leaders, team-leaders or, unfortunately, policewomen. The last in particular (but also some other functionaries) were not chosen from among the Polish 'politicals'. Some of the policewomen were not Poles at all, but of German origin, *Volksdeutsch*, and by their disgraceful behaviour while bearing the initial P brought dishonour on the name of Poland. The French women had forgotten (or wished to forget) with what enthusiasm they had been received by the Poles when they arrived in Ravensbrück, and how the Poles always shared their food parcels with them. Parcels received by the French were few and modest. Above all, they had forgotten how generously Poles working in the kitchen helped the French with food supplies for the block, at great risk to themselves.

Perhaps this unpleasant tension might not have become so acute, had it not been for the fact that the Polish women, almost the only prisoners with a knowledge of languages, were giving orders to the French. In any case, I was painfully conscious of the situation and I had no patience with their ironical ill-will and constant opposition. Meanwhile, it was only when I fully grasped the meaning of 'concentration camp' that, for me, Ravensbrück began in earnest. Apart from anything else, I was unable to continue with my 'lectures' for lack of time. I had one consolation all the same, which was a daily delight. That was a visit to the sickbay. After morning and evening roll-call, I listed the names of prisoners who reported sick and conducted them to the sickbay. There they had to stand in the yard outside, in rain or freezing weather, and wait their turn. I was on good terms with the policewoman on duty, a Czech, and occasionally – though rarely – I managed to get my patients under cover. After that, they sometimes had to wait hours before we eventually came face to face with the nurse, a German, who decided the fate of the sick. *Schwester* (Sister) usually looked at the patient from as far away as possible and pushed her out with a yell, usually after giving her a single aspirin. A great deal of persuasion and determination was often needed to get *Schwester* to allow a sick person to be seen by the woman doctor, a prisoner herself. The best thing that could happen to a patient was to be examined by Zdenka.

Zdenka Nedvedova-Nejedla was one of the camp 'characters', of whom we each of us cherish a radiant memory. For those on whom she bestowed friendship, that friendship will remain a moral privilege. Zdenka embodied in herself traits of character sufficiently rare, even singly. She was very intelligent, very good and very energetic. Moreover, she had a merry disposition and the sunny smile rarely left her pretty face. Personally, she was very unhappy for she had lost her beloved husband in Auschwitz, but she thought it improper to burden others with one's private pain. It was only later, when we became very close friends, that she sometimes spoke to me about him, revealing then a soul torn by suffering. She was a convinced Communist who had no idea what Communism was really like, but put her own noble theory into practice in the light of her shining ethics. I often told her that if everybody in the world was her kind of Communist, it would be paradise on Earth. She was the only Czech doctor who recognised no national or class differences of any kind. Her sole concern was for the patient as such, and she devoted her whole strength to saving her. She commanded a great deal of respect among the Germans, who were impressed by her iron devotion to her work and her inflexible attitude. She helped me to save both French and Jewish women.

Salvation depended above all on raising the patient's temperature, which had to exceed thirty-nine degrees for the patient to be eligible for a 'bed-card' in the hospital block, and so come under the care of the prison doctors. ('Bed-cards' were no longer allowed in the prisoner blocks.) Zdenka fought hard for patients to be granted the bed-card, because it assured them of a couple of days bed-rest with no roll-calls, and the sick person had some hope of being treated by her fellow prisoner, the Czech doctor. The French women in particular often became ill, having little resistance to the Ravensbrück climate, so different from that of their homeland. I often thought that this was another reason for their dislike of the Poles, who were always so healthy. The French women felt bad physically, which weakened their morale still further. It was completely wrong, though psychologically understandable, that they were galled by the superior resistance of the

Poles, whereas one or two of the French prisoners would go down with pneumonia after every roll-call in the freezing weather.

There was still one other way of shielding the aged and the weak from work. On the basis of an examination by a German doctor, the sickbay could issue a so-called pink card inscribed '*Bedingt tauglich*'[40] with the prisoner's number and the doctor's signature. A person producing such a 'permit' could not be assigned to physical labour. Candidates for the pink card could be recommended by block- or room-leaders. The majority of the French women categorically demanded pink cards, whereas the rest of us never liked to apply for them, distrusting the purpose of those lists of the oldest and weakest, which were meticulously prepared as the cards were being handed out. This was a ground for endless complaints against us by the prisoners. Doria Dreyfus suffered inflammation of the lungs on two occasions. I used to believe that it was sheer strength of spirit that kept this woman going, unbowed by calamity, though, when she was young, the Germans had killed her father and her first husband and now she had just lost a son-in-law and, above all, a much-loved son. I trembled for her life when I took her to the sickbay for the second time, comparatively soon after her first admission with pneumonia. But again she returned, firm in the belief that she would see France again some day.

The hours spent every day in the sickbay were for me a source of strength, because by being there it was possible to engage directly in the struggle to save prisoners' lives. During the long hours of queuing at the sickbay, the prisoners behaved quite differently from when they were in the block. I never needed to compel them to do anything, nor were they rebellious – quite the opposite. They appreciated the help and support. Though sick and unhappy, they were warm and kind-hearted. When the sickbay hours were over, I returned to the block with the usual dread at the thought of having to go now and collect bread or a meal. One of the most unpleasant duties of a room-leader was to chase the prisoners out to collect bread and containers of food for themselves and for those who would shortly be returning from the workshops. The prisoners cursed us. They also cursed the 'green' Viennese woman, calling her a 'German swine'. The Austrian was mortally offended – but only by the first word. She came to me bitter and resentful, demanding to know what she had done to justify their calling her a German.

The *Brotkammer* (bread store) used to close at twelve o'clock. If a block was late, it got no bread, but sometimes it was impossible to get the women prisoners out in time to fetch the food. One had literally to throw them out of the hut, otherwise not only they, but their colleagues who had been hard at work, would go hungry. The struggle over carrying the containers of food was even more difficult. The containers were heavy and the French women prisoners were weak, so their resistance in this case was entirely understandable. But nothing could be done about it.

Roll-call, repeated daily before dawn and after dusk, was a hideous performance. First, one had to get them all out of the block, not forgetting all the lavatories, washrooms and the top bunks of the 'three-deckers', where people used to hide before roll-call. Then they had all to be led on to the camp-square where, as the least disciplined of the blocks, ours had to parade under the very windows of 'authority'. There, usually in pitch blackness, they had to form up ten deep, while the ranks were constantly getting confused and agitators could be heard exhorting them in stage whispers: '*Faites neuf rangs, faites onze rangs*!'[41] One had to run around, pleading, counting heads, screaming. Then the Schutzhaftlagerführer, Binz or some other creature would come up and join in: '*Natürlich die Französinnen! Fünf Sonntage kein Mittagessen!*' or '*Stehen nach dem Appell!*'[42] That meant another few cases of pneumonia!

Seeing no end to it, I made up my mind to escape from this hell at all costs. I reported to the authorities, declaring that since I was unable to influence my fellow prisoners, they should take away my green armband and give me some other kind of assignment, even physical work. At the same time, I dropped a hint that since I had a knowledge of languages, I could perhaps be useful in the sickbay. The last sentence did the trick. Binz ordered me to report to the sickbay and ask the *Oberschwester* whether she had a place for me. If so and she saw fit, would she please report a need for my services. I cannot describe the sensation of happiness that overwhelmed me when the application came through from the sickbay. I now felt certain that this was the beginning of a new era of camp life for me. I was reminded of the short but rewarding days of hospital service in the Lwów prison. Once again, my great, long-standing interest in nursing, which in my youth had once almost blossomed into a professional pursuit, was reawakened. What a joy it would be to exchange this repulsive green armband, which ostensibly elevated but in reality so degraded, for the yellow badge of a hospital orderly. On top of all this, I had a secret understanding with the newly arrived Dr Maria Kujawska*, who was about to take charge of the hospital block, that as soon as I joined the medical staff she would submit a request for my transfer, as a student nurse, on the strength of my language skills. 'I can teach you everything you need to know and you can help me with my work . . .' Maria Kujawska, with her two daughters and a group of about fifty Polish women, appeared in the camp in January 1944. The crime for which these women were being punished was having chanced to be in Yugoslavia when the Germans occupied the country. They were arrested at night and told they would be sent back to Poland. On the way, they were separated from their husbands and boys, who wrote later from Dachau concentration camp, while the women came to us. In this group were two cousins of mine, Zofia Potocka* and Róża Tyszkiewiczowa* with their daughters, together with Marysia Kujawska. For a long time we entertained the illusion that efforts at foreign intervention, which we knew were under way, would succeed in rescuing the whole group from Ravensbrück. It was only when I learned that the wife of the Camp Commandant, Suhren, was wearing my cousins' diamonds, that I knew there was no hope for them.

Almost the entire group went out to work in the Neu-Brandenburg factory. Dr Kujawska and her daughters, meanwhile, began a campaign for more humane treatment of the sick. To the end she believed in the eventual triumph of Good over Evil, and in the ideals to which she had vowed allegiance the day she qualified as a doctor. She was a woman of such conviction, but at the same time so naïve, that she was simply unable to believe in Evil. I was afraid for her and restrained her whenever I could see that there was not the slightest hope of success.

'What do you mean? How can you suspect a doctor – even a German one – of approving the terrible things that are happening here? I am going to tell him all about it. Things have got to change!'

Only after long weeks of perilous struggle to save the abnormal and the insane, of whom a few dozen were kept in small cubicles without clothes and almost without food, and only after the *Oberschwester* had described her as 'bitten by this humanitarian bug' (*Humanitätsfimmel*), did Dr Kujawska become dejected – amazed that people could be so evil. She was further appalled when they began murdering the 'madwomen' and when she came into contact with their executioner, Carmen Mory.[43] This woman – prisoner and Swiss spy – made a shattering impression even on me with much less faith in humanity. She had hair and eyes as black as a raven, a very wide, thin-lipped mouth and a heavy jaw. At first sight, the expression on that face – neither human nor animal – gave me such a surprise that I could not recall where I had seen it before. It was only later that I retrieved the prototype from my memory of the she-devils painted by Hieronymus Bosch, that tragic caricaturist of the Flemish Renaissance.

But even Carmen Mory could not for long shake or frustrate the faith and energy of Maria Kujawska. She constantly dreamed of turning the sickbay into a true haven for the sick, and I dreamed about helping her achieve it. I was growing impatient, for I was still living in that terrible block and there was still no order to release me and thus clear the way for my transfer to the hospital block. Suddenly one day after roll-call I was told that I was to stay where I was. A colleague working in the camp secretariat as a cleaner read a letter she found lying on a desk. It came from Himmler's Berlin chancellery and it concerned my own case. The letter categorically forbade any change of assignment for me. It was forbidden to take away my green armband, since I had asked to be deprived of it, and I was to continue working as a room-leader, exclusively on the most difficult blocks with the French or the Gypsies, and excluding, in particular, the Polish blocks.

That was undoubtedly the bitterest moment of my entire captivity, the only one in which I felt truly unhappy. By forcing me to wear the green armband I had come to hate, coupled with the ban on mixing with fellow Poles, so ensuring that I remained in an atmosphere of ill-will, the Germans had at last succeeded in 'punishing' me.

In opting for the sickbay, I had thought I was saving myself. Now that hope lay in ruins . . .

So I gritted my teeth. There was nothing left for me to do except flounder on through that cold, wet spring of 1944. Anyway, it all had to end one day . . . Meanwhile, more and more new transports of prisoners were arriving, among them many French women 'politicals' of high intellectual calibre, for whom the impression reputation earned for French women by Block 27 was inexpressibly painful. Even Madame de Montfort, a friend of Poland whom I begged to intervene with her compatriots, could get no good of them. Nor could Tante Yvonne (Madame Leroux, widow of a French admiral), though she impressed us all tremendously with her grace and her bearing.

One of the main problems was the fact that almost none of the more eligible French women knew German. That made it difficult to propose them for the post of room-leader. We only once managed to get round this stipulation when there was a question of getting Doria Dreyfus to work with us officially. Somehow, the Germans agreed and Doria doubled and tripled her efforts to raise the general standard. However, this tower of moral strength turned out to have a very sensitive psyche and suffered excessively from the unsparing malice of her compatriots.

Many Belgians also arrived at about this time, among them two women by the name of Gommers from Brussels, a mother with her daughter who was a Latinist, extremely tall, with great personal culture and the exemplar of a beautiful, quiet, yet radiant Catholicism. Unfortunately, both women soon left our block, together with a large group of French and Belgian 'politicals', who were accommodated with the 'rabbits' in Block 32, under the care of a very brutal German block-leader, Käthe Knoll. The documents of these French and Belgians were stamped with the letters NN, which seemingly stood for *Nacht und Nebel*.[44] Their presence in the camp was intended to be kept secret from their people at home. They were not allowed to receive any parcels or write letters. With the departure of the NN prisoners, our Block 27 lost, in large part, its recently acquired complement of 'good' inmates.

Among those remaining, the most unusual personality was Mère Marie, Madame Skobzoff, a Russian émigrée who had lived for years in Paris and was arrested there, which is how she came to be included with the French deportees. She was an Orthodox nun. As a married woman and a mother, she separated from her husband, who became a priest, and she herself joined a missionary congregation. Mère Marie was very probably the only person in Block 27 who did not in the least complain about being in Ravensbrück. She had an exceptional amount of work to do and laboured indefatigably in her vocation among the Ukrainian and Russian prisoners, especially the Red Army women soldiers. She spent every Sunday with them and all her spare time, apparently achieving some impressive successes. She converted a whole series of girls, very many of whom heard from her, for the first time, who Christ was. At the same time she made no pretence of her contempt for Europe, in which she did not believe. She told the French in her block exactly what she thought of them with unusual sincerity and bluntness, reproaching them for want of endurance and above all for lack of gravitas, for frivolity. To be fair to the French, despite all this, they had a great deal of respect for her. She did not despise the Poles, though – simply as a Russian – she hated them sincerely. She was very good to me personally and we had many – for me – very interesting conversations about the illusions of many Poles concerning the West. She explained in her faulty, though rich French that she had lived in Paris for twenty-five years and therefore knew that, neither from Paris nor anywhere else in the West as a whole, could any creative spiritual currents emerge. The future lay with Asia – more precisely, with Russia, which would be transformed. Europe, however, was finished for good. One got the impression that Christianity, in which this exceptional woman believed unshakeably, embraced only her powerful intellect, while remaining totally alien to her Asiatic soul.

News from the outside world came through to us fairly regularly. We knew that great events were under way – but slowly, for the Germans were fighting a tough defensive action. They boasted that they would not allow the enemy into Rome, and that Monte Cassino was still in their hands. The news we received from the east was rather sketchy, and all the more worrying for that. How will the Russians behave when they cross into Polish territory? What will the Allies do to safeguard our rights? These were the questions we continually asked one another, each assuring the other that, since all the western governments were supported by moral rights, they could not themselves hold back and simply let the Russians into the heart of Europe! One thing was uppermost in all minds: our belief that the end was near . . .

Individually, we were beginning to face the fact that some us could not hold on much longer. Our physical strength was starting to give out. Feet and hands were swelling. We got up every morning streaming with sweat. Sometime in May, I myself landed in the sickbay with a high temperature (not artificially induced). My throat was so swollen with laryngitis that I could hardly breathe. I was suffocating, and I kept thinking that my prisoners would not get up for roll-call because I could not shout, and that Binz was on her way to us. This absurd 'room-leader's nightmare' very soon receded, however, to be followed by a high temperature and debility that lasted two weeks. Maria Kujawska looked after me and other Polish women came to see me, if only through the window beside my bed. Within the hospital block, women of all nationalities were living in harmony. At last they had time for often interesting conversations and a 'free' exchange of views. All round them there was suffering – a very great deal of it – but the fact that the women were now receiving at least a modicum of medical attention had a soothing effect on everyone. Obviously this relaxation of tension was very much a relative matter. The leader of the sickbay block was the same Carmen Mory who constantly spied on everybody and reported everything to the Germans. So callers outside my window would disappear at a given signal, and all conversation among patients was carried on in whispers. Despite the fact that Mory and her protector, the *Oberschwester* – who always made her surprise appearances after being summoned by Mory – shrieked and yelled, imposed punishments and chased people away, the sick still managed to get some rest.

Doria called in every day. As a room-leader, she could always invent an operational excuse for dropping into the hospital block. She looked very poorly but, like the rest of us, she was full of hope. We knew that this time we were not deluding ourselves: the Germans were done for. Monte Cassino had fallen.[45] The invasion of northern France was expected at any moment.

Suddenly one day, out of the blue – improbable, unimagined, almost incomprehensible – the news burst upon us. Polish women rushed about among the bunks, whispering in the ears of sick compatriots an item of information so electrifying that patients who, a moment before, had been lying prone and helpless, sat up in their beds, wanting to hold back by force the bearer of such news. But the messenger had already raced past and was leaning over the next bunk. The whole block was whispering, but it was not long before the Polish women were speaking aloud, constantly repeating to themselves and others the words that crowned their new and unexpected joy: 'Monte Cassino was taken by the Poles!'

Two weeks after that, dropping into the outpatients' surgery, which was crowded at the time, Dr Treite, the senior physician, announced loudly that the invasion had begun. Five minutes later the news was all over the camp. During the next weeks and months the national groups of women prisoners from the West – France, Belgium and Holland – waited as their countries were liberated, one by one, from German occupation. The Polish women prisoners, too, were waiting, but their fears for the fate of their homeland grew greater every day . . .

Not long afterwards Doria told me she was feeling ill with a terrible headache. I was seriously concerned by the mere fact that the invincible Doria was complaining at all, and persuaded her to go to the sickbay. She insisted that she would prefer to wait till I had recovered, so that I could take her there, because then, she said, everything was bound to go well, as it had twice in the past when she had almost died. She spoke about France and invited me to stay with her for a holiday. Finally, she went away, after saying goodbye with more emotion than usual. The next day she let me know that she was feeling too ill to come to the sickbay that day, but would visit me again without fail the day after. The next morning she was carried to the sickbay unconscious. A couple of hours later Zdenka came to tell me that Doria was dying. A brain problem. In less than twenty-four hours she was no longer with us.

When I returned to the block some time in July, I found Bortnowska, as block-leader, very busy and I was sorry not to be strong enough to help very much. It was not long before I contracted a dry inflammation of the lung, but without fever – so no sickbay. That was the only stage at which I thought I might die in Ravensbrück of natural causes.

Now more and more prisoners were arriving at the camp. The transports from all over were more numerous, and the newcomers predicted an ever more speedy end to the Reich. Came 20 July and the news of a successful attempt on Hitler's life. It was not till the next day that we learned the truth. A few weeks after that, some German women who had been indirectly concerned with the bomb-plot reached the camp. These serious-minded persons stated that the Katyń massacre had been the work of the Germans. From this we could appreciate how successful Communist propaganda in Germany must have been with all the opponents of Hitler, completely irrespective of personal conviction, if these women – having nothing in common with Communism – could lend themselves in this way to acquitting Moscow of one of the most atrocious crimes in its history.

Many prisoner transports were arriving from Poland. All the women spoke of the atmosphere at home being 'electrically charged' and they were all looking forward to great events in the immediate future. We had known for a long time that General Grot Rowecki had been arrested the previous year, that his successor as Commander-in-Chief of the Home Army resistance was General Tadeusz Bór Komorowski, and that the Home Army was expecting great battles to come. The latest arrivals told us that Russia's attitude was unclear and nobody knew what was happening on that front . . .

We often used to sit at night with Bortnowska in her private office doing our best, with the help of these scraps and fragments of information, to put together a picture of the Polish situation. We said repeatedly that we probably did not know the most important thing of all, because all the pieces of information that we had – considered logically – appeared self-contradictory . . . We could never have guessed at the time that even our worst apprehensions were wildly optimistic.

Suddenly, about 8 August, another sensation in the camp was the news brought in by 'outside' workers – at first, just a puzzling rumour, unconfirmed, hazy. Within a couple of days, however, there was no longer any doubt about the reports: Warsaw was fighting. From that day, for long weeks on end, none of us – working hard and ever harder – had a moment to spare, what with pushing the women out for roll-call, struggling to get them attended to in the sickbay, and receiving new transports. But never for a moment were we without the ceaseless mental accompaniment – like a hammer beating in the brain – of that one word: Warsaw, Warsaw, Warsaw . . .

At the end of August the order was given for the immediate evacuation of Block 27, now destined to become a reception centre for new arrivals in transit. Within twenty-four hours the French and Jewish women were distributed among the other blocks, already overcrowded, while our old block was cleaned and, as far as possible, deloused.

While this feverish work was under way, in the sharp heat of the August sun, a new transport arrived. It stopped beyond the wire, to the rear of the hospital block. For two days and nights we could hear the shouted appeals for help, for water, for straw and to be rescued: yells and screams that more and more people were falling sick and nobody knew what was wrong with them. The clamour was interrupted only by the barking of police-dogs. Talking it over with Niuta Bortnowska in the block, we agreed that in view of my fluency in German, I should again go and see Binz. On my way there, I tried to work out in advance what to say. I went into her office and, aware at once that she was not delighted to see me, announced my arrival in a very loud voice. This was the stage at which those in authority were beginning to lose their heads. Binz stretched out her hands: '*Was ist denn schon wieder los?*'[46] she demanded. I replied, with all the solemnity I could muster, that the whole camp was in the gravest danger, in view of the threatened spread of an epidemic that barbed wire was powerless to stem. Detecting a look of sheer panic in Binz's eyes, I gave an increasingly vivid account of what we had gleaned from the shouts and screams that had reached us, adding that this was a matter of the greatest urgency. 'But what can we do?' Binz asked despairingly.

'First of all, order the dogs to be locked up. Then let me have a few of the Polish women to take with me, and an appropriate guard, so that we can leave camp. We'll carry buckets of water and containers with food from the kitchen, find out what is happening out there, then, presently, I'll be back with my report.'

At this, she tossed her head dismissively. 'Why all the fuss? That's nothing,' she shouted. But I could see that her fear of contagion would save the situation. She issued the necessary orders for everything I wanted to be done. But, as I was leaving, she warned me on no account to come near her on my return.

Out we went and found a few women in very poor shape. The sickbay would not take them because, as new arrivals, they had no numbers. Another great commotion. Once again, those in charge capitulated – out of fear. We laid hold of stretchers ourselves and carried the women to the sickbay. Later, it turned out to be scarlet fever that they had. One or two died; one or two recovered. The healthy ones were given something to eat and drink, and a latrine was dug for them. While work was in progress, we showered them with questions.

All the women appeared to hail from Wola[47] – a mixed bunch of shopkeepers and tradeswomen, who assured us repeatedly that they were 'totally innocent' and had 'nothing to do with politics'. They implored us only to safeguard the gold which they seemed to have brought with them in large quantities. But there were also women from all walks of life and of all ages, gritting their teeth in silence. When they did open their mouths, it was to ask only one question: 'Are we going to have to work for the Germans?' There was one thing on which they all seemed to agree. When we asked them what was going on in Warsaw, their only answer was: 'There is no Warsaw any more.'

'What do you mean – no Warsaw?'

'Warsaw is burning. The whole city's on fire. Nobody will get out alive. It's not a city any more. Nothing but ruins. There is no Warsaw any more.'

Returning to our block with Niuta Bortnowska, I was furious with these women. 'Look at the effect of mass hysteria! The way they go on talking round in circles about there being no Warsaw, instead of just telling us what's going on.' Wiser than myself, Niuta said nothing. I looked at her and saw that every drop of blood had drained from her face . . .

From that day till midway through September there was a stream of transports arriving day and night. Not only were they now camping in the open behind the hospital block, but living in a marquee. Unable to cope with the influx of women prisoners, the authorities had put up an enormous tent on the only open space inside the camp. There, often for a week at a time, without fresh air or water, the 'evacuees' from Warsaw were huddled together. The camp authorities no longer raised any objection when a group of Polish block- and room-leaders made contact with them. We took them food and water, removed the sick or dead and plied the newcomers with questions, while searching for relatives or friends.

Cultural levels among them varied very widely. Some of the transports contained a high percentage of criminals, who had managed to escape from civil prisons and loot an incredible amount of gold and jewellery from Warsaw in flames. The Germans confiscated the lion's share of these immensely valuable commodities, but a little seeped into the camp to demoralise it still further. The process of 'organisation' blossomed anew. For a long time, the arrival of every transport was an opportunity for the bath-house orderlies, and, indeed, for anyone who could get close to the newcomers, to make a lot of cash. It was not always easy, for the wardresses kept a very close watch, taking the best of everything for themselves. Formerly, everything belonging to members of each fresh intake was sent to the *Effektenkammer*, the storeroom for prisoners' personal effects. Immense deposits of private clothing were held there till the winter of 1944–45, when they were seized for distribution to German citizens 'who had lost their belongings as a result of enemy air-raids'. The transports now pouring in from Warsaw brought with them such quantities of goods that people who happened to be passing by outside the bath-house at the time could help themselves. There were badges and brooches with images of Our Lady or the Polish Eagle, powder-boxes, watches and evening dresses, prayer books, pots and pans, silver spoons, whole lengths of expensive material, mirrors, eiderdowns and violins, beautiful silk underwear and peasant kerchiefs – all higgledy-piggledy: a macabre, monstrous flashback to the bygone days of the capital. And still more women came pouring in.

One group consisted of an unimaginably cantankerous gaggle of elderly Byelorussian women from some old people's home in Warsaw. By comparison with these, the Cumaean Sibylla[48] of the Sistine Chapel was full of youthful charm. There were women with children and some pregnant women, who gave birth to their babies in Ravensbrück. That activity was now permissible in concentration camps, but the majority of the newborn died anyway of weakness. For the pregnant women I managed to wheedle a distribution of milk out of Binz, on the grounds that these women were just evacuees, 'not criminals like us'. That presentation of the problem helped to produce some milk, but supplies were meagre and irregular.

The women often arrived in such a state of nervous distraction that it was difficult to converse with them. A mother or daughter or sister might be crammed into different carriages for the journey, only to find on arrival that one or other carriage was missing, having been sent to another camp. A certain Mrs Baranowska told me that she had left two children behind in Warsaw because the Germans had taken her without them. The woman's neighbours whispered to me that they had seen her eight-year-old son killed before their eyes by a bomb. I implored them not to say anything to the mother there and then, because who knew who might walk out of that inferno alive. It was no use. That afternoon we heard a terrifying shriek from the dormitory. Mrs Baranowska had learned of the child's death.

Another woman woke everyone up once or twice each night with an almost animal scream. She finally confided the secret to somebody. As a rule she could not sleep a wink, but lay open-eyed in silence. The moment she fell asleep, she would at once dream in full detail of what she had watched with her own eyes: the rape of her seventeen-year-daughter by Vlasov's soldiers,[49] followed by the girl's murder. On another occasion, when during early morning roll-call a young woman vomited, her mother standing beside her felt weak. I brought her a stool to sit on. 'I'm sure my daughter is pregnant,' she whispered, 'she's constantly feeling sick. She was raped a few times by Vlasov's men . . .'

The flow of transports from Warsaw kept pace with the fall of Warsaw's various districts: Wola, the Old Town, Mokotów, Żoliborz, Śródmieście. More than half of the trains bound for Ravensbrück called at our block before travelling on. A minimal percentage of the Warsaw women were given work on the spot. The Germans allocated the vast majority of them to various factories or airfield construction projects. At that final stage of the all-out effort to wage total war, the demand for extra labour was enormous.

In order to prevent people from being drafted who, for ideological reasons, did not want to work for the German war industry, various quite often high-risk stratagems had to be adopted by block- and room-leaders, some of whom were masters of the art. Foremost among them was Niuta Bortnowska. For her, making life difficult for the Germans (apart from being her duty) was precisely one of the sources of her inexhaustible moral strength, in such strange contrast to her physical weakness. She had already saved many of the French 'politicals' she had in her Block 24 from being sent to a munitions factory. These included a young niece of General de Gaulle,[50] whom Bortnowska saved on several occasions – once in the nick of time – from being sent out. Success depended on making sure that a given person's name was not on the list for a transport. The procedure was as follows: the block-leader would be sent a list of numbers of those required to report to the *Arbeitsamt* (Labour Office) at a certain time. Those listed, who were not meant to go, would simply not be taken to the Labour Office. However, this could happen only if the list was received twenty-four hours in advance and the persons concerned could succeed in becoming 'seriously ill' the same day, and being sent to the hospital block for a day or two. To this end, we had recourse to the most varied methods of raising the body temperature artificially – for example, by inserting garlic into the rectum, and suchlike.

When the block- or room-leaders paraded the prisoners in fives, according to the list in front of the Labour Office, there would appear (sometimes at once, but sometimes only hours later) the 'buyers' accompanied by Arbeitsführer[51] Pflaum, with his live merchandise on offer. This coarse, pot-bellied individual had a special aversion to Bortnowska and me. At the sight of me, he would shake his fist and yell: 'You are cheating on these transports. I know you're twisters – you and your little block-leader! Just wait till I catch you.' Fortunately, Hitler's downfall was not long enough delayed for him to see through our tricks.

In the autumn of 1944 the activity of the Labour Office was expanded, due to a great influx of women prisoners. Our task became more difficult as a result, for the 'evacuation' of Warsaw brought whole families our way: sisters, though more often, mothers and daughters – in short, persons who simply refused to be separated in any circumstances. Many women, having no ideological inhibitions, willingly went to work in the factories, knowing that their living conditions there would be better. But they would insist on taking an old mother with them at all costs. It once happened that a 'buyer' was sufficiently humane to take a mother as well, since the daughter was right for the job, but that was an isolated case which did not recur.

Occasionally, also, when Pflaum was very drunk, it proved possible for us to directly persuade a factory owner, who had selected a mother, that her feeble daughter was also a particularly able worker. That succeeded, however, only because of an extreme shortage of labour and that, too, was a rare case. It was a common sight to see the meticulous inspection of hands and feet, followed by the selection of the more serviceable goods on offer and the rejection of those less appealing, amid scenes previously known to us only from the pages of *Uncle Tom's Cabin*. The 'conscripts' were then sent to the sickbay for a medical inspection. They had to strip naked and stand in the open, sometimes for an hour or two. From what I observed, SS men (who were clearly not doctors) would always make a point of walking past the queue, often more than once. After an hour or two, the women would parade before Dr Treite, who almost never rejected anyone already earmarked for a transport. Then the sickbay staff would draw up lists, and Polish women in the sickbay, regardless of the nationality of those sent away, omitted from the list the numbers of those who did not want to go to work, for ideological reasons. That scheme entailed a great deal of risk for all involved. In fairness, it must be admitted that on a few occasions the Austrian woman in the Labour Office and one German woman, Ilse, who worked there, joined in and, at the last moment, contrived to 'lose' a prisoner for whom we had asked.

By that means, in the autumn of 1944, quite a number of women members of the Polish Home Army[52] avoided being forced to work for the German war industry. They continued to 'loaf about' in camp. There were women among them who told us that, if we could not save them, they would die rather than consent to go straight from a clandestine Polish munitions factory or the barricades of Warsaw to work in a German armaments factory. Unfortunately, we were not able to protect all of them. That was the most painful thing of all.

Those on the final list for the transport would arrive at the appointed time (usually about 11 p.m.) at the bath-house. There, each prisoner had everything – absolutely everything – confiscated, in a much more thorough fashion than at the outset. Wardress Knopf (nicknamed the Sparrow, and known for her strange, squeaky voice and immense brutality) was in charge of transports. Often quite serious fights broke out. I remember a Ukrainian woman who was prepared to be kicked till she bled, rather than surrender her rosary. Other women fought heroically to be allowed keep the photograph of a child. For a room-leader to safeguard the property of someone leaving camp, who was in the bath-house, was fraught with much peril for all concerned. For that final dodge to work, quick-witted partners were essential.

At last, towards dawn, stripped of everything and clad, even in November, only in skimpy flowered summer dresses – the supply of convicts' striped overalls having long since been exhausted – without even stockings or coats, the women were marched out of camp in fives. If they were bound for remote workplaces, administered by other camps, we lost sight of them, but if they went to factories regularly serviced with labour by Ravensbrück, they would return later, sometimes hideously wounded, if the factory happened to have been bombed.

Air-raids were becoming ever more frequent. People were glad they were 'nightlies'. More often than not, this meant two hours off work. We used to sit in the block-leader's little office, looking and listening. One evening, the silence was broken by Krystyna Dunajewska, room-leader and mother of two pilots: 'It could be my own sons flying over me,' she said. A few times during raids, the whole camp was lit up. We assumed they were photographing us from the air. Soon we had confirmation of this in the form of four green balloons that seemed to be hovering in the air at each of the camp's four corners. Bombs fell around. The results of this 'heavenly' protection were unexpected. Gestapo dignitaries started arriving from Berlin to live at our camp headquarters. We were furious . . .

Even when the flow of transports from Warsaw ceased, activity in the camp was hardly reduced. The more the boundaries of Hitler's empire shrank, the more numerous were the transports arriving from other directions. The Germans began sending women prisoners to Ravensbrück as they withdrew from the various occupied countries. From all over Hitler's *Festung Europa* they came: French, Belgian, Dutch, Yugoslav, Italian, Polish and Hungarian.

In the late autumn a transport of some fifty Greek women arrived. It was a troublesome situation, because they knew no language but their own. We were struck by the way they pointed out the P on our sleeves to one another. They behaved very cordially towards the Poles, but in a respectful and disciplined way. They appeared to be rather simple women, with the exception of one whose orders they obeyed like lightning. Her name was Sula and she was a nineteen-year-old law student from Salonika. Her refined figure, innate pride of bearing, purity of profile and the proportion of her features were all clearly reminiscent of her immortal ancestors. Later we learned that she was the commander of a small military unit, captured, fully armed, in the Greek mountains. Sula was also their interpreter because she was said to 'know' French. In fact, though she spoke it almost fluently, she understood very little. The trouble was her very strange pronunciation, but I eventually got used to it. She never complained, although she and her companions in their summer dresses had to parade for roll-call, turning blue with the cold, in that Mecklenburg autumn.

One day, to please her, I recited a few lines of Homer. Sula's reaction was unexpected. She threw back her beautiful head of black hair. Her eyes shone with inexpressible pride, as for a moment she felt herself to be the representative of the eternal heritage of Greece. She stood in front of me and began to declaim long passages from the

Iliad. The throngs of women around us fell silent. Squabbling and yelling ceased. They did not understand the words, but they gazed with admiration at the tall figure of the girl and at the expression on her face of both solemnity and ardour. They clearly sensed that this voice, and these lines in a foreign tongue, had nothing in common with the world of humiliation and ugliness surrounding us. We listened to the monumental hexameters of that heroic poem and, for the time being, it seemed to us that everything around us that bore the seal of our captivity had ceased to exist.

Another time, Sula explained to me that the Greek women felt at home in Ravensbrück because they were under Polish leadership. They had been told by the instructors in their military organisation that the Polish people had made the greatest sacrifice for the common cause and that only the Poles had offered total resistance to the invaders. They also knew that Poland had suffered immense human losses through the sacrifice of so many of her sons and daughters. At first, I did not know quite what to say to all that, especially in view of the language difficulties. Finally, I quoted to them the one sentence by Thucydides that I happened to know by heart from a speech of Pericles: 'The whole earth is the graveyard of enlightened men.' Sula gave me a long, intense look, then ran back into the block, from which she later emerged, accompanied by two other Greek women. I understood that she was explaining to them that although the Poles, away to the north, lived so very far from the Greeks, they nonetheless knew who Pericles was and what the freedom of Athens had meant for the world. She then recited the most important extracts from the speech, which two and a half thousand years later had still lost none of its power, proclaiming the love of Freedom and Fatherland as the greatest cultural values of humanity.

Almost all the Greek women were then detailed for transport to other places. Only a few sick were excluded – among them Sula, who happened to be unwell at the time. When we returned to the block, she threw her arms round me and begged me to 'wangle' a place for her on the transport. That was something I had not expected. So many women of all nationalities were constantly wanting to dodge the transports at any cost, in order not to cast bullets to kill their own brothers – and here was Sula keen to go! Seeing that I could not understand her, the girl gritted her teeth and whispered the single word 'sabotage'. Her eyes narrowed and at that moment, to my surprise, I saw a flash of totally alien ferocity on that noble face. A moment later she added that she must go at all costs, because she was under orders. It was just not permissible to separate her from her comrades . . . They were good and courageous women, but there were certain things they did not know. In this case, the honour of Greece was at stake . . . It proved possible to grant her request.

In the evening, just before the transport moved off, and when the staff were no longer on hand, the Greek women said goodbye, in honour of the Poles, by singing their songs of freedom. Tears poured down their cheeks, but their voices never faltered as they sang those songs full of nostalgia and passion.

The blocks were now overfilled to the point where additional three-tiered bunks had to be set up in the mess halls, so that the prisoners ate and spent all of their free time on their bunks, sleeping three to a bunk. This, given the prevalence of ulcers and sores, was unspeakably disgusting. Only those working in the sickbay or the kitchens, as well as block- and room-leaders and the most senior prisoners, kept a bunk each right to the end. This, it must be admitted, was an immense privilege, all the more precious, the greater the congestion. In these conditions, trying to de-louse the block was like the struggle of a drowning man against the waves.

The drainage, designed to cope with 15,000 persons, was having to serve three times that number. As a result, the system was almost uninterruptedly out of order. Prisoners therefore relieved themselves in the open, near any block, as long as it was not their own. Inmates were severely punished if a passing official should take it into her head to penalise the contaminated block.

All of that was as nothing compared with what was going on in the tent. That was where, in late autumn, they put more than 4,000 women evacuated from Auschwitz (Oświecim); mostly Hungarian Jewesses. There was nowhere to breathe because there was no air; nowhere to lie down because there was no room; and nowhere to relieve oneself because the temporary latrines were unusable. Consequently, a stream of urine and excrement seeped out from under the tent, surrounding it, as it were, with a wreath of stinking puddles. Moreover, day and night there issued from the tent the ceaseless wailing and shrieking of 4,000 women, which could be heard all over the camp. The formerly relaxed and serene tent block-leader, Hanka Zaturska, now had a strangely permanent expression in her eyes, wide-open with horror. She said little about what was going on in her tent, referring only to many technical difficulties to do with the removal of bodies, identification being out of the question. Once she told me almost casually: 'We had another problem today. A young and very pretty Hungarian girl suddenly went berserk. Despite the total lack of space, she succeeded in jumping on to the corpses, addressing them and dancing around.'

Sometime towards the end of October there was a change in my own situation. I was transferred as block-leader to Block 32, which housed the NN prisoners, the Soviet Russians and, above all, the 'rabbits'. I was sincerely pleased about this, for the 'rabbits' had been badly treated by the previous block-leader, Käthe Knoll. I was happy to think that I would be with them, if dangerous times for them lay ahead.

For Niuta Bortnowska and me, it was not easy to part. We had worked together for so many months in the closest cooperation and, although we were very different, we got along exceptionally well. I had been immensely impressed by her intelligence, so rarely combined with an indomitable personality. Niuta was arguably the toughest of us all. She resisted the Germans, at risk to herself, everywhere, always and at every step. They hated her in particular. The chilly pride with which she behaved towards them irritated them greatly, for it pricked their inferiority complex. The Germans, moreover – of all nations possibly the most arrogant, but the least proud – are infuriated by nothing so much as an innate pride, which they usually dismiss as impertinence, though it impresses them profoundly. I do not recall which of our girls met with the reproach: '*Sie brauchen ja nicht so frech sein, weil Sie ein P tragen!*'[53] The whole group at the time received this compliment with much satisfaction.

Among the women in 'protective custody', Bortnowska had many affectionate and devoted colleagues, but there were also those who were not so affectionate, particularly because Niuta had spoken to them roughly, was sometimes stand-offish and was never genial with everybody. Some of the women felt ashamed in front of her, well aware that Niuta did not know the meaning of the word 'compromise'. A few days after I left, the Germans working in camp headquarters accused her of ill-treating German women in the block. That was not true. In fact, the Germans in her block received no favoured treatment of any kind. That was what angered them. I no longer remember all the details of the affair, but I do know that she once got her face slapped by a wardress at roll-call in front of the whole block, and for a few days had to stand outside the camp office, where I slipped her some Sympatol tablets stolen from the sickbay, because I was awfully afraid her heart might fail. Niuta was as tough as ever. They threatened her with being sent out to work in a factory, but we hid her among the patients in the block sickbay, where she rightly belonged after her most recent experiences.

Things did not go well for me immediately after my shift to my new workplace. The composition of the block 'population' differed greatly from that of all others in the camp. The three basic groups of *Häftlinge* – the NN, the Soviets and the 'rabbits' – kept rather apart from one another. Among the NN (as, indeed, in the whole camp) the Norwegians distinguished themselves by their standards, discipline and worthiness – in short, their culture. They were the only national group (though small in number) that consisted entirely of women 'politicals'. They were also treated as deserving of every respect by the rest of the camp. The French and the Belgians were also of a far higher standard than in Block 27. They were strongly Communist but, at the personal level, relations between us were correct. Obviously, getting them out on parade for morning roll-call was unpleasant, but that was almost the only bugbear of the day. Block 32 was also spared having to collect bread or food. Everything was delivered by the Soviets, who had meanwhile been formed into a supply column for distributing food to all the sickbays, and of course their own block as well.

After roll-call, only one other danger threatened those in custody. Those who had no permanent jobs and were known as 'disposables' had to parade in fives before the Labour Office officials on the camp-square and were taken away to work. In my block the only 'disposables' were French and Belgian. The 'rabbits' did not work, and all the others had permanent assignments. While escorting the French to the Square, you dared not take your eyes off the prisoners for a moment, or they would run away and you would be left with nobody to parade. However, to my standard response that, in the pitch-black light of dawn (roll-call was at 4.30 a.m.), I could not be responsible for workers whom I could not see, I was above all sworn at as an incompetent and threatened, but never punished, for the situation was growing more chaotic every day. Finally, work was found for the 'disposables'. They went willingly, since the work was light and plenty of things could be 'organised' – particularly clothing. The French reported that in the early days they were ordered to sort out large quantities of new goods, very obviously arriving from shops, including kitchen utensils, clothing, furniture and boots. They managed to make off with several pairs of shoes bearing the names of Warsaw firms. After quite some time, the sorting out of new items came to an end and they were set to work arranging the most varied assortment of used goods, which were then dispatched in railway wagons. Nothing was lacking from this latest assortment, absolutely nothing – from curtains to porcelain, from silken coverlets to children's toys.

One of the Polish women, Mrs Anna Lasocka, who was busy at the dump, came across some of the furnishings of her own apartment in Warsaw. The owner did not help herself to any of her own belongings, but many women did manage to clothe themselves and thereby save their lives. Nobody was asking any questions by this stage. It was a general free-for-all. The steady influx of new transports, the disorganisation of everything due to almost uninterrupted air-raids in the neighbourhood and, above all, increasing fear among the Germans created an atmosphere in which there could no longer be any question of the former draconian discipline. But there was no improvement in prisoners' conditions. Unbearable overcrowding, and the ceaseless noise and turbulence of the throng, were accompanied by acute shortages of everything, while the whole camp became unspeakably filthy and infested with lice. Bedding had long since disappeared. There were hardly any blankets and often not enough food, not to mention the disappearance of potatoes, leaving us only turnips in hot water and no more Saturday slices of sausage or margarine.

Food parcels – our only real source of nourishment – stopped arriving, the further the Germans retreated. Only the International Red Cross continued to remember us, though for several months the Germans imposed a *Paketsperre* – a ban on the receipt of parcels by prisoners. A huge pile of our parcels began to accumulate at the camp headquarters, which later on the Germans themselves, eagerly, if not without some difficulty, managed to take with them as they left. At this stage, only informers and lady friends of Ramdohr, the camp police chief, received the contents of Swiss food parcels for services rendered. Sometime during the winter the Germans suddenly began to distribute food parcels once more. As a result, some of us were again a little less hungry than we had been, and the health of our gums improved slightly. But, in this huge camp, that was no more than a drop in the ocean.

In connection with all this, the general state of health steadily worsened. The women prisoners grew most perceptibly weaker, and finally some kind of dysentery – presumably contagious – gained a grip and spread through the whole camp. The disease had the effect of totally weakening the intestines, so that any food raced straight through the system without nourishing it in the least, and the sick became hungrier than ever. Because this type of dysentery caused no increase in body temperature, the women could not be admitted to the sickbay, were sick in the block and made to stand for roll-call, after which the square was covered in stinking excrement and at night whole trails connected the dormitories with the non-operational lavatories. Shouting and squabbling could often be heard at night when the topmost tier began to dribble on the lower bunks. The outside walls of the block were soiled all round to a height of about eighty centimetres.

Something peculiarly hideous now ensued. That was the way in which the French women started dying. They perished without a struggle, no death-throes, often in their sleep. Increasingly often at dawn, just before roll-call, a neighbour would come running up with the news: 'Madame XY has died!' 'When?' 'I don't know, we were still chatting together at dawn. Then I got up and now I've just found her body, already cooling off!'

I rushed up to the front of the parade to alter the total number of prisoners that I had already given in advance of the roll-call. One was not allowed to write simply '1 dead' for, as a matter of principle, it was forbidden to die in the block. That was what the sickbay was for. One was therefore required to write '*1 kommandiert*'. In fact, one was allowed to add the word '*tot*'[54] in brackets. That was regarded as the ideal solution. Some blocks failed more than once to report a prisoner's death in time and had to parade for roll-call with the corpse.

Once, I remember, on a Sunday, old Madame de Ganay died. She had been a long-term prisoner, always disciplined and kind-hearted, reminiscent in bearing and disposition of those noble French ladies at the time of the French Revolution. She had all her wits about her and asked me not to let her be carried to the sickbay, because she wished to stay with friends till the end. I knew that her state of health was already such that the sickbay would have to receive her, though she had no temperature. However, a person with only a few hours to live would certainly not be given a bed. In all the block sickbays, the sick ended up half-naked on the floor. The French women begged to keep Madame de Ganay with them in the block. I knew that at 2 p.m. there was to be a general roll-call at which all prisoners, alive or dead (sickbay patients excepted) must be present. On top of that, the sick who had not been taken to the sickbay in the morning would not on any account be received later. I hesitated, deeply undecided, and went to fetch Dora Rivière, a French doctor friend of mine. Dora examined the sick woman and expressed the opinion that she would probably not live till two o'clock. So I decided to risk it and keep the old lady with us. At one o'clock she was still alive and I began to reckon with the probability that I would have to carry her to roll-call, when, at one-thirty precisely, the Supervisor came running in from the camp office, bellowing the order for a general roll-call . . . But Madame de Ganay had already been 'drafted' – to heaven.

It was hardly surprising that the whole group was stricken with pre-mortal fear, so to speak. Even the toughest among them were finding it very hard to keep going. But the dauntless *Zimmerdienst*, Simone Lahaye above all, and others struggled to the very end to maintain the group's morale. It is one thing to look death in the eye, but quite another to be in constant contact with corpses. To make matters worse, fresh transports were arriving with French women from prisons where they had been for a year. These women, for the most part older people with lowered resistance, both physical and psychological, paraded for roll-call two or three times, caught pneumonia or dysentery (or both together) and died off like flies in the autumn. In the group were two or three English women who had been captured in France. They were a particular headache, because whenever they fell ill, they categorically demanded the special treatment and nursing that they required. To all the explanations and reasoned persuasion of Simone and me, pointing out that we were in Ravensbrück and there was nothing to be done, they always replied with one and the same sentence: 'But I am British . . .' They, too, died in the end.

The arrival of still more Franco-Belgian transports led to serious problems in relations with the Red Army women. These girls, having been treated from the beginning with special esteem, were now – as the victors of tomorrow – becoming daily more audacious. When the French arrived tottering with exhaustion, the Russian women, who each had five or six blankets, refused to part with even one each for the French. I had to insist on a reasonably fair distribution. Once again, when I told them one at a time that I was not a Communist, but I still considered it wrong for one person to freeze while her neighbour had six blankets, the Russians agreed with me. However, once they were together, not only did they threaten me, but they frightened the French as well. Only Simone was not afraid of them. Her bearing and courage had won her great authority, but she, too, was exposed to her undisciplined colleagues.

The blankets were no help. The French went on dying. The corpse (or rather the skeleton) had to be stripped naked in the block, and the number – the only thing of any importance – had to be written on the deceased's chest with an ink pencil and the remains taken to the mortuary. No stretchers were available. So the dead had to be carried in an old blanket, like a sack, or more often on a (rarely washed) closet door. As far as possible I used to deal personally with the remains in order to spare the closest colleagues of the deceased. Besides, I still remained physically stronger than the majority of the French women. So I had no alternative.

I was once told that a Madame Thierry had died, but there was no need to write her number on her chest. It seemed she got up an hour earlier, washed herself, wrote the number on her skin, then lay down again and died. 'She was certainly not psychologically weak,' I reflected. 'There are various kinds of heroism.' And I took the remains of Madame Thierry to the mortuary. Strictly speaking, the sickbay was supposed to certify every death, but with 120–30 people dying every day, that was impossible. It therefore depended on the conscientiousness, intelligence and experience of the block-leader to avoid the ultimate catastrophe – namely, the inclusion of a living person with the corpses. Apparently, that had happened more than once.

On one occasion I remember, when we were conveying somebody's remains to the mortuary as usual, I was set upon with wild shouts by some people from another *Leichenkolonne*[55] consisting of some German women, but mainly Gypsies. The air was thick with dreadful abuse, most of which I could not understand. Finally, I managed to ask them what it was all about, since 'There's never been any trouble between us before.' This provoked renewed uproar. 'You bloody So-and-So, we know you well! You always put the hands of your corpses like this –' (here they placed the claw-like hands of a corpse as though for prayer, 'or like this' (hands crossed). 'We know what that means, we know very well!'

This was followed by another torrent of abuse. In the midst of this appalling hubbub, I was overcome by a strange sense of calm. I waited for a little, then said very quietly but distinctly: 'You cannot imagine how happy I am, how immensely pleased I am that you know what this is all about. There is nothing in the world of greater importance, and it is a great joy to know the meaning of this sign.' Silence. They stood there motionless, as though thunder-struck, gazing at me in shock. Then they lowered their black eyes to stare fixedly at the ground, and their black locks hung over their foreheads. Silence. Then I wished them well and returned to the block with my colleague, carrying our door. From then onwards, the *Leichenkolonne* treated me with the greatest respect, not devoid of a certain fear. Later, thinking it over, I wondered whether there had not been, in the life of those unfortunates, a moment when, through the narrowest of cracks, they had glimpsed the radiance of the Truth?[56]

There were some nurses capable of surrounding a dead person's remains up to the last minute with appropriate respect – washing, laying out the body, closing the eyes. But others no longer could. They hadn't the strength.

Outside the entrance to the sickbay, during that last winter of the war, stood or rather tottered about or lay in the biting cold rows of curiously swathed figures, for long hours on end. Every day, some of the waiting sick would die before they reached the nurse, thus shortening the queue. Even Zdenka broke down at times and simply wept. 'How is anyone to heal the sick with no beds, no medicine and no energy?' How, indeed, could these spectral creatures be treated by doctors, when it was already impossible to believe that they had once been women?

In this hopeless locale of the dying and the dead there remained to us one great source of strength, which constantly gained intensity – that was the ever-growing need to escape into the realm of intellectual riches. In this connection a great delight came our way. One of the Polish women brought with her from Auschwitz a treasure that, because she was travelling on with the transport, she had to leave with us. That was a one-volume edition of Shakespeare's complete works in English. The book was stamped with the number of an officers' prisoner-of-war camp, from which it had by some miracle been smuggled to the Auschwitz-Birkenau camp. Shakespeare was now secreted in my straw mattress, from which I used to lend him out to the occasional reader. There were days when reading was out of the question. I had neither the time nor the energy, but for us the mere awareness that *King Lear* or *Richard II* was with us was proof that the world still existed.

Requests for 'lectures' multiplied. Apart from the 'rabbits', I had also a set of five serious girls, whose leader and inspiration was Halina Wohlfarth*. They were particularly interested in the ancient classics and regularly took notes at my lectures. Once, a particularly zealous wardress found one girl's notes and hoped that she was at last on the track of a conspiracy – something increasingly feared as everything began to disintegrate. The situation was serious and the consequences could be very grave. The girl said that she had noted down a number of localities and details given to her by a much-travelled colleague, so that one day she could go there and see for herself. She thought the affair was about to blow over, when the wardress discovered in the notebook, as she thought, proof that her suspicions were correct. The proof was the word 'amphitheatre'. The girl came out of it alive, thanks only to the efforts of many people. As for the seriousness of the students, perhaps the best group I had in the camp was the result of the powerful influence of Halina on her colleagues.

One day, soon after New Year, Halina was taken away to the Bunker together with a few others, among whom was the room-leader Zosia Lipińska*, Doctor of Law. All had previously been arrested, almost four years ago in Warsaw, on a grave charge, that of operating a secret printing press.

The next day, 5 January 1945, in the evening, they were escorted out of the Bunker under the eyes of their colleagues. They crossed the camp-square and were leaving by the main gate when they met two prisoners, German women returning from the Commandant's office. 'Where are you going?' they asked, shocked to see the group going out at that hour with a strong escort. Zosia Lipińska pointed a finger heavenwards.

Two days later, one of the members of my study-group asked me: 'Are you going to go on teaching us? Are you going to leave us now that – that . . . Halina's . . . not here any more?' I replied that, of course, I would give my normal Sunday lecture on sixth-century Greek culture. I had meanwhile to decide on the shape of this lecture. At the last minute I managed to get hold of a small book with reproductions of some Rembrandt paintings. When I climbed on to the three-tier bunk where my listeners were waiting, I said, not looking them in the eye: 'If you don't mind, I am going to interrupt our classics course for today, and instead I would like to say a few words about the religious paintings of Rembrandt.'[57]

The execution of 5 January was the last in a long series. It brought the number of Polish women who lost their lives in Ravensbrück to 144.

A week or two later, the Viennese woman who was friendly towards Poles came to me. I knew she wanted to tell me something, so I waited.

'Have you a little time?'

'Of course – if it's important.'

'Go to the main office. There's nobody about just now. In that small room beside the secretariat, you'll find a newcomer.'

'Polish?'

'No, the wife of the Mayor of Cologne. Go there – I've asked her to tell you everything she knows about politics.'

'Something interesting?' I asked, wrapping a scarf round my head.

'It certainly is.' As I went out, she added: 'Only grit your teeth.'

In the little room beside the secretariat I found a rather young, tall and energetic-looking blonde. We greeted one another and I asked her what was going on in the world. She looked at the letter P on my arm and asked: 'Do you know the terms of the Yalta Agreement?'[58]

I left the room fifteen minutes later as a person without a homeland . . .

Within a few days we got to know the names of the main members of the Lublin Committee.[59] We passed them round by word of mouth, for there were Polish women of all social and political shades in Ravensbrück, coming from all parts of the Republic. Despite that, there was not a single one of them who knew even one of the names that reached us. We could not fathom it. Bierut? Osóbka-Morawski? Gomułka? Who is he? Who were these people nobody had ever heard of? So it was that our fear for Poland's fate grew day by day. This apprehension was predominant in our hearts and souls, but other, equally natural, though more egoistical feelings were beginning to creep in. For every Polish woman imprisoned in Ravensbrück for serving the independence of her country and the ideal of human freedom, the personal sacrifice had counted for nothing. It was something very unpleasant, but also very natural, that she should be here and possibly die here: it was quite usual, not very interesting or, at any rate, not all that important – *provided the aim was achieved.* Now, however, if Poland had been sold out and the world's freedom trampled underfoot, the individual sacrifice made by each of us suddenly began to appear as something terrible, because pointless. Now, and only now, did our personal misery, and the memory of our sisters who had fallen in battle or died here, begin to weigh crushingly upon us.

Suddenly, some of us older ones (Niuta and myself in particular) began to feel aware of a new obligation – a burning and rather difficult compulsion. Our young people at this time were being overtly bombarded by Communist propaganda. One had to do everything within one's power to counteract it by doing what was often very difficult namely, *telling the truth*, by explaining to those who asked the exact nature of Communism. Amongst the older ones, opinions were divided on this subject. I will never forget one evening conversation I had with Marysia Kujawska. She called for me and took me over to her sickbay. There in her 'study' she came straight to the point.

'You're making anti-Communist propaganda among the young people.'

'With all my strength,' I replied.

'You simply must not do it! You see what's happened. For some time to come, we have got to coexist with Communism and the Soviets. It certainly won't be easy, but we must find a *modus vivendi*, and it's therefore not permissible by any means to incite the young to hostility against Russia or its system.'

I was well acquainted with Marysia and I knew that her intentions were of the purest. I also knew, however, that honourable people who are unable to imagine *Evil* can be very dangerous. I therefore answered gently, but inflexibly. No use. Finally, when Marysia insisted ever more forcibly, I told her calmly that, as an academic teacher, I had special duties to the young, which I intended to fulfil – to the end. We parted without resolving our differences. We went on seeing one another as before, but relations between us had changed.[60]

In the camp, meanwhile, changes had taken place – at both personal and general levels. Thanks to the scheming of German women in the camp secretariat, who first overcame the resistance of Bortnowska, the Polish room-leaders were transferred from my block, including Jadzia Wilczańska, with whom I got along very well. In exchange, I was given two persons whose job, I knew, was to spy on me: a German, the loquacious soothsayer from the Bunker, and, for the Russian women, a Soviet Russian émigrée who pretended to be a 'Caucasian princess', which impressed the Germans not a little. Though the star-gazer proved to be thoroughly malicious, she was just a harmless lunatic, all said and done; the 'Caucasian princess', on the other hand, poisoned my life by inciting the Soviets against me, of whom (like most people in the camp, including the German authorities) she was increasingly afraid. The intrigues eventually resulted in my being transferred as a room-leader to a neighbouring camp, known as the *Betriebshof* or workshop centre. The block-leader and the second room-leader were Germans and showed themselves ill-disposed towards me, all the more so because my prisoners, most of them 'black' or 'green', soon noticed that, since my arrival, they had begun receiving larger helpings of food. Since I was not allowed to visit the neighbouring camp, I was afraid that when the moment of decision arrived, I would not be able to rejoin my sisters. However, a fortnight's bout of flu, with a temperature (slightly enhanced), enabled me to return once more to the sickbay.

There, on 4 February, my successor, the present block-leader of the NN prisoners and the 'rabbits', called in to tell me that she had received an order forbidding her to allow the 'rabbits' to leave the block. In the past, such an order had preceded every execution.

In the afternoon I was visited by two of the 'rabbits', who had come to say goodbye. Some of the 'rabbits' were convinced that for them there was now not a shadow of hope. Others were in favour of each defending herself individually to the last breath. After a while, two of the Soviets came in and whispered: 'Miss Karla, we won't surrender the "rabbits",' and off they went. That day, a campaign for the defence of the 'rabbits' got under way, with a large part of the camp joining in. To gather the sixty women and remove them from the camp by force would be no easy matter for the authorities at that stage. Since their transfer from Block 32, the 'rabbits', now in block 24, did not sleep there, and appeared only during the day for short periods and in groups. Roll-call was the greatest danger. Two days later the authorities surrounded all the women of block 24 with a cordon of wardresses and SS men. It seemed that all was lost. Meanwhile, the Soviets who maintained the camp's electrical installations engineered a brief short-circuit; all the lights went out and confusion reigned, during which the 'rabbits' broke through the ring with the help of the Russians, while the authorities were overcome by panic.

The defence of the 'rabbits' at this critical juncture by the Red Army women was undoubtedly an extremely ethical action, but it was also a propaganda coup of the first order, which won them the sympathy of the whole camp. Apart from that, the Germans took fright and understood that they would not be able to take the 'rabbits' by force. The girls, too, changed the numbers on their armbands and paraded for roll-call with other blocks, which, in exchange, sent their Polish women to attend roll-call at Block 24. Confusion grew and roll-calls were cancelled for some days in a row. One group of 'rabbits' hid in a cave near room-leader Mietka's block, from which they emerged sick. It was clear to us that it might be possible to prolong their lives by such measures, but sooner or later they would surely be killed, unless some extraordinary event intervened.

It looked just then as though something extraordinary was indeed about to happen in the very near future. By night the thunder of the guns was coming appreciably closer to us and we had the impression that the Red Army was no distance away. We had reached the point of praying, as we lay there listening at night, that the Muscovites – since they were coming anyway – would arrive before the Germans had time to murder the girls.

But the approach of the front line also had other consequences, crucial for the camp. Mass transports were passing out through the camp gates in an unbroken chain. At the same time, innumerable children of every nationality, who had recently been wandering around, getting into mischief and playing about during roll-call or round the Bunker, had been disappearing from the camp. It was said officially that Ravensbrück was to become a *Musterlager* (Show Camp) for 10,000 women. From one day to the next, the huge tent disappeared and trees were planted round the blocks. We gazed at all this in amazement – only the Dutch smiled knowingly: 'It's a good sign – very good,' they said. 'That means it won't be long now. In our camp in Holland, just before the Allies invaded, they built a special, children's block and painted the walls inside with scenes from fairy-tales. The pictures were still wet when they evacuated us.'

Fifteen of the 'rabbits' managed to leave the camp with these departing transports, masquerading under the numbers and names of dead prisoners.

Apart from that, we did our best to make sure that Binz got to know that the outside world was fully informed about the affair of the 'rabbits', thanks to Aka Kołodziejczak, whose father (an American citizen) had managed to get his daughter out of Ravensbrück and, via Switzerland, to the United States. Then the authorities summoned two of the 'rabbits' for an interview: Jadzia Kamińska and 'Bajka' (Zofia Baj), both of them brave, quick-witted and with a good command of German. They were received by Binz and Johann Schwarzhuber*, the new officer in charge of the 'protective custody' camp, who informed them that the 'rabbits' were simply being moved to a safer camp. (He mentioned, almost casually, Gross-Rosen in Silesia, where fighting was already in progress!) The two 'envoys' got a strong feeling that the object of this conversation was to glean information about Aka Kołodziejczak. Actually, none of us knew how much Aka had in fact been able to achieve, but over the years, by various channels, we had been sending information back to Poland, as a result of which, seemingly, the 'rabbits' had been referred to in radio broadcasts. Binz, whose name apparently had also been mentioned, was in any case terrified – a reaction to which Jadzia and Bajka eagerly contributed.

At last, after many long days of struggle, the camp Commandant

Fritz Suhren who, until then, had not been involved in the 'rabbit' affair, sent for one of them, Marysia Plater. Jadzia and Bajka went along with her 'as interpreters'. Suhren showed Marysia a piece of paper, promising to release her if she would sign it. The document certified that the scar on her leg was the result of an accident in a factory. Marysia refused, and stated that she did not wish to be released at that time. Since it was not possible for her to return to Poland, she preferred to remain with her friends. A long discussion ensued, in the course of which Suhren promised to write to Berlin and to give the 'rabbits' a final answer regarding their fate. It goes without saying that no answer was ever received by the 'rabbits', but their struggle for life continued.

Suddenly one evening, while I was still lying in the sickbay, a wardress appeared at my bedside and ordered me to get dressed immediately and go with her to the Commandant. As I was putting my clothes on, I just had time to tell my neighbour that the reason was quite clear: the Commandant never summoned anyone at that hour. The fact was, this was execution time. As we left the block, the sight of a second wardress waiting to join us seemed to confirm my supposition. They were both small women. Walking between them, I thought we must look like a triptych. After passing through the gate, however, instead of turning right towards the forest, we made for the Commandant's headquarters. After a short wait, I entered Suhren's office and reported myself present. He received me standing, as on the first occasion when I was still a *Sonderhäftling* (privileged prisoner). This puzzled me. He enquired after my health. Hearing that I was sick, he expressed the hope that it was nothing serious.

Now I understood. Only a very high-level intervention could have produced such a result. I had read a couple of months before in the *Völkischer Beobachter*, which the wardress in our block office used to receive, that Carl Burckhardt*, a Swiss historian and a friend of long standing, had become President of the International Red Cross. At that moment, as I stood in front of Suhren, I suddenly felt the prestige of an international organisation and, above all, the strength of human friendship, protecting me like a shield raised between him and me. He asked me whether I had any wishes. Was I short of clothes? Food? He was behaving like a shopkeeper offering his goods. I said there was nothing that I needed. At that, he grew impatient and repeated the question. At last, I was led away again. When I got back to the block, they were all awake. The Polish women were praying. 'It's her! She's back and still smiling!' I felt faintly ridiculous, having gone to my death and been offered a choice of free gifts instead.

After being discharged from the sickbay I was appointed room-leader in Block 31, with block-leader Hanka Zaturska. I had hardly been there a couple of days when I was sent for by Dr Treite. So I went. At the sickbay door, my friend, the plump Czech policewoman, was waiting in a state of excitement. 'Treite sent for you but, first, go quickly and see Zdenka. She's expecting you!' As though she meant to drag me there by force, she dug her none too gentle fingers into my skinny arm and pushed me in the direction of Zdenka's room. As I went in, Zdenka slammed the door behind me and began to whisper very fast: 'Karla, you're going to be released!' At first, I thought Zdenka was out of her mind. But she went on whispering: 'Treite mustn't know that you've been to see me. He asked me about you and your health and then said something very quietly to the *Oberschwester*. Now, go into him, then come back to me, only don't let him see you. If you don't come back, I'll die of sheer curiosity.'

I returned presently to tell her that Treite had questioned me closely about my health and had looked to see that my feet were not swollen. Despite my assurance that I was safely over my flu, he ordered me to go to bed at once in Ward No. 1, where they only took cases under his personal supervision.

'Have you got friends abroad?' Zdenka asked.

'I have. The President of the International Red Cross is a friend of mine.' She flung herself round my neck. 'But Zdenka, it's unthinkable! Leave here alone, without you all. Absolutely out of the question!'

'You've no right to think like that. Your release could save the rest of us. Now run for it, and don't let anyone see you.'

So I went to Ward No. 1. On the way there, I heard the whimpering of Gypsy women who had been sterilised. There, in a room designed for six patients, a bed was made up and waiting for me. Seriously ill fellow prisoners were lying in top bunks and had to climb down to wash, and I – with nothing the matter – by special order of the *Oberschwester* had a bottom bunk, with nobody above. I lay down and waited to see what would happen next. I did not have long to wait. A nurse brought in something out of this world: a glass of milk. In the evening they started feeding me Vitamin C, and the next day the *Oberschwester* herself arrived with a large bottle of cod-liver oil. Meanwhile, all possible tests were carried out on every organ in my body that might have suffered attack. I succeeded in convincing my carers that I needed exercise and fresh air and must go for a walk. I was therefore able to resume my teaching, while sharing out my cod-liver oil in small bottles. (As a reward for drinking so much of it, the *Oberschwester* brought me still more . . .) Suddenly, after about ten days, the whole comedy ended abruptly. I returned to Block 31. We assumed that the intervention from abroad must have failed, but we did not think about it all that much. We had other, more urgent things to worry about.

The camp was gradually emptying. The Jewish women, among them Frau Strassner, had been sent to Belsen, the NN to Mauthausen and the women 'evacuees' from Warsaw had just been 'released'! Their numbers had been taken off, they had been issued with plain dresses and sent out as civilians to work in the factories. For many people this was a moral tragedy, for it was even harder to work for the Germans, when ostensibly free, than as a prisoner. The weakest and oldest were housed in the former *Jugendlager* (Youth Camp). The young German women were unexpectedly moved from there on about 20 January. A day or two later, women who were listed as having been given pink cards in the past were told that the former Youth Camp was now reserved for them. There would be no more roll-calls and they could lie in bed all day and rest. Dora Rivière, the doctor, and some nurses went with them. For ten days all went well. Then Dora, the nurses and the medicines were sent back to the main camp. The Youth Camp had roll-calls that lasted five or six hours daily, during which the women's coats were taken away from them.

On 5 February the new Director of the Youth Camp, Fräulein Neudeck, appeared with a lorry, collected a load of women and drove away. The lorry returned spattered with blood, and the following day the camp 'store' received a large number of blood-stained garments with pink cards in the pockets. From that day onwards, Fräulein Neudeck – a tall, good-looking blonde, aged not more than twenty-four, who was almost always drunk – regularly chose groups of women from the Youth Camp, whom she ordered to strip to their underwear and write their numbers on their chest with an ink pencil. She then locked them in a separate block, from which they were collected by lorry the following day. Neither the lorry nor the clothes were later seen to be blood-stained but, uninterruptedly, from the chimney of the big, new crematorium flames mounted skywards, lighting the whole camp at night. One was reminded of the beginning of the *Iliad* when plague overtakes the Achaeans: '*Eternally flamed the undying fires of the dead . . .*'

The suffocating stench of burned bodies and hair was unbearable. The gas oven functioned efficiently from the beginning of February to 1 April.

In February, Dr Winckelmann* came to Ravensbrück – a man well known to the women from Auschwitz, who Marysia Kujawska insisted up to the last was not a doctor, because 'He couldn't possibly have been.' Winckelmann selected all the seriously ill women from the sickbays and handed them over to Fräulein Neudeck, who drove them away in her lorry. From that moment, we started hiding the sick in the blocks to prevent them being sent to the sickbays.

Eventually Winckelmann, usually accompanied by Labour Officer Pflaum and a couple of wardresses, began to appear in the ordinary blocks, where all the inmates, singly or in pairs, were made to parade in front of the doctor at a distance of eight to ten paces. Often very ill women, barely able to stand, struggled to straighten up with what strength they had left, so as to march as firmly as possible past Dr Winckelmann. They wanted to live! Cripples and crocks pulled themselves together, but the 'doctor', with a nonchalant wave of his hand, consigned them: right – to work; left – to death. Women with grey hair or swollen feet were irretrievably doomed. The last desperate struggle for life by the women of Ravensbrück had begun. A certain group of us block- and room-leaders pressed hard to be allowed to 'help preserve order' in the blocks while the selection was being made. We 'helped' by mixing up the ranks and switching prisoners from the left lane to the right.

I remember once, in the absence of Labour Officer Pflaum who usually never took his eyes off me, Winckelmann, during the selection, condemned to the Youth Camp two young and very debilitated women – one Polish and the other Jewish – while their respective mothers walked 'to the right'. The two girls standing in the 'death' lane quietly begged me to save them. I told them to stand behind me for a moment, then I grabbed the pair of them roughly by the arms and hauled them in front of Winckelmann.

'Herr Doctor,' I bellowed (Germans are always impressed if shouted at), 'these two young healthy layabouts have slipped in over here, where you said the sick women were to stand. They don't want to work. *Unerhört!*'

'*Unerhört!*' Winckelmann yelled after me, '*Sofort zur Arbeit!*'[61]

I pushed the two girls over to the right, where they collapsed into the arms of their mothers, half swooning with terror. Now it was my turn to take fright, but the executioner was already busy with fresh victims.

After the selection, we broke through the cordon separating the women who had been condemned, on the pretext of bringing them a few necessities, since they were supposed to be 'going to have a rest'. We then helped them to climb through the windows of neighbouring blocks, where they hid for an hour or two on the topmost tier of three-tier bunks, often having their grey hair dyed black with greasy liquid of some kind. Protecting the sick from being marked down for execution became the most important part of our activity. Sometimes – since the Germans are systematic not only in crime, but in chaos – it was possible to guess which block Winckelmann would be visiting. The sick were then carried to the sickbay of the block he had visited most recently and there 'stowed away'. I remember with gratitude the loyal cooperation of the majority of sickbay personnel in what was none too safe an operation. In fairness it must be added that, in exposing ourselves to the risk of discovery, there was a degree of selfishness on our part. It was simply the only way we could carry on without going mad.

There were moments when the sheer grotesquerie of it all was comic. Once, one of the German women from the Commandant's office brought me an order. 'You must help me quickly to draw up a list of French and Polish women with hereditary titles.' I was convinced that the woman, a Socialist of long standing, was out of her mind. I must have looked aghast, for Fräulein Thury assured me spontaneously that she was still quite sane, but had been instructed by Johann Schwarzhuber, the new man responsible for prisoners in 'protective custody' to provide him with such a list.

'Obviously,' she said, 'they don't want to gas people of that sort, so we must broaden the list as far as possible.' When I tackled the French on the matter, I elicited much merriment, particularly on the part of Marie-Claude Vaillant-Couturier, with whom I got along well. I was able to add quite a few *marquises* and *vicomtesses* to my list. A few other persons who were particularly vulnerable we invested with especially resounding titles, but unfortunately these could be fabricated only in very small numbers, rather than wholesale. Nobody whose name was on our list was subsequently gassed.

It was the only time that I had not cursed the green badge on my arm, but we none of us had any illusions that our help was anything but minimal. We succeeded in saving a certain number of human lives, true, but it was only a drop in the ocean. Seven thousand women, at that time, went to the gas ovens almost before our eyes. We were especially helpless in the face of the gassing of the sick and wounded after the air-raids on factories. There were many fatal casualties among those who had been evacuated from Warsaw. I remember once in the late evening I was walking near the bath-house, when somebody recognised me in the dark and called out to me by name. I went over to where a group of women were lying on the ground outside the bath-house. 'Madame, they've sent us back from the factory as sick. What are they going to do with us?'

'Oh, I'm sure they will find you somewhere to rest in one of the blocks,' I replied, but no sooner had I spoken than I had the impression that the voice was not my own. Then suddenly a wardress ran up and chased me away. That night, no block played host to the French transport – only the flames of the crematorium leaped high . . .

Sometimes, by day, one would meet a party of women collected from the blocks without warning, who never got as far as the so-called Youth Camp. I remember once, when I happened to be passing close to one such group, somebody waved goodbye to me with a serene smile. It was Mère Marie. There were also a few German women among them, including the loquacious astrologer.

A day or two after those people disappeared from the camp, the secretariat received from the Commandant's office a list of their numbers and names, with the observation that those listed had been transferred to the *Schonungslager* (camp for convalescence) at Mittwerd in Silesia. Incidentally, we all knew that the whole of Silesia was already in Russian hands.

Once, in the closing days of March, larger groups were being rounded up, comprising Poles and French, who were not even given time to take anything with them. That was a fatal blow to their morale. Fellow prisoners persuaded the comparatively decent wardress Seltmann to escort us, and even let us take their odds and ends with us. In so doing, we hoped to smuggle a little bread to them as well. She agreed, and we scrounged a barrow from somewhere, loaded it up with our bundles and off we went to the Youth Camp, pleasantly sited in a pine grove, within 300 metres of the main camp. Women flocked around us when we arrived and told us all that had happened there. When, after distributing their various belongings, we came to leave again, an elderly grey-haired French woman clung to me. I remember that she was a midwife called, I think, by the common surname of Madame Durand.

'Madame Karla, I am from Block 27 and I know how the French

tried your patience. I watched everything that was going on there and the way you became ill. Today I am here and I know, as you do, what awaits me. Please tell me that you are not angry with me personally, because I never did you any wrong.' I remembered her very well. She was always good and kind. I cannot describe the emotion that overcame me at that moment.

We returned to the camp, leaving behind us the pine wood with its death-blocks.

There was one extraordinary symptom of life in this place of death. The denser the smoke that billowed from the crematorium, the closer and the more immediately each of us looked death in the eye, the greater grew our need for spiritual sustenance, our intellectual craving. It was not possible to satisfy all the demands, as requests for 'lectures' multiplied. Every afternoon there was a lecture for the 'rabbits' on the third floor. For that hour, a group of girls would return to the block and, once look-outs were posted, I would begin my cultural history lecture on the age of Charlemagne or a talk on Gothic art. The audience, who never knew whether or not this was the last day of their lives, nevertheless listened with great concentration and genuine interest. Sometimes, I had three groups a day. Squeezing my debilitated memory like a lemon, I managed to keep talking. Today, I can only express the hope that I gave my listeners, if only in part, what I received from them – the chance to tear oneself away from the moral and physical squalor, putrefying matter, dysentery and humiliation surrounding us and return to those values that once constituted my own very special world.

Easter week was approaching when I was visited by Marysia Grocholska Czetwertyńska, huge of build and as great of heart as Podbipięta,[62] whose Christianity was unshaken even after some months in the *Strafblok* (punishment block). It was said that nobody who had not been in the *Strafblok* could know what Ravensbrück was really like, nor could anyone who had been there emerge morally sound. However, not only did Marysia emerge unbowed; in addition, she had won the admiration of her fellow inmates – the dregs of camp society. She came to tell me that I would have to devise (especially for the 'rabbits') a course of lectures based on Easter week. When I said that this was beyond me, she was so insistent that I finally surrendered to her gentle persuasion: 'After all, it is possible – even probable – that this will be our last Easter week, especially for the "rabbits"! It must not be allowed to pass unnoticed!'

I did not quite know what to do. So I began to tell my listeners how the great artists of the past had represented the principal scenes of our Lord's Passion. For Maundy Thursday, I chose Leonardo's *Last Supper* and Tintoretto's treatment of the same theme; for Good Friday and Easter Saturday I chose suitable works and poems by Michelangelo, with a description of the great religious events of the last period of his life. The new lectures were very well received and made more of an impression than I had supposed they might. I had to repeat them to several groups. For Easter Monday I had prepared 'Emmaus in the art of Rembrandt', but there was a hitch and the lecture had to be postponed. At noon, during lunch, the Viennese woman from the Labour Office called into the block with an order for me to go at once and stand with the French outside the bath-house. That morning, 400 'healthy' French women had been selected and told to go for a shower. Rumours were circulating about an exchange of prisoners with France. Now I was to go with them. At first, I did not believe it and pointed out that this was the second (not the first) of April, and I'd like to drink my soup in peace.

'No, you can't. Hurry up, Commandant's orders!'

'Commandant's orders?' I repeated automatically and looked at my fellow prisoners. They regarded me in silence. I got up, went outside and stood with the French women in front of the bath-house, just as I had done as a 'new arrival' twenty-seven months before.

Then came a thorough medical inspection. Any women with swollen feet, a symptom of starvation, were sent back to the blocks. Three hundred of us were accepted. We were bathed, dressed in clothes without numbers or marks of any kind, and put into a special block surrounded by barbed wire. But nobody was paying any attention to discipline by that time, so I let myself out the next day and returned to my block, where I gave my lecture about Emmaus and a talk about something or other as well. News from outside about the German catastrophe was by then such that our departure seemed increasingly doubtful. However, on the afternoon of 4 April we were told that the following morning reveille would be at 4 a.m., followed by a special roll-call . . .

I ran to see my closest friends, who gathered to say goodbye to me: Bortnowska, Grocholska, Zdenka and a few others. I was memorising totals, so as to be able to tell people roughly how many prisoners there were of each national group in Ravensbrück at that time. I had other pieces of news apart from that. The camp gas oven had been removed on 2 April and, in exchange, a vehicle well known to women prisoners in Lublin as 'the bus' appeared in the little wood close to the Youth

Camp. A hundred persons at a time would take their 'seats', then a little chimney on the roof started to revolve: death was instantaneous. It was clear that the lives of all the remaining women prisoners were still under threat, and great hopes were hanging on my release. 'You will get us out!' they said. But some were pessimistic. Marta Baranowska came to see me off and said: 'I don't believe that we will get out alive, but it will be easier to die with the knowledge that one of us, at least, will live to tell our tale in Poland.'

The next day, 5 April: roll-call – the last. There was a new and this time quite dramatic selection ceremony. A few of the French prisoners had fallen ill in the past two days and were now replaced by 'healthy' comrades. The procedure took ages and was horribly distressing. At last, we began marching in fives towards the gate. I was the very last. Suddenly, someone ran up behind us: Halina Chorążyna. We exchanged a short, almost rough kiss on the march. I was now passing the Polish blocks. Along my route, windows and doors opened and women waved goodbye. The same words were shouted again and again, echoing from block to block: 'Remember us! Don't forget about us!' At last, I reached the camp-square where Bortnowska, Grocholska and a group of 'rabbits' stood waiting.[63] Grocholska was as ever calm and serious; Niuta, usually solemn, was smiling today, though tears were streaming down her wise, emaciated face; the 'rabbits' had only one thing on their minds and they were deeply uneasy. 'Do please remember in all this excitement, don't forget at the last moment to turn round and walk out backwards, facing us. That means you'll get us out. It would be terrible to forget that!' It reminded me of Stanisławów.

The French women were already outside. Walking behind them, I was the last to pass through the gate of Ravensbrück, stepping backwards, hands outstretched towards the camp. I turned at last and walked along that road built by Polish women four years earlier. How many times had we gazed through the bars at that stretch of road, winter and summer, imagining the eventual Day of Liberation, when we would all leave together – for Poland! Now I was leaving alone, the only one of my group to do so. And I was heading west, every step taking me further still from Poland. At a bend in the road, I turned once more for a last sight of that group of my sisters in the early morning, spring sunshine. Their hands were reaching out to me through the barriers, which had already been lowered. That cruel moment beggars description.

Round the bend, we left the main road in the direction of that stunted forest. No more than 300 paces away stood a convoy of white lorries with the Red Cross emblem. We had seen that sign so many times on German vehicles, but now we were looking at a different sign: a white cross on a red shield. Jesus and Mary! It was the symbol of Switzerland, a free country, which had remembered us – prisoners with nobody to care for them and protected by no convention. The bonnets of the lorries were inscribed: '*Comité International de la Croix Rouge – Genève*'. Then it was true – it really was true – they had been sent for us.

I read that inscription for a second time, as though with difficulty. It was, in fact, hard to understand. They were urging me to hurry up and take a seat. The French women had already boarded the large white lorries. The camp authorities were present in the flesh, but so different from normal was their behaviour that I kept thinking they could not be the same persons. But they were, in fact: Suhren, Schwarzhuber, Pflaum and a throng of wardresses. Only now, nobody was screaming, kicking or clouting. They were behaving like normal human beings, and even with studied politeness towards a single civilian stranger who was present and who behaved just as normally. Who might this civilian be? 'That is the Swiss delegate,' somebody said. I gazed at him as though at an almost exotic specimen. This is a free man, I kept telling myself, neither blinded by his own totalitarianism, nor by that of a foreign invader . . .

Suddenly the obese Pflaum, Labour Officer, caught sight of me and bounded across with a playfully jocose gesture: 'What? You're going as well? I'm so delighted you won't be here any more, driving me mad!'

At 9.05 a.m. the convoy set off. We were finally on the move, leaving behind us in Ravensbrück the living and the dead.

All day long we drove through a countryside totally deserted. There was no sign of people or cars on the *Autobahn* and in the forests along the way, only a lot of tanks and concealed military equipment, in the woods alongside the road, in stark contrast to the millions of violets and anemones which, at that season, covered the blood-soaked soil of Germany. In the evening we reached Hof in Bavaria, where we were given lodging for the night in the municipal theatre of the small town, Ober-Kotzau. There, closely supervised by the Gestapo, we had to wait three days for petrol.

From those three days I recall a minor incident, the significance of which I failed to understand at the time. We were sitting on the floor of the auditorium, on clean (!) straw, relaxing . . . At a given moment, one of the French women came and told me that Tante Yvonne would like to speak to me. The widow of an admiral, Madame Leroux was an outstanding person who commanded great authority among the cultured French ladies and had always shown me particular goodwill. I stood up and went over to where Tante Yvonne was lying. She was very weak. After greeting me warmly, she said: 'I want to tell you something. If you should ever have problems of any sort in future, do please let me know at once. Here's my address.' She handed me a visiting card with the details. I could not imagine what kind of future problems might necessitate an appeal to this venerable old lady. Obviously, I thanked her profusely and left, not wishing to exhaust her, for she looked terribly ill. Indeed, on her return to France, she died almost at once.

(Not long after my release, I was to find out just what kind of 'problems' Madame Leroux had in mind. I, in the West, and Niuta Bortnowska in Poland, were both accused, in widely differing quarters, of having collaborated with the Germans in the maltreatment of fellow prisoners. Separated as we were by the Iron Curtain, it was some time before we both realised that this was simply a question of revenge for our respective ideological influence on the young. Whereas I had to suffer 'only' slander and defamation, Niuta was put in prison. She was rescued by our friend Zdenka Nedvedova, Communist *par excellence*, who made a special journey from Prague to obtain Niuta's release from jail in Warsaw.)

Meanwhile, the petrol we had been waiting for in Ober-Kotzau finally arrived and we were able to resume our journey. Now we were driving through thickly populated southern Germany, along the Danube. We passed through Ulm, or rather a shapeless expanse of rubble bearing that name. Appalled by the sight, I was trying to make out the ruins of the famous cathedral, when suddenly (from the back of a covered lorry, one could see only what the cab had already passed) there reared up before our eyes that magnificent cathedral: intact, untouched, not a mirage, but a concrete, architectonic reality, if one may speak of such a Gothic masterpiece as a 'concrete reality'. The mighty spire pointed heavenwards, as though to demonstrate the victory of the only power that really matters.

We reached the Swiss frontier that evening. The mountains of the Free Country were clearly visible in the distance by the light of the setting sun.

At 10 p.m. our lorry, which was the last in the convoy, stopped at Kreuzlingen, a small border town. We were told to disembark and form fives. I was in the last row. Ten paces away we could see a large open gate. Beside it stood a row of men, including our Gestapo escort. The French women marched in fives through the open gate. Our group – the last – was held back. Suddenly I was approached by a man who introduced himself as the German Ambassador in Berne. He said he was happy at my release and hoped that I was *ein guter Mensch*,[64] although it would seem that I was very bellicose. I was flabbergasted. However, at that particular moment I was not in the mood for yet another quarrel with the Germans. I replied merely that if love of one's country was proof of bellicosity, then I must agree: I was bellicose.

'Such a good command of the German language could be put to better use,' said the Gestapo man behind the Ambassador. I was hastening to assure him that I also spoke English, when for the last time I heard the word '*Los!*'[65] We crossed the border. We were alone. Behind us, on the far side, the Gestapo men were left with the Ambassador and, with them, the Third Reich.

'*Bonsoir*,' said somebody from the side. It was the Swiss sentry. Opposite us groups of Swiss locals stood waving handkerchiefs and shouting: '*Soyez les bienvenues!*'[66] We were all lost for words. We could greet them only with gestures. Then the church bells began to ring. The Mayor of Kreuzlingen had given the order for a free country to celebrate our release in such a way – the simplest and the most solemn. I can testify that it is far easier not to break down during three years' captivity than it is to withstand such a reception. They gave us a meal and a bed. They surrounded us with touching care and attention, which proved all the more necessary for, despite the rigorous weeding-out process at Ravensbrück, some of the French women were already fighting for their lives. The sick were left in Kreuzlingen and the following day we caught the train. The French women were returning to their liberated homeland, while I got out at Geneva. There to greet me at the station were my brother Antoni and the President of the International Red Cross, Carl Burckhardt, my saviour.

Chapter 8

ITALY

After a brief exchange of greetings, I told my brother that I must send a telegram at once to the Red Cross in Warsaw to let them know that I had left Niuta Bortnowska behind in Ravensbrück.

'Telegram to Warsaw?' he repeated. 'You mean to London,' he added hurriedly. Our eyes met, then he looked away. I understood that he did not feel like telling me everything in the first minute of our reunion, but I knew at once that the most dreadful thing of all had happened. From that moment, I was no longer a prisoner, but had become an exile.

The next day I entered on a period of what, in other circumstances, would certainly have been a pleasure, namely 'returning to life'. As things stood, however, it was bound to result in a clash. I was obliged to adapt myself inwardly to certain standards required of people living 'normally'. Such norms, I think, are difficult to understand, certainly for anyone who has been divorced from them for a long time – indeed, marginalised from life as a whole. I suppose that 'resurrection' can never be an easy matter. But one might think that returning to a free country, together with all those who have suffered for the common cause, would be such a tremendous experience that any private difficulties in adapting to necessary external manners and customs (however laughably outdated and pointless they might seem) would be a mere bagatelle at such a time. In my case, however, everything was so very, very different. Not only was I not returning to a free Poland, but I had emerged alone, without my sisters, into a Swiss wonderland that had not known war. I needed to go and buy a dress, shoes, a hat (!) and to eat in a restaurant. All of that seemed not only ridiculous, but monstrous, while others 'over there' might be going to their death.

There was only one thing left – only one important thing: how to rescue them.

Although, within a couple of days of my arrival, communications with Ravensbrück had broken down, so that a second rescue expedition had to turn back halfway, I had the pleasure of knowing that my report for the President of the Red Cross helped with the organisation of a so-called Swedish expedition. A large number of women were collected from Ravensbrück, conveyed to Lübeck and from there to Sweden.[1] Besides that, Geneva had known nothing about the presence of the French and Belgian NN prisoners in the Mauthausen camp. Vehicles were sent off at once, which fortunately got through and returned, bringing the NNs safely with them.

Immediately after my arrival, Burckhardt received a letter about me from Himmler's deputy, SS General Kaltenbrunner*. The letter (reproduced on page 298) was unexpected proof of the truth, so far as my encounter with Krüger was concerned.

After the first two weeks of hectic emotion, every possibility – even the most indirect – of getting help to the women in Ravensbrück ceased to exist. The curtain had fallen. Consequently I had no further duties and was left with only my own safety to think about. In the circumstances, that safety evoked a particular sensation of distaste and bitterness, which even the proximity of people dear to me and the touching hospitality of the Swiss were unable to counteract. The tension of being in danger is itself a great source of strength. When that suddenly ceases, in respect of oneself but not the Cause, nothing is left but a painful sense of emptiness, followed by a humiliating depression.

It is not in the storm, or in the strife
We feel benumbed and wish to be no more
But in the after-silence on the shore
When all is lost except a little life.[2]
Lord Byron

The world situation at the time was best described by Burckhardt, whom I met on the day of the ceasefire. To my question as to what he thought of the noisy jubilation all around us, he replied tersely: 'One of the Hydra's heads has been torn off – the stupider one, unfortunately!'

How wise the remaining second head proved to be we saw more clearly every day, as our former Allies in the West bowed low before the purposeful and predatory will of the 'Great Ally in the East', signing their assent to its 'right' to half of the Polish lands and recognising in the other half a make-believe 'government' headed by a 'President' whose real name nobody can remember to this day.

How fortunate was that Poland of the nineteenth century, in whose name nobody had the right to make lying speeches, and whose refugees, for the whole civilised world, came to symbolise man's struggle for freedom![3]

Instead, we Poles had now become the 'enemies of peace' for refusing to play the leading role in a historic première in which, after winning the war, the victorious Allies bury one of their number.

In this political and, above all, moral chaos, everyone was seeking an anchor. For many, that anchor was the Polish Forces, for the time being untouched by the catastrophe – above all, the victorious 2 Corps, then stationed in Italy.

So it was in those scorching July days, aboard an army lorry in the wake of thousands of 'liberated' exiles, that I sped through France towards the Adriatic. For me, too, a fresh chapter had begun.

We passed through Bologna, recently taken by our forces, undamaged, and approached the sea. Now, we repeatedly saw warnings written in Polish on makeshift signposts, as we were making a detour to avoid a bridge that had been blown up. More and more vehicles passed us with the Mermaid[4] insignia of the 2 Army Corps, till finally, at Forlì, we came upon a major motorised detachment of the Polish Forces. Trucks, tanks, weapons – all gleaming in the sunlight. Soldiers, sun-tanned, strong and fit, smiled at us as we drove past. The closer we came to the Adriatic, the more densely crowded the roads were with Polish military and the more soldiers climbed aboard asking for a lift to the nearest township. They were polite and kindly, incredibly experienced and well-informed after their lengthy wanderings in so many foreign lands. The innate intelligence of the Polish peasant – particularly those from our eastern regions – had at last found unexpected opportunities for development. That was evident from the soldiers' conversations during this, my first 'active service' road journey. They talked of Iraq, Iran, Palestine, Egypt, about General Anders, Monte Cassino, Ancona, Bologna. They told their tales with verve and emotion while I looked and listened. One's own experiences seemed so meagre and prosaic compared with that rich blend of *Tales of 1001 Nights*, *The Adventures of Robinson Crusoe* and Xenophon's *Roads.*

I was struck by the fact that they said little about Russia. I asked what the camps there were like. I got the impression that they preferred not to talk about it, not wishing to dwell on their suffering. But hatred of Russia was expressed spontaneously. It was not easy to store that away out of sight in one's mind, or even in one's heart. A person who has been denied external impressions for three years, and whose life during that period has been the very opposite of colourful, is by no means proof against such emotions. I was at that time just getting to know what Poland had been awaiting for so many years, but had still not attained. That day, I saw and experienced the saga of 2 Corps – reminiscent of a Sienkiewicz[5] epic – reliving it with all the intensity of someone who had the sensation only then, of at last coming back to life.

A couple of days later, in a lorry and already in uniform, I drove along the Via Salaria into Rome . . .

I was posted to the Forces Education Department and was given the job of organising higher studies for soldier-students of 2 Corps. It was the start of a difficult but engrossing task.

One day, I was visited in Rome by a young person, newly arrived from Poland, who brought me warm greetings and news from Adam Szebesta.

'He asked me to tell you that his young son is praying for you every day.'

That item of information struck me with the force of lightning. At that moment, I suddenly realised that the words of the poet Juliusz Słowacki applied equally to me: I SHALL NOT BE GOING HOME!

An innocent child in my country was made
To pray for me daily though now it is plain
That never my ship which so widely has strayed
Shall sail home again . . .[6]

EPILOGUE

In the early days of 1967 I learned completely by chance from the London Polish newspaper *Dziennik Polski* that the trial was to take place in Münster, Westfalen, of Hans Krüger, former Chief of the Gestapo in Stanisławów, Poland, charged with the mass murder of Jews. I sought advice from our lawyer, Dr Chmielewski, and wrote a letter, dictated by him, to the appropriate German judicial authorities, offering myself as a witness. Two of my registered letters in turn remained unanswered. It was not until I wrote to say that I would be publishing my letter in the *Zürcher Zeitung* that I received an immediate invitation to appear as a witness.

I asked the distinguished advocate Chmielewski to accompany me. We set off together. In Münster we were welcomed at the station by a young German lady of short stature. She announced that she was to look after me. We went to the hotel. The trial was to begin the following morning at ten o'clock. I asked my 'minder' to take me to church early. After Mass, the three of us went to the court.

Three judges were seated on the podium and, at each side in a semicircle, sat members of the jury, including some women. To their left, in the dock, were Krüger and eight Gestapo men, formerly his subordinates. Some of them I recognised. Beside them were seated their defence counsels. The Prosecutor was on the right. I was directed to a chair and a small table in the centre of the hall, close to the podium.

Behind me were seated a few score members of the public, among them my advocate Chmielewski.

As I walked in, the President of the court greeted me politely and, after formally stressing the responsibility of a witness and the importance of an oath, asked whether I would agree to let my answers be recorded on tape. Obviously, I agreed. Then he put the formal question to me: '*Also, Sie waren in Stanislau?*'[1] I answered affirmatively and described my various visits to Stanisławów, my arrest, the conditions in the prison, and finally my interrogation by Krüger, when he told me that he had murdered the professors of Lwów. I pitched my statement in the form of a 'report'. When I finished the account of my experiences in Stanisławów and came to the case of the Lwów professors, the Judge politely but firmly interrupted me, saying that this trial concerned only Stanisławów and I must therefore confine myself to saying what I wished about Stanisławów. That worried me. I tried to carry on speaking in telegraphic style, but without omitting anything of importance. Suddenly the entire jury stood up, walked over to the President of the court and said something to him, rather quietly but energetically. I was much afraid that they did not want to hear about Lwów.

When they had returned to their seats, however, the President interrupted me once again and said: 'The jury have asked that you should not leave out anything you were planning to tell the court. I therefore withdraw what I said earlier.' Obviously, in view of that, I spoke for considerably longer than I had intended – an hour and five minutes all told.

At the end of my address, the President announced a brief adjournment, during which I drank a large coffee in preparation for the anticipated major battle with the defence lawyers and the accused.

When we returned to the courtroom, the defence counsel was called to speak. To my utter astonishment, he declared that he had nothing to say. At that, the Judge turned to the accused and asked him what he had to say, in view of what he had heard from the witness. Krüger was silent . . .

Then the President himself asked me a few rather banal questions, which clearly displayed his total ignorance about the situation in Poland during the German occupation. He then gave the accused a second chance to speak, but Krüger again kept his mouth shut. The Prosecutor rose to speak. Turning sharply towards me, he asserted among other things that the Polish underground resistance cooperated with the Soviets by hiding Bolshevik parachutists, as Krüger would confirm. Flabbergasted by this, I asked for permission to speak and said: 'Mr Prosecutor, the Bolsheviks are – and were – the greatest enemies of Poland, and the Polish people have nothing in common with Communist Russia.'

To this the Prosecutor declared that Krüger said otherwise. I turned to the President, spread my hands and shrugged – without a word.

Suddenly Krüger jumped up in his box and raised his hand. The Judge invited him to speak. With that wild yell I knew so well, he addressed the Prosecutor, screaming: '*Aber Herr Staatsanwalt!*[2] What I said was that the Ukrainians were helping the Soviets. I could never have said any such thing about the Poles. The Poles hated the Soviets. You're talking nonsense!'

Then the Prosecutor himself started screaming at Krüger. Meanwhile I sat there calmly, between the pair of them shouting their heads off, waiting to see what would happen next. One thing was clear: the Prosecutor, whose key witness was me, wanted at all costs to dispel the impression that my accusation might make on those present, but he knew nothing about anything and was driving the accused mad with his compromising twaddle.[3] When at last the President managed (not without difficulty) to silence the row, he asked me a few more trite questions, after which, for the third time, he asked Krüger whether he did not have something to say. For the third time, Krüger said nothing.

Then, a crucifix on a pedestal was raised. The Judge asked me whether I would swear an oath on the crucifix that what I had said corresponded to the absolute truth. I did so, repeating after the Judge the clear and simple form of words. The hearing was at an end.

The three of us left the courtroom: Chmielewski, the 'minder' and me. Considerably later it dawned on me why the other two had not left me on my own for one moment, either in the street or in the restaurant. I understood that there were plenty of people in Münster who would not have been at all happy about my testimony.

In the afternoon, journalists, Jews and non-Jews were waiting for me at the hotel. They asked a lot of rather banal questions. The case of the Lwów professors, so important to me, interested them rather less. They mainly asked questions about the Jews, and I was able to enlighten them on various details. One of them told me that my evidence had placed Krüger in a difficult situation, particularly since my name had already been mentioned at the beginning of the trial. Krüger had declared then that he would immediately have been cleared of all charges, if only the Countess Karolina Lanckorońska were alive, for she was well aware of how much he had done to help the Poles and the

Jews. Unfortunately, he said, that lady had perished in Ravensbrück . . .

Later, we went to church to visit the grave of Cardinal Clemens August Count von Galen*, whose heroic letters to Hitler were formerly circulated throughout occupied Poland. They were for us precious proof that among that unhappy nation – submerged in crime – there were nevertheless some magnificent individuals.

The next day I left Münster, having written a detailed report for Professor Z. Albert* in Wrocław, who was leading an action from the Polish People's Republic on behalf of the widows and orphans of the murdered professors. Shortly afterwards, I went to Vienna to meet Szymon Wiesenthal*. He received me very kindly, but was insistent that the Lwów professors were murdered not by Krüger, but by Kutschmann, who, he said, had other crimes on his conscience also and was now hiding in Argentina. I expressed the opinion (which was also my private impression) that Kutschmann, as Krüger's subordinate, might well have cooperated with his superior, but it was difficult to imagine that Kutschmann alone would have carried out the deed. I said that before capturing Kutschmann, it was absolutely necessary to prevail upon the Germans to mount a fresh trial of Krüger for the murder of the twenty-five professors of Lwów University. Wiesenthal greeted this suggestion with reserve.

Meanwhile, I learned that Krüger had been sentenced to life imprisonment for the murders at Stanisławów. I then wrote to the German judicial authorities at all levels, asking to be examined again as a witness at a trial concerning the Lwów crime. I received no reply. From Paris, the nephew of 'Boy' Żeleński, Mr Władysław Żeleński, has been and still is making very energetic efforts to bring about the trial – so far without any result. Wiesenthal's people meanwhile finally ran Kutschmann to ground in Argentina, but the Germans failed to request his extradition, in view of which the Argentines set him free again.[4] The case of the twenty-five murdered professors of Lwów remains open.

Rome, 1967

Appendices

1 Names of the Lwów professors murdered by Krüger
2 Letter from SS General Ernst Kaltenbrunner to the President of the International Red Cross, Carl Jacob Burckhardt: photocopy of the original and an English translation.
3 Biographical Notes

Names of the Lwów professors murdered by Krüger

Cieszyński, Antoni, prof. UJK* (medicine)
Dobrzaniecki, Władysław, prof. UJK (medicine)
Grek, Jan, prof. UJK (medicine) with his wife and guest, 'Boy' Tadeusz Żeleński, prof. (French) at Ukrainian Ivan Franko Univ.
Grzędziecki, Jerzy, doctor UJK (medicine)
Hamerski, Edward, prof. Lwów Academy of Veterinary Medicine (medicine)
Hilarowicz, Henryk, prof. UJK (medicine)
Korowicz, Henryk, prof. AHZ† (economist)
Krukowski, Włodzimierz, prof. Polytechnic (electricity)

---

* UJK Univesity of Jan Kazimierz.
† AHZ Academy of Foreign Trade.

Longchamps de Berier, Roman, prof. UJK (law) with his three sons: Bronisław, Zygmunt and Kazimierz
Łomnicki, Antoni, prof. Polytechnic (maths)
Mączewski, Stanisław, doctor UJK (medicine)
Nowicki, Witold, prof. UJK (medicine) with his son, Jerzy (doctor)
Ostrowski, Tadeusz, prof. UJK (medicine) with his wife and guests: Dr Adam Ruff with his wife and son and Father Komornicki
Pilat, Stanisław, prof. Polytechnic (chemistry)
Progulski, Stanisław, lecturer UJK (medicine) with his son Andrzej (engineer)
Rencki, Roman, prof. UJK (medicine)
Ruziewicz, Stanisław, prof. AHZ (maths)
Sieradzki, Włodzimierz, prof. UJK (medicine)
Sołowij, Adam, prof. emeritus UJK (medicine) with his grandson Adam Mięsowicz
Stożek, Włodzimierz, prof. Polytechnic (maths) with his two sons, Eustace (electrical engineer) and Emmanuel (chemist)
Vetulani, Kazimierz, prof. Polytechnic (maths)
Weigel, Kasper, prof. Polytecnic (maths) with his son Jozef (lawyer)
Witkiewicz, Roman, prof. Polytechnic (mechanics)

Later information provided by Elżbieta Orman:
To the author's list I have added the name of Kazimierz Bartel, professor of the Lwów Polytechnic School, who was shot on 26 July 1941. In the same month of that year, in the presence of Hans Krüger, the SS *Einsatzkommando* police, commanded by Brigadeführer E. Schöngarth, arrested and shot a total of twenty-five Polish professors in Lwów, together with twenty other people, family members or guests, who happened to be staying with the professors at the time. Most of these persons, including twenty-one of the murdered professors, were executed at dawn on 3–5 July, on Wulecki Hill. From the start, the crime was shrouded in secrecy by the Germans who, even when the truth became known, did everything to hush it up. On 9 October 1943 they exhumed the corpses and burned them in the Krzywczyc Forest, grinding the bone remains in a mill and scattering the ashes over the forest floor. To this day, despite efforts, notably by Władysław Żeleński and Karolina Lanckorońska, the German Public Prosecutor has not elucidated this crime. In 1986 Professor of Medicine Zygmunt Albert, a pupil of one of the murdered professors, published a book in Wrocław entitled *The Execution of the Lwów Professors in July 1941*, which contains all his research and documentation on the subject.

Translation of a letter from SS General Ernest Kaltenbrunner to the President of the International the Red Cross

Dr Ernst Kaltenbrunner
SS-Obergruppenführer
General der Waffen SS und der Polizei

Berlin SW11, 2 April 1945
Prinz-Albrecht Str. 8

Dear Mr President,

I am pleased to be in a position to report to you that the Reichsführer-SS has granted your wish and has released Countess Lanckorońska from preventive custody. As I gather from the facts of the case, Countess Lanckorońska was placed in preventive custody as long ago as 1942, on account of serious activity contrary to the interests of the German occupying power. This in itself would have fully justified more severe punishment. However, the official responsible for the interrogation behaved in a very inappropriate manner towards Countess Lanckorońska in an attempt to make himself appear more important and interesting, by telling her about the full extent of his 'personal authority' and 'deterrent measures' employed in combating opponents. In view of these aberrations, not only did the official have to be punished, but a general relaxation took place in the conditions of the preventive custody itself.

Permit me to remind you once again of your personal undertaking to instruct and influence the Countess Lanckorońska, who is going to stay with her brother in Switzerland, to conduct herself loyally with regard to the interests of the Reich as long as the war lasts.

In order to fulfil your wish as quickly as possible, I have asked your delegate Dr Meyer – despite the discomfort of this means of conveyance – to take the Countess on the first transport.

With best wishes and high esteem, yours ever,

Ernst Kaltenbrunner

Dr. Ernst Kaltenbrunner
SS-Obergruppenführer
General der Waffen-SS und der Polizei

Berlin SW 11, den 7. April 194 5
Prinz-Albrecht-Str. 8

Sehr geehrter Herr Präsident !

Ich bin in der angenehmen Lage, Ihnen berichten zu können, dass der Reichsführer-SS Ihrem Wunsche stattgegeben und die Gräfin L a n s k o r a n s k a aus der Schutzhaft entlassen hat. Wie ich aus dem Tatbestandsbericht entnehme, wurde die Schutzhaft über die Gräfin Lanskoranska schon im Jahre 1942 wegen starker Aktivität gegen die Interessen der deutschen Besatzungsmacht verhängt. Es wäre an sich eine härtere Bestrafung vollauf berechtigt gewesen; jedoch hat sich der Vernehmungsbeamte der Gräfin Lanskoranska gegenüber sehr ungeschickt benommen und sich ausserdem wichtig und interessant zu machen versucht, indem er ihr von "Machtbefugnissen" seiner Person und "abschreckenden Methoden" der Gegnerbekämpfung erzählte, so dass schon wegen dieser Entgleisungen nicht nur der Beamte bestraft werden musste, sondern insgesamt eine entgegenkommende Handhabung der Schutzhaft stattfand.

Ich

An den
Präsidenten des Internationalen Komitees vom Roten Kreuz
Seine Exzellenz Herrn Gesandten Prof. B u r c k h a r d t
G e n f / Schweiz

Ich darf mich noch einmal auf Ihre persönliche Zusicherung berufen, die Gräfin Lanskoranska, die bei ihrem Bruder in der Schweiz Aufenthalt nehmen wird, dahin zu belehren und zu beeinflussen, sich auf Kriegsdauer gegen Reichsinteressen loyal zu verhalten.

Um Ihren Wunsch möglichst rasch zu erfüllen, habe ich Ihren Beauftragten, Herrn Dr. M e y e r , trotz der Unbequemlichkeit dieser Beförderungsart gebeten, die Gräfin Lanskoranska schon beim ersten Transport mitzunehmen.

Mit meinen besten Grüssen und vorzüglicher Hochachtung

Ihr sehr ergebener

Kaltenbrunner

Biographical Notes

Albert, Zygmunt (1908–2001) Anatomical pathologist, professor and assistant lecturer at the University of Lwów during the war. After the war, Rector of the Academy of Medicine in Wrocław. Author of *The Execution of the Lwów Professors in July 1941* (Wrocław, 1989).

Anders, Władysław (1892–1970) General who fought in the 1920 Polish-Soviet war and the German-Polish war in 1939. Taken prisoner by the Soviet forces which, on 17 September 1939 under the Ribbentrop-Molotov pact, invaded Polish territory as the second army of occupation. Released in July 1941 after the signing of the Sikorski-Majski agreement and became Commander of the Polish Army in the USSR. In the autumn of 1942 he was evacuated to Iran with this army. Commanded the Polish 2 Corps, as part of the British Eighth Army, and fought in the 1944 Italian campaign (Monte Cassino, Ancona and Bologna). Lived in London after the war.

Barda, Franciszek (1880–1964) Latin Rite Bishop of Przemyśl from 1933.

Bolesław, Father: see **Huczyński, Augustyn**

Bor: see **Komorowski, Tadeusz**

Bortnowska, Maria (Niuta) (1894–1972) After the outbreak of war in 1939 and the occupation of Warsaw by the German Army, directed the Information Bureau of the Polish Red Cross. Arrested by the Gestapo on 23 September 1942, and transported in 1943 to the German concentration camp at Ravensbrück. Released with the last transport of Polish women prisoners in July 1945. In 1947 she was arrested in Warsaw by the Communist authorities and accused of wartime collaboration with the Germans. Sentenced to three years in prison, but freed in 1948 as a result of intervention by former fellow prisoners in Ravensbrück.

Brachyneć, Andrij (Brakhynets, Andrii) (1903–63) Ukrainian historian of philosophical and socialist thought, and a Marxist. Lectured at the University of Kharkov (1937–9) and in Lwów (1939–46).

Bujak, Franciszek (1875–1953) Professor of Economic History at the

Jagiellonian University in Kraków (1909–18) and at Warsaw University (1919–20). In 1920 Minister of Agriculture and State Lands. From 1921 till September 1939, Professor at Jan Kazimierz University in Lwów. Lectured during the Soviet occupation of 1939–41 at the Ukrainian Ivan Franko University. After the war Professor at the Jagiellonian University.

Burckhardt, Carl Jacob (1891–1974) League of Nations High Commissioner in Gdańsk (1937–9). President of the International Red Cross, Geneva (1944–8).

Caetani, Roffredo (1871–1961) Composer and pianist, a descendant of the wealthy Italian family. Great-grandson of the Polish aristocrat Wacław Rzewuski. The shared ancestry of Karolina Lanckorońska and Caetani with the Rzewuski family dates from the seventeenth century.

Chorążyna, Halina, née Starczewska (1895–1986) Chemical engineer, employed by Warsaw University and Chemical Research Institute. During the German occupation was a member of the secret military organisation, the Union for Armed Struggle, in Warsaw. Arrested in 1940, and transported to Ravensbrück concentration camp in 1941. Taught chemistry and the German language illegally to young women prisoners. Prepared a so-called 'spoken journal' in the camp, based on the German press. Participant in clandestine preparations for self-defence by women prisoners, in the event of the camp being liquidated. After the war returned to work in the Warsaw of Chemical Research Institute.

Cieński, Father Włodzimierz (1897–1983) Roman Catholic parish priest of St Mary Magdalene in Lwów. After the outbreak of war in 1939, during the Soviet occupation of Lwów, was chaplain to the underground independence organisations. Arrested in 1940 by Soviet security and transported to the heart of Russia. Released under the Sikorski-Majski agreement in 1941. Chaplain to General Anders' Polish Army. After 1945 active in Polish parochial work in Great Britain. In 1955 joined the contemplative Order of Trappists in Bricquebec, France.

Dąmbska, Aleksandra (Lesia) (1902–88) Nursing sister. In wartime belonged to the underground military organisation, the Union for

Armed Struggle/Home Army and assisted in the distribution of aid to prisoners by the Main Council for Relief (RGO) in Lwów.

Dyboski, Roman (1883–1945) Professor of English Philology at the Jagiellonian University, Kraków. Also lectured in Prague and at London University (School of Slavonic Studies). During the Second World War, when the Germans closed down Polish secondary and higher schools, he worked as a labourer and taught in professional training schools.

Dzidzia: see **Krzeczunowicz, Maria**

Fedorowicz, Father Tadeusz (1907–2002) Canon of the Roman Catholic chapter in Lwów, and Secretary of the local 'Caritas'. During the Soviet occupation, in June 1940, he decided to travel voluntarily eastwards with one of the transports of Poles forcibly deported to the depths of the USSR. Worked felling trees in a forest in Kazakhstan while secretly ministering as a priest. In autumn 1941 became chaplain to the Polish Army with General Anders and, after the departure of the Anders Army, continued as chaplain with the second Polish Army under Soviet command. In 1946 moved to Laski near Warsaw as chaplain to a Foundation for the Blind, run by Franciscan Sisters. In Communist times this was an important meeting place for independent Polish intellectuals.

Frank, Hans (1900–46) Close henchman of Adolf Hitler. From 1939 to 1945 was General Governor of that part of Poland occupied by the German Army, but not incorporated into the Third Reich, with its headquarters in Kraków. Ruthless in carrying out German plans for the elimination of the Polish intelligentsia and Polish culture, as well as the extermination of the Jews. After escaping from Kraków in January 1945, he was arrested by the American authorities and condemned to death as a war criminal in 1946 by the International War Crimes Tribunal at Nuremberg.

von Galen, Clemens August, Count (1878–1946) Cardinal Archbishop of Münster, who openly opposed Nazism by widely circulating the 1937 Encyclical of Pope Pius XI, *Mit brennender Sorge* (*With Ardent Concern*), which condemned the Hitler regime.

Gansiniec (Ganszyniec), Ryszard (1888–1958) Classical philologist and professor (1920–40) Lwów university. During the German occupation he earned a living by working as a bricklayer and clerk. Post-war, Professor of Classical Philology at Wrocław University and from 1948 at the Jagiellonian University, Kraków.

Gebhardt, Karl, (1897–1948) SS Brigadeführer. Friend and personal physician of Heinrich Himmler, and Director of the German Red Cross.

Gębarowicz, Mieczysław (1893–1984) Art historian. Pre-war librarian and curator of the National Ossolineum Institute in Lwów. During the Soviet occupation (1939–41) was Director of the Art Department of the Ukrainian Academy of Sciences and from 1941 to 1944 worked in the State Library. After 1945, when Lwów found itself no longer in Poland, he remained as one of the few Polish intellectuals in the city. From 1946 to 1949, at the Ukrainian Ivan Franko University, he directed the Department of Theory and History of Art, later working with the Ukrainian Academy of Sciences (1951–5) as well as the Museum of Ethnography and Industrial Art (1955–63).

Goetel, Walery (1889–1972) Professor of Geology and Palaeontology at the Mining Academy (later the Academy of Mining and Metallurgy) in Kraków. Rector of this institute (1937–9 and 1945–50). During the war took part in clandestine teaching. From 1944 to 1946 was a local member of the Home National Council – the provisional Polish Parliament, dominated by the Communists.

Gołuchowski, Agenor, Junior (1849–1921) Polish aristocrat. Minister of Foreign Affairs, Austro-Hungary (1895–1906).

Grabski, Stanisław (1871–1949) National right-wing activist. Professor of Political Economy at Jan Kazimierz University of Lwów (1910–39). Minister of Religious Denominations and Public Education (1923 and 1925–6). Autumn 1939, was arrested by the Soviets and imprisoned in the Lubianka, Moscow. Released in 1941 under the Sikorski-Majski agreement, he travelled to the UK. Head of the émigré National Council in London (1942–5). Returned to Poland after the war. Deputy leader of the provisional, Communist-dominated Home National Council Parliament (1945–7) and Professor at Warsaw University.

Grekowa, Maria, née Pareńska (d. 1941) wife of Jan Grek, doctor of medicine, professor at Lwów University. Murdered together with her husband on the Wulecki Hill in Lwów on 4 July 1941.

Grot: see **Rowecki, Stefan**

Hess, Rudolf (1894–1987) Personal secretary to Adolf Hitler from 1933, and his deputy as leader of the Nazi Party. In 1939 was declared second deputy to Hitler (after Hermann Goering). After fleeing to the UK on 10 May 1941 with the aim of negotiating a peace, was relieved of all functions and expelled from the Nazi Party. Sentenced to life imprisonment in 1946 by the International War Crimes Tribunal at Nuremberg.

Himmler, Heinrich (1900–45) Chief of the Gestapo, the secret police of the Third Reich. Joint architect of the Race and Settlement SS, responsible for developing the concept of transforming the Slav lands into German 'living space' (*Lebensraum*) in Eastern Europe. During the war supervised the activity of the concentration camps. In 1943 Minister of Internal Affairs and from 1939 to 1945 Reichskomissar for Consolidating Germanisation, chief architect of the so-called 'Final Solution of the Jewish Question'. After his arrest by the British, he committed suicide.

Horodyska, Jadwiga (Wisia) (1905–73) Sculptress. In wartime an active member of the clandestine movement for independence, at first in Lwów and later in Kraków. After the war, lecturer in the Architecture Department of Kraków Polytechnic.

Huczyński, Augustyn (Father Bolesław) (1904–44) Prior of the Carmelite monastery at Rozdół, an estate belonging to the Lanckoroński family. During the Soviet occupation in 1939 was arrested and taken away by the Soviet security police. Released after the Sikorski-Majski agreement in 1941 and joined the Polish Army of General Anders as an army chaplain. Later, while serving with the 2 Corps, was killed on the Italian front in 1944.

Jaworski, Jan (d. 1991) Officer of the Polish Army. After the Polish defeat in September 1939, he made his way to Lwów, then under Soviet occupation, and engaged in Polish underground activities. May 1940 was arrested by Soviet security, sentenced to five years in a labour camp. Released in 1941 under the Sikorski-Majski agreement and became an Intelligence Officer with General Anders' Polish Army. After 1945 he settled in Turin, Italy, where he was active in the Polish émigré community.

Kaltenbrunner, Ernst (1903–46) Austrian Secretary of State for Security (1938–40), who initiated the construction of Mauthausen concentration camp. In 1943 succeeded R. Heydrich as Head of Reich Security and Chief of Security Police in the Third Reich. All concentration camps in Europe were placed under his command. Sentenced to death by the International War Crimes Tribunal at Nuremberg and executed.

Kochaj, Jan (1896–1942) Surgeon, and Director (1935–9) of the hospital at Stanisławów (now called Ivanofrankivsk). When the town was taken over by the Soviet Army in 1939, he was removed from his position as Director and practised as a surgeon. He operated on (among others) wounded German airmen shot down over Stanisławów, saving their lives. Arrested at the beginning of 1942 together with about 250 representatives of the Stanisławów intelligentsia by Hauptsturmführer SS Hans Krüger, and shot soon afterwards in a mass execution.

Koegel, Max (d. 1946) SS Obersturmbannführer. Commandant of the women's concentration camp in Ravensbrück (1939–42).

Komornicki, Father Władysław (1911–41) Biblical scholar, lecturer at the Priests' Seminary in Lwów and chaplain at the Surgical Clinic of Professor Tadeusz Ostrowski. Arrested by the Germans on the night of 3 July 1941 at Professor Ostrowski's home and shot at dawn the following day with the Lwów professors.

Komorowska, Irena (Renia) Countess (1904–68) Daughter of the Polish general, Robert Lamezan-Salins, descendant of an old Franco-Austrian family. In 1930 married Tadeusz Komorowski. From the beginning of the 1940s worked with the Polish Red Cross in Kraków. After the war lived with her family in London, managing an upholstery firm.

Komorowski, Tadeusz, Count, codenames Bór and Prawdzic (1895–1966) Officer of the Polish Army. After the Polish defeat in the

German-Polish war, in September 1939, was active in the anti-German resistance. From 1941 deputy Commander-in-Chief of the ZWZ (Union for Armed Struggle) and, after the arrest of General Stefan 'Grot' Rowecki in July 1943, leader of the largest underground military organisation in Europe, the Home Army (AK). Took the decision to launch the Warsaw Uprising against the Germans (1 August–5 October 1944). After signing the capitulation, was imprisoned by the Germans. Freed in May 1945, he joined Polish emigration in London. Commander-in-Chief of the Polish Armed Forces in the West (1945–6) and Prime Minister of the Polish Government-in-Exile (1947–9).

Kornel: see **Macieliński, Emil**

Kornijczuk, Oleksandr (1905–72) Ukrainian writer and Deputy Prime Minister of the Ukrainian SSR; husband of Wanda Wasilewska, Polish writer and Communist activist.

Kot, Stanisław (1885–1976) Historian of education and (1953–4) activist in the Peasant Movement. Professor at the Jagiellonian University in Kraków (1920–34). Removed from his teaching posts for criticising the Pitsudski regime. In September 1939 he organised, with Zygmunt Nowakowski, a Refugee Relief Committee in Lwów. From December 1939 in Paris was Minister for Home Affairs in the Polish Government-in-exile and Ambassador in Moscow (1941–2). After the war, Ambassador of the Polish People's Republic in Rome (1945–7). In 1947 he emigrated to the UK.

Kozłowski, Leon (1892–1844) Professor of Archaeology at Jan Kazimierz University of Lwów. Minister for Agricultural Reform (1930–2); Premier of the Polish Republic (1934–5). Arrested in September 1939 by the Soviet authorities, deported to Moscow and sentenced to death (commuted to ten years in prison). Released following the Sikorski-Majski agreement and joined General Anders' Polish Army in October 1941. In November 1941 defected to the German side and was sentenced to death *in absentia* as a deserter, by a court martial of the Polish Army. Interned by the Germans in Berlin, where he died of a heart attack during an Allied bombardment.

Krüger, Hans, SS Hauptsturmführer. In 1941, as a member of Special Commando Schöngarth, participated in the murder of more than a score of university professors in Lwów (4 July 1941). In 1942, as Gestapo chief in Stanisławów, sentenced to death 250 Polish members of the local intelligentsia. Also responsible for the death of more than 10,000 Jews. His betrayal of a 'professional secret' to Karolina Lanckorońska, concerning the murder of the Lwów professors, resulted in his recall from Stanisławów and trial in Berlin. After the war, he stated that he had also been punished at that time for hostility to the Hitler regime. As a result of a jury trial in Münster in 1967, he was condemned to many terms of life imprisonment for the murder of the Jews. The German prosecutor discontinued pursuit of the case against Krüger for the murder of the Lwów professors, despite the depositions against him by Karolina Lanckorońska and the Polish intelligentsia of Stanisławów. On the grounds of judicial economy, the Prosecutor argued, since Krüger had already been sentenced to life imprisonment, further pursuit of the crimes duly acknowledged in the legally valid verdict (so-called additional crimes) would be pointless.

Krzeczunowicz, Maria, codename Dzidzia (1895–1945?) Sportswoman. During the German occupation, she was active in underground independence organisations; confidential courier of Colonel Tadeusz Komorowski to Hungary and Rome (1941). Sent to Bucharest with Andrzej Sapieha in March 1945 and thence to Belgrade, they were last seen on the streets of that city in July 1945 and then disappeared without trace.

Krzemieniewski, Seweryn (1895–1948) Botanist, and professor at Jan Kazimierz University in Lwów, where he was Rector (1931–2). During the Soviet occupation of Lwów (1939–41) he lectured at the Ukrainian Ivan Franko University. During the German occupation (1941–4) worked in the Research Institute on typhus and viruses. Professor at the Jagiellonian University, Kraków (1945).

Kujawska, Maria (1893–1948) Doctor of medicine. Joined in the Silesian uprisings against the Germans in 1919–21, then became a deputy in the autonomous Silesian Diet in Poland. As a known Silesian activist, had to flee from the Germans after the outbreak of the German-Polish war in 1939. In Yugoslavia she organised and ran refugee camps. Arrested with her daughters in January 1944, she was transported to Ravensbrück concentration camp, where she worked as camp doctor. Returned to Poland after the war and lived with her family in Pszczyna in Silesia, where she continued to work as a doctor.

Kulczyński, Stanisław (1895–1975) Botanist and professor at Jan Kazimierz University, where he was Rector (1936–7). Resigned his post in protest against discrimination against students of Jewish descent. During the Soviet occupation of Lwów (1939–41) he lectured at the Ukrainian Ivan Franko University. During the German occupation worked at the Research Institute on typhus and viruses. Active in the Polish underground. In 1944 he lectured at the clandestine Jagiellonian University in Kraków. After the war was professor at the University of Wrocław (1945–69) and Rector (1945–51). Occupied important political posts in post-war Poland, among others, member of the Sejm (1952–72) and Deputy President of the Council of State (1956–72).

Kuryłowicz, Jerzy (1895–1978) Philologist and polyglot (fluent in thirty languages). Professor at Jan Kazimierz University in Lwów. During the Soviet occupation of the city he lectured at the Ukrainian Ivan Franko University. From 1941 to 1944, under German occupation, taught languages in clandestine schools. After the war lectured at Wrocław University; from 1948, at the Jagiellonian University, Kraków, and later Hamburg (1960), Harvard University (1964–6) and Madrid (1970).

Kutrzeba, Stanisław (1876–1946) History of Law Professor at the Jagiellonian University, Kraków, and Rector (1932–3). President of the Polish Academy of Sciences in Kraków. Arrested on 6 November 1939 by the Germans, together with 183 professors from colleges of higher education in Kraków, and transported to Sachsenhausen concentration camp. Returned to Kraków in 1940 and from then till 1945 taught at the underground Jagiellonian University. A local member of the National Home Council (1945–6), the temporary Polish Parliament, dominated by the Communists.

Kutschmann, Walter (1914–1986) SS Untersturmführer. Probably in charge of the execution of Lwów professors on 4 July 1941. In 1942 was the Commissar of Police in Lwów responsible for suppression of the Polish resistance. After deserting from the German Army in France (1944), he went to Argentina. Hid under the assumed name Pedro Ricardo Olmo and worked as sales manager of the Buenos Aires branch of the international electrical firm Osram. In 1975 assistants of Szymon Wiesenthal, engaged in hunting down German war criminals all over the world, succeeded in finding him. Arrested on charges of massacring

Jews in Brzeżany and Podhajce in 1942. However, the German authorities did not apply for Kutschmann's extradition and he was set free. In later interviews he called Wiesenthal's accusations lies.

Lanckorońska, Małgorzata Eleonora, née Lichnowsky (1863–1957) Daughter of Prussian cavalry general Karol Count Lichnowsky and Maria von Croy-Dülmen. In 1897 married Karol Lanckoroński (she was his third wife); a year after the wedding their first daughter Karolina was born (1898) and in 1903 the second daughter Adelajda. Her great-grandfather was Beethoven's patron: Carl Lichnowsky, grandfather of Edward Lichnowsky, author of the eight-volume *History of the House of Habsburg* (1836–44). Małgorzata's brother, Karol Maximilian (1860–1928), was German Ambassador in London (1912–14).

Lanckoroński, Antoni (1893–1965) Son of Karol Lanckoroński and his second wife, an Austrian, Franziska Xawera von Attems (who died giving birth to their son). A landowner and entrepreneur, he administered, in the period between the wars, estates at Wodzisław, Jagielnica, Rozdół and, in Austria, Frauenwald (here, also, after 1945). From 1939 to 1945 worked with the International Red Cross in Geneva and, after the war, with the Comité Suisse d'Aide médicale à la Pologne.

Lednicki, Wacław (1891–1967) Historian of Russian literature at the Jagiellonian University in Kraków; also lectured at the Free University in Brussels. Early in 1940 he travelled to Brussels but, a few weeks after he began lecturing, had to escape from the Germans, who were looking for him. Moved to Lisbon and from there to the USA, where he settled permanently. Lectured at Harvard University and at the École des Hautes Études in New York (1940–4). After the war, Professor of Slavic Studies at the University of Berkeley, California.

Lipińska, Zosia, real name **Zofia Szulcowa née Bortnowiczów** (*c.* 1907–45) Lawyer and Democratic Party activist in Warsaw. During the defence of Warsaw in September 1939 she was among close collaborators of the city Mayor, Stefan Starzyński. Worked with the Prisoners' Welfare Society 'Patronat' and in the anti-German underground. Arrested in 1941, sent to Ravensbrück in 1942 and shot in the last execution to take place at the camp on 5 January 1945.

Longchamps de Berier, Roman (1883–1941). Descendant of an old French Huguenot family that settled in Poland in the eighteenth century. Professor of Civil Law at Jan Kazimierz University in Lwów, and Rector (1939). From 1938 was President of the Polish Law Society in Lwów. On the night of 3 July 1941 was arrested by the Germans with his three sons, and shot with them and the other Lwów professors at dawn the next day.

Macieliński, Emil, codename Kornel (1892–1941) During the Soviet occupation of Lwów (1939–41) was active in the secret underground Polish organisation, the Union for Armed Struggle (ZWZ). From June 1940 served as Commandant of the Lwów Region ZWZ. Twice arrested and twice set free, he was instrumental in bringing about a wave of arrests among underground members in Lwów. Charged with treason, he was sentenced to death by military court of the ZWZ High Command and shot, in December 1941, in Warsaw.

Mandel, Maria (1912–1947) Chief wardress at Ravensbrück concentration camp from April to October 1942.

Marczenko, Mychajlo (1902–83) Ukrainian historian and professor at the Pedagogical Institute of Kiev (1937–9). During the Soviet occupation of Lwów, Rector of Ivan Franko University. Lecturer at the Pedagogical Institute of Novosibirsk (1941–5) and, after the war, in Kiev.

Nowicka, Olga, née Schuster Wife of Witold Nowicki, professor of anatomical pathology at Lwów University.

Ostrowski, Tadeusz (1881–1941) Surgeon and Director of the Surgical Clinic of Jan Kazimierz University, Lwów. During the Soviet occupation (1939–41), Director of the Surgical Clinic at Lwów Medical Institute. One of the pioneers of organ transplants, he introduced many innovative surgical procedures. President of the Society of Polish Surgeons and a well-known Lwów art collector (his home contained a number of works of art deposited by the aristocratic Jabłonowski and Badeni families). On the night of 3 July 1941, he was arrested by the Germans with his wife and friends, who were in his house at the time, and shot with them at dawn the next day, together with the other Lwów professors. The Ostrowski residence was pillaged by the Germans shortly afterwards.

Peretiatkowicz (Peretjatkowicz), Janina (1890–1963) Teacher of geography and educational activist. On the staff of Warsaw University. After the Polish defeat in September 1939 she was an underground teacher. Arrested in November 1941 by the Gestapo and imprisoned in Ravensbrück in 1942, where she secretly taught astronomy, geography, geology and mineralogy, enabling many young women prisoners to obtain a *Matura* certificate while in the camp. After the war became Director of the Earth Museum in Warsaw. In December 1949 was arrested by the Communist authorities and remained for four years without trial in Stalinist imprisonment, until rehabilitated in 1956.

Podlacha, Władysław (1875–1951) Art historian and professor at Jan Kazimierz University, Lwów. During the Soviet occupation (1939–41) lectured at the Ukrainian Ivan Franko University and during the German occupation (1941–4) worked at the Museum of the History of Lwów. After the war, professor at Wrocław University.

Polaczkówna, Helena (1881–1942) Historian and archivist. From June 1941 her home was the base of the wartime underground Information and Propaganda Bureau of the Union for Armed Struggle (ZWZ). Arrested by the Gestapo in August 1942 and executed in Lwów that autumn.

Potocka, Zofia, née Tarnowska, Countess (1901–63). Landowner, and wife of Andrzej Potocki (1900–39), who fought in the German-Polish war of September 1939 and was murdered by Ukrainian peasants during the retreat of Polish forces in the Wielkie Oczy district.

Prawdzic: see **Komorowski, Tadeusz**

Ramdohr, Ludwig (1909–1947). Officer of the criminal police in Ravensbrück concentration camp, and head of Department IV, concerned with women political prisoners.

Rencki, Roman (1867–1941) Professor and Director of the Clinic for Internal Diseases at Jan Kazimierz University, Lwów. Organiser of an anti-TB campaign among youth. President of the Society of Doctors (1922–39). After the capture of Lwów by the Red Army in September 1939, he was arrested and imprisoned by Soviet security. At the end of June 1941, when the Germans took Lwów, succeeded in escaping from prison. On 3 July was again arrested, this time by the Germans, and executed at dawn the following day with more than a score of Lwów professors.

Reynaud, Paul (1878–1966) French Premier, Minister for Foreign Affairs and Defence in 1940. Opposed French capitulation to the Germans and was interned by the Vichy Government. Later imprisoned in concentration camps.

Rękas, Father Michał (1895–1964) Hospital chaplain at the Institution for the Psychically Ill in Kulparków, near Lwów, founding the *Apostolate of the Sick*. During the Soviet and German occupations of Lwów, was active in charitable work among the sick, the wounded and refugees. Lectured in a clandestine Roman Catholic priests' seminary. After the war was hospital chaplain in Katowice, and Editor of *Apostolate of the Sick*.

Ronikier, Adam (1881–1952) Landowner, social and political activist, in the National Party. During the First and Second World Wars was one of the managers of the charitable organisation, the Main Council for Relief (RGO). President of the RGO (June 1940–October 1943). The object of the RGO was the distribution of charitable aid and various types of intervention with the German authorities (e.g. Karolina Lanckorońska, as a functionary of the RGO, had permission from the German authorities for bulk distribution of foodstuffs to prisoners in all prisons of the General Government). Left Poland in January 1945 for a short visit to Rome and travelled to the USA.

Rosenberg, Alfred (1893–1944) Ideologist of Hitlerism, and author of the book *The Myth of the Twentieth Century* (1930). Minister of the Reich from 1941 for the occupied territories of the USSR. In 1946 was sentenced to death as a war criminal by the International War Crimes Tribunal at Nuremberg.

Rowecki, Stefan, codename Grot (1895–1944) Brigadier General of the Polish Army, who fought for Poland's independence in the First World War and the Polish-Russian war of 1920. After Polish defeat in the German-Polish war of 1939, was Commander-in-Chief from 1940 of the underground independence organisation ZWZ (Union for Armed Struggle) throughout all occupied Poland. From February 1942 was Commander-in-Chief of the Polish AK or Home Army, the largest organised secret army in Europe for the struggle against the

German occupation. Arrested by the Germans in June 1943, he was confined in Sachsenhausen concentration camp (not far from Ravensbrück). In August 1944, a few days before the outbreak of the 1944 Warsaw Uprising organised by the Home Army, he was murdered by special order of Himmler.

Sapieha, Adam Stefan, Prince (1867–1951) Metropolitan Archbishop of Kraków (from 1925). During the Second World War, after the Primate August Hlond left Poland, he became one of the leading authorities in Polish society. Supported the activities of the RGO (Main Council for Relief), as well as maintaining liaison with the representative in Poland of the Polish Government-in-exile and the leadership of the Home Army (AK), and informing the Holy See about crimes committed by the Germans in Poland. After the war, on 18 February 1946, was made a cardinal. On his way to Rome he met soldiers of General Anders' 2 Corps and visited the cemetery of Monte Cassino. Karolina Lanckorońska devoted a number of articles to Cardinal Sapieha.

Schebesta (Szebesta), Adam (1893–1973) Doctor and neurologist. Fought in the German-Polish war of September 1939. After defeat of the Polish forces was Commandant of the Hospital Centre at Zamość (set up by agreement with the Germans, and active until December 1939), during which time more than 3,000 wounded soldiers were cared for. From 1940 was deputy plenipotentiary of the Polish Red Cross (PCK) for the Kraków region. As Health Inspector of the Main Council for Relief (RGO), he organised aid for prisoners in the concentration camps of Auschwitz and Majdanek, as well as the prison in Montelupich Street, Kraków. He was chief of health services for the Polish underground organisations. In 1943 was one of a group of Polish Red Cross representatives present at the exhumation of the remains of thousands of Polish officers murdered at Katyń in spring 1940, by order of Stalin. After the war, continued to work with the Red Cross in Katowice (1945–9). For taking part in investigations of the Katyń crime and for cooperation with the Home Army, he was briefly arrested and imprisoned by the Communist authorities.

Schwarzhuber, Johann, SS Obersturmführer. After the Auschwitz concentration camp was evacuated in January 1945, he came to Ravensbrück as a specialist in the mass murder of prisoners.

Seyfried, Edmund (1889–1968) Lawyer. Between the wars was Director of the Polish Society of Railway Bookshops, 'Ruch', in Lwów. During the German occupation worked with the RGO (Main Council for Relief), and was Deputy Director from February 1941 and Managing Director of the Central Bureau in Kraków from July 1943. Worked closely with Archbishop Sapieha. In 1943, was a member of the team that inspected the remains of the Polish officers murdered in Katyń by Stalin's order in the spring of 1940. After the war, in 1948, he was arrested and sentenced to ten years in prison by the Communist authorities. After being released from prison, worked in the administration of the Catholic periodical *Tygodnik Powszechny* in Kraków.

Sikorski, Władysław (1881–1943) General and politician. Fought for Polish independence in the First World War and the Polish-Soviet war of 1920. Chief of General Staff of the Polish Army (1921) and became Prime Minister in 1923. Withdrew from politics after 1928, following a dispute with Marshal Józef Piłsudski. Prime Minister of the Polish Government-in-exile and Commander-in-Chief of the Polish Forces in the West (1939–43), fighting in alliance with Britain and France. On 30 July 1941 signed an agreement with the Soviet Ambassador in London, Majski, by which Polish-Soviet diplomatic relations were restored, having been broken off on 17 September 1939 when the Soviet Union, by virtue of the secret Ribbentrop–Molotov pact, occupied eastern Poland. Sikorski also obtained agreement on the formation by General Anders of a Polish Army on Soviet soil (comprising the thousands of Poles forcibly deported to the heart of the Soviet Union in 1939), under the control of the London Polish Government-in-exile. Perished on 3 July 1943 when his aircraft crashed in Gibraltar in circumstances that remain obscure to this day. On 17 November 1993 a coffin containing his ashes was laid to rest beside the tombs of Poland's kings in the Wawel Cathedral in Kraków.

Slipyi, Josyf (1892–1984) Greek Catholic Archbishop of Lwów. Formerly assistant to the Greek-Catholic Archbishop, A. Szeptycki, of Lwów. After war broke out in September 1939 and the capture of Lwów by the Red Army, was secretly consecrated as Bishop and nominated a coadjutor by the Vatican. In 1941 became a member of the Ukrainian National Council and supported the creation of a Ukrainian Division as part of a German SS formation. After the death of Archbishop Szeptycki in 1944, he took over the archbishopric. In 1945 was arrested by the Soviet authorities for collaboration with the

Germans and agitation against the Red Army, and sent to a labour camp. Pardoned in 1963 and given permission to go to Rome. Created a cardinal in 1965.

Smaczniak, Father Józef (1896–1942) Roman Catholic parish priest of Nadwórna. After war broke out and the occupation of eastern Poland by the Red Army, he organised aid for Polish refugees from Silesia and western Małopolska, as well as persons forcibly deported into the depths of Russia. Cooperated with the Polish underground organisations. Was unmasked (according to some accounts, by local Ukrainians) and arrested on 17 August 1941; murdered in prison in Lwów in 1942.

Sołowij, Adam (1859–1941) Gynaecologist, and professor at Jan Kazimierz University, Lwów. On the night of 3 July 1941 was arrested by the Germans together with his grandson Adam Mięsowicz. Both were shot at dawn the next day, with the other Lwów professors.

Studyns'kyj, Kirylo (Studziński Cyryl) (1868–1941) Ukrainian literary historian. Lectured at the Jagiellonian University, Kraków (1897–9), and was a professor at Lwów University (1900–18). President of the Ukrainian National Council (1921–2). During the Soviet occupation of Lwów (1939–41) he was Dean of the Philosophy Department and Pro-Rector of the Ukrainian Ivan Franko University.

Suhren, Fritz, SS Hauptsturmbannführer. Commandant of Ravensbrück concentration camp (1942–5).

Szebesta, Adam: see **Schebesta, Adam**

Szeptycki, Andrzej, real name **Roman** Count (1865–1944) Greek-Catholic Metropolitan of Lwów (from 1900). Descended from an old Ruthenian-Polish noble family and grandson of the distinguished Polish comic writer, Count Aleksander Fredro. Promoter of the Uniate campaign among the Orthodox in Russia, Byelorussia and the Ukraine, and supported the independence aspirations of Ukrainians. During the Second World War he accepted the cooperation of Ukrainian organisations with the Germans, but in a pastoral letter ('Thou shalt not kill') of 21 November 1942 condemned murders committed with the participation of Ukrainian nationalists.

Tomaka, Wojciech (1875–1967) Roman Catholic Suffragan Bishop of Przemyśl. From 1939 to 1941 he administered that part of the Przemyśl diocese under Russian occupation.

Twardowski, Bolesław (1864–1944) Metropolitan Archbishop of Lwów of the Latin Rite (from 1923). During the war he sheltered Jewish families in the Archbishop's Palace.

Tyszkiewiczowa, Róża, née Tarnowska, Countess (1898–1961). Landowner, and wife of Władysław Tyszkiewicz (1898–1940), deported to the depths of the USSR and never found. After WWII, she settled in London.

Weichert, Michał (1890–1967) Lawyer, critic and theatrical producer, Director of the Kraków Jewish Theatre. President (1940–2) of the Jewish Social Self-Help, cooperating with the Main Council for Relief (RGO). In 1945, he was cleared by the court of the Central Committee of Jews in Poland of a charge of dishonesty in distributing transports of aid to the Jews. (During the war he had been forced to prepare false statements about supplies, which had in fact been seized by the Germans.) After WWII he was accused of collaboration with the Nazis, cleared by the state Court but condemned by the Jewish common court in Poland. He moved to Israel in 1957.

Wiesenthal, Szymon (1908–2005) Architect and native of Lwów. Prisoner in Nazi camps in Lwów, Płaszów, Gross-Rosen, Buchenwald and Mauthausen (1941–5). After the war, he founded the Vienna Jewish Centre for Documentation of the Holocaust period. His activity contributed to the arrest and prosecution of many Nazi war criminals.

Winckelmann, Adolf Doctor. After the liquidation of Auschwitz concentration camp, he was posted to Ravensbrück, where he contributed to the death of thousands of women prisoners.

Wohlfarth, Halina (1916–45) Physical training instructress and activist in the Scout movement. After the Polish defeat in the 1939 German-Polish war, she was engaged in the Polish clandestine resistance movement, the Union for Armed Struggle (ZWZ), in Warsaw. Worked in a secret printing press and took part in the distribution of an illegal newspaper. On 9 September 1941 was arrested by the Germans and sent in 1942 to Ravensbrück concentration camp, where on 5 January 1945 she and four fellow women prisoners were executed.

Zanowa, Teresa, née Dowgiałło (*c.*1883–1944) Landowner and proprietor of the Dukszity estate in the Wilno region. Worked in the library of the Stefan Batory University in Wilno. From 1940 was actively engaged with the work of a ZWZ (Union for Armed Struggle) cell in a Warsaw prison. Arrested in 1941 and imprisoned for a year in the Pawiak prison (she helped fellow prisoners, making use of her excellent command of German). Transported in 1942 to Ravensbrück, where she died in autumn 1944.

Żebrowski, Władysław, codename Żuk (Beetle) (1883–1940) Colonel of artillery, Commandant of Lwów Cadet Corps. After war broke out in 1939 and the capture of Lwów by the Red Army, he served from December 1939 as Commandant of the underground resistance organisation, the Union for Armed Struggle (ZWZ), in Lwów. Shot on 25 April 1940 while trying to cross the frontier.

Żeleński, Tadeusz, literary pseudonym 'Boy' (1874–1940) Translator of French literature, theatre critic and writer. Trained as a paediatrician, he abandoned medicine for literarure. Contributed to the Kraków cabaret *The Little Green Balloon*, for which he wrote satirical verses. His enormous output as a translator, comprising well over a hundred and a few score volumes of French classical literature, appeared in the series he published entitled *The Library of Boy.* As a publicist, he fought against clericalism and bourgeois prudishness and was a leading figure in the cultural life of Kraków and Warsaw. After war broke out in 1939, he lived in Lwów. During the Soviet occupation lectured on French literature at the Ukrainian Ivan Franko University. After Lwów was taken by the Germans, 'Boy' was arrested on 3 July 1941 and, together with the family of Professor Grek and a couple of dozen other Lwów professors, shot at dawn the following day on the Wulecki Hill in Lwów. When the war was over, his nephew living in Paris, Władysław Żeleński, attempted to give wider European publicity to the crime against the professors of the Lwów universities. However, his efforts to organise a trial in Germany of surviving participants in the crime had no success.

Żuk: see **Żebrowski, Władysław**

Notes

Introduction

1 From a speech delivered in the Polish Embassy in Rome on being awarded the Grand Cross of Polonia Restituta, 27 May 1991.
2 1569, Act of Union between Poland and Lithuania founded 'The Most Serene Commonwealth of the Two Nations'. In 1795 Poland was partitioned between Russia, Prussia and Austria.
3 S. Cynarski, *History of the Lanckoroński Family from the 14th to 18th Centuries*, Warsaw-Kraków.
4 R. Taborski, *The Poles in Vienna*, Wrocław, Warsaw, Kraków, 1992.
5 See the Biographical Note on page 308.
6 A. Wysocki, *Half a Century Ago* (*Sprzed pół wieku*), Kraków, 1974.
7 J. Suchmiel, 'Research activity by women at the University of Lwów up to 1939', Częstochowa, 2000, pp.225–7.
8 She completed work on her *Wartime Memoirs* in Rome in 1946. They are now appearing in English for the first time.
9 Address by Karolina Lanckorońska on receiving her award of honorary doctorate at the Jagiellonian University, Kraków, 27 May 1983.

Preface

1 Professor Karolina Lanckorońska decided to publish her wartime memoirs in 2000.

Chapter 1 Lwów

1 Germany invaded Poland from the west on 1 September 1939. The Soviet invasion from the east took place on 17 September.
2 Asterisks refer to entries in the Biographical Notes (see pages 299–316).
3 Literally: 'patricides' – perhaps 'chokers'.
4 After the death of her father in 1933, Karolina Lanckorońska became the last owner of Komarno.
5 'Monument salvaged from a shipwrecked Fatherland.'
6 On 6 November 1939, in Kraków, the Germans arrested 183 professors of the Jagiellonian University, the Academy of Mining and the Academy of Trade and Commerce, who were subsequently imprisoned in Sachsenhausen-Oranienburg concentration camp.
7 The Hermitage art gallery in Leningrad (now St Petersburg).
8 Karolina Lanckorońska lived at 19 Zimorowicz Street, Lwów.
9 A classic patriotic drama by Poland's national bard, Adam Mickiewicz.
10 Quote from Book 11 (*The Year 1812*) of *Pan Tadeusz* by Adam Mickiewicz: 'O Spring! Who saw Thee at that season in our country [. . .] rich with events, pregnant with hope.'
11 The Nazi swastika.
12 A legendary eighteenth-century Ukrainian bard and seer who foretold the destruction and resurrection of Poland.
13 The Russian–Finnish War broke out on 30 November 1939.
14 'Have a safe journey!'
15 'Have a good stay!'
16 Karolina Lanckorońska was the foundress and patron of this church.
17 'Give me God!'
18 'Bitter Sorrows', a seventeenth-century series of sung reflections on Christ's Passion.
19 Both deeply patriotic hymns with great historical and cultural significance for Poles, as expressions of protest against oppression. To defeat bans, harmless words were sometimes sung to the traditional music.

20 In 1996 his daughter found his Christian name and surname on one of the most recent lists of victims of the Katyń Forest massacre (1940), when thousands of Polish officers were murdered by the Soviet NKVD.
21 I had not known him personally, because Komarno belonged to the neighbouring diocese of Przemyśl and not to the Lwów archdiocese (K.L.).
22 The Germans broke through the Norwegian defences on 10 April 1940.
23 Note dated 30 October 1996: reading these memoirs through to check their accuracy, I notice that in several instances I have written in praise of, or in gratitude to, people whom I could not name at the time for their own protection – names which I now, of course, cannot recall (K.L.).
24 Note dated 30 October 1996: at that time I had no idea of the prophetic significance of those words (K.L.).

Chapter 2 Kraków

1 'Out with the rats!'
2 'Germans only.'
3 The underground resistance movement loyal to the Polish Government-in-exile – first in France, then in London. The movement later formed part of the AK or Home Army.
4 A Polish national holiday commemorating the adoption by the Polish Government of the revolutionary new Constitution of 3 May 1791. This so alarmed the rulers of neighbouring Russia, Prussia and Austria that they embarked on the gradual partition and absorption of the Polish State, which, at least technically, ceased to exist from 1795 to 1918.
5 The German forces invaded Belgium and Holland on 10 May; a month later, on 10 June 1940, Italy declared war on France.
6 The unconditional capitulation of France was signed at Compiègne on 22 May 1940.
7 'Zygmunt', the historic bell of Wawel Cathedral, named after King Zygmunt (Sigismund) I, or the Old, was cast and blessed in 1520. Traditionally it was rung to celebrate great national events.
8 'The originally German city of Kraków.'
9 *Dante Saw Nothing.*
10 At Grünwald in 1410, Poles and Lithuanians defeated the Teutonic Knights. At the siege of Vienna in 1683, victorious

Polish forces led by King John Sobieski ended the Turkish threat to western Europe.

11 The Battle of Britain began on 8 August 1940.

12 Polish forces defeated and repelled the invading Soviet army in 1920, almost at the gates of Warsaw – a victory attributed by many Poles to divine intervention.

13 A favourite promenade with bushes, trees and flowerbeds, planted to replace the original city walls.

14 Presumably 'Say not the struggle nought availeth'.

15 The date was 17 August 1940.

16 In November 1939.

17 The Hel Peninsula garrison, which fought on for almost a week after the fall of Warsaw on 27 September 1939, was one of the last Polish strongholds to surrender to the German invaders after heroic resistance.

18 Juliusz Słowacki, 'Pogrzeb Kapitana Meyznera', lines 49–54. On 27 May 1991, while in Rome, I met the Speaker of the Senate, Professor Andrzej Stelmachowski. That day, I received by his hand the Order of Polonia Restituta, which I had been awarded. On our way to the Polish Embassy together, I asked him whether perhaps he was related to the young hero of the Hel Peninsula, of the same name, who had died in my presence in Kraków in October 1940. The high dignitary turned out to be the younger brother of my patient. The Speaker was deeply moved by this uncanny encounter. He referred to it in his speech, which lent the solemn ceremony a thoroughly human note. In my boundless gratitude I once more recalled that prayer by Słowacki, which has been answered in our day: the daylight has streamed 'through heaven's portals wide' (K.L.).

19 From families of German origin living in Poland.

20 This is very unpleasant to record, but I think it should not be passed over in silence (K.L.).

21 Small or great, these constant annoyances on the part of the Ukrainians used to keep me awake at night. I was viewing these pinpricks in a far wider context, convinced that when the Germans eventually left Poland, we and the Ukrainians would be left on our common soil. From early youth, I had known that we *must* somehow get along together and reach agreement, otherwise life would be impossible. But the Germans had made the situation even worse (K.L.).

22 'Sweet Mother Mary'. The original, highly patriotic words were

replaced by an innocent hymn sung to the same melody, so as to avoid criminal charges.

23 'When I was King.'

24 An old Polish custom. At Christmas or New Year, for example, when people meet family members, friends – and strangers, at home or at parties – they may exchange scraps of one another's wafers while wishing each other the compliments and blessings of the season.

25 'And there was I thinking a countess would be a cultured person.'

26 'Till the next Polish freedom struggle.'

27 Krystyna died as a nurse during the Warsaw Uprising, in August 1944 (K.L).

28 Count Fernando Álvares de Toledo, Spanish Governor of the Netherlands (1567–73).

29 'But we Germans build libraries.'

30 'Where are the carpets? Hurry up!'

31 Major Jan Cichocki, Chief of Staff, Kraków District.

32 The then codename of General Komorowski, derived from the Polish for 'truth'.

33 Burial site of General Tadeusz Kościuszko (1746–1817), a Polish hero who fought in the American War of Independence, later returning to Poland to lead the first unsuccessful revolt against Russian rule in 1794.

34 Lieutenant Colonel Jan Cichocki, Chief of Staff, Sector IV Kraków, was arrested on the night of 17 April 1941 at No. 6 Sławkowska Street.

35 Major Leon Giedgowd, codename Leon, was arrested on 20 April 1941.

36 The Kraków prison (K.L.).

37 Worried.

38 General Tadeusz Komorowski, threatened with arrest, hid for two days in the author's flat, No. 1 Wenecja (Venice) Street.

39 'Brilliant, but hopeless.'

40 During the night of 3–5 July 1941, twenty-five high-school professors, together with members of their households and tenants, were shot on Wulecki Hill in Lwów. In October 1943, in an attempt to destroy all traces, the Germans exhumed the bodies and burned them in Krzywczyc Forest, in the Lwów suburbs.

41 The RGO, an important pre-war Polish relief and welfare organisation, was allowed to function for a time in the German-

occupied zone (the General Government), but was later suppressed.

Chapter 3 On Tour in the 'General Government'

1 The heartland of German-occupied Poland, where the brutal Nazi General Governor, Hans Frank, was committed to the systematic destruction of the Polish State, the annihilation of the Jews, as well as all Polish intellectuals, and the exploitation of the remaining Polish population for slave labour.
2 'It is sweet and honourable [to die for the one's country].'
3 The name of the Committee Chairman in Nowy Sącz was Jan Piotrowski.
4 Party birds: a Nazi Party term.
5 Promoters of culture.
6 Due to my lack of a foreign accent when speaking German (K.L.).
7 'On the point of death from starvation.'
8 The first two Polish dynasties (ninth to sixteenth centuries).
9 After the death of Karol Lanckoroński in 1933, Rozdół was inherited by his son Antoni*.
10 'The Return of Galicia to the German Reich.'
11 The family of Professor Stanisław Kulczyński*, Rector of Lwów University 1936–7.
12 Roman Longchamps de Bérier was shot together with his three eldest sons: Bronisław, Zygmunt and Kazimierz.
13 'Ethnic Germans.'
14 Which, of course, they never did (K.L.).
15 Professor Stanisław and Maria Kulczyński.
16 'In a safe place.'
17 St Charles Borromeo, Cardinal Archbishop of Milan, 1538–84.
18 'Impossible! Impossible!'
19 Stefan Żeromski (1864–1925), novelist and poet, left-wing neo-Romantic, sometimes called 'the conscience of Poland'.
20 'Ravens and crows will peck us to pieces . . .'
21 'Yes, but they go very well with my suite of furniture.'
22 'Not so well with your officer's code of honour.'
23 Cyprian Norwid (1821–83), one of Poland's finest poets. The lines are from his 'Song of our Homeland'.
24 The January uprising (1863–4) in Poland against the Russian occupation was ruthlessly suppressed and was followed by mass executions and deportations.

25 'How on earth could the General . . . ?'
26 Wodzisław was the Polish estate to remain for the longest period in the hands of the same family, 1370–1945 (K.L).
27 This monumental tomb was the work of Antonio Canova, who was working in Vienna at that period. The son of the deceased, Antoni Lanckoroński, would naturally have commissioned him to sculpt the beautiful memorial and would have arranged to have it brought to Wodzisław (K.L.).
28 'They are all long since dead!'
29 'Krüger shot them before I arrived, without legal basis or court of law. Do you know what that means for an attorney?'
30 Father Augustin Huczyński* (name in the Order: Bolesław), padre of the Polish 2 Corps, buried in the Polish Forces cemetery on Monte Cassino.
31 Some of the paintings and other precious objects were in the Drohobycz Museum at Stryj and the Lwów Art Gallery.
32 'Ode to Youth' by Adam Mickiewicz, a rapturous salute to youth and freedom by Poland's national bard.

Chapter 4 Stanisławów

1 'I must subject you to a security police interrogation.'
2 'I don't care for your attitude. I don't want you in my Reich!'
3 'You are in the gravest danger!'
4 'So, at last!'
5 'Take a note!'
6 'Since when?'
7 There was a clock hanging on the wall (K.L.).
8 'Never heard anything like it. Write it down!'
9 'Or are you really very shrewd, all said and done?'
10 He died in Auschwitz concentration camp (K.L.).
11 'You are under arrest, after all.'
12 'A subhuman Pole', an ironic reference to Nazi racist dogma.
13 Friedrich Schiller (1759–1805), German playwright and poet.
14 'Life is not the most exalted good;
The greatest evil, though, is surely guilt.'
15 That was how I knew that I had already been sentenced to death (K.L.).
16 'I shall treat you in a chivalrous manner.'
17 'Turn round!'
18 He did it each night. I shall never forget it (K.L.).

19 Soviet State secret police.
20 *Armia Krajowa* (Home Army), the consolidated Polish military resistance loyal to the 'Polish Government-in-exile in London. AK embodied the ZWZ, of which Karolina Lanckorońska was an active member.'
21 'Kill me!'
22 *Hours of Our Lady.*
23 I forget her surname, but I remember that her father, a railway official, lived at 28 Rzeczna Street, Przemyśl (K.L.).
24 He had instructed Karolina Lanckorońska to concentrate exclusively on her social relief work and break off all other contacts.
25 'I don't want you in my Reich!'

Chapter 5 The Łącki Street Prison in Lwów

1 'Police Commissar Kutschmann*. Polish political affairs.'
2 'No charges.'
3 Wacław Rzewuski (1785–1831) was a noted Polish orientalist and traveller in the Arab world and Turkey. A Romantic figure, he commanded his own detachment in the 1831 Polish Uprising.
4 It was only after the war that I discovered the unimaginable way in which Caetani came to learn of my arrest. My brother in Geneva heard about it on the Ukrainian radio! He informed our friends in Rome (K.L.).
5 'Unwarranted.'
6 In a letter of 21 July 1942, Himmler wrote that Karolina Lanckorońska abused the trust of the German authorities by openly declaring herself an enemy of Germany. In view of her 'anti-German instigation' he considered her arrest to be necessary.
7 Himmler, as SS-Reichsführer.
8 The Historical Museum and Library, founded in Lwów in 1817. Now established in Wrocław, where it houses the national collection of manuscripts by Poland's major classic writers.
9 'What's going on here?'
10 'Ascension squad' – i.e. executions would be taking place. Grim humour based on the German for 'Ascension Day' (literally: Journey to Heaven Day).
11 The prison where, at the time of the French Revolution, Louis XVI and his wife Marie Antoinette awaited the guillotine.
12 Shakespeare in the original English.

13 'O man, you have been a citizen of the great City, go now with a peaceful heart.'
14 'The wanderer.'
15 Obviously, we knew all classical literature only in the original (K.L.).
16 'I am not Jewish. Please ring Pełczyńska [Gestapo HQ number, and room number], otherwise it will be too late. It's a misunderstanding, I am not Jewish.'
17 This line (from Shakespeare's *King Lear*) was printed in large letters and underlined twice in Karolina Lanckorońska's notebook.
18 Ashes and shadow.
19 *Ananke*: circumstances, needs; *moira*: fate.
20 But not as I want . . .
21 *Julius Caesar*, Act I, Scene iii.
22 A well-known professor of Greek studies at Lwów.
23 'Listen to me, silverbow.'
24 In the Salvator cemetery at the foot of the Kościuszko Mound, with its splendid view of the Vistula and Kraków, there stands a great wooden cross on the grave of the playwright Karol H. Rostworowski (1877–1938).
25 How much longer?
26 Italicised words written in English.
27 After the war, I learned that one of my smuggled messages had reached the Commander and he was fully informed (K.L.).
28 After the war, through the mediation of Cardinal Slipyi*, with whom I had an audience, I succeeded in tracing his family in Canada and was able to let them know how splendidly he held out to the end and that he had not been tortured, but died on the spot (K.L.).
29 Consequently, love is the perfect fulfilment of the Law.
30 'Krüger has been toppled.'
31 That night of bloodshed in Lwów.
32 'I had to stiffen your resolve' (literally: give you the necessary spine).
33 'For all the atrocities.'
34 Release on parole.
35 These notebooks still exist. They are not suitable for publication, but I have made use of them in writing the present memoir (K.L.).
36 'Believe me, I mean that final wish very seriously.'

37 Lwów ever-faithful.

Chapter 6 Berlin

1 Formerly known by the German name of Breslau, the city was returned to Poland at the end of the Second World War.
2 'Madam Sergeant.'
3 Shameful deeds or atrocities.
4 Madam Sergeant-Major.
5 'How very curious!'
6 'Judge attached to the office of the SS Leader' (Heinrich Himmler).
7 'A judicial impression.'
8 *The Young Captive*: 'I am only 18 years old . . .'
9 'Quick, this is for you . . .'
10 'What are you in for?'
11 'Contacts with Russia. My girl-friend's already been beheaded.'
12 The Fascist leader of Italy, then still Hitler's ally.
13 Hitler's autobiography, *My Struggle*.
14 Nazi concentration camp for women (1934–45).
15 'Whether you're not in your cell.'

Chapter 7 Ravensbrück

1 The master-race. According to Nazi German racial dogma, Slavs were 'sub-humans'.
2 'Get out!'
3 'You are Polish.'
4 The Polish term *króliki*, 'rabbits' is in this context the equivalent of 'guinea pigs' in English.
5 A sanatorium for wounded SS officers.
6 Consorting with Germans.
7 'Get up!'
8 From the German *aussen*, meaning 'outside'. The name given to prisoners employed daily outside the camp.
9 Antisocial element.
10 Society of International Bible Students (Jehovah's Witnesses).
11 'Shut up, you cheeky individual!'
12 Ancient underground cemeteries in Rome, where early Christian converts took refuge and were buried.

13 Deputy Director of the RGO and a leading Polish Red Cross official.

14 Wife of General Tadeusz Bór Komorowski, later Home Army Commander-in-Chief. His second son, Jerzy, was born in 1944 and the author (K.L.) became his godmother.

15 'Prisoner in protective custody.'

16 'Lovely, isn't it?'

17 'What are all these pilgrim [foreign] swords doing here?'

18 *The Myth of the Twentieth Century.*

19 On 12 April 1943 the Germans announced the discovery of the bodies of more than 4,000 Polish officers in Katyń forest near Smolensk. For this, and other mass executions of Polish officers taken prisoner by the Russians, the guilt of Stalin's KGB was finally acknowledged after the collapse of the Communist regime in Russia.

20 Officer in charge of the protective-custody camp.

21 The name of the gardeners' team-leader – Zan – was that of a celebrated early nineteenth-century patriot and fellow student of Poland's national bard, Adam Mickiewicz, author of a classic verse epic 'Konrad Wallenrod', whose heroine was Aldona – the codename used to alert Karolina Lanckorońska.

22 'Pillage committed outside the frontiers of a given tribal society does not incur dishonour for the participants; they maintain that it serves to train the youth and aids the struggle against idleness' (*De Bello Gallico* VI, 23).

23 'Heavens, a raw onion!'

24 A State prisoner in the Bastille in the reign of Louis XIV. He wore an iron mask covered in black velvet and his identity remains a matter for speculation.

25 'A visit by a VIP.'

26 The first concrete indication that I am meant to die here (K.L.).

27 From 'Hymn' by Juliusz Słowacki (1809–49):

> . . . I saw storks flying overhead, airily spaced
> And remembered the day
> When storks above Poland's ploughed acres I'd see:
> Sad heart of me!

28 'The other name of your honour is loyalty.'

29 Rank of Sergeant-Major or Inspector.

30 3 September 1943.

31 'Fortress Europe.'

32 Christiane Mabire was not released at that time, merely transported to the Tyrol and imprisoned there until May 1945, as she told me when we met after the war (K.L.).

33 Karolina Lanckorońska's message reached General Tadeusz 'Bór' Komorowski in November 1943.

34 Karolina Lanckorońska learned after the war that the President of the International Red Cross had raised her case several times: 'Himmler ordered a reply to the effect that, in view of the seriousness of my case as well as my provocative and chauvinistic behaviour, he begged them not to refer to the matter again. My Italian relatives received the same answer from Ribbentrop' (Copy of a report by Karolina Lanckorońska on the reasons for her imprisonment in Germany in 1942, PAU Archive, Kraków).

35 We were speaking the language of the camp, a frightful Polish-Ukrainian-Yiddish mixture (K.L.). 'Miss Karla, are you a religious person [a believer]?'

36 Adam Mickiewicz, author of *Pan Tadeusz* and the historical, patriotic drama *Dziady (Forefather's Eve)*. This contains *The Great Improvisation* (Part 3, Scene 2) in which the poet hero, Konrad, reproaches God for indifference to the (Polish) people's suffering and begs for a share of divine power over souls, so that his inspired poetry may create order and happiness on Earth, even against people's will.

37 *Chorąży* in Polish means 'ensign'.

38 Jadwiga Horodyska, the 'liaison officer', had caught an eye infection, which, thank God, passed off and she was able to decipher my 180 words in 'dot code'. The message got through to General Komorowski, who told me about it after the war (K.L.).

39 Frau Strassner later died in Belsen concentration camp (K.L).

40 'Conditionally fit for work.'

41 'Form nine rows, form eleven rows!'

42 'It would be the French! No lunch for five Sundays!' 'Remain standing after roll-call!'

43 Carmen Mory was sentenced to death at Nuremberg and committed suicide in her cell.

44 Literally: night and fog; figuratively: 'Dead of night'.

45 After a battle in which Polish units played a major role, Monte Cassino was captured by the Allied forces on 18 May 1944.

46 'What's the matter this time?'
47 An outlying district of Warsaw.
48 Apollo granted her wish to live for a thousand years. Unfortunately, she failed to ask for eternal youth at the same time and finished up as an ugly little creature in a bottle.
49 Soldiers of an army created by the Russian General A. Vlasov, which served with the German Army and had a reputation for particular cruelty.
50 London-based Commander-in-Chief of the Free French Forces, later French President.
51 Labour Manager.
52 These women were among survivors of the sixty-three-day Warsaw Uprising of August to October 1944, in which about 200,000 civilian lives were lost and the centre of Warsaw was razed to the ground by order of Hitler.
53 'You've no need to be so impertinent just because you're wearing the letter P!'
54 'One drafted' and 'dead'.
55 A party charged with escorting a corpse to the mortuary.
56 Years later, I had the honour of mentioning this episode to His Holiness John Paul II (K.L.).
57 In the typescript recounting her experiences in Ravensbrück (preserved in the PAU Archive, Kraków), Karolina Lanckorońska, writing of the change in her lecture, adds: 'It was the only mourning ceremony by which we could honour the memory of Halina.'
58 At the Yalta Conference (4–11 February 1945) Roosevelt, Churchill and Stalin agreed, among other things, on the post-war frontiers of Poland and recognised Central and East Europe as a zone of Soviet influence.
59 The Polish Committee of National Liberation, self-proclaimed in December 1944 and later the Soviet-sponsored nucleus of Poland's first provisional post-war government, was installed with Soviet backing after Germany's defeat in May 1945.
60 Maria Kujawska, while still working in Poland in 1945 and 1946, sent me by three separate routes identically worded copies of the following message: 'Karla, I apologise with all my heart. You were right – not one hundred but one thousand per cent.' Today, when she is no longer alive, I think with immense gratitude of her touching gesture (K.L.).

61 'Unheard of! Off to work with you at once!'
62 Saintly hero of a celebrated historical novel by Henryk Sienkiewicz, *Ogniem i Mieczem (With Fire and Sword).*
63 Karolina Lanckorońska brought out of the camp with her a list of all the women who had undergone experimental operations (written on the hem of a handkerchief), which she passed to the International Red Cross authorities in Geneva.
64 'A good person at heart.'
65 'Get going!'
66 'Good evening. Welcome!'

Chapter 8 Italy

1 Years later, while I was still in London, I was visited a few times by former fellow inmates of Ravensbrück who had come out through Sweden. They said the Swedes had a list of those Polish women who were to be evacuated in the first batch. The Swedes were asked where they had got a list of so many people 'suspected of Bolshevik' sympathies. The Swedes said the list was in a telegram from Geneva. They reckoned that this list could have come only from me. I then understood how right Zdenka had been to insist so forcefully that I had to go! And how difficult that had been! (K.L., 23 November 1994).
2 From the poem 'Lines on Hearing That Lady Byron Was Ill' (9–12).
3 Throughout the nineteenth century and until the end of the First World War, Poland was divided between and administered by Russia, Prussia and Austria, with varying degrees of repression.
4 The Mermaid was adopted officially as the symbol of Warsaw only a year before the outbreak of the Second World War, though the association stems from a medieval legend recounting the appearance of a mermaid in a tributary of the River Vistula.
5 Henryk Sienkiewicz (1846–1916), Poland's most celebrated historical novelist, was best known abroad as the author of *Quo Vadis* and at home for his trilogy about Poland's seventeenth-century struggles against the Cossacks and the Swedes. He was awarded the Nobel Prize for Literature in 1905.
6 Juliusz Słowacki (1809–49): lines from his poem 'Hymn' ('*Smutno mi Boże*') written at sea, off Alexandria, one of the most poignant evocations of Polish exile nostalgia.

Epilogue

1 'So, you were in Stanisławów?'
2 'But, Mr Prosecutor!'
3 Not long afterwards I met a Professor of Church History, whom I already knew well, Father Professor Dr Hubert Jedin. I mentioned that I had been at the trial and he immediately asked: 'How did the Prosecutor behave himself? It is sometimes said they are instructed to present their chief witnesses in a negative light.' I replied: 'Very unfavourably, where I was concerned, but he didn't succeed because he did not know the difference between Poles and Ukrainians.' Much later I was to learn that, in German trials of this kind, prosecutors often tried to get Nazi criminals acquitted!
4 Kutschmann later died of a heart attack in Argentina.

Index of Names